OCCULT ABC

Books by Kurt E. Koch

Christian Counseling and Occultism

Demonology, Past and Present

The Lure of the Occult

Occult ABC

Occult Bondage and Deliverance

Occult Practices and Beliefs

OCCULT ABC

Exposing Occult Practices and Ideologies

KURT E. KOCH

kregel
PUBLICATIONS

Grand Rapids, MI 49501

Occult ABC: Exposing Occult Practices and Ideologies

© 1978, 1986 by Kurt E. Koch
Second edition 1986

Originally published as *Occultes ABC* by Kurt E. Koch
Translated into English by Michael Freeman in 1978 as
Satan's Devices.

Published in 1986 by Kregel Publications, a division of
Kregel, Inc., P.O. Box 2607, Grand Rapids, MI 49501.
Kregel Publications provides trusted, biblical publications
for Christian growth and service. Your comments and
suggestions are valued.

For more information about Kregel Publications, visit our
web site: www.kregel.com

Cover design: Frank Gutbrod

Library of Congress Catalog Card No. LC-78-566

ISBN 0-8254-3031-3

Printed in the United States of America

11 12 13 14 / 03 02 01 00

CONTENTS

Introduction 1

A. FORMS OF OCCULT MOVEMENTS and DEVICES   5
   1. Acupuncture 5
   2. Anthroposophy 11
   3. Astrology 18
   4. Baha'i 21
   5. Biological Feedback and Mind Control . . . 24
   6. Black Mass 26
   7. Blood Pacts 29
   8. Charismatic Movements 29
   9. Christian Science 35
  10. Clairvoyance 38
  11. Color Diagnosis and Color Therapy 41
  12. Conjuring Tricks 43
  13. Death Magic 45
  14. Demon Possession 47
  15. Descent from the Ape 52
  16. Drug Abuse 54
  17. Edgar Cayce 57
  18. Exaggerated Doctrines and Theological Constructions 60
  19. False Christs and False Prophets 65
  20. Fortunetelling and Soothsaying 70
  21. Freemasonry 75
  22. Ghosts 77
  23. Goblins and Elves 82
  24. Group Suggestion 84
  25. Halloween 87
  26. Hari Krishna 88
  27. Healing Fanaticism 89
  28. Homosexuality 92
  29. Hypnotism 95
  30. Iris Diagnosis 100
  31. Jeane Dixon 104
  32. Jehovah's Witnesses 107

33. Kathryn Kuhlman 110
34. Legalism 121
35. Levitation 125
36. Magic 126
37. Magic Charms 133
38. Maoism (Chinese Communism) 140
39. Meditation 143
40. Metamorphosis 146
41. Neo-rationalism 146
42. Ouija Board 152
43. Parapsychology 154
44. Peditherapy 159
45. Poltergeists 160
46. Pornography 168
47. Predictive Dreams 170
48. Processeans 172
49. Queen of Darkness—Queen of Black Witches . . 175
50. Rock Music 180
51. Rod and Pendulum 185
52. Rosicrucians 192
53. Satan Worship 194
54. Scientology 200
55. Sensitivity Training 202
56. Sixth and Seventh Book of Moses 203
57. Soul Force 205
58. Speaking in Tongues 206
59. Spirit of the Age 210
60. Spiritism 215
                    Extrasensory Perception
    a) Spiritist Visions 217
    b) Spiritist Prophecy 217
    c) Table Lifting 218
    d) Ouija Board 218
    e) Speaking in Trance 219
    f) Automatic Writing 220
    g) Spiritist Soothsaying 221
    h) Conversation with Spirits 221
    i) Excursion of the Soul 222
    j) Astral Traveling 222
                    Extrasensory Influence
    k) Materialization 223

l) Transfiguration 224
m) Translocation 224
n) Apports 224
o) Deports 225
p) Levitation 225
q) Telekinesis 226
r) Spiritistic Aggressive Magic 226
s) Spiritistic Defensive Magic 227
t) Spiritist Operations 227
u) Spiritist Miracles 228
v) Dematerialization 229
w) Teleplasm 229
Extrasensory Apparitions
x) Spiritist Apparitions 230
y) Spiritist Cults 232
z) Spiritist Lodges 232
aa) Spiritist Churches 232
bb) Spiritism Among Believing Christians . . . 234
61. Spiritist Healing 234
62. Spiritist Operations 236
63. Superstition 239
64. Symbols of Peace 241
65. Television 243
66. Transcendental Meditation 247
67. Translocation 249
68. Uri Geller 250
69. Vampires 253
70. Weleda Medicines and Herbal Remedies . . . 255
71. Yoga 256

B. EFFECTS OF OCCULT MOVEMENTS and DEVICES   261
1. Mediumistic Affinity 263
2. Resistance to the Things of God 266
3. Distortion of Character 270
4. Emotional Disorders 272
5. A Breeding Ground for Mental Illness . . . 275
6. Oppression of Descendants 277
7. Frequent Suicides 278
8. Ghosts and Poltergeists Result from Sins of Sorcery 278
9. Frequent Diseases 280

C. DELIVERANCE   283

   1. Come to Christ   287
   2. Destroy All Occult Objects   288
   3. Break Off All Mediumistic Contacts and Friendships   290
   4. Recognize and Confess Your Guilt   292
   5. Renounce and Declare Yourself Free From
        Satan and the Sins of Sorcery of Your Forebears .   294
   6. Accept Forgiveness by Faith   297
   7. Don't Get Stuck Half Way   297
   8. Seek Out a Counsellor Who Has Spiritual
        Authority Before Whom to Declare Yourself Free   300
   9. Join a Prayer Group   301
  10. Practice Praying and Fasting   303
  11. Place Yourself Under the Protection of Jesus' Blood   305
  12. Command the Enemy in the Name of Christ . .   306
  13. Make Diligent Use of the Means of Grace . . .   309
  14. Put on the Spiritual Armor   310
  15. Realize Victory of Jesus Over Powers of Darkness
  16. Guard Against the Return of the Demons . . .   314
  17. Be Willing to Dedicate Yourself Fully to Jesus . . 316
  18. Deliverance Is Possible Only Through Christ .   317
  19. Obey the Lord in All Things   318
  20. Be Filled With the Spirit!   319

D. IN THE CONQUEROR'S TRAIN   322

   1. From the Satanists to Christ   322
   2. Astrology and Christianity   326
   3. The Magician   328
   4. Conquest of the Mighty   330
     a) From Macumba to Christ   330
     b) From Voodoo to Christ   331
     c) From Yoga to Christ   332
     d) The Country Devil Becomes a Christian . .   333
     e) A Muslim Sorcerer Becomes a Christian . .   333
     f) It's Your Fault!   336
     g) Blood Pacts   336

E. SUPPLEMENT

  72. UFO   338
Footnotes   343

INTRODUCTION

Readers usually skip the introductions and prefaces to books. Admittedly, they are generally boring. But readers of this book would be well advised to read this introduction to avoid misunderstandings and wrong impressions.

Some people may be shocked when they read the list of contents. What, for example, is a chapter about meditation doing in a book directed against the occult? The answer is very simple. This book deals only with abuses; and in the instance of meditation, there are more occult forms than genuine forms. Prayerful thought about a Bible passage, of course, has nothing to do with the occult. I am attacking only those forms of meditation which lead people away from Christ.

Another feature of the book is that it deals not only with occult movements and Satan's devices, as the title suggests, but also with other extreme movements, ideologies, and opinions of the present day.

The German reader will find reference to many movements with strange-sounding names. That is because the book is being translated into English. I have therefore included the American movements. Again, a publisher in Quebec, Canada, has asked permission to translate the book into French; so various Canadian movements will have to be taken into account. In any case, it has for years been true to say that trends in North America appear in Europe ten years later. Even things unknown to Europeans today, or those hard for us to understand, will be familiar in ten years.

This book is the outcome of constant demand for my previous book *Der Aberglaube* (*Superstition*), which is now out of print. The only thing, however, it has in common with *Der Aberglaube* is that the subjects are dealt with in alphabetical order. The content has been reworked and rewritten from beginning to end.

The numerous case histories from my own counseling will once again raise the question of confidentiality. I have been accused in the past of breaking the seal of the confessional. This allegation I strongly deny. Up to now I have worked, by God's grace, in 130

1

countries, including the South Pole. It is impossible for anyone to determine the source of any particular illustration. I have omitted, where necessary, all reference to place names, or the names, ages, and occupations of counselees. My chief comment on these allegations is that I have only used case histories where I have permission to do so.

Other objections have been raised by parapsychologists like Professor Bender of Freiburg. He alleges that my examples are of no scientific value, only of personal value, because all statistical data have been omitted. There are three things I would say in reply to this:

1. I have statistical data in my files.

2. Exact details have been omitted for the very purpose of guarding confidences.

3. In the field of parapsychology, spontaneous occurrences provide more powerful evidence than experiments. Spontaneous occurrences are manifestations far stronger than anything found through experiments. Professor Bender will reply that my opinion is refuted by the fact that it has been possible to record the Rosenheim ghost on film. My answer to that is that the Rosenheim ghost is a spontaneous occurrence and not in any sense an experiment. Other questions along these lines are dealt with in the chapter on parapsychology.

Another criticism is sometimes raised among believing Christians, who certainly deserve to be taken seriously. They ask whether we do not give the devil too much honor by writing books against the occult. This criticism has been made against me in America, in the Christian magazine *Eternity*. I reply that Paul could write to the Corinthians, "we are not ignorant of his [Satan's] devices" (2 Corinthians 2:11). Today it would have to be said that we are ignorant of Satan's devices. Many Christians have no inkling of all that is going on in the occult. Such ignorance, confusion, and short sightedness make Satan's task easy. I will give three examples which have caused me much distress.

1. When my book *Christian Counselling and Occultism* appeared, Pfarrer Fischer was the principal of the Bible school at Unterweissach. He said there was no need for such a book. If a Christian suffers from the occult influence, one should earnestly pray with him, and then he will be freed from all the effects of such influence. Fischer's opinion revealed boundless ignorance. There are Christians who suffer for years, even decades, from occult influence that has

been caused by sins of sorcery committed by their ancestors or by themselves.

2. The same book *Christian Counselling and Occultism,* which has now been through twenty-three editions, including those in other languages, has been condemned by Dr. Wasserzug of the Beatenberg Bible School. It was put on her index of books that Beatenberg students were forbidden to buy or read. But when I was preaching in Interlaken, students and teachers from Beatenberg came to me for counseling about their problems with the occult.

3. My third experience was in Basle. Pastor Gilgen, leader of the Free Church in Basle, was a man whose Christian witness God had blessed. When my books on the occult were published, he said, "We do not need these books; there are no problems with the occult in Switzerland." In Switzerland, however, the canton Appenzell is well known for its occult, magic, and spiritualist healers. There are tens of thousands of people in Switzerland, who are suffering severely under the effects of occult practices. It is beyond comprehension that a man can preach the Word of God and counsel people for forty years without being confronted with such problems.

A proper view of the occult lies somewhere between two extremes. One extreme has already been illustrated. Some Christians believe that, when someone turns to Christ, all effects of the occult end at that moment. This is a view I have often heard in North America. But it is a false view based on lack of experience.

The other extreme is to exaggerate the occult. There are some Christians who think everything they do not understand is from the occult. Such people can even develop a kind of occult neurosis, which makes them ascribe everything unusual in their lives to occult influence. It is important to be levelheaded about the occult, to stick to the facts.

I must also give the reader a warning. Anyone who has weak nerves, or is very easily influenced, would be better advised not to read this book. At most they should have Christian friends tell them some of its contents. Some people are so sensitive that they apply everything they read to themselves. Even those who are mentally and emotionally strong are advised to pray constantly that they may be under the protection of Christ and shielded by His precious blood. The devil always tries to attack us at our weakest point. If you go onto a battlefield, you will be shot at. I have found this to be true even in writing this book. One illness followed another and many accidents took place. One day I had such acute pain in my right arm that I was prevented from using the typewriter, and I had to stop writing for several weeks.

I have intentionally avoided writing in a scientific style like my other book, *Christian Counselling and Occultism*. I have been told many times that it was too technical for lay people. A popular book that does not minimize the problems but does not exaggerate them was needed. In this book I have tried to provide just that.

If I were asked what I hoped this book will achieve, I would reply with the following illustration.

Ex 1 Some years ago a teacher told me how she had escaped from great danger. She had climbed a mountain one afternoon. It was dark when she began to climb down. She took a wrong turn and lost her way. Being a Christian, she asked the Lord to protect her. Suddenly she saw a bright light on the other side of the valley, which also lighted up the path in front of her. To her consternation, she saw that she was at the edge of a great chasm. If the light had not come at the right moment, she would have fallen down a precipice. The object of my book is simply to fulfil the function of that light. I want to illuminate some precipices so that the unwary may not fall into chasms.

Warning and illumination, however, is only one side of the matter. The other aim of this book is to point to the only One who can help—Jesus Christ, the Son of God—who, on the cross of Calvary, crushed the ancient serpent's head. He came into this world to lighten our darkness. The Son of God appeared to destroy the works of the devil (1 John 3:8). Whoever links himself to Jesus and accepts Him as Lord of his life is on the victory side. Paul says in 1 Corinthians 15:57, "But thanks be to God, which giveth us the victory through our Lord Jesus Christ."

One more point about the arrangement of the book. The three long chapters on magic, spiritism, and fortunetelling contain only a general survey with a few examples. The important points are dealt with again in the specialized chapters. That, for the sake of the observant reader, is why important problems like the use of ouija boards, pendulums, and other occult utensils appear twice in the book.

Finally, I commend the readers of this book and all those whose experiences are published here to the protection and preserving grace of God.

A. FORMS OF OCCULT MOVEMENTS AND DEVICES

1
ACUPUNCTURE

The material used in the following account has been collected from every continent. It is impossible for me to use every example that has come to my notice in counseling.

As far as the abundant literature is concerned, one book that gives a good historical and technical introduction to the subject of acupuncture is Marc Duke's *Acupuncture* (Suhrkamp). This book, however, must be read with some caution, for it does not deal with the psychic aspect of acupuncture. It is this latter that constitutes the main problem for the Christian who is considering the use of the treatment. The preface to the book is by Dr. Köhnlechner, and the final chapter by Dr. Scheel. Incidentally, neither of these scholars have noticed the mistake in the opening line of the book. The word "acupuncture" is compounded from two Latin words: *acus, -us,* fem. = needle and *punctum, -i,* neut. = prick—not *punctua,* as stated in the first sentence. That grates on the Latinist. Several introductory examples about acupuncture follow:

Ex 2 In Tokyo, I was the guest of Dr. Eitel, who was for about thirty years chief consultant of a hospital in Changsa, Hunan Province, in China, until he was driven out by the Mao revolution. I asked this experienced surgeon, "What do you think of acupuncture? You know that this form of treatment has a background in astrology. Yang represents the solar system, Yin the lunar system."

Dr. Eitel replied, "In the course of 5,000 years—which is the length of time acupuncture has been going—the astrological background has completely disappeared. Christians do not need to worry about that. What is clear is that here in East Asia, acupuncture has achieved some startling successes."

Ex 3 In September 1974, I was the guest of Dr. Hill, a medical doctor in Sherbrook, Quebec, Canada. Dr. Hill is a committed Christian. I asked him his opinion of acupuncture. He gave his answer in the form of an illustration. A believing Baptist minister was unable to move one of his arms, due to rheumatism in his wrist. In his congregation there was a Christian doctor from China, who had studied acupuncture in Hong Kong. The doctor treated the pastor

5

with needles. As a result, the minister was able to move his arm again.

Ex 4   An excellent example of unimpeachable reliability is the account by Dr. Mildred Scheel, wife of the president of the Federal Republic of Germany. We find it in Duke's book, under the title "Caesarean section in full consciousness."[1]

The president had to make a journey to China, and his wife expressed the desire to see an operation with acupuncture. Her wish was fulfilled. In a hospital in Peking, she watched a Caesarean section performed; the only anaesthetic was the piercing with needles. Four needles, each 3 inches long, were pushed into the lower leg. Then two more needles, 5½ inches long, were inserted near the navel. All the needles were then linked up to electric terminals. 2,400 shocks per minute caused the surface of her abdomen to vibrate, and 140 shocks per minute caused the legs to vibrate. During the incision of skin, fat layer, and sinews, a doctor handed the patient pieces of apple. The two surgeons even conversed with the patient during the operation. The baby was born. It was a fascinating experience. This account is undoubtedly of great value to doctors in the Western world.

These first three examples are positive. In the case of acupuncture, we are faced with a method developed by experience and success. Even the Chinese doctors who use it are unable to give a scientific explanation. The Russians, on the other hand, think they are on the way to explaining acupuncture.

Most doctors in the West are skeptical about acupuncture. In the USA, this form of treatment is forbidden. In the spring of 1975, I saw a TV program in which a young girl was anaesthetized by needles before an operation. After the operation there was a discussion for and against acupuncture. It is evident that up to the present time, German and Swiss doctors in particular either reject or are at most noncommittal about the development of this Chinese method of healing and anaesthesia.

We can see that there are two camps. This was true even in China as long as Chiang Kai-Shek was president of the Chinese mainland. Chiang, who was a Christian, wanted to forbid acupuncture by law. Mao knew how strongly the people clung to their ancient method of healing. After he came to power, he introduced it and favored it everywhere.

The origin of acupuncture goes back to the Emperor Huang Ti, about five thousand years ago. Huang Ti concluded through study of the stars, that harmony and balance reign in the universe. His next conclusion was that man as the microcosm must correspond to the macrocosm. In other words, physical and mental processes must be put in tune with one another. This insight has found new emphasis in the psychosomatic school of our own century. The basic concept of acupuncture is thus philosophical in character, with a leaning to astrology.

The next step came when Emperor Huang Ti worked out a theory as to how this harmony could be brought about or maintained in the human body. He called the energy or life force of a man "Ch'i." This was said to flow into the body at birth and to go out again at death. The Ch'i flows through the body in two systems: Yang and Yin. Yang is the male principle (the sun), Yin the female principle (the moon). The flow of Yang and Yin throughout the body is through a system of canals, the meridians. These meridians have nothing to do with the circulation of the blood, nor with the lymphatic system, nor with the nerves. For this reason, Yang and Yin are rejected by Western critics as being nonexistent.

The third step is knowledge of how the meridians are arranged. They are said to go under the skin and around the body. The fourteen main meridians are linked by fifteen Luo canals. Branching off from the main meridians are forty-seven subsidiary ones. The meridians pass close to the skin at 365 points. These are the places where needles can be inserted.

What is the idea of inserting the needles? In the entire body, and in every organ, a balance must be maintained between Yang and Yin. If either form of energy is too strong in an organ, then illness results. If, for example, the Yin, or female principle, is too strong, a gold needle is inserted in the appropriate place in order to strengthen the Yang, or male principle. If the Yang is too strong, a silver needle is inserted.

Present-day specialists in acupuncture no longer content themselves with the classic 365 points, but use up to a thousand. A modern example:

Ex 5 In the German magazine, *Bunte Illustrierte,* there is an article about one form of acupuncture under the sensational heading "Five Needles in the Ear Makes You Give Up Smoking." The astonished reader is presented with a powerful antidote to the smoking habit. A German woman has specialized in auricular acupuncture, that is, acupuncture of the ear. In the ear, there are said to be over a hundred places from which illness can be influenced by the insertion of a needle. Five of these are supposed to represent the center of addiction. This practitioner claims that more than 90 percent of her patients have been freed from smoking by this method. She takes special pride in four medical students whom she names as having given up smoking under her treatment. Her prize example is the German TV speaker, Dieter "Thomas" Heck, who used to smoke about eighty cigarettes a day until completely freed from the habit by means of acupuncture.[2]

Perhaps I may be allowed one or two lighthearted observations. If a chain smoker has a car accident and flies through the windshield, getting his ear cut off by the glass in the process, then he will be freed from his habit. The center of addiction has been removed.

We live in the age of organ transplants. In the case of the ear, a transplant would be particularly easy. My brother is a smoker. I am a nonsmoker. If I exchange ears with my brother, he will be freed from smoking; and I will be plagued with a longing for cigarettes.

But these, of course, are as I said, lighthearted conclusions about this mysterious method of treating an addiction. In case chain smokers place too much hope in the method, another example ought to be mentioned:

Ex 6   The actor, Richard Harris, underwent acupuncture of his ear in New York in the hope of becoming master of his smoking habit. The treatment was unsuccessful. Mr. Harris said afterward, "I'm afraid they found the wrong nerve. I still smoke 100 a day."

Let us conclude our study of the so-called scientific side of acupuncture by mentioning the greatest error in the classical theory of acupuncture. The ancient Chinese doctors believed that the spleen performed the functions which medicine ascribes to the brain. The brain had a minor role in their view. This gives us something of a yardstick by which to assess how "scientific" the system is.

Let us consider the extremely serious problem raised by acupuncture, which is not mentioned in the book by Marc Duke nor in the majority of books about acupuncture, namely,

The psychic factor

The Western view of the world is rational, the Eastern is what is called psychic. This is a subject which we cannot here consider in detail. It is my intention to deal with it in a forthcoming volume. Here I will give some brief comments.

The ancestor cult and all the religions of the East have a spiritistic or an animistic background. The result is the development of psychic powers. It is extremely difficult to define this term "psychic." It means an openness to that which transcends the mind, to the metaphysical, the supernatural—the demonic.

Missionaries and Christian researchers who have lived in Asia for many years claim that between 95 and 98 percent of the non-Christian population have psychic powers. These vary considerably in strength, depending on the extent to which the person has been involved with the occult practices of Asiatic religions.

The Western view of life is predominantly based on reason. In the West the percentage of people with psychic powers is the reverse of that found in the Eastern world: between 2 and 5 percent of the population are psychic. Only in those areas where magic is practiced is the proportion a higher one.

What then have psychic powers to do with acupuncture? It is a fact of experience that acupuncture is much more successful with psychic doctors and psychic patients than with those who are not psychic. Many Chinese doctors have indirectly acknowledged this, for a great many of them will not treat Western patients by acupuncture. There are of course exceptions, for in the Western world also there are psychic people. Psychic sensitivity, for the most part unconscious, is the catalyst for successful results in acupuncture.

It should be mentioned in passing that psychic powers enhance meditation, suggestion of every kind, hypnosis, narcosis, telepathy, and the ability to go into a trance. Practically all spiritistic and magical practices are impossible without psychic powers.

In many cases, acupuncture is a form of psychic anaesthesia (lack of feeling, deadening of pain). Whether this is true in all cases, I do not know.

As far as psychic anaesthesia is concerned, I have seen it practiced in East Asia and have taken photographs of it. In the cases I have observed, there was no need for any piercing with a needle.

Ex 7 During a pagan festival in Kuala Lumpur, the capital of Malaysia, I came upon a procession. Many of those taking part had stuck bamboo sticks through their cheeks, their eyebrows, their ears, the skin of their temples, or the muscles of their upper arms. The procession lasted six to eight hours, during which time the sticks were piercing their bodies. Those who participated claimed they felt no pain. When the sticks were pulled out, the wounds did not bleed and healed up within two hours.

Ex 8 I was particularly fascinated by one impressive scene. A

Hindu stuck a knife in between the two bones of his forearm. He said that he could do it by means of a semitrance. He was able by mental concentration to make his forearm insensitive to pain. Here, too, there was no pain, no bleeding, and swift healing. It was not a trick, as Western rationalists would have us believe. In one case, a similar act of putting a knife into the body was recorded by an x-ray photograph.

I know psychic people who can bring about psychic anaesthesia in themselves or in other people. Needles are not necessary, but they can be used in order to enhance the psychological effect.

These examples from East Asia suggest a possible explanation for those cases in which treatment by acupuncture was eminently successful.

There are not many Christian workers in the West who are familiar with the problem of psychic anaesthesia. I will mention a few who are friends and particularly well known to me:

1. Emil Kremer (of Colmar in France) deals with the subject in his book *Geöffnete Augen,* 14th Edition, p. 73.

2. Gottfried Eisenhut, of the Central Mission in Blekendorf, Germany, is very familiar with this subject.

3. Vim Malgo of Pfäffikon, Switzerland, should also be mentioned.

4. The book *Eine gefährliche Unwissenheit* by Walter Wilms (Schriftenmission Essen) I also recommend.

In North America, too, there are Christian workers who warn us against all occult practices, including acupuncture.

Ex 9 One Christian brother in California is deeply involved in the fight against occult practices. His life has already been threatened by Satanists and occult practitioners, and therefore I will not mention his name. Among other things, he has written a letter to the California state prosecutor, Evelle J. Younger, demanding that he come out against the spread of occult practices and institute proceedings against the organizers. Unfortunately, Satanists and occult practitioners sometimes threaten judges and lawyers, and so silence them. The Satanists are naturally not concerned about one more murder.

All these movements which come from the East remind us of the words of Revelation 16:12-14:

"That the way of the kings of the east might be prepared . . . For they are the spirits of devils, working miracles, which go forth unto the kings of the earth and of the whole world."

Finally we come to two questions. Can Christians also be psychic?

When a person is converted and turns to Christ, the psychic powers he may have inherited or acquired do not always disappear. Because inherited psychic powers are not usually known to those who have them, such Christians experience negative effects in their life of faith without understanding their origin. Christians like this can also be influenced by practitioners of the occult. Perhaps the second example in this chapter comes under this category.

The other question which I am often asked is, May a Christian believer allow himself to be treated by acupuncture? I cannot speak for anyone else. Everyone must make his own decision. If a Christian has been undergoing ordinary medical treatment for years without success and thinks that acupuncture will help him, he is making a serious decision. But under all circumstances he should pray that he may be under the protection of Christ. Psychic powers are dangerous.

Additional note:

What are we to make of electro-acupuncture? I have encountered two forms. In the first, the needles are connected to an electric supply at small voltage with a high frequency, with the object of bringing about vibration in the body of the patient. This form deserves the name of electro-acupuncture.

The second form has really nothing in common with acupuncture, and it is misleading to call it electro-acupuncture. I have seen the second form used by two fully qualified German doctors. To diagnose the patient's complaint they placed in his left hand the electrode of a meter. With his right hand, the patient, guided by the doctor, tested various medicines. The electric meter gave various readings during the test. The doctor chose the medicine which had produced the optimum response, and knew at once what was wrong with the patient. How this form of diagnosis and therapy came to be called electro-acupuncture, I am unable to fathom. Methods of healing become stranger every decade.

2
ANTHROPOSOPHY

Some opposition is bound to arise when readers compare the title of this book with its contents. At this point the question will be asked, What does anthroposophy have to do with the occult and Satan's devices? The answer is simple.

The theological collection *Religion in Geschichte und Gegenwart* has this to say: "Anthroposophy, the wisdom of man, or, as it calls itself, the study of the human spirit, is the most complete form of *occultism.*"[3]

The founder of this twentieth century movement or philosophy was Rudolf Steiner. He found followers among many educated people, especially doctors. Steiner tried to bring together in a universal system many religious movements such as Buddhism, Christianity, Theosophy, Gnosticism, Mysticism, Idealism, and also Spiritism and magic. His aim was to create a unity among them.

To describe this new system would require a philosophical essay, and would therefore go beyond the limits of this book. In this chapter, I will do no more than relate some of my own experiences.

Ex 10   As I was driving past the highway junction at Ulm West, I stopped for a hitchhiker. In the course of the journey to Karlsruhe, I asked him, "What is your job, that you cannot afford to travel by train?" "I am an anthroposophist priest," he replied.

Feigning ignorance, I asked, "What is that? What do you believe? What is your main teaching?" My passenger was very willing to tell me. "One of our central doctrines is reincarnation. We believe that a man returns to the earth approximately every 800 years, for further development."

"That is also taught by the Eastern religions," I commented. My curiosity was not yet satisfied, so I asked, "Can a person know what he did 800 years ago?"

"Yes," replied the priest, "we can draw conclusions from his inclinations, his likes and dislikes, his attitudes. What do you like or dislike the most?"

Being in the mood for a joke, I said, "Vicars and theology students make my blood boil." (I ought to add, by the way, that I love my Christian brethren among the theologians!)

The priest answered immediately, "This prejudice reveals that 800 years ago you were a professor of theology." The logic that led to this conclusion was not quite clear to me. I was amused.

Now it was my turn. I told him that the doctrine of reincarnation cannot be reconciled with the Bible. Our one life here on earth is decisive for eternity. But my companion was not satisfied. He replied that John the Baptist had been the reincarnation of Elijah. It is true that in Matthew 17:12 Jesus compares John the Baptist with Elijah. But the Baptist was certainly not a physical reincarnation of Elijah; he was simply equipped with the power and authority of Elijah. Similarity of divine commission does not mean that in this world flesh and blood return in a new form. Resurrection to a new kind of body is a future event which will not take place until the return of Christ.

We must firmly maintain that the Bible says nothing about a second or third chance. Our one life, and our attitude to Jesus Christ, are what determine where we will spend eternity.

The doctrine of reincarnation and with it anthroposophy have gained some fresh impetus in recent decades as a result of some unusual experiments.

Ex 11 A Swedish psychiatrist asked a woman who was under hypnosis to describe her life. His intention was to pursue the questions back to her birth and beyond. In this experiment the woman said that she had experienced something in the previous century. She gave a name, full address, and many circumstantial details that proved to be correct. Neither the psychiatrist nor the hypnotized woman knew beforehand about the information given under hypnosis.

A number of such experiments have now been recorded. A hypnotist in Zürich conducted the same experiment with the same result.

I do not lend great credence to newspaper articles. Press reports are often given added color in order to increase their sensation value.

I will give two examples of such articles, simply to illustrate. On January 22, 1975, the following report appeared in the *Rhein Neckar Zeitung:*

Ex 12   Murdered as Gretchen Gottlieb?
An American under hypnosis speaks of her former
life—new sensation from the "occult front."

An American history professor is at present trying to discover whether in the last quarter of the nineteenth century a young girl by the name of Gretchen Gottlieb lived in Eberswalde, Germany. He thinks that she may have been murdered during the religious struggles of Bismarck's *Kulturkampf.* The starting-point of his unusual research project? Fifty-two-year-old Dolores Jay, from Elton, Virginia, USA, swears she has never learned a word of German in her life—yet under hypnosis spoke in German of her former life as this Gretchen Gottlieb, and of her murder at the age of sixteen at the hands of several men in a forest.

According to a report in the *Washington Post,* Mrs. Jay was hypnotized several times by her husband, a Methodist minister, because of back trouble. In one of these sessions in 1970, he asked her whether she was still in pain, to which she unexpectedly replied with the German word "nein" ("no"). When her startled husband asked her if she felt well, the reply was again in German, "ja" (yes). During the three years following this, Mrs. Jay was repeatedly hypnotized and questioned by professors of German and scientists. She and her husband also underwent a number of lie detector tests without negative results. Various relatives testified on oath, that the woman had never learned German, nor had she ever had anything to do with German-speaking people.

The picture of Gretchen Gottlieb, which Mrs. Jay gave in the course of several sessions of hypnosis, is described by her husband. "Gretchen was about sixteen when she died, and she lived in the 1870's. She could neither read nor write. Her father was burgomaster of a town called Eberswalde, and she lived there with her father and a cook called Frau Schilder or Schiller." Gretchen was murdered while waiting in the forest for her uncle, who had hidden some horses to enable them both to get away. A group of men had discovered her before that could happen, and she had been killed.

When questioned by various history professors, Mrs. Jay kept returning under hypnosis to "church problems." "She has a fear of death and talks a lot about problems with the church," her husband said. Gretchen's father had been imprisoned because of these church problems. These references cause historians to suggest that the church problems in question are the bitter struggles of the *Kulturkampf* between the Prussian state and the Catholic church, which gave rise to isolated acts of violence. Although there are several places in Germany by the name of Eberswalde, Mrs. Jay is evidently referring to the market town of Eberswalde near Berlin.

Mrs. Jay's maternal forbears were Germans. Although her mother spoke no German, one of the explanations for the "Gretchen reminiscences" suggested by her husband is that they are possibly "a kind of genetic memory."[4]

Ex 13   A second article concerns itself with the work of the Munich therapist, Th. D. His practice is carried on under the name of the Institut für auBergewöhnliche Psychologie (Institute of Unusual Psychology). This man experimented with hypnosis and magic while still in his boyhood. He is therefore excellently qualified, not to cure his patients, but to subject them to occult influence. His therapy consists of hypnotizing his patients and, by hypnosis, removing their hang-ups, depressions, and the results of faulty development.

Th. D. is convinced that every person comes into this world at least twice. When a patient says that he is willing for an experiment to be made, he is hypnotized back to the time before his last birth. The hypnotist goes still further back, into his first life. He records the utterances of the patient on tape.

Some "prenatal" hypnotic experiments have been observed by the Munich psychology professor, Dr. Fuchs. Just a few examples:

Ex 14   Charley Baum, a radio program director from Saarbrücken, was hypnotized by Th. D. in the presence of Professor Fuchs. Baum declared, "I was born in 1732. It was at Tirgenberg in Swabia. My name is Karl Moritz Tebben. I sell black cloth. In 1769 I was struck down by the fever . . . my arms and legs became black. The doctor gave me something to drink. The only other thing I can remember is wood being knocked together, and then darkness." The whole conversation was broadcast over the "Saar European channel." This is a further example of how the public is being influenced in a negative way by the mass media.

Ex 15   Twenty-two-year-old Margret Näher was put into a deep hypnosis by D. Then she began to speak, "I am called Anna Schmidt, and I was born at Eggenburg in Austria on September 3, 1810. In 1828 our farmhouse was burned down. I was rescued by a neighbor. My mother's name is Josefine, my father's Andreas. In 1828, I moved to Berlin, where I later married an engine driver named Wenzel. In 1871, I died."

That all sounds interesting. The snag in the story is that there is no record of the birth of an Anna Schmidt in the register of 1810 at Eggenburg.

We have not, however, finished with the problem of reincarnation. How are we to judge this matter of people being hypnotized back beyond their birth and conception?

My opinion of hypnosis will become apparent in the chapter devoted to that subject. At this point, however, we must briefly touch on one or two questions. Where does this knowledge come from, which the hypnotized persons have about a supposed former life? Various explanations are offered:

1.   Buddhists and anthroposophists say that it is evidence that the hypnotized person has lived before. This theory is unacceptable to the Christian.

2.   Rationalists, who reject anything supernatural, seem satisfied to dismiss such evidence as deceit. They find corroboration for their

view in cases like that of Margret Näher (Ex. 15 above), where statements have been checked and found false.

3. Parapsychologists will perhaps assume a gift of retrospection on the part of the hypnotist. By this is meant a clairvoyant's ability to see the past.

4. Others will answer along the lines of Eduard von Hartmann and Hans Driesch, who talk of tapping the world soul. Anchored in this world soul are the facts about the lives of all men. This, too, is a theory which cannot be proved. For the Christian, God is the world soul, and He does not allow practitioners of the occult to tap His knowledge.

5. When I wrote to Professor Köberle and asked his opinion about these utterances, he replied that the first thing which came to mind was a tapping of Jungian archetypes. Professor Köberle is a serious theologian and a believing Christian, and this suggestion must therefore be investigated.

Undoubtedly Carl Gustav Jung is the most well-known depth psychologist to date in the twentieth century. His studies of the individual, family, and collective unconsciousness have become common in psychology.

It may appear presumptuous to try and pick holes in the views of one so famous. One or two quotations, however, will make Jung's spiritual position clear. In his book, *Über die Psychologie des Unbewuten,* we read, "The collective unconscious contains the experiences of the human race and of its animal forebears."[5] Our animal forebears?

In *Symbolik des Geistes,* Jung says that a spiritual God is nothing more than a personifying projection of unconscious elements into the realm of metaphysics.[6] God, a projection of the human mind?

If the penny has not yet dropped, let it be known that Jung has described the God of Job as a malicious tyrant *(Antwork auf Hiob).* With all due respect to Jung, the scientist, it is obvious that he cannot be a guide for the Christian believer.

Nevertheless, an answer must be given to those who speak of the tapping of the archetypes.

The archetypes are, according to Jung, the structural elements, the formative symbols of the collective unconscious. What he is talking about are simply dispositions, motives, inclinations, dominant principles. No amount of tapping of the archetypes of a present-day person could reveal the life history of a person of former days. Date of birth, Christian name, surname, place of residence, occupation, circumstances, and date of death are not recorded in the archetypes, if indeed these often-mentioned archetypes exist at all. The explanation suggested by Professor Köberle goes beyond what Jung himself taught.

6. How then are the "prenatal" experiences revealed under hypnosis to be explained? An indirect answer is given to us when we look at the history of the Munich psychotherapist who conducts these experiments. Anyone who undertakes experiments with magic or hypnotism becomes psychic, even if he does not realize it. This therapist is not tapping archetypes, but the powers of which Paul warns us, "For we wrestle not against flesh and blood, but against . . . spiritual wickedness in high places" (Ephesians 16:12). "Prenatal hypnosis" is, if no deception is taking place, contact with the spirits, or spiritism. Through these experiments, both hypnotist and subject come under an evil influence. "Prenatal" hypnosis presents us indirectly with the problem of possession. An example will illustrate:

Ex 16 In France, a minister brought a woman to me who had symptoms of possession. If anyone prayed with her, she fell into a trance. Then another voice came from her, which claimed to be that of her grandmother. Not only this, but the second voice identified itself also with the granddaughter who was in the trance.

If a psychiatrist examines a woman with these symptoms, he speaks of a split consciousness, or personality. The dissociated parts of the unconscious, he will say, have made themselves independent. This is a common feature of the schizophrenic syndrome. Yet there are very considerable differences between a spiritist trance and schizophrenic disintegration. I refer the reader to the chapter on spirit possession.

Few pastors have been able to counsel people who are possessed. Those who are most frequently named around the world are Motherwell in Australia, Ruark in Canada, Rosteck in the USA, and Kremer in France.

When a possessed person dies, the demon goes out and tries to enter another member of the family. Relatives of possessed persons are often themselves psychic, and so open to invasion by evil spirits. Sometimes a possessed person cannot die until the demon which has been inhabiting him has found another home. If one of these spirits succeeds in gaining possession of a grandchild, a certain family tradition is set up. A hypnotist who hypnotizes such a person back beyond his birth is in fact making contact with these family spirits, and it is from them that the knowledge about the ancestors is gained.

This all sounds like an absurd construction. Even real Christians who have no experience of spirit possession, find it incredible and impossible to understand. But anyone, who has spent years counseling those who have come under occult influence, is familiar with such experiences. The fact that unbelieving, unregenerate psychiatrists, hypnotists, parapsychologists, and modernist theologians scoff at it does not invalidate the truth.

It is significant that in various English translations of the Bible the term *familiar spirits* is used in Old Testament references to sorcery. Although this expression in its natural sense means intimate, well-known spirits, it could also be taken in the original, literal sense of the word to mean *spirits of the family*. There are some families which are ruled for many years, even centuries, by such spirits.

The evil spirits enjoy deceiving and misleading men and women. The "prenatal hypnotists" are without exception to be counted among their victims.

3

ASTROLOGY

Astronomy is a reputable science, concerned with the study of galaxies, fixed stars, and planets. Astrology is the interpretation of human destiny, and a man's future, by reference to the position of the stars at the moment of his birth. Astrology is therefore a form of fortunetelling. It has existed for five thousand years. The Sumerians, Accadians, the Chaldeans, Babylonians, Greeks, and Romans all had their astrologers. A hexameter listing the signs of the zodiac has come down to us from Roman times:

They are aries, taurus, gemini, cancer, leo, virgo, libra, scorpio, sagittarius, capricorn, aquarius, pisces.

Astrologists are eager to cite the three Wise Men from the East as justification of their dark art. The three Wise Men from the East, however, were God-fearing men who let their knowledge of the stars be used to lead them to Christ. In those days, no distinction was drawn between astronomy and astrology. The distinction was first made at the time of the enlightenment, in the middle of the eighteenth century. Thus we have no right to use the wise men from the East as a justification for this astrological fortunetelling. Let us look at a modern example.

Ex 17 In October 1975, when visiting the Catholic church at Bad Wiessee, I noticed that the face of the clock on the tower was decorated with the signs of the zodiac. I wrote to the priest, saying that it was incompatible with the Christian faith to portray the signs of the zodiac on a Christian church. The priest replied that the zodiac was a symbol of the glory of the creator.

It is grotesque evidence of muddled thinking to take symbols used for fortunetelling and use them to glorify God. I wrote again to the priest, citing several Bible verses, including Isaiah 47:12-14, where we are told that astrologists are under the wrath of God and will not escape the judgment.

Ex 18 At a certain party, a Lutheran pastor met, among others, a lady of thirty-five. She showed him a horoscope which had been made for her by an astrologer. This Lutheran pastor is also known for his astrological predictions. He said to her, "You are a teacher with a good position. You have a great longing to get married, and yet you are not willing to. You have had a number of affairs. At present you are going with a man who is twenty years older than you are. He is an officer, probably a staff officer. Your relationship has a serious crisis to undergo, and will come to an end." The woman admitted this was so, and said, "The relationship ended the day before yesterday." The teacher was a stranger to the pastor. They had never met before this big party. The pastor himself told me of the incident, attacking me for my rejection of astrology. Just as with the Catholic priest, I directed him to Isaiah 47:12-14. His reply, "That does not apply to us. The book of Isaiah was written for the Jews of that time." That is a strange way of expounding the Bible. On that principle the letters of Paul have no validity for us, since they were written to Romans, Corinthians, Philippians, Galatians, and to other churches. Here we see a theologian artfully dodging the claims, the commands, and the prohibitions of Holy Scripture.

This example demonstrates first the thoroughly wrong attitude and behavior of this pastor. But it also reveals that not all fortunetelling is swindle and humbug. This Lutheran pastor was able, with the aid of astrology, to give accurate information. This is equally true of other forms of fortunetelling such as palmistry, card-laying, fortunetelling by rod or pendulum, and other occult arts. Accurate statements are made in perhaps 5 to 8 percent of cases. This does not mean that we ought to use astrology. The Old Testament says, "Soothsayers and sorceresses you shall not allow to live." Obviously in the twentieth century we cannot put up stakes and burn the astrologists and fortunetellers. We must, however, reveal their practices, warn people, and show the victims of astrology the way to deliverance.

Fortunetelling is dangerous, whether or not its predictions come true. I will illustrate this with an example from my own counseling.

Ex 19   A young man of twenty asked an astrologer to cast him a horoscope. One of the things it said was that he would not be happy with his first wife. He would only achieve marital harmony with his second wife. The young man married early, and on his wedding day he said to his brother, "The woman I am marrying today is not the right one. Only my second wife will make me happy." His brother was angry with him and rebuked him.

This first wife proved to be a true and reliable person. His parents were very happy with the match.

The couple had three children. Then the man left home and abandoned his wife and three children. His Christian parents and other family members were very sad. His father disinherited him and gave title to the house to his three grandchildren. Not long afterward the man married again, and thought that this was the wife with whom he would be happy. The second marriage, however, lasted only a year. His second wife became a Jehovah's Witness and went to extreme lengths to try and win her husband to the sect. He, however, wanted nothing to do with such rubbish. He left his second wife, and now he hopes that he will find in his third wife the person who will make him happy.

The horoscope's prophecy of a happy second marriage was wrong. The second marriage lasted a shorter time than the first. What is obvious from this example of astrology is that the young man was influenced to his own downfall by suggestion through the horoscope. Many people say that astrology is humbug. But even humbug can have suggestive power. This suggestive power influences the behavior and decision of superstitious people to their disadvantage. There really ought to be a law prohibiting this and all other forms of for-tunetelling. Astrology has been responsible for a number of suicides and murders.

Ex 20   Another example came to my attention in a church in Brazil where, over the years, I have conducted three evangelistic campaigns. A young woman who was engaged to be married sought out an astrologer and had her horoscope cast. The astrologer wrote the following prediction: "Your engagement will break up. This man will not marry you. You will not marry at all, but remain single." The girl was stunned. She was very much in love with her fiancé and could not bear the thought of losing him. She was constantly wor-ried that the engagement would break up and that she would never marry. She became overpowered by melancholia and resolved to put an end to her life. On the day when she was planning to carry out her resolve, she was stopped by a friend of her fiancé. Upon that one's advice, she came to me for counseling, confessed the whole story, repented, and surrendered her life to Christ. Not long afterward, her fiancé came to be counseled, too. He was also ready to give his life to Christ. They were married, and today they have several children and are enjoying a happy marriage. In this case, Christ prevented the disaster which had been set afoot by the astrologer.

My best experience in counseling in the field of astrology can be found in a special section in the last chapter, *In the Conqueror's Train*. Let us close with the words of the prophet Isaiah, chapter 47:12-14:

> Stand now with thine enchantments, and with the multitude of thy sorceries, wherein thou hast laboured from thy youth; if so be thou shalt be able to profit, if so be thou mayest prevail. Thou art wearied in the multitude of thy counsels. Let now the astrologers, the stargazers, the monthly prognosticators, stand up, and save thee from these things that shall come upon thee. Behold, they shall be as stubble; the fire shall burn them; they shall not deliver themselves from the power of the flame: there shall not be a coal to warm at, nor any fire to sit before it.

4
BAHA'I

The Baha'i religion originates from Islam. In about 1800, the Arab Sheikh Ahmed founded the sect of the Sheikhs, which was eschatological in emphasis. They awaited the return of the last Imam (spiritual leader and interpreter of the Koran). In 1844, the Sheikh declared himself to be the Bab (gate of truth). His followers called themselves Babi. Persecuted by conservative Muslims and driven into a corner, the Babi separated themselves in 1848 from Islam. In 1850, the Bab was shot. Martyrs of any sort unquestionably give added impetus to a movement.

The Bab found a zealous and highly gifted successor in Mirza Husayn Ali, who was born in 1817 in Teheran, the son of a government minister. His life too was marked by persecutions, arrests, and even attempts to poison him. On the basis of revelations which he had while in prison, after his release he called himself Baha u'llah, the glory of God. He was a very talented man. When he died in 1892, his written works filled 100 volumes.

In his will, Ahmed appointed his son Abdul Baha as his successor. He had inherited some of his father's talents. Although Abdul had never been to school, he spoke Persian, Arabic, Turkish, and had a wide knowledge of philosophy and theology. It was his achievement, in great journeys across the world, to carry the Baha'i faith to the Western world. Baha'i temples were set up in Ishkabad (1902), Kampala (Uganda), Sydney (Australia) and Wilmette, near Chicago (USA); and these temples served as mission centers. I have been to all these temples except the one at Ishkabad. The Wilmette temple is architecturally the finest of all. While I was in Chicago on a lecture tour, Pastor Plaum took me to see this "drafty" building. For us Christians this temple makes one Baha'i tenet very clear: Christ has a place alongside Mohammed and Abraham. He is one religious leader among others and not the Savior of mankind, the one and only ground of our salvation.

This brings us to the religious content of the Baha'i religion, insofar as it can be of any interest to the Christian. All religions, they say, are relative and express only a part of the truth. They find their unity and fulfilment in the Baha'i revelation. The Baha'i teaching is the highest, and expresses the solidarity of all religions. Therefore Buddha, Moses, and Jesus stand on the same level as Mohammed: as founders of religions.

What we have here is religious syncretism, with Baha'i as the umbrella organization. As far as Biblical teaching is concerned, this is unacceptable. Jesus says in John 14:6, "No man cometh unto the Father, but by me." Further light on the Baha'i system is shed by the Dodecalogue, or twelve leading principles (cf. Decalogue, the Biblical Ten Commandments). Outside the temple in Sydney is a tablet with the following inscription:

Baha'i

World-embracing faith

Twelve fundamental doctrines of the Baha'i

We teach:

1. The unity of all mankind
2. Independence of inquiry into the truth
3. All religions have the same origin
4. Religion must be the cause of unity
5. Religion must be in agreement with science and reason

6. Equality between woman and man
7. Prejudices of every kind must be ignored
8. Universal peace
9. Universal education
10. A spiritual solution to economic problems
11. A unified language
12. An international court of law

These twelve guidelines are extremely illuminating. Many parallels to them can be found. Think of Kant's *Religion Within the Limits of Reason Alone*.[7] The Baha'i principles could have been drawn up by adherents of modern theology; most of them would be accepted by the ecumenical movement. Indirectly, therefore, Baha'i doctrine is gaining ground rapidly.

This can even be noticed in a simple newspaper advertisement, like that in the *Schorndorfer Blatt* of May 15, 1975. This reads:

> The Baha'i are members of a world community which includes people of every nation, race, and class. They have as their basic aim the unification of all nations on this planet. Baha'i—the religion of unity.

Behind the advance of Baha'i there is much more hidden. It is nothing less than a first-class preparation for the coming Antichrist, who will reduce everything to one common denominator: a single official language (in the West at least), a single currency, a single centrally financed government, a single political system with a single head (the Antichrist himself), a world court of justice, a single tax system. Every citizen will have a registered number, without which he will not be allowed to buy or sell; and there will be one universal world church. Anyone who refuses to take part in this universal system is finished, and will have no right to exist.

If we consider things in this light, it is not surprising that some Christians are saying that the Antichrist will come from the Baha'i religion. There are various views about the origin of the Antichrist. Luther said he would come from the papacy; others see Communism as his breeding ground. The majority hold that he must come from the Jews. Others again think that the Antichrist will come from the ten kingdoms which will rise in the territory of the former Roman Empire. The future will reveal who was right. Since the Antichrist is to appear in company with a False Prophet, it is quite possible that he will use a follower of the Baha'i faith as his religious helper in order to bring about his plan for a universal church. These events cannot be predicted with certainty. We merely observe the present world religious scene and conclude that, both in Baha'i and in the ecumenical movement, tendencies are appearing which will one day play a part in the Antichrist's final substitute for religion.

"He who has eyes to see, let him see!" (Matthew 13:13)
"He who has ears to hear, let him hear!" (Matthew 11:15)

5
BIOLOGICAL FEEDBACK AND MIND CONTROL

In 1929 the German physiologist, Hans Berger, discovered that the brain produces weak electrical impulses, which are related in frequency to the varying degrees of consciousness. At the time the medical world took little notice of this discovery. It was not until twenty-five years later, when encephalograms began to be used to register electrical activity in the brain, that Berger's findings were rediscovered. The following table illustrates the significance of the various frequencies:

1. beta waves, 13-30 cycles per second—our normal conscious state in doing things; eyes open; feeling of concentration or tension.

2. alpha waves, 8-12 cycles per second—feeling of "relaxed well-being and inner awareness"; eyes closed; a letting go of tension. (This is the state of day-dreaming or hypnosis.)

3. theta waves, 4-7 cycles per second—the state just before sleep.

4. delta waves, 0.5-3 cycles per second—deep sleep. New born babies are often in this state.

In the USA, various movements have developed, using these calculations and their relation to the level of consciousness as a basis. One of these is "biofeedback research." In charge of this is Dr. J. W. Hahn of Los Angeles. The term biofeedback means biological renewal of life, enhancement of vitality, strengthening of energy.

More than sixty firms in California have developed machines for regulating the electrical activity of the brain in connection with the method and goal of this research. In particular the aim is to loosen excessive tension in the beta state. The idea is that people should live more in the alpha state. Hence the name of these technical devices: "alpha control" machines. Their program is defined as descent into alpha.

Biofeedback is thus a new form of therapy. The aim is not only to bring the brain waves under control but also to control other unconscious body processes.

At first sight this appears to be a scientific method. But when one reads the literature about it, one becomes skeptical. Yogis, magicians, hypnotists, and other workers with the occult are constantly mentioned. A small example from an article by Dr. Hahn:

Ex 21 Dr. Elmer Green at Menninger Foundation showed that, by using biofeedback, humans could learn to differentially control the temperature of their hands: one hand hot, the other cold. Yogis practice exactly the same exercise at the second stage.

The occult element is still more obvious in the case of a second movement of this type, known as Silva Mind Control. The founder is José Silva, a former electrical engineer from Texas. He never had any formal education, yet he is discussed on university platforms.

The news sheet *Mind Control* reveals the deliberately occult program of the movement. Like biofeedback, it is based on the varying frequencies of electrical impulses in the brain. The Silva people do not use technical apparatus. They do everything by means of concentration.

Everyone who studies this method has to undergo a four-day introductory course, for twelve hours each day. The nature of the course is reminiscent of transcendental meditation or of yoga. Silence alternates with the monotonous repetition of sentences, or of a "mantra." This is followed by breathing exercises. Finally a mild form of group hypnosis is attempted.

Let us hear what experts and members of the Silva movement have to say by way of explanation.

Ex 22 Catherine Bigwood writes: " 'Mind Control is neither a religion nor a philosophy,' says Silva. 'Yogis looked for control over the mind and called it Yoga; Zen Buddhists called it Zen; hypnotists called it hypnosis. These are all just different techniques for going to the alpha level. Mind Control is a way of using more of our brain, a way of consciously learning how to use the subconscious. . . . Mind Control's main goal is subjective communication or ESP. . . .' " ESP is extrasensory perception, an occult phenomenon.

There is no need for us to look for further evidence of the occult nature of the Silva method. Its adherents admit it openly. It is true that Silva regards ESP as harmless. That is the mistake made by all occult movements.

Their news sheets provide every conceivable type of material. Silva, the founder of the movement, is a medium. His followers practice *psi* communication, for example, telepathy, and train themselves in clairvoyance. The number of followers has grown so enormously, that today, Silva Mind Control is the largest association in the field of parapsychology.

The contradictory character of the reports on this movement is demonstrated by the example which follows. Ms. Bigwood writes that Mind Control is not a religion. Robert Taylor, another adherent, says, "Conscious control of the subconscious—the peace that passes all understanding, practiced by Christian and Hebrew mystics, Muslim sufis, Indian yogis and Zen masters—is available to Western culture."

What a dreadful hodgepodge! The peace which passes all understanding comes from Silva, the occult electrician from Texas! Christians are mystics, who pursue the same goal as yogis, sufis, and zen buddhists? No. This is not true! Christians have Jesus Christ, the Son of God, the Redeemer and Judge of all men, who will one day put an end to all occult and demonic movements.

What is absolutely tragic is that several hundred pastors have already practiced this occult method. They delve into the occult because their theology does not teach personal salvation through Christ. These pastors then carry this sublimation of the occult into their congregations.

Here the greatest help is to be found in Hebrews 4:12:

> For the Word of God is quick, and powerful, and sharper than any two-edged sword, piercing even to the dividing asunder of soul and spirit, and of the joints and marrow, and is a discerner of the thoughts and intents of the heart.

On the one side we have the living God; on the other is Satan with all his wiles. Let every man decide for himself to whom he wants to belong.

6
BLACK MASS

Every satanic cult of history and of today has celebrated the black mass. There are only a few exceptions, for instance, the Processeans.

Those who celebrate the black mass are Satan's elite troops. The purpose of the black mass is to mock God, to blaspheme against the Trinity.

Ex 23 Some years ago a great sensation was caused by some theology students in Münster, West Germany. They celebrated the black mass in a church. On the altar they had bottles of schnapps. In the prayers they substituted the name of Satan for the name of God. They were asked why they were studying theology. Their answer: "To destroy the Church."

Ex 24 When I was in Cornwall, England, I heard of the black masses in that area. A naked woman serves as an altar. The members of the cult practice perversions on her. The horrible things which are done cannot be repeated in a book. I have heard the confession of a professional man who has not been able to find inner peace since practicing these horrible things. Sometimes the Satanists break into churches and use the monstrance for their black mass, or take a crucifix and cover the figure of Christ with their excrement.

Ex 25 In the USA, the Satanists use the blood of animals for their black mass. Very exclusive groups of Satanists mix bread and wine with a substance taken from a man and a woman. In Haiti, the high priest drinks the blood of children at the annual festival. In the Macumba groups in Brazil, the same thing is done at the initiation of a Mae de Santo (cult mother).

To lovers of the peace symbol, let it be known that the black pope, Anton La Vey, projects a peace symbol onto a large screen before the commencement of his satanic rites in San Francisco. Yet the naive Christians of Europe and USA wear the peace symbol on a chain around their necks or on the sleeves of their jackets!

7
BLOOD PACTS

Blood pacts provide some of the most difficult problems in counseling. I have record of about a hundred cases in my files. What is a blood pact? A person takes a piece of paper, scratches his finger until it bleeds, and then signs himself over to the devil. From that day on such people are no longer approachable on spiritual issues. They become totally opposed to the church, the Bible, prayer, and to every kind of spiritual influence. I am surprised that such people come for counseling. It evidently shows that they are not happy with their master and are looking for something else to satisfy them.

Ex 26 In Canada, I was speaking at a youth conference. In the group was a seventeen-year-old girl who took part during the day in the Bible study and the prayer meeting. At night, however, she had confused dreams, and her roommates could hear her cursing herself and saying: "I hate Jesus. I love the devil. He is my lord." Yet this same girl, who cursed herself and had sold herself to the devil, could come to me for counseling and ask for help.

Ex 27   A young teacher came to me for counseling. He suffered from depression and suicidal thoughts, and asked me for advice and help. In the course of the conversation, the following facts came to light. In a fit of despair he had signed himself over to the devil in his own blood. He took the paper to a cave, went inside, placed it on a ledge of the rock and put a stone on top of it. Then he left the cave. A few minutes later he began to regret what he had done in his desperation. He ran back and reentered the cave, intending to pick up the paper and destroy it. The paper was gone. There was no one in the cave who could have taken the paper. It could not have been blown away by a gust of wind, for he had put a stone on top of it. He now became very anxious, and his anxiety brought him to me for counseling.

A psychiatrist would say that he was an unstable character. But, in spite of his depression and his instability, he was telling the truth. It was his earnest desire to find the way to Jesus. It took considerable time before this teacher found inner peace. He made a general confession of sin, and was able, in faith, to accept the forgiveness of Christ. Then he did something I have never advised anyone who has made a blood pact to do. He scratched his finger again and with his blood wrote a statement declaring himself free from the devil. I repeat that I never advise anyone to do this, although I know there are some counselors who tell people to do so.

Blood pacts create a terrible block. People who have signed them find it extremely difficult to find the way of salvation. The story which follows makes this frighteningly clear.

Ex 28   A woman belonged to a spiritist circle and had signed herself over to the devil in her own blood. She happened to go into a mission meeting. She was convicted by the Spirit of God and made a general confession in the course of being counseled afterward. She wanted to follow Jesus, come what may. From that moment onward, terrible struggles began. The satanic attacks reached their climax in a red tatto which appeared on her breast one night. She showed this to her sister. It was in the shape of a horseshoe with an S in the middle. A prayer group began to intercede for this troubled woman. She was delivered.

Ex 29   What concerns us more than the power of Satan is the victorious power of Jesus. A man who had made a blood pact went to see a friend of mine. This counselor, who is a fully qualified pastor, heard his confession and advised him to write another statement in his own blood declaring himself free from the devil. This bold piece of advice was followed by the blessing of the Lord. The man became free.

8
CHARISMATIC MOVEMENTS

Let us briefly sketch the history of the modern movements in which speaking in tongues has emerged.

At the age of nineteen, George Fox (1624-1691) broke with the church because he was repelled by its laxity. The spiritual system he adopted depended on experience. He heard a voice say to him, "Not the outward Word of Scripture, not the teaching of the church, not the outward Christ can lead you, but only the inner light, the inward Christ."

Fox was the founder of the *Children of Light* or *Society of Friends*. Their enemies called them Quakers. This nickname has remained with them to the present day. A dangerous, extremist view can be seen in the origin of the Quakers: the inner light and the voices from above were more important than the written Word of God. The door was open for all kinds of false teaching. In the early days some groups also practiced speaking in tongues. Since then some things have been clarified among the Quakers, and things have settled down. I have addressed Quaker meetings in places like Kotzebue in the Friends' Mission Church.

Another group which teaches speaking in tongues and other ecstatic forms of expression are the Irvingians. They call themselves the Catholic Apostolic Church. The founder was Edward Irving. Among his circle of friends was one Mary Campbell, who began speaking in tongues in 1826. Various charismatic manifestations such as faith healing, visions, and prophecies attracted people for whom traditional churches no longer had any significance. The Irvingians spread rapidly in England, Holland, USA, and especially in Germany, where their center was in Augsburg; but their largest congregation was in Stuttgart. By the year 1900, they had fifty thousand members.

Among ecstatic movements we must also number the Mormons, the Latter-Day Saints. Their founder was Joseph Smith (1805-1844), who was born in the state of Vermont, USA. This movement is marked by visions, revelations, speaking in tongues, and healing. In 1823, Smith had a vision of the angel Moroni, who showed him a chest containing some golden tablets on Mount Cumorah. Smith claimed to have received these tablets in 1827. For the Mormons, the words written on these tablets have the same authority as the Bible. The length to which this labyrinth of false teachings took Smith is shown by his insistence that he had been consecrated to the Aaronic priesthood by John the Baptist. Peter, James, and John had later raised him to the priesthood of Melchizedek. Smith was murdered in 1844.

Everything that claims to possess an equal authority to the Scriptures is false teaching. For the Mormons, authority is found in the Bible and in the Book of Mormon. In the Catholic Church, authority is found in the Bible, but also in church tradition and the doctrinal pronouncements of the Pope. In some extremist circles, it is the Bible and the revelations and prophecies of those with "gifts of the Spirit."

We may thank God for reminding us through Martin Luther that authority is *sola scriptura,* in the Scriptures alone.

Even in the cold climate of Russia a tongues movement appeared. In the Armenian village of Kara Kala (lovely and beautiful) a charismatic movement woke to life in the Russian Orthodox Church. The Orthodox Church was in the habit of forcefully suppressing all who thought differently. They persecuted the Stundists and the Gospel Christians.

The speakers in tongues left Armenia, moved to the USA in 1900, and settled in Los Angeles. A few years later, this group joined the fellowship in Azusa Street, Los Angeles, who also spoke in tongues. Various charismatic groups gradually became established, mainly in America. To list them briefly, we note:

In 1899, the Reverend Parham, at a small Bible school in Topeka, Kansas, formed the conviction that speaking in tongues is the evidence of the baptism of the Holy Spirit.

In 1900, this small movement came to Los Angeles, a city whose atmosphere of spiritism makes it a breeding ground for any ecstatic movement.

In 1906, a former student of Parham, W. J. Seymour, worked up a strong tongues movement at 312 Azusa Street, Los Angeles.

In 1908, this enthusiastic movement was spread to Norway by Barrat, and to Hamburg and other towns by E. Meyer. The unedifying scenes which resulted led to the Berlin Declaration of September 1909.

In 1959, a new charismatic movement began in Los Angeles. It affected not only the Pentecostal churches but all denominations. Los Angeles has been, since 1850, the starting point for all kinds of occult and extreme spiritual movements until the present day.

In 1967, the Jesus People movement began, again in California. This movement is not all of one mold. Among the extreme groups are also some small groups of genuine Christians who cannot hold their own against the general movement.

Parallel to the Jesus People movement is the so-called charismatic movement, which has a much wider scope than a tongues movement. Here it is not merely a matter of speaking in tongues, but of faith healing, visions, prophecies—in short, all the gifts of the Spirit.

One can understand the starting point of those who belong to the charismatic movement. Cold congregations, with traditional and uninspired forms of worship, are not able to satisfy the spiritual hunger of many Christians. If this hunger and seeking had remained within Biblical limits, the charismatic movement would have brought great blessing to Christendom. In reality, however, this so-called charismatic movement has issued a great sea of confusion, depending on evidences of power which owe much to religious suggestion, hysteria, hypnotic and occult influence. This pseudocharismatic awakening has become a worldwide threat and a confusion to true Christians. The pseudocharismatics are the élite, the advance guard of Satan, who would use them to attack the best members of the church of Christ. I must, however, warn anyone who would use these hard but frank words as an excuse for his own unspiritual attitude.

Within the charismatic movement, there are tens of thousands of true Christians who will one day inherit the kingdom of God. On the other hand, there will not be a single modernist theologian in Heaven, unless he repents, receives Christ as Son of God and his own Savior, and throws his theology overboard, as Dr. Huntemann has done.

Why are genuine Christians found in the ranks of the pseudocharismatics? They must lack the gift of distinguishing between spirits, otherwise they would leave this movement. It is a common experience that, in the circles where gifts of the Spirit are most talked about, they are least to be found.

After this introduction, let me give a few examples:

Ex 30   Some years ago in Kevin Ranaghan's book, *Catholic Pentecostals,* I read: "Baptism with the Holy Spirit leads to a greater love of Mary, a greater veneration of the Pope, a greater submission to the Catholic Church, a more frequent attendance at Mass, and a greater authority in witnessing to these matters."[8] The Holy Spirit leads us into all truth, not into false doctrines.

Ex 31   Another experience contains a similar lesson. Some years ago I gave several lectures in a church in Rock Island, Illinois, USA. The pastor told me he had been invited by the Jesuits in New York to come and speak about the gifts of the Spirit. This group of Jesuits belonged to the charismatic movement. The pastor declined the invitation with the comment, "I should first address Jesuits on the subject of the second birth and conversion before I could deal with the subject of the gifts of the Spirit." This pastor said to me, "The Jesuits have gone straight into speaking in tongues without being born again, and that is not Scriptural."

Ex 32   Another example is from Vim Malgo's publication *Mitternachtsruf*. Notice that I am not alone in my assessment of the charismatic movement. "A lady who belonged to the Roman Catholic charismatic movement prayed for a long time for the baptism of the Spirit. Nothing obvious happened. She did not speak in tongues. Finally she cried out to the Lord in desperation, 'I have now been asking You so long, and You have not given me my request. If You do not give me the baptism of the Spirit, I will speak to Your mother about it.' At that very moment she began to speak in tongues."

Vim Malgo adds: "Here again we cannot speak of a baptism of the Spirit, but rather of baptism with spirits." I am thankful for the clarity of the view here expressed by Vim Malgo.[9]

Ex 33   In the *New Covenant* magazine I read the following caption: "The Holy Spirit: My Hope."[10] The article was written by Cardinal Suenens. Apart from the content of the article, the title itself is unscriptural. The New Testament tells us that Jesus Christ is our hope for eternal life. It is characteristic of the charismatic movement that the center of emphasis is shifted at this point. When people add to or subtract from the statements of the Holy Scriptures, the result is false teaching.

Ex 34   Also in *New Covenant,* Archbishop George Pearce of the

Fiji Islands is reported as saying, "I owe to the Spirit, and to him alone, the fact that I have been given a new life."[11]

Here again the focus has been shifted from its rightful place. Jesus says in John 10:28: "I give unto them eternal life." And in Romans 6:23 Paul testifies that "the gift of God is eternal life through Jesus Christ our Lord." We must not deduct anything from the work of the Holy Spirit, but neither must we move Him into the center of the work of salvation, as is done by the charismatic movement.

Ex 35   The worst example of which I have heard, took place in Batu, East Java. The Dutch evangelist, Hugenduyk (senior), was giving some lectures at the Batu Bible School. Among other things, he said, "We now no longer need speak of the cross of Jesus, of His blood and His redemption, but only of the work of the Holy Spirit." A woman missionary from Batu told me of this.

Ex 36   In H. A. Baker's book, *Visions Beyond the Veil,* the following appears: "Where is the Holy Spirit who was to come to carry on His [Jesus Christ's] *uncompleted task?*"[12] The uncompleted task of Jesus Christ? The apostle John tells us in John 19:30 that on the cross, Jesus cried out "It is finished." In order to justify their actions and intrigues, members of the charismatic movement are prepared to declare the work of Jesus Christ incomplete.

This list of examples may be concluded with an excerpt from an illuminating report from the missionary G. A. Birch. In his report, this appears under Case 8. People who come for counseling are not, of course, cases—but it is difficult to find another word.

Ex 37   Mark (not his name) was a Christian in a church that he thought was formal and dead. He went to a Pentecostal church, where hands were laid on him, and he was what they called "slain in the spirit." He was lying on the floor in a trance. When he came out of it, he was praising Jesus in a loud voice, and he continued praising Jesus.

While attending this Pentecostal church, Mark also received a gift of tongues. The name of the spirit of the tongue was "Domenigaio." Here are some of the notes taken when this demon was cast out in the name of the Lord Jesus Christ.

> "Domenigaio, how many associates are with you in Mark?"
> "I am alone."
> "When did you enter him?"
> "When he was slain in the spirit."

"Who sent you?"

"The devil, from the pit."

"Do you acknowledge our authority over you in Christ Jesus our Lord?"

"I do."

"What is your commission from Satan?"

"To deceive."

"How?"

"In his love for the Lord Jesus; ruin his faith; have him follow Satan."

"You were posing as the Holy Spirit, weren't you?"

"Yes."

Mark denounces this demon in the name of the Lord Jesus Christ, and he is cast out into the pit in the name of the Lord Jesus Christ.

The name "Jesus" keeps coming into Mark's mind, so we command in the name of the Lord Jesus Christ that, if there is a demon in him named Jesus, he come forward and give his name.

Answer, "Jesus."

"What Jesus?"

"Jesus of the devil."

"What is your work, what did Satan commission you to do?"

"To fool him; to steal the glory from God."

"When did you enter into him?"

"When he was slain in the spirit."

This demon had to acknowledge his defeat by our Lord Jesus Christ, through the blood of the cross, and was cast out and into the pit, in the name of the Lord Jesus Christ.

We see here again that demons sometimes claim to be Jesus. Further, it here becomes evident that the so-called *baptism of the Spirit* in the charismatic movement is usually an opportunity for demons to enter.

Experiences with the so-called charismatic movement teach us to pray more than ever for the gift of discerning of spirits. These experiences also warn us to be led, in faith and obedience by the Word of God and the Holy Spirit, into all truth.

9
CHRISTIAN SCIENCE

My information about this movement has been gained largely from the two major works of its founder, Mary Baker Eddy. They are entitled *Science and Health* and *Miscellaneous Writings,* covering the years 1883-1896. I have also visited the center of the organization in Boston, USA. The building is a twenty-seven-story skyscraper. Much of my material has come from my counseling meetings and discussions with followers of this occult healing movement. As could be expected, the term *occult* in connection with this movement has brought strong attacks upon me.

Ex 38 In 1974, I gave lectures on Haiti at mission stations and at an international missionary conference. When I mentioned the occult healing methods of Christian Science, one person sprang up in a rage, interrupted me, and would not let me continue. He said that he and his sister had been healed by Christian Science practitioners. He was not going to allow anyone to run down this church in his presence. The chairman intervened and called the heckler to order, pointing out that he could discuss the matter with me afterward. After the address was ended, a pastor from California came up to me and said, "Don't be too upset. That man is a troublemaker wherever he goes. And yet he is the pastor of a church." I replied, "I am not surprised. In my experience all those who have been healed by Christian Science have received some kind of oppression or emotional damage."

Ex 39 On another occasion, I received a sharp attack in Germany. In one of my books, I had observed that sometimes practitioners—as the active workers in Christian Science are called—use their mental powers to harm people whom they have something against. Mary Baker Eddy mentioned this in her books. She called this reversal of healing powers into harmful powers *malpractice*. My assailant maintained that he had read neither the idea nor the word *malpractice* in Mary Baker Eddy's books. I am still amazed at such an assertion, and yet perhaps not. There are Christians who do not read their Bibles. Similarly, there are Scientists who do not read the books of their founder. Since the Scientist mentioned above accused me of misrepresenting Mrs. Eddy, saying that the expression *malpractice* does not occur in her writings, I am compelled to give some page references.

In *Science and Health,* malpractice is mentioned on pages 105,

375, 410, 419, 451, and 459. In *Miscellaneous Writings* reference
is made to malpractice on pages 31, 40-41, 55, 222, 284, and 368.
One of these many passages is as follows (pp. 40-41): "An element
of brute-force that only the cruel and evil can send forth, is given
vent in the diabolical practice of one who, having learned the power
of liberated thought to do good, perverts it, and uses it to accom-
plish an evil purpose. This mental malpractice would disgrace mind-
healing, were it not that God overrules it."

Ex 40 The following is one of my most significant examples.
A Christian Science practitioner admitted his error and left the
movement. From the center in Boston, he received a letter saying that
he would regret it. Shortly afterward, he developed a dreadful
skin disease which no dermatologist was able to cure. The patient
shed his skin like a snake. This happened three times. The third
time, he died. It cannot be proved that this severe illness was the
result of the united malpractice of several psychic practitioners. I
can only truthfully record that such things have been confessed to
me in connection with other occult movements. For some time there
has been in the USA a movement which makes use of *soul force*
to bring back an *erring sheep,* causing problems like that previously
mentioned.

Mary Baker Eddy's doctrines are very complicated. What is clear
from her books is that this system of teaching is not in line with
the Bible, although Biblical quotations are used. Mary Baker Eddy
simply does not believe that sickness and death are real. It is only
necessary to have the right inward attitude to be able to overcome
both sickness and death. The power controlling everything is said
to be "Mind."

I must keep my treatment of Christian Science brief, and will
therefore touch on just three aspects of this doctrinal system.

1. *Death*

Eddy actually thought that it was possible to overcome death.
Thus in *Miscellaneous Writings,* she wrote: "In 1867, I taught the
first student in Christian Science. Since that date, I have known
of but fourteen deaths in the ranks of my about five thousand
students."[13]

Since then, of course, all five thousand have died.

The followers of Eddy believed that their revered leader would
escape death. It is said that after she died, a mannequin dressed in her
clothes was driven around in a carriage in order to deceive her fol-

lowers. When the fraud was unmasked, tens of thousands left the movement.

2. *Healing*

Those who had studied under her became practitioners all over the world. These people could heal directly or from a great distance by the power of their minds or "knowing the truth." They called this "praying," or "working" for somebody. This form of healing has nothing to do with prayer as the Bible teaches. The practice comes into the category of suggestion, autosuggestion, religious suggestion, and, most commonly of all, mental suggestion (remote influence by suggestion). The frequent Bible quotations and all the supposedly Christian trimmings are nothing but camouflage.

This is no insinuation. We read it from the pen of Mary Baker Eddy in *Miscellaneous Writings:* "Who is the Founder of *mental* healing?"[14]

Reference is also made to healing at a distance: "Mind is not confined to limits,"[15] that is, not limited by distance. On the use of medicines, Eddy says, "No man can serve two masters,"[16] that is, either mind-healing or healing by drugs, not both.

The word *mind-healing,* which Eddy used hundreds of times, is proof that what we have here is not a Biblical healing process. It is the mind, the power of thought, the thinking spirit of man, that she believed to be the basis of healing, and not Christ. In any case, in any genuinely Christian movement, the salvation of man, and not his physical healing, stands in the foreground.

3. *Malpractice*

Mary Baker Eddy states that mind-healing, the spiritual concentration on a sick person, is true healing, and that its opposite is malpractice. What she means by the latter is the use by a practitioner of his mental powers to make a person ill or to harm him in some other way.

The conclusion that mind-healing is Scriptural is false. When a Christian prays for a sick person, his attitude is, "Lord, Thy will be done." In Scriptural healing, it is from Christ that the healing power comes. In mind-healing, the source is the practitioner "working spiritually."

Thus, from a Biblical standpoint, even the "good form" of mind-healing is malpractice, since it depends on a psychic—indeed an occult—power. Practitioners who are not psychic are unable to effect cures at a distance.

What Eddy calls malpractice is therefore a double negative form of healing. It is magical. Eddy is familiar with this evil form and mentions it very often.

There is, therefore, according to the teaching of Christian Science, both a good mental practice and a malpractice. Neither is in harmony with Scripture, however hard Christian Scientists may seek to prove it is.

Christian Science is an occult movement against which Christians must be warned. It is all the more necessary because of the fact that the Word of God is used thousands of times as a jumping-off point for the system.

The finest flower of Christian Science is Agnes Sanford's book, *Healing Light*. This book has such a plausible Bible framework, and the ideas of Christian Science are so sublimated, that many Christians, indeed even a bishop, have been deceived by it.[17]

10

CLAIRVOYANCE

Clairvoyance, or second sight, is an area where the Biblical and the demonic are constantly confused. Biblical prophecy is of divine character. Second sight has roots in the occult. If one observes the development of a clairvoyant, the psychic, occult nature of his activity always becomes evident.

Ex 41   Let us take as an example Pastor Delbert Larkin. He lives in the USA, where he is head of a psychic research center. He was ordained as a pastor by an international association of spiritists.

Larkin discovered his gift of second sight when he was only fifteen. He foresaw the death of one of his schoolmates. When asked about the source of his abilities, Larkin gives three answers:

1. He inherited them. His mother, brothers, sisters, and grandmother were all mediums.

2. It is a gift from God to help other people.

3. Guidance from spirits, who reveal everything to him.

These three indications make the position clear. This gift of second sight is not a gift from God. Larkin is a religious spiritist. People who are advised by him come under an evil influence.

How accurate are his prophecies? The Catholic Loyola University in Chicago checked out Larkin's predictions, and said he has an accuracy of 87 percent. I am not convinced. If we go through his most important prophecies in July 1973, we find:

a) Many senators will commit suicide in connection with the Watergate affair. Not one did so.

b) In 1973, the American and Russian forces will unite and attack Cambodia, Vietnam, and Red China together. It never happened.

c) Before the end of November 1973, Chicago will be struck by an earthquake. Wrong again!

d) Before May 1974, one of the greatest fires of history will destroy the northern part of Chicago. Once again, fortunately, no more than a fancy.

None of these four prophecies contained a shred of truth. If all clairvoyants went in for such clumsy bluff, they would be hounded out with scorn and derision.

After this introduction, let us now go into detail. We will not consider the card experiments of Prof. Rhine of Duke University. Throughout this book we are concerned *only* with the spontaneous cases which occur from time to time.

Three types of clairvoyance may be distinguished, if we consider the time reference: retrospective clairvoyance, telaesthesia, and precognition. These terms are used, respectively, for extrasensory perception of the past, knowledge of hidden things in the present, and prediction of future events.

The question of retrospective clairvoyance is the subject of much debate at the present time. It has already been mentioned in the chapter on anthroposophy.

Ex 42 In Erich von Däniken's book, *Erscheinungen,* similar experiments are mentioned. An American woman named Ruth Simmons was hypnotized and questioned about events before her birth. She said that she had lived before under the name of Bridey Murphy. The dates of this lady's birth and death were checked, and, according to Däniken, they were correct.

My answer to such experiments is a clear *no.* The Scriptures tell us that we have only one life. Anyone who undertakes experiments of this kind becomes the victim of deceiving spirits (Ephesians 6:12).

Däniken also believes that the dead can make contact with us. We cannot justify this from 1 Samuel 28 (the appearance of Samuel), nor from Matthew 17 (the appearance of Moses and Elijah). When God acts, it is different than what happens when a man tries blasphemously to draw aside the veil which hides the unseen world.

Sometimes clairvoyants can give a limited degree of help. Holland has a well-known clairvoyant by the name of Croiset. Both Professor Tenhaeff of Utrecht and Professor Bender of Freiberg University have conducted experiments with this clairvoyant. I have counseled people suffering from the ill effects of this man's gift.

Ex 43 A taxi driver ran over a boy. In court, the driver claimed the boy had already been lying in the road. The driver could not, however, prove his innocence. The relatives of the accused counted money no object and consulted Croiset. The clairvoyant meditated on the accident (put himself into a semitrance) and gave the following information, "I see a green Volkswagen. I can only make out two letters of the registration number." The statement sufficed. The police were able to trace the Volkswagen. After a long interrogation, its driver admitted he had run over the boy. The taxi driver was acquitted. But that is only one side of the story. The other side is the effect on the minds of those who make use of Croiset's help. I have often made this known, but as far as the parapsychologists are concerned, I am preaching to deaf ears. No one makes use of occult powers without harm.

Telaesthesia is remote vision of an extrasensory kind.

Ex 44 One evening a farmer's daughter did not return home from her work in the field. Her parents were anxious and sent out a search party. The next day, many people joined in the search. Finally, one of the villagers brought the matter to the attention of a man in the next village who could do more than other people. The man with the "sixth sense" was called in. In the living room of the farmhouse the girl lived in, he touched a piece of the girl's clothing. He began to stare strangely. Then he said, "Go to the brook behind the wood. There is a single willow by the waterside. The girl has become caught in its roots." The statement was true. The girl had taken her own life.

Precognition, the prediction of future events, creates difficult problems. A prediction is possible only if everything is already determined, or foreordained. There are some schools of thought in theology, particularly in Calvinism, which accept predestination. This book is not an appropriate place to go into this question.

One philosophical explanation of precognition would be the concept of timelessness. If past, present, and future all lie on one plane, there is no absolute before and after. In eternity, our concept of time ceases. Revelation 10:6 can be translated: "Time will be no more" (cf. AV "there should be time no longer").

It is very difficult to imagine timelessness. I have found a simple example at the South Pole. All around the South Pole are scientific centers. Each center keeps the time used at home. When the Americans go to bed by American time, the New Zealanders are getting up. At the South Pole, and of course at the North Pole also, there is no local time; so any time reference is valid. If you find that hard to comprehend, look at a globe, and you will find that all the lines of longitude (by which time is fixed) meet at the poles.

The problem is to explain how some clairvoyants are able to tune into timelessness. This ability does not lie within the scope of the human mind. I have found it only (but in hundreds of cases) with workers in the occult who make use of powers from below.

Amid the chaos of confusing fantasies there are some genuine predictions. How high the percentage is, one can only conjecture. It is certainly not as high as 90 percent as Jeane Dixon claims, nor 87 percent, as claimed by Larkin. Possibly only 2 percent of such predictions are unquestionably genuine. I have records of one or two as a result of a very extensive counseling. An example:

Ex 45 A woman told me that as a girl she had been friendly with a professor. She asked a clairvoyant for advice concerning the relationship with him. She was told, "You will not marry this man. He will be buried alive. One day you will get a lovely child." The girl replied, "I do not believe that I will get a child. I am not cut out for it." The clairvoyant replied, "It will not be your own child."

This information that her friend would be buried alive made the girl think there was going to be a war. Two years later, the Second World War broke out. During an aerial attack on Würzburg, the professor was in fact buried alive. Also, an American family who came with the army of occupation gave her a lovely child to look after.

If God has hidden the future from us, it is of His own mercy. We would not be able to relax at all if we knew what would happen to us tomorrow. We should be content with what our Lord Jesus says in John 10:28: "Neither shall any man pluck them out of my hand." The only question that matters is whether we have yet surrendered our life to Jesus Christ.

11
COLOR DIAGNOSIS AND COLOR THERAPY

It is no secret that colors can have a helpful or an inhibiting effect on the human psyche. I have often wondered why modern architects build tower blocks and rows of houses in plain concrete. The color gray has a depressing effect, and after a few years the concrete houses look dirty and oppressive, even hideous. Why do our skilled architects

not reckon with the psychological effect of their work? The circumstances of our day are gray and oppressive enough already.

Colors can enliven or depress. When I look out my office window
and see a green garden or a stony waste, my energy for work is increased or diminished accordingly.

Warm colors warm one's feelings. Cold colors harden one's sensitivity. There are some people who have made a study of this subject.
I will mention some men and movements from three countries.

1. *Switzerland*

The Swiss psychologist, Max Lüscher, has developed a color test
which enables him to discover the way a person behaves, his tendencies, his conflicts, and his unconscious motivations. In this
color test, it is a question of which colors the subject prefers. There
is certainly a grain of truth in this diagnostic method, though one must
guard against any exaggeration.

2. *Germany*

Such exaggeration and oversubtlety is found in the views of a
German color diagnostician, B. J. (I will not give his full name, because I do not wish to attract any further customers to this diagnostician and amateur astrologer), who calls his method of diagnosis
and therapeutic treatment *Psycho-Grafik*.

If Dr. Lüscher can be described as a scientist, B. J. is without
doubt an occultist. For his diagnoses, he has painted twelve picture
charts, to which he has allotted the twelve signs of the zodiac. The
patient chooses the chart which pleases him most or least. From
this, conclusions are drawn as to his character. Those who require
more details must give their birth date, so that a horoscope can be
cast. This is proof of the occult nature of this type of color diagnosis.

3. *New Zealand*

I have twice traveled extensively through New Zealand and collected
material about the theosophical, spiritist, and occult movements. In
this chapter I am concerned only with color diagnosis and color therapy. I cannot go into this problem in great depth. I have already dealt
with it fully in my book, *Uns, Herr, wirst Du Frieden schaffen.*[18]

The color therapists of New Zealand maintain that every human
body and every organ in it has a certain frequency band of its own.
Spiritist mediums can see this frequency band as an *aura*. In case of
illness or strong changes of character, the frequency band is altered.
These alterations can be detected with a rod or pendulum. The New
Zealanders also have a technical pendulum machine which they call
a *motor scopus*. According to the diagnosis made, the altered fre-

quency is corrected by means of colored threads and bags.

New Zealand scientists call this inordinate humbug. But some people are, however, determined to be deceived. A few examples will show how the process of improving the frequency is carried out.

A student at the Palmerston North University told me, "I went to the color therapist. He told me what was wrong with me by using a pendulum. Then he gave me a little bag with a colored thread. He told me to wear this bag on the diseased part of my body, and I would then be healed."

Another patient told me, "The color therapist gave me a cotton reel with some colored thread. Then I was instructed to wave this cotton reel around my body in straight and circular movements, in order to increase the diminished frequency of the diseased organ."

A farmer with whom I was staying showed me a tin can containing a colored thread which he had to bury under the cowshed to prevent the cows from calving prematurely or becoming sick.

As a means of guarding against cancer, these color therapists give people an amulet containing a colored thread. This amulet must be worn around the neck. The list of examples could be continued.

In connection with this color therapy we find all manner of humbug, deception and superstition; also the use of rods, pendulums, spiritist aura—in short, many forms of occultism combined. And modern, enlightened, twentieth-century people allow this rubbish to be served to them as if it were a great discovery!

Assuredly those who do not have their vision directed to Jesus Christ, the light of the world, fall victim to the most absurd ideas.

12
CONJURING TRICKS

Conjuring tricks have nothing to do with real magic. Tricks are a matter of sleight of hand, which has to be practiced for many years. Nevertheless, it has become evident that those who perform conjuring tricks for entertainment often have associations with real magic. The two things are not always clearly distinguished.

This short chapter about conjuring is necessary because of a man who has become well known in the USA and other English-speaking lands. In the USA, he is regarded as the greatest master of conjuring. His name is André Kole. Whenever I have traveled in the USA on speaking tours, I have been asked about this man. I have not heard him myself. I have only seen various articles written by him and about him. The best article is one he wrote entitled, *Magic and the Bible*. I agree with what he says in this article. André Kole tries to make a clear distinction between the magic which the Bible condemns and his own tricks. A second article I have read and studied is called *Mr. Magic*. The subtitle is *André Kole has been sawing his wife in half for twenty years*. There is a picture of this on the title page. A third article, dated September 1973, is entitled *Counsellor*. In this account, André Kole is called "The World's Greatest Magician." In addition to these three articles, I have letters from American friends who have been urging me for years to say what I think about André Kole.

It is not my duty to criticize other Christian workers. On the other hand, we have a general commandment from the Bible to test everything. For several years now, I have been doing that with regard to the novel and remarkable witness of André Kole.

My basic position is that, if God uses André Kole with his particular gifts in the service of the gospel, we have nothing to say against it. God has many unusual servants. Let us, however, look at what is said in the various articles I have mentioned. In the report of "The World's Greatest Magician," it is said that as a schoolboy André was able to undo locks and hypnotize birds, snakes, and people. I know from long experience that people, who have practiced amateur hypnosis in their youth, are occultly influenced. When they come to faith in Christ and are freed from their occult bondage, they can work unhindered for God's kingdom. There are, however, some conversions in which the occult influences are not cleared away. The reason this happens so often is that occult subjection is unconscious, even though it has certain evident effects. André Kole ought therefore to ask himself whether he has been completely freed from the hypnotic powers which he used in earlier years.

A second point which causes me much thought is André Kole's statement that "most of the tricks and illusions are produced by natural means." I find myself wondering if *most* of his tricks are on a natural basis, might there be also some tricks which do *not* belong to the category of sleight-of-hand? Kole's statement was made after he had begun to use his tricks in the service of the gospel.

The third thing which disturbs me somewhat is one statement in *"Magic and the Bible."* He writes that for several years about a thousand students have found Christ through his ministry every week. I have often attended mass meetings in America and have seen how people have been influenced by the emotional appeal of an enthusiastic address to stand up or to raise their hands when the call to decision has been made. When such people are visited later and asked about their attitude to Christ, they give a confused answer. A few weeks or months after their decision, they show that they are not disciples of Jesus Christ. Young people are easily influenced by emotion. Mass decisions, too, are catching. I have my doubts therefore as to whether these thousand young people who are won every week have really experienced regeneration through the Holy Spirit.

A fourth point on which I have reservations is the question whether one can preach the gospel by means of magic tricks. The realm of magic is so notorious today that even harmless conjuring tricks are viewed in a dubious light. André Kole perhaps realizes this himself, for he sometimes says at the end of his address, "The decision for Christ is of course not a trick, but a reality."

I have only mentioned my reservations here, but I must repeat again what I said at the beginning. If God uses André Kole, we conservative people must be silent and support him with our prayers.

13
DEATH MAGIC

The various forms of magic have been described in my books on occultism. Generally speaking, death magic is not often found in civilized countries, although it is sometimes practiced. In pagan areas, on the other hand, this sinister, devilish mischief finds its full expression.

In my book, *Unter der Führung Jesu,* I have distinguished death magic from crime on the one hand and death by autosuggestion on the other. I have learned what to do about death magic from counseling experience in mission areas. Former sorcerers sometimes come for counseling and surrender their lives to Christ. When they do this, they confess their terrible sins.

Death magic, the most devilish of all the forms of magic, is directed against both animals and human life. In the Batu Bible School in Java, a man named Brown was employed as chauffeur for three months. He was able to kill small animals by means of magic. This chauffeur, who had learned his black art in Mecca, had to be dismissed.

Worse still is the death magic which is directed against people. I have encountered such activities among the Shamans in Alaska and on St. Lawrence Island, among the voodooists of Haiti, and the Macumba spiritists of Brazil. Death magic is also found in connection with Zombiism in Africa, with Muslim black magic all over East Asia, with the Saugumma cult in New Guinea, the Hilots in the Philippines, and the Kahunas of Hawaii. There is no pagan country that is free from these devilish practices. An example I have not mentioned before in any of my books is the criminal activity of the Alauts on the island of Timor, where God has been sending a wonderful revival since 1965. In connection with this revival, several hundred practitioners of this death magic came to faith in Christ and then confessed their crimes.

Ex 46 The Alauts combine spiritist excursion of the soul and materialization with death magic. They acquire their powers through various ceremonies and by signing themselves with their blood to the devil. In the night, they put themselves into a trance and split off part of their energy. They have two ways of seeking out the victims whom they wish to hurt or kill. Sometimes the split-off energy, in the form of a small spirit, rides upon an owl and so flies to the victim's house. The other method is for the energy actually to transform itself into a night owl. This mysterious bird then sits on the victim's house and puts a spell on the people who are to be attacked. Then a kind of spiritist operation takes place. A cut is made with a small knife in the victim's abdomen, and a piece of his liver is then cut off. The hole is sometimes filled up with leaves. The Alaut then eats this liver for breakfast.

Before the days of the revival, these Alauts were greatly feared in Timor. There was no way of protecting oneself against them. The police did nothing, for fear of being victimized by the Alauts themselves. It was even known for pastors to become Alauts, in order to protect themselves and their families.

Reports of this magic are unacceptable to rationalists. On the other hand, these know-it-alls reject even the reports in the Scriptures. In Exodus 6-7, Moses, acting on the command and in the power of God, changed his rod into a snake. The Egyptian sorcerers imitated him, using the power of Satan.

Those who have seen the sorrow and genuine tears of repentance in sorcerers who come to confess their sins—and I have seen this— know that what such people say in confession before God is the truth.

I must not fail to point out that born-again Christians cannot be hurt or killed by Alauts. I have observed this also with voodooists in Haiti and the Macumba people in Brazil, and I have come to attach great significance to it. The dark powers of Satan are powerless in the face of the great power of Jesus Christ.

Someone may object: why then did pastors on Timor join the Alauts? The answer is very simple. They were nominal Christians who did not put themselves under the protection of Jesus Christ.

In connection with this, I would also refer the reader to those chapters on "Metamorphosis" and "Spiritist Operations."

14

DEMON POSSESSION

It was more than twenty years ago that Professor Bender had invited me to speak at his Institute in Freiburg on the problem of demon possession. He had also invited several psychologists, some Catholic theologians, and a professor from the psychiatric hospital. After the lecture there was a discussion about a woman patient in the psychiatric hospital who showed symptoms which were unfamiliar to the psychiatrist. She would suddenly cry out and say that she was being beaten by unseen powers. Bruises appeared on her body. Another time it seemed as if she were being crushed by a large snake. The marks of the snake's coils were photographed by an assistant doctor. The psychiatrist explained these phenomena as psychogenic dermatography (marks in the skin originating in the mind). On one occasion a nurse tried to protect the patient by putting her arm around her. The nurse was herself beaten. The psychiatrist put this down to psychological induction. Sometimes male voices came from the patient, describing themselves as seven devils. The psychiatrist called this process dissociation (or splitting) of the unconscious into seven independent parts. Occasionally examples of clairvoyance occurred.

The professor asked the Catholic theologians present for their opinion. They declared, "It is demon possession." The psychiatrist was somewhat irritated by this and said: "That is what your bishop suggested in his covering letter. I do not believe it. I think it is, at the most, a case of hysteria, although in a form that I have never met before." Then he asked me for my opinion. I replied by asking him, "Do you know whether this woman has had anything to do with magic or spiritism?" The reply was affirmative. Then I expressed my conviction that this was a case of possession. Later, I discovered that this woman had signed a pact with the devil with her own blood.

It is quite understandable that scientists should be hesitant about recognizing a case of demon possession. Possession is not a medical problem, but a religious one. What is difficult to understand is why the majority of theologians let the psychiatrists and psychologists take them in tow. I am not referring only to the modernist theologians, but also to many who have a good name in the church of Christ. Thus, for example, Professor Vicedom declared before 2,500 people in the Michaelis Church in Hamburg: "The demonic is the subhuman and the superhuman part of us." At that time Friedrich Heitmüller was still alive. In his hall at Holstenwall, he tried to put Vicedom right, saying: "The demonic is neither the subhuman nor the superhuman part of us, but the extrahuman factor."

The scorn of competent scientists is also the reason scarcely one theologian dares to write a book about possession. Anyone looking for books about demonology must look beyond the circles of the official church.

Among non-Christian contributions one might mention, *Die Dämonen—Wesen und Wirkung eines Urphänomens,* by Robert Müller-Sternberg. It is written from a historical and philosophical point of view, but not in the light of the New Testament. A believing Christian will not find it much help.

From a Biblical point of view, the book by Adolf Rodewyk, a Jesuit, has considerably more to offer. His book is called *Dämonische Bessessenheit heute.* What is here described by Rodewyk is familiar to me from my own experience in counseling. It has long been evident to me that the Catholic Church has more practical experience in dealing with the possessed than Protestant ministers have. True, there are some laymen in the Evangelical Church who devote themselves to the possessed, but their numbers are small.

What I cannot accept in Rodewyk's book is his tendency to give too much emphasis to baptism. Second, it is impossible for a Christian who bases his faith on the Bible to accept that one human can take another's sins on himself and make atonement for them. This is stated in Rodewyk's book.[19] There is only one act of atonement, the atoning death of Jesus Christ on the cross of Calvary. Furthermore, there are in this book some typically Catholic passages which cannot be harmonized with the Bible. All the same, Rodewyk and I have many experiences in common. In performing exorcism, for instance, he uses the same prayer I do: "In the name of Jesus Christ, the Son of God, I command you unclean spirits to leave this person." This prayer must not be thought of or used as a formula. It can be formulated in other ways; the important thing is that we have the courage to claim the authority which Jesus gave to His disciples according to Luke 10:19: "Behold, I give unto you power to tread on serpents and scorpions and over all the power of the enemy: and nothing shall by any means hurt you."

In America, there is more Biblically based literature about demon possession than is available in Europe. It is impossible to mention here all the important books. Of particular value are the following: Nevius, John L. *Demon Possession.* Grand Rapids, Mi.: Kregel, 1968. Unger, Merrill F. *Biblical Demonology.* Wheaton, Il.: Scripture Press, 1952.

— *Demons in the World Today.* Wheaton, Il: Tyndale, n.d.

There are also many second- and third-rate books written by people with extreme views, which cause more confusion than they remove.

A full reply to the psychiatric viewpoint would require more space than can be given here. It would also achieve nothing. A psychiatrist who is not a Christian, or only a nominal Christian, cannot be convinced of the fact of demon possession. Several arguments, however, should be mentioned.

1. Psychiatrists declare that Jesus and His disciples were children of their own age. They did not know any better. What they regarded as demon possession was in reality mental illness. I have heard this argument so often that I am weary of it. It is so easy to refute. Jesus, His disciples, and the writers of the New Testament were well able to distinguish sickness from demon possession. They are clearly distinguished in the following passages: Matthew 4:24; 8:16; 10:1, 8; Mark 1:32; Luke 9:1-2 and elsewhere.

2. The reactions of mentally ill persons and those who are demon possessed are different. I will not repeat here what I have already publicized in other books. In my book *Demonology Past and Present,* page 136, I have listed eight symptoms of possession. Here I mention only three of the chief ones:

> a. Attacks of madness which occur only when spiritual counsel is offered. Several Christian workers can testify to such incidents. I was called in to see a woman who began to rave every time someone prayed with her. The same thing happened when I did so. In such cases it is my practice to command the spirit in the name of Jesus.
>
> b. The trance. If one tries to pray with people who have come under an evil influence as a result of spiritism, they go straight into a trance.

Ex 47 A minister in Zürich brought a woman to me for counseling. When I prayed with her, she went into a trance and stuck her tongue out at me. When I said "amen," she came to herself. I asked her whether she had been to any spiritist séances. She said she had. She had belonged to a spiritist group for the past nine years.

c. Speaking in unknown languages. In the Rituale Romanum speaking in an unknown language is also regarded as a sign of possession. One day a young man came to me for counseling. While we were praying, he went into a trance and the voices which came from him used foreign languages which he had not learned. This is the strongest argument against the view of the psychiatrists. A person who is mentally ill does not suddenly speak foreign languages which he has not learned.

The symptoms of mental disorders differ from those of demon possession. The signs of possession are only recognizable by a person who has experienced a second birth through the Holy Spirit. The demons do not react in these ways to nominal Christians. This all sounds arrogant and hard, and yet it is clearly in line with the teaching of the Scriptures.

A gleam of light can be seen in a book called *Ergriffenheit und Bessessenheit,* edited by Jürg Zutt (A. Francke Verlag, Bern/Munich, 1972). The contributions in this volume are from psychiatric and anthropological papers produced for the Conference of the World Association of Psychiatry and the Werner-Reimers-Stiftung for anthropological research. At the congress, psychiatrists, psychologists, sociologists, theologians, medical historians, and anthropologists all had their say. One result of this conference was the declaration: "For the present we must be willing to allow an independent assessment of emotion and possession in their religious aspect, and not to label them over-hastily as mental illness." This is an astonishing admission. But it is something which believing Christians have known for a long while, without having studied medicine, psychology, and anthropology. By a long and devious route, science is gradually coming to the same position which believers have held for two thousand years on the basis of the Bible.

One question is hotly disputed among believing Christians. This is the question whether or not a Christian can be possessed. Many years of experience lead me to the conclusion that those who have no experience of dealing with the possessed say *no.* Those, who have counseled many possessed ones, know that even believers can be controlled or ruled by demons. These facts do not follow anyone's preconceived ideas. Our ideas must be formed, rather, on the basis of the facts.

I have had many discussions on this subject, particularly in America. I am therefore all the more thankful for the men who confirm my own experience. Among these are Dr. Edman, former president of Wheaton College, Professor Unger, already mentioned, the psychiatrist Dr. Jackson, of Milwaukee, who is a doctor both of medicine and of theology, the psychiatrist, Dr. Reed, and others. When I lectured in various countries, there were other men in conversations who declared they had counseled more demon-possessed believers than unbelievers. I must also mention Pastor G. Birch. In a letter of September 21, 1973, he wrote: "My wife and I had experience in Borneo of casting out demons in the name of the Lord Jesus Christ. But here at home (Canada), we have seen 120 people delivered from demon possession in eighteen months. All these people were Christians." My friend Pastor Birch is not an extremist. You will find his name mentioned again in the chapter on *Speaking in Tongues.*

My most detailed account of a case of possession is to be found in my book, *Unter der Führung Jesu,* beginning on page 250. Dr. Lechler, an experienced psychiatrist who, like me, recognized the fact of demon possession, described this account as the best-established example of possession in modern times.

In England I have also found a few psychiatrists who share my conviction. Several years ago I was invited by Dr. Martyn Lloyd-Jones to address some psychiatrists at Westminster Gate on the subject of possession. In the discussion, one psychiatrist came up with the usual argument, that what the Bible describes as possession would today be regarded as a mental illness. I did not have to try and correct this view. Two of the other psychiatrists contradicted him. One of them said, "I have had seven cases of possession in my practice." The other said, "And I had eleven cases of possession." This last-mentioned psychiatrist became a friend of mine. We held a seminar together for 200 Anglican clergy. During the week, this fellow believer told me: "Your book, *Christian Counselling and Occultism* confronted me with the problem of possession. I have now, for several years, observed typical cases which cannot be classified in the normal language of psychiatry. It was there that I discovered the truth of the thesis you maintain."

If there were no demons, Christ could not have disarmed (spoiled, King James Version) them (Colossians 2:15). If believers can never be misused by Satan as his mouthpiece, Jesus would not have had to say to Peter, "Get behind me, Satan, Thou art an offense to me" (Matthew 16:23).

We know of the enemy's power. We know how easily believers are tempted, but we know still more of the victory of Jesus Christ. The triumphal cry of the apostle makes hell shudder: "Thanks be to God, who gives us the victory through our Lord Jesus Christ!"

15
DESCENT FROM THE APE

One of my daughters came home from school one day and said that her teacher had told them that man comes from the ape. This is only one instance of the thousands of statements to this effect made daily in schools, universities, books and articles.

It is not my task to unravel this whole question of descent from the apes, although I have often encountered it on my tours.

Ex 48   A Swiss named M. Le Coc told me about Darwin as he flew me around Patagonia in a single-engine Cessna. The often-quoted scientist spent two years in Patagonia searching for the missing link between ape and man, without success. The high mountain range in Patagonia was called the Darwin Mountains in his honor.

In the extreme North, inside the Arctic Circle, I found something similar. Some archaeologists were digging out an old Eskimo settlement and claimed that the bones they had discovered were twenty thousand years old. I was somewhat skeptical about this claim.

Another time I was in Mexico. I visited various pyramids. One of them was said to be fifteen thousand years old. I did not believe it. Sometime later I found out how right I had been. I saw in a newspaper that some parts had been found in the fifteen thousand-year-old pyramid which could be burned. The C 14 test showed that the pyramid was not fifteen thousand, but only three thousand years old.

I have great respect for archaeology, but I often doubt the accuracy of the figures given. The Pithekanthropus is supposed to be six hundred thousand years old. The Homo Heidelbergiensis, found near Mauer (which is only 14½ miles from where I live), is said to be one hundred thousand years old. Why doesn't someone cut a piece out of these specimens, burn it, and establish its age by the C 14 test? Even that test allows for a given margin of error. My other question is whether these are human bones at all, and not animal bones.

In thousands of cases, archaeology confirms and illuminates the Scriptures. In dubious cases, where some scientist's statements do not coincide with the Bible, I come down on the side of the Bible, which was written under the infallible inspiration of the Holy Spirit (2 Timothy 3:16; 2 Peter 1:21). That may be called unscientific, but it is more certain and reliable than science, which changes its theories every ten years. The Holy Scriptures have never yet had to revise any statements.

Let us consider a classic example of how scientific experts contradict themselves. I quote from *Bibel und Gemeinde*.

> Just how valueless are the conclusions drawn from individual skulls, one or two facts will show. The famous Engis skull, found in 1831, is held by Professor C. Vogt to be distinctly ape-like; Lyell thinks it Caucasian; Professor Huxley, the Darwinist, finds it on the other hand so beautiful that it 'could have belonged to a philosopher,' and Theodor Landzert, the anatomist from Petersburg, compares it with the classic heads of the great Greeks (Ranke, Der Mensch, p. 443).
>
> The equally famous Neanderthal skull, which was at one time said to be the typical example of ape-like, antediluvian man, comes in for this comment from Virchow: "Even if it is regarded as typical of a race, which is an assertion I think completely unreliable, it is quite improper to deduce from this skull a similarity to any type of ape." Dr. Pruner-Bey has emptied it and discovered that the capacity is greater than that of an average man today. He considers it to be the skull of a Celt within the historical era (Figuier, L'homme primitif, p. 101). Professor Davis on the other hand regards it as the skull of an idiot, possibly someone who fell to his death in the chasm in modern times!
>
> Professor Fraas, himself an expert, rightly pours scorn on such findings, and adds: "These views of the scholars provide the clearest evidence that we know as good as nothing about the oldest inhabitants of our world" (Vor der Sintflut, p. 478). "Skulls do not carry, any more than other bones or flint axes, their date of manufacture; and in every age there were round

skulls and long skulls, gifted heads and stupid heads, and also cripples and idiots."[20]

This is the judgment of an expert, Professor Bettex, who simply uses the results of research to put together this very important collection of statements by leading scientists!

As long as there are people who despise the Bible, the legend of the ape will not die out. The fact that many modern and orthodox theologians believe this legend is proof that they and their theories stand in need of demythologizing. The tragedy is that thousands of believing parents must send their children to school to be taught by such teachers and theologians.

Conclusion: If you absolutely insist on coming from the ape, rejoice in your ancestors, and go to your relatives in the jungle and eat bananas.

Disciples of Jesus Christ know their pedigree: "God created man in his own image, in the image of God created he them" (Genesis 1:27).

16
DRUG ABUSE

Nearly every day there is some newspaper report concerning drugs. The drug problem has spread worldwide. The same day I wrote this chapter, our own newspaper carried two stories which may be briefly related as an illustration of the drug problem.

Ex 49 Morphia tablets, which were among medical supplies sent from Germany to Bangladesh during the great flood disaster, have been available for some time on the black market in Copenhagen. The pills, which weigh about 0.2 grams and contain about 84 percent morphine, cost sixty to seventy crowns each ($10-$12). This diversion of German aid has now been uncovered by the head of the Copenhagen drug squad, Svend Thorsted. In the home of a twenty-two-year-old American and his eighteen-year-old Danish girlfriend, the police found three hundred thirty "Pakistan pills," as they are known among drug dealers, and confiscated them.

Ex 50 Five young people, among them a fourteen-year-old boy and an eighteen-year-old girl, were arrested in St. Louis, Missouri. Under the influence of drugs they had sexually assaulted two boys aged fourteen and twelve, multilated them horribly and then murdered them. The two bodies were found in a gutter.

Drug addiction is a complex problem. Let us consider some aspects.

1. The *epidemic growth* of drug addiction in the whole of the Western world must first capture our attention. In 1970, I could still write that whereas New York had about two hundred thousand drug addicts, Germany had only ten thousand. Now, five years later, the picture is much blacker. The age at which young people begin to take drugs, at one time eighteen, is now ten. Responsibly-minded parents do not know what to do. It is alarming that the number of girls dependent on drugs is growing most rapidly at the moment. In our local town there is a high school in which whole classes smoke cannabis. If you ask the teachers, they know nothing about it. If you get a young person to ask one of the children, you will be told where to get the drugs and how much they cost. It may further be observed that the drug craze is not limited to the towns, but has reached even the smallest villages.

2. Drug abuse causes *chronic ill health.* Young cannabis smokers who progress to hard drugs like heroin, morphine, cocaine, and opium thus ruin their health in eight to twelve years. The body is systematically destroyed. This leads to early retirement. Young people of twenty-five to twenty-seven become unable to work because of drugs and so become a burden on the state, that is, the taxpayer. One paper reported recently that by 1980, every German worker will have one invalid to support. We are all, therefore, drawn into this problem, affected by it, burdened by it.

Drug addiction increases the numbers of accidents and crime.

Ex 51 A twenty-year-old was preparing his dose. His little brother of five saw the "sugar" which had been prepared and laid out on the table. He quickly put it in his mouth and died several hours later from poisoning.

Ex 52 Depression or carelessness? A daily newspaper reported the finding of a forensic medical expert in a West German town that two young people had died from an overdose of drugs.

Ex 53 A young man who was once a drug addict and has been delivered by Christ told me that on ninety occasions he had broken into a chemist's shop to get opiates. His skill in doing so is shown by the fact that not once was he caught.

More serious than breaking in are the many cases of violent robbery by addicts who are trying to get money to pay for their drugs.

3. The use of drugs is apparently tied up with a *religious problem* also. There are some drug addicts who maintain that drugs help to produce a religious feeling. They claim to get nearer to God by this means. In other words, they find "the god of the chemical re-

tort." The devil is so good at disguise that he can even make religious capital out of drug abuse.

4. Drug abuse could also be used in *political* and *military* strategy. What I mean by this can best be explained by an illustration. Switzerland is not only a neutral but also a peace-loving country. Let us imagine that some country should attack Switzerland and force her to defend herself. If half her soldiers were drug addicts, her powers of resistance would be halved. It would be an added advantage to the attacker.

This illustration is not far-fetched. In 1969, I was in Vietnam at the time of the first big offensive by the Vietcong. I was told by an American missionary that about 60 percent of the American soldiers were addicted to drugs. Some were unable in their stupor to recognize the enemy. Others had hallucinations and shot at phantoms, enemies who were not there.

Communist countries use this method to weaken the defenses of other countries. Western intelligence sources say that in 1975, Red China smuggled more than fifteen million kilograms of drugs into the West. The purpose of this was the physical and mental undermining of the West, to make it ready for communism. The USA has difficulties in stopping drug traffic from Cuba.

5. Drug addiction is a symptom of the degeneration of the Western world. Red China does not have this problem among her youth. But it is more than this. The drug epidemic is an *eschatological* problem. Satan has begun his final battle. He is using his many-sided arsenal of weapons, to bring men to ruin and destruction.

The time has begun of which Paul tells us in 1 Timothy 6:5, when there will be men of depraved mind.

The most important question for us is whether there is any way of halting this drug epidemic. Medical science has tried many methods of dealing effectively with this addiction. Pharmacists, for instance, have developed the drug called methadon. This drug causes addicts to lose their appetite for other drugs. The addict becomes addicted to methadon, but methadon addicts are fit to work. It is not a cure, but a means of diverting the addiction.

There are also religious means of diverting addiction. I read a book by a Pentecostal minister in which he says that young people have become free under his ministry through the gift of speaking in tongues.

I have encountered one such case in my own counseling. A young man took to speaking in tongues and so freed himself from drugs. Four months later he fell back into drug addiction.

Genuine liberation does not come by speaking in tongues but through Christ alone. Those whom the Son makes free are free indeed (John 8:36). I will give one example from the USA of this liberation.

Ex 54 I have had several opportunities to speak in the Rev. John White's church in Grand Rapids. John is a youth evangelist whom God has blessed. He is not content to invite young people to his services. He says: "The young people don't come to us, so we go to them." He goes out on the streets with a team and speaks to those he finds there. He puts into practice the words of Luke 14:23: "Go out into the highways and hedges." He has been privileged to have many experiences on these fishing expeditions. One evening a young man was sitting before me who had come from a life in the drug scene. He had found Christ through the ministry of John White. He had also experienced deliverance and a call to full-time Christian work. He went to a Baptist seminary and is now pastor of a Baptist church.

Genuine deliverance is found when the Lord takes hold of a person and grants him a new beginning.

17
EDGAR CAYCE

Much information about this spiritist is in the book, *Edgar Cayce, the Sleeping Prophet*. In addition, I have been involved both in counseling and in discussions concerning this man.

In speaking of the dead, one is normally guided by the old Roman principle *de mortuis nihil nisi bene* (not to speak ill of the dead). It, however, cannot be regarded as universally valid as we can see from two examples: we cannot say good things about the mass murderers Stalin and Hitler simply because they are dead.

Edgar Cayce was no mass murderer. He did, however, bring much harm to his patients and still does to those who read his biography.

Cayce was born in Kentucky in 1877. At the age of seven he displayed clairvoyant abilities. Because of these gifts, he decided while he was still a boy, that he was going to help mankind. He was very active in the Christian church to which he belonged, and eventually became a Sunday school teacher. It was his very commendable habit to read the Bible through each year. He continued to do so faithfully for forty-six years, until he died in 1944 at the age of sixty-seven years.

At the same time as reading his Bible so faithfully, he was practicing his occult gifts. For this reason the *Association for Research and Enlightenment* elected him as their president. We are faced here with a strange mixture of Bible study and magic. It is one of Satan's specialties to hide under a Christian disguise.

The fact that Cayce discovered his psychic abilities at the age of seven proves that he inherited these occult powers. His parents must have had some dealings with magic.

One of Cayce's main teachings was reincarnation. This is the view that a man is born several times, in order to develop further. Cayce claimed that he had lived about nineteen hundred years before, in the days of the Bible. He had been the nephew of Luke, the physician, who wrote the Gospel and the Acts of the Apostles.

How did Cayce come to be known as the *sleeping prophet?* Cayce had used his clairvoyance to diagnose diseases of every kind. He was able to make startling diagnoses which were verified by doctors.

One occult ability followed another. He developed the power of mental suggestion. He could transmit healing impulses to the patient. In connection with spiritistic experiments, he practiced his ability to go into a trance. And all the time he was a faithful Bible reader and Sunday school teacher. Such confusion can Satan bring about!

How did Cayce view these psychic powers? He mistakenly believed them to be a gift of God, indeed the working of the Holy Spirit. What an extraordinary confusion—to mistake gifts which come from the realm of darkness for the actions of God! Many Americans remember Cayce with gratitude, because he healed them.

How did diagnosis and healing take place? When a sick person came to him for help, Cayce would go into a trance for a few seconds. After four or five seconds, he was able to tell the patient the nature of his disease. Then Cayce prescribed a medicine which the patient could obtain from a chemist. In some cases, he gave not only a trance diagnosis, but also, as mentioned already, a healing impulse by means of mental suggestion. In this case, no medicine was needed.

This is what may be called a clairsentient diagnosis, analagous to clairvoyance. Both clairsentient diagnosis and mental suggestion are occult in character. The effectiveness of the cures was not doubted.

Cayce's son maintains that his father gave effective treatment in 85 percent of the cases.

For the Christian counselor, the problem is the evil effects of such healings. They are paid for by disorders and blocks of various kinds. Spiritual life is hindered or stopped. Help for the body is obtained at the cost of difficulties in the life of faith.

Cayce's activity was not limited to occult healing. He also practiced telepathy, fortunetelling, clairvoyance, and possessed a strong power of suggestion. Not least, he revelled in revelations and visions, which cannot possibly be made to agree with the Bible.

We may name several of his false teachings:

a. Jesus Christ was only a reincarnation of Adam, Melchizedek, Joshua, Zend (the father of Zoroaster) and many other important figures of the pre-Christian era.

b. God includes in one person both a male and a female principle. He is a Father-Mother God.

c. Jesus and His mother Mary were twin souls. (The Catholic church will rejoice over this statement).

d. Mary was not begotten by a man but by the Holy Spirit. (This is the Catholic doctrine of the Immaculate Conception. It teaches that Mary's mother, Anna, conceived her child by the Spirit of God. Although this is taught in the Catholic church, it is a pernicious heresy. We do not find it in the Bible.)

e. God does not know the future.

f. Many human experiences can be explained by reincarnation and by vibrations from other worlds.

g. Union with God is our own doing. In other words, we redeem ourselves.

We should not really be surprised at this last doctrine. It is part of the doctrine of reincarnation. Man is sent back to the earth again and again until he has freed himself, as it were, from all the dross, he then becomes so finely purified that he is fit for union with God.

There is no place in such a scheme for the redeemer, Jesus Christ. We must therefore issue a warning in the strongest terms against Cayce's books and ideas.

What the apostle John wrote remains true for all eternity:

"He that hath the Son hath life; and he that hath not the Son of God hath not life" (1 John 5:12).

18
EXAGGERATED DOCTRINES AND
THEOLOGICAL CONSTRUCTION

Among believers there is to be found a great deal of forced exegesis (interpretation) of the Scriptures. The result is often the erection of barriers which are a great hindrance to the church of Christ. Let us take a brief look at some examples of taking texts out of their context, or making forced interpretations.

1. Eternal security is one such idea which is discussed excessively by English Christians. To avoid misunderstanding, I will declare at once that I also believe that Jesus loses none of those whom the Father has given Him (John 6:39).

Overemphasis of the doctrine of eternal security, which is often done by English and American Christians, can create superficiality, lukewarmness, and lethargy in the believer's spiritual life. It also leads to legalism.

I know a missionary who was sent home from the mission field by his board and dismissed, because he opposed the excessive emphasis on eternal security. In Europe, and especially in Germany, there is a healthy fear of this expression *security*. We prefer to use instead the term *assurance*.

Exaggerated emphasis of eternal security also leads to distorted interpretations of Bible passages. Thus in the USA, I have often heard it said that King Saul was not rejected, although the Bible says clearly that he was. Moses said that those who make contact with the dead are an abomination to the Lord and will be driven out (Deuteronomy 18:12). Saul sought out a medium at Endor, and he was rejected by God.

A grotesque interpretation of the Scriptures was made by a widely known Baptist preacher in Canada, whom I know very well. He said, "Judas, the betrayer of the Lord, was not lost; he only forfeited his reward and his crown." The Bible, however, states that Judas was the son of perdition (lostness) (John 17:12).

2. Another English specialty is the suggestion that at the wedding at Cana (John 2) Jesus did not turn water into wine, but into fruit juice! Here again I must guard against misunderstanding. We must oppose by every means the misuse of alcohol, but this does not mean that we are to change the meaning of the Bible in that cause. Let us consider the problem by first looking at the meaning of the New Testament "wine texts" and then at the philological aspect.

a. The first point to note is the reaction of the steward of the feast. He says in amazement: "Every man at the beginning doth set forth good wine; and when men have well drunk, then that which is worse; but thou hast kept the good wine until now" (John 2:10). Would not a steward know the difference between fruit juice and wine? And since when do people lose their powers of discernment from drinking fruit juice?

According to the *juice theory* Paul advised Timothy: "Use a little fruit juice for thy stomach's sake" (1 Timothy 5:23).

The Good Samaritan would have poured oil and juice into the wounds of the injured man (Luke 10:34). In a hot climate, juice would have fermented early in a single day's journey. What a lot of infection the well-wisher would have added to the victim's pain by pouring juice into his wounds!

It was not without reason that the Pharisees accused Jesus of being a winebibber (Matthew 11:19). Jesus was, of course, no winebibber. A man is not a winebibber or drunkard because he occasionally drinks a glass of wine.

b. The philological aspect is equally clear. The Greek language has only one word for wine: *oinos.* For juice, on the other hand, it has four words: *to hygron,* meaning fruit extract or the fluids of the body; *chymos, chylos,* and *opos,* juice in a fruit or plant.

The counter-argument to the juice theory is to be found in the inspiration of the Bible. In case I am immediately accused of heresy, I will declare at the outset that I believe in the inspiration of the entire Bible. For me, the Bible is God's Word.

The Bible schools which maintain the juice theory believe, along with many other places of theological education, in verbal inspiration —that the words of Holy Scriptures were dictated by the Holy Spirit. There is no room here for a discussion of the question of personal inspiration and verbal inspiration. The doctrine of verbal inspiration runs into difficulties in view of the nature of the 500 Biblical manuscripts we have (including both majuscule and minuscule). These various manuscripts which underlie the Bible text as we have it contain hundreds of variations. Those who maintain the doctrine of verbal inspiration overcome this problem by assuming that there was only one original manuscript, which was verbally dictated. This original manuscript has not been discovered up till now. Those who hold to the juice theory should be asked to explain why none of the manuscripts which have so far come to light uses the word *juice.* Why, under the inspiration of the Holy Spirit, was none of the four words for juice chosen, but only the one word for wine?

Arguments, however, are of no use. Those who are "stiff for juice" regard Christians who disagree with them as lacking in deep moral earnestness. I know some Bible schools which are so legalistic that they demand their students to believe that *juice* is meant. In my collection, I have the ninety-sixth lesson of such a Bible school. The rigid requirement, that students must believe and preach that Jesus turned water into juice, led one courageous student to leave the school and go to another.

On my many lecture tours on every continent, I have observed that the churches with Calvinistic tradition frequently practice a rigid, or even legalistic interpretation of the Scriptures. The churches with a Lutheran tradition are sometimes more influenced by the gospel.

There are dangers in both directions. Narrowness can lead to legalism and tyranny. Broad-mindedness can produce lukewarmness and lethargy.

3. There is no movement today which produces so many theological constructions and exaggerated interpretations as the tongues movement and the neo-charismatic movement. The appropriate chapters in this book should be read in this connection.

Anyone who expounds the Scriptures must be guided by the following texts: "Ye shall not add unto the word which I command you, neither shall ye diminish ought from it" (Deuteronomy 4:2); and "If any man shall add unto these things, God shall add unto him the plagues that are written in this book: and if any man shall take away from the words of the book of this prophecy, God shall take away his part out of the book of life" (Revelation 22:18-19).

Add nothing—take nothing away! What minister is so arrogant as to say that he is open neither to the one danger nor to the other on any point of Holy Scripture?

In the following section, I hardly need to say on which side I stand. Hundreds of experiences and examples have convinced me that today's extreme movements do not come from the Holy Spirit. This, however, is not to say that in my own camp no mistakes are ever made in the interpretation of the Scriptures.

Let us begin with the extreme right, with those who believe in dispensationalism. They maintain that all the gifts of the Holy Spirit ceased at the end of the apostolic era. For example, Bullinger wrote: "Those who claim that these signs might continue or ought to have continued . . . are deceived by the great enemy of the Word of God."[21] Bullinger claims that the apostolic miracles came to an end with the conclusion of Acts 28. This chapter was written earlier than the one about speaking in tongues, 1 Corinthians 12-14.

Dispensational theology contains many elements of truth. I am referring only to the exaggerations.

On the half-right wing, that of the opponents of the so-called charismatic movement, there are several problems. Here it is a question of the theological interpretation of 1 Corinthians 13:8. A doctoral thesis could be written on this one verse. It is impossible now to go into the whole range of questions raised by it.

First, let us quote the verse in question: "Charity never faileth: but whether there be prophecies, they shall fail [*katargēthēsontai*]; whether there be tongues, they shall cease [*pausontai*]; whether there be knowledge, it shall vanish away [*katargēthēsetai*]" (1 Corinthians 13:8).

The Greek is given in the brackets. These Greek words have been the subject of long and wearisome discussions. We cannot go into these problems here. It is a matter of theological constructions. And I have met more than my fill of them.

In the course of two lecture tours in New Zealand, I learned of several publications directed against the tongues movement: *The Modern Tongues and Healing Movement* by Carrol Stegall and *The Doctrine of Tongues* by W. G. Broadbent. What these writers and I have in common is resistance to the tongues movement. What repels me about them is their rigid system of interpreting the Scriptures, a method bearing similarities to a mathematical proof. Those who use human logic and mathematical methods of proof in Bible interpretation are in constant danger of distorting the Bible message.

Since then, Broadbent's book has appeared in German with an appendix by Fritz Hubmer. The title is *Heute Hoch in Zungen Reden?* (Speaking in Tongues Today?) and has been published by the Liebenzell Mission.

A fatal mistake appears in Broadbent's book. Fritz Hubmer, whose books are highly regarded in the Christian community, writes: "Indeed, even the exorcism of demons is, according to the Scriptures—strange though it may seem—a manifestation of Satan's power."[22]

In writing this sentence Hubmer is attacking Pastor Blumhardt, the man whom God equipped with such spiritual power, and many other men of God. Blumhardt cast demons out of Gottliebin Dittus, and that was a manifestation of God's power, not Satan's. I have read this statement of Hubmer's many times, and I simply cannot understand how a writer with such a knowledge of the Bible can write something like that.

We are not, however, discussing this fatal remark, but the question of interpreting 1 Corinthians 13:8. Both Broadbent and Hubmer believe that the gifts of prophecy, tongues, and knowledge disappeared when the New Testament Scriptures were collected to form the canon. The formation of the canon took place at the synods of Jamnia and Joppa and was finalized in A.D. 201. Broadbent and Hubmer maintain that the other six gifts of the Spirit, mentioned in 1 Corinthians 12:7-11, have continued in the church. Bullinger stated that all the gifts of the Spirit ceased in A.D. 60.

On the extreme left are those who speak in tongues and the followers of the charismatic movement, who maintain that all the gifts of the Spirit have continued to the present day. The results of this unscriptural theology are to be seen all too clearly all over the world, and they present a frightful spectacle.

This is not the place to discuss gifts of the Spirit. I have already dealt with that subject in my paperback *Charismatic Gifts* (Kregel, Grand Rapids, Michigan). Here, I am only concerned to issue a warning against theological constructions, however well meant. 1 Corinthians 13:8 is variously interpreted by godly people. This shows that here too our knowledge is only in part.

Dr. Karl Heim, one of the leading theologians of his day and a God-fearing, born-again Christian, took this passage to refer to the return of Christ. He knew the Greek text better than Broadbent or Hubmer. In his lectures, he would point out the various meanings of the Greek conjunction *eite . . . eite.* This verse could also be translated: "Even if prophecy, tongues and knowledge were to cease, love would remain." In other words, the question of when the cessation takes place is left open.

Helge Stadelmann, a young theologian at the Dallas Theological Seminary, USA, wrote to me,

> Regarding glossolalia (speaking in tongues) Paul's choice of words in 1 Corinthians 13:8-11 seems to me significant: prophecy and knowledge will be taken away *(katargēthēsontai)*. Both are described as "in part" *(ek merous)*. This imperfect revelation *(prophēteia + gnōsis)* will be taken away *(katargēthēsetai)* when the *telos* (clearly the future consummation, not the canon, as we are often told here in America) comes. Amid this consistent usage, we find the short phrase *"eite glōssai pausontai."* Paul

here uses a quite different word *(pauomai)* and moreover does not say that this gift will be "taken away" when the *"telos"* comes. Is it permissible to draw the exegetical conclusion that glossolalia will have ceased to some extent on its own initiative (the verb is in the middle voice!) before the coming of the *telos?* This interpretation would leave open the question of when Biblical "speaking in tongues" will end, for the Bible gives us no information on that point; but a certain tendency toward the disappearance of glossolalia would be confirmed.

These words are free of the usual narrowness. When the Bible leaves a final question open, we should not try to answer it. Our task is exposition (bringing out the meaning) and not imposition (reading a meaning in).

We have no need of elaborate constructions to help us reveal the unscriptural, often demonic character of the charismatic movement. There are sufficient spiritual criteria by which it has been demonstrated.

19
FALSE CHRISTS AND FALSE PROPHETS

In Matthew 24:24, Jesus makes the following prediction about the last days: "For there shall arise false Christs, and false prophets, and shall shew great signs and wonders." One of the characteristics of the last days is that men, inspired by Satan, will claim to be Christ, or his prophets.

In the USA, there lived, until a few years ago, a man known as "Father Divine." He claimed he was God and that his son was Christ.

Another strange bird has been flying around the United States. He claims to be Christ returned. He is a seventeen-year-old East Indian, who has the reputation in Christian circles of leading a considerable night life in the bars and questionable night clubs. Even his own mother is said to have described her son as a playboy. The surprising thing is that all these false Christs have gathered a following.

In France, a former post office clerk, named George Roux, let it be known that he was Christ come back to earth.

A fisherman in Sweden and a sailor in Holland made similar claims.

A certain Korean has become well known. I was told by Pastor Ludwig Heinemeyer that "the leader of the 'Society for the Unification of World Christendom' is a Korean by the name of Moon. His followers claim that he is the coming Messiah. His book *Die Göttlichen Prinzipien* (Divine Principles) shows clearly that what we are dealing with is a false Christ."

The most remarkable *messiah* at the present time is to be found at camp Manujothi Ashram in the desert in South India. It is the extreme American evangelist, William Branham whom Christians have to thank for this false messiah. His name is Paluser Lawrie Mathukrishna. When Branham was on tour of India, Brother Lawrie became a disciple of his, and Branham described him as the Son of God and Christ returned.

Brother Lawrie has established a kind of commune with his followers in South India. Those who join give up all their possessions to the group. I know a woman from Germany who sold all she had inherited from her father and went to India with DM.60,000. After a few years, she came back to her husband in Germany without a penny.

It is strange how this latter-day sect attracts people from all over the world. Germans and Americans are especially welcome, since they usually bring with them large sums of money.

One of Lawrie's main teachings is that the world will be destroyed in 1977. Before that, however, his followers will be taken up from the earth. The *brides of Christ* are already preparing themselves for this rapture by a process of spiritualization of the body.

At the time of writing, this community numbers seven hundred. No more are being accepted, although there are nine hundred applicants. Brother Lawrie says that the spiritual development of the seven hundred is now so far advanced that the new members would not get there. Only the seven hundred "firstfruits" will be taken up.

The activity of Lawrie's representative in Germany, Herr Mengel, is also of interest. At first he lived with his wife and four children in Lawrie's commune, but then he returned to Germany in order to make Lawrie's ideas known in Europe. Herr Mengel claims to be one of the two witnesses who are mentioned in Revelation 11. After three and one-half years, he says, he will be murdered, but then he will be raised.

It is strange how people can be filled with such a spirit of error, that they really believe these things. Let us wait and see what lies they will tell us, because the prophesied destruction of the world in 1977 did not happen.

Parallel to the false Christs is the activity of the *false prophets*.

Lying visions and false prophecies were and are always the accompaniment of satanic deception in extreme circles.

The false prophetesses Berta Dudde and Sister Marguerite, through whom Christ is supposed to speak in the first person, have already been mentioned in passing. It would take up too much space to give examples of their revelations, especially since these are on subjects of no importance and much too vague. Instead, I will give three other examples of precise but false prophecies.

Ex 55   In the fifties, I came to know a preacher and his family. I also spoke several times in his fellowship meeting. He had been trained at Chrischona. In order to avoid any misunderstanding, I should say that I have a high opinion of this missionary training school. It has a clear, Biblical foundation. This makes the story all the more surprising. The preacher's wife said to me one day that Christ would come in 1964. I asked how she knew this. She replied that a woman who had the gift of genuine visions had been given the following revelation from the Lord. God had called the prophet Mohammed to Himself and had given him the task of informing the Mohammedan priests that Christ would come again in 1964. They should make themselves ready.

I said to the preacher's wife, "Has God then made a point of calling to Him that religious swindler, Mohammed, and of leaving genuine men of God out of account? The falsity of this vision is quite obvious. Anyway, no one knows the day or the hour."

I have mentioned this example, not to expose Chrischona, but to show that even in good movements, such invasions by a lying spirit are possible.

Ex 56   The example which follows is more tragic, since it caused an untimely death.

In the chapter on healing fanaticism, I shall give an illustration told me by Pastor Hans Bösch, of Affoltern, Breitenstr 477. It concerns a man who took his wife out of hospital just before she was due to have an operation for cancer. Here I will mention the prophecy behind this act.

The prophecy came from a group calling itself the *Revival Fellowship* in Bonstetten near Zürich. On January 16, 1966, a message came for Brother Albert (the husband of the woman with cancer):

> The Lord says: My son, in My grace I have covered you. Trust Me in all things and you will have the assurance that it is I who have so led and ordered everything. Take your wife away

now. Do not leave her there as a guinea-pig to be experimented on, for it will bring her to death. Take her to the children of God in the high place [the reference is to the Maison Bethel house in Orvin], where she will be nursed and cared for under My word. It is a home for tired and burdened souls. There she will be strengthened in body, soul, and spirit, and she will also recover again from her illness. Bring her out at the right time [from the hospital]. I am the Lord your God, who leads you aright.

The words in brackets were added by Pastor Bösch for the sake of clarity. This lord, who spoke in the first person through this modern prophetess, was not Christ or God, but a lying spirit of Satan. This lying spirit brought the patient to an early death.

Ex 57 A lying prophecy which has become known throughout the world is written in Fritz Hubmer's book. I quote:

In the year 1952, the following prophecy, purporting to come from a German Christian worker in Pentecostal circles in Canada, was published. It was also forwarded to the *Gnadauer Verband*. The prophecy from Canada ran as follows: Say to your brethren, it is about the Berlin edict. The leading men who drew that up and signed it roused My great displeasure and so brought a curse on their land, for they misinterpreted My work and made rules for My Spirit. The same number of leading brethren must come together and confess like Daniel: "We and our fathers have sinned and have been rebellious. We confess and recant the wrong that we have done to Your people, for we have built a dam against your gracious visitation and with it have quenched the fire of revival. Please be gracious to us again, according to Your mercy, and forgive what we have done" (Daniel 9). This confession must be made public by those who have signed it in the same way in which that wicked declaration was made known. Otherwise, a nation-wide revival will not come until the fifth generation. But I know whom I will make responsible if that happens.[23]

In my experience as a counselor all prophecies, without exception, in which Christ speaks *today* in the first person through the mouth of a believer, are false prophecies. Moreover this *anti-Berlin declaration* smells extremely strong of a hoax. But there will be simple minds which will believe something like this.

Satan's art of deception becomes more and more dangerous and threatening as the return of Christ approaches. We should pay more heed to God's Word, which contains all the prophecy which we need for life and for death:

"Take heed that no man deceive you" (Matthew 24:4).
"Be not deceived" (1 Corinthians 6:9).
"But evil men and seducers shall wax worse and worse, deceiving and being deceived" (2 Timothy 3:13).

Additional note on Moon:

This book was prepared for printing when a fuller report on Moon, the Korean mentioned above, reached me. Moon claims to have seen a vision of Christ at the age of sixteen. In this vision he was given the task of bringing the Christians of the whole world together.

I obtained further information from a television program on Monday, November 15, 1975. In 1954, Moon founded a society in Seoul for the unification of world Christendom. Since 1972, this organization has also existed in Germany, under the name *Vereinigungskirche*. This church is international, interdenominational, and interracial.

Conferences are held in the Taunus region of West Germany with the object of building up an international leadership. Other centers in Germany are found at Frankfurt, Freiburg, and Tübingen. The Moon followers hold occasional services with sacred music, prayers, and talks.

Moon comes from South Korea and is opposed to communism. The particular characteristic of this new religious leader is his strong messianic consciousness. His followers play this down, saying that he is only the forerunner of the Messiah.

In the USA, the mainstay of the movement is an *International Cultural Foundation,* which is encountering growing opposition. The opposition is flaring up for two reasons:

a. The parents of young people who have been led astray by the sect have formed anti-Moon groups, and are amassing evidence to prosecute the movement.

b. The strongest opponents of the Moon movement are young people who have succeeded in freeing themselves from the grip of this religious fanaticism. These former members speak of treatment which is reminiscent of brainwashing. The uninterrupted sessions of instruction amount to physical and psychological torture.

20
FORTUNETELLING OR SOOTHSAYING

Since I have written about fortunetelling in other books, *Between Christ and Satan* and *The Devil's Alphabet,* I will give only a brief account here.

1. *History*

The oldest form of fortunetelling is the use of rod and pendulum. (See 51 in this section.) Rod and pendulum can be traced back six thousand years. The second oldest form is astrology (see 3 in this section). Astrology may be traced back five thousand years. The third form is palmistry, which goes back about four thousand years. Palmistry was practiced by the priests of ancient Babylon. The fourth form of fortunetelling is that involving the use of cards. The Romans had little wax tablets with symbols carved on them, which they used for telling the future. The practice of card-laying is about two thousand years old. A fifth form of fortunetelling is psychometry. Here the fortuneteller holds an object belonging to the person in his hand and then gives information concerning the person. A sixth form is fortunetelling with the aid of a crystal ball. A good example is that of Jeane Dixon, about whom there is another chapter herein.

Every pagan nation practices fortunetelling. In the Old Testament, too, we have continual warnings against taking part in these pagan activities. One thinks of passages like Deuteronomy 18: 10-12, or Leviticus 19:31, 20:6, 20:27. I will quote the last three passages: "Regard not them that have familiar spirits, neither seek after wizards, to be defiled by them: I am the LORD your God. . . . And the soul that turneth after such things as have familiar spirits, and after wizards, to go a-whoring after them, I will even set my face against that soul, and will cut him off from among his people. . . . A man also or a woman that hath a familiar spirit, or that is a wizard, shall surely be put to death: they shall stone them with stones: their blood shall be upon them."

2. *Examples*

I shall *not* here deal with the forms of fortunetelling to which special chapters in this book are devoted. Let us begin instead with palmistry.

The fact that palmistry is related to astrology is evident from the division of the palm into seven planet mountains. From the index finger to the little finger these are the Mercury mountain, the Apollo mountain, the Saturn mountain, and the Jupiter mountain. Below the thumb is the Venus mountain and the Moon mountain. In the lines of the hand, four main lines are distinguished: the heart line, the head line, the life line, and the line of destiny. According to this system, one can speak of intuitive palmistry and suggestive palmistry.

In this account, we are concerned only with genuine cases, not with suggestive or fraudulent cases.

Ex 58 My informant is a Christian woman with a university education. Her cousin lives in Rügen. One day a gypsy woman came to him and read his palm. "Your father," said the gypsy, "will win a great sum of money one day. Then he will die at the age of sixty." The young man laughed, and then she said: "And you will have to die at the age of twenty-seven."

One day the young man received a letter telling him that his father had won DM.50,000. Then, on the father's sixtieth birthday, a telegram arrived to say that the father had had a fatal accident. The son became anxious. He was afraid that he would die when he was twenty-seven—and that is what happened. Here we have a genuine example of prediction of the future.

Ex 59 When I was preaching in Graz, a doctor's wife came to me for counseling. This woman had studied medicine. While she was a student, she had joined a student group going to Hungary for the weekend to taste the Hungarian wine. On the way back they met a gypsy woman. The young people were in hilarious mood and let the gypsy examine their palms and tell their fortunes. In the case of one young man, the gypsy refused to say what the future held for him. The group went on their way. A young lecturer who was with the group went back to the gypsy and asked, "Why did you refuse to tell the young man's fortune?"

"This young man will meet a violent death in the next six weeks," replied the gypsy woman. "I did not want to tell him that."

The young man was not told about this prophecy. He was not, therefore, influenced by suggestion. The six weeks went by, and then the young man received a telegram calling him to go and see his father who was dying. Two of his friends went with him to Graz railway station. He got on the train for Salzburg. A few hours later, a special anonuncement was made that the two rear coaches of this train had been derailed. Among those who had died in the accident was the student. Here we have another example of genuine prediction of the future.

I return to the doctor's wife who told me this story. She too was told her future by the gypsy woman. The prediction caused this woman many years of unhappiness. I will not go into the details.

Occasionally fortunetellers give a person genuine information, for which the person will pay dearly. The effects of occult practices are the subject of the second part of this book.

Questions are also raised by what is known as psychometric clairvoyance. The clairvoyant who uses psychometry concentrates on an object for a few seconds and then gives information about the circumstances surrounding the object and the past, present, and future of its owner. Some parapsychologists like Rüsche, Osty, Price, Gumpenberg and Gatterer, think that a person impregnates his clothing and all the objects he uses with aspects of his personality. On this view psychometric clairvoyants have the ability, when in a trance or semi-trance, to read and interpret these mental impressions. One would have to admit the possibility that this theory might explain statements made about a person's past. But psychometric clairvoyants are also able to give information about the future. And the future cannot be tied up in a person's clothing. It is impossible to account for this phenomenon of psychometric precognition in terms of parapsychology. One could more readily accept the theory of Carl Gustav Jung that at a higher level, past, present, and future are all present. If one goes on to ask how a person can reach this higher level, Osty and Hartmann would reply by saying that people who are psychic have the ability to attain a mystic union with the world soul. The world soul contains all the plans and life histories of men, and these can be discovered by tapping it.

From a Biblical point of view, this is an impossible process. For us, the world soul is the living God, and He does not allow fortunetellers to pry into His secrets. It is always the same. Learned men bring out the most absurd theories in order to escape facing up to the truth. The Bible describes the whole complex of fortunetelling as a demonic practice which stands under the judgment of God. Those who get their guidance from the Bible will not be impressed by these strange parapsychological theories.

I will give two examples of psychometric soothsaying. One of them concerns a pastor's family, the other a doctor's practice.

Ex 60   A French pastor's wife came to me for a talk. She had been suffering for years from depression. The depression could not be accounted for medically. The pastor's wife told me the story of her life. It included a case of fortunetelling. One day when her son (now grown up) was ill as a baby, a man from the parish came to the door of the house. "I know that your son is ill," the man said.

"Please give me something that belongs to the child. I am able to heal him."

"What do you want to do?" asked the pastor's wife. "We have a doctor. I should like to talk it over first with my husband. He is away at the moment."

"I have heard," said the man, "that your child has a high temperature." The mother replied that the baby's temperature was 104° F. The man said, "You can see how urgent it is. If the child dies, you will be responsible, because God has given me the ability to heal diseases."

A mother who is anxious about her beloved child is, under some circumstances, open to persuasion. So she went into the house and brought one of the baby's dresses. The man went home with it. A short while later, the fever abated and the child recovered.

But the child's development was unusual. He was not normal. He was very clever and went to the high school. But when he came home from school he would stand against the wall and, for about two hours, knock his forehead against it. He could not be persuaded to stop this. His mother also had spiritual problems. She was hardly able to pray or to read the Bible, and she started to suffer from depression.

Ex 61 Now for the example from a doctor's practice. It is not only quacks and amateur healers who use occult methods of diagnosis and cure; there are also a few occultists among doctors. The doctor in question is not only a fully qualified M.D., but is also a psychometric clairvoyant, clairsentient, and fortuneteller. He takes a drop of blood from his patient. This blood sample is not tested in a laboratory. It suffices for the doctor to hold the drop of blood up against the light and to concentrate on it. Then he gives his complete diagnosis. Undoubtedly many diseases can be diagnosed by examination of the blood. I have had a blood test myself. The doctor had the blood tested in forty different ways in the laboratory. It is not possible to do that with just one drop of blood, and some of the laboratory checks take a long time. This doctor is an occultist. All the patients who undergo this occult diagnosis come under a ban.

While we are talking about doctors, I will mention another example. I was told in the course of counseling about a school doctor who asked for samples of urine. He does not make the usual urine tests for protein, sugar, hemoglobin and so on, but he uses it like the doctor in the last example. He concentrates for a few seconds on the urine, without sending it to the laboratory for examination, and then makes his diagnosis and prescribes his cure accordingly. This too is a case of occult diagnosis.

Thus it is not only quacks and healers who use occult methods. There are doctors who do the same thing under cloak of their professional qualifications.

I will give one more example, this time of card laying, and then make some final comments on the whole subject of fortunetelling. Basically, the problem is always the same: people make use of dark powers at the cost of their inner peace or even their salvation.

Ex 62 A minister took up card laying as a hobby. I do not mean ordinary card games, but fortunetelling with the aid of cards. He used the cards not only to guide himself and his family, but also his church, for many years. The effects were evident. His wife became addicted to alcohol, and his daughter became interested in white and black magic. When the girl was seventeen years old, she became deranged and was admitted to a mental hospital. Card laying was the ruin of the minister's whole family.

3. *Warning against the various forms of fortunetelling*

It is not enough to issue a warning against the various forms of fortunetelling. There is another problem tied up with the whole complex of divination. It is the question of whom we trust, of to whom we are willing to entrust our lives. It is easy to understand why people seek guidance when they are in a difficult situation. It is also easy to understand that people are afraid of the future and its threatening events. But we must take this fear and anxiety to the right place, to the One who said: "Neither shall any man pluck them out of my hand" (John 10:28). It is Jesus Christ who has given us the promise: "Lo, I am with you alway, even unto the end of the world" (Matthew 28:20). The Bible contains thousands of promises to encourage us, promises which are strong enough to take away all our fear. The Psalms, in particular, are a great treasure house from which we can daily take all that we need. Think of the most well-known psalm, Psalm 23: "The Lord is my shepherd; I shall not want." I often use it when praying with my children. Or consider Psalm 37:5, "Commit thy way unto the Lord; trust also in him; and he shall bring it to pass." Read through the Psalms with a red pencil in your hand, underlining all the verses which give courage and strength or which offer protection concerning the unanswered questions of life.

21
FREEMASONRY

It is about ten years since my book *Der Aberglaube* was first published. The third edition has now been sold out, and it will not be reprinted. The book aroused a great deal of opposition. A judge in South Germany wrote, threatening to take me to court, if I would not alter my article about freemasonry. A minister supported him in his protest and told me that what I had written about the Freemasons was not true. Since then I have counseled others who have been involved with Freemasonry. I have had no occasion to alter my opinions, even though I might receive more threatening letters.

First, let us consider the history of the masonic movement. In some cases, the masons trace the origin of their secret society back to the guilds of masons who worked for King Solomon. Historically, of course, this is untenable. In Europe, 1717 is named as the foundation year of the first great lodge. Lodges in Germany began in 1738, when Frederick the Great became a member. In the USA, I have been told that there are about five million Freemasons. In Germany their numbers are estimated at fifty to eighty thousand.

It is impossible to describe the organization and ideas of all the lodges in the same terms. In some lodges, magic and spiritism are practiced, but there are others in which a cult of friendship and light is fostered and in which they engage in philanthropic works.

What has surprised me most in the USA is that there are Methodist ministers, high-ranking officers of the Salvation Army, and bishops who belong to masonic lodges. I have preached in a church where the masonic symbols were displayed behind the altar. I said to the pastor of this church: "If I had known beforehand that this was a masonic church, I should not have accepted the invitation." It is encouraging that in the USA, the Lutheran Church Missouri Synod has forbidden its ministers and elders to belong to a lodge. This is one observation I think it my duty to mention. It is the experience of many spiritually alive ministers in North America, that churches whose ministers are Freemasons are spiritually dead. It is also difficult to preach the Gospel in such churches. One has the impression that some kind of ban has been put on the whole church.

There follow a few examples from my own work.

Ex 63 My most recent experience was a meeting with a high-ranking mason from St. Petersburg, Florida. After I had spoken in Dr. Kenneth Moon's church, a man came to me for help who had reached the thirty-second degree of masonry. The highest grade is the thirty-third, that of the Grand Master. His request was that I should help his wife, who suffered from depression. I asked him to bring his wife to me, since one cannot counsel someone through another. During the conversation I asked him about his own relationship to Christ. He gave a vague answer, saying that he believed in God. Through the questions that I asked, the conversation came round to a central point, and I discovered that the man was hindered by a spiritual blockade. He was not in a position even to understand the facts of salvation in the New Testament, much less to accept them. I was unable to help this man.

Ex 64   During an evangelistic campaign in Switzerland, I heard that the secretary of a Swiss lodge had become a Christian. From that moment, he knew that he would have to leave the masonic movement. No one had told him this. It had become obvious to him by the act of deciding for Christ.

Ex 65   One of my acquaintances is the son of a Swiss building contractor. The father was originally a Freemason. For some reason, he left the lodge. From that time on, the banks refused him credit. The reason was that the directors of the bank were themselves masons. The building contractor's business was ruined.

I have other information of a more serious nature, showing how those, who have resigned from lodges, have been persecuted by their former colleagues. But I have no desire to be taken to court. The threats of that South German judge have thus had their effect on me. At the same time, such threats throw some light on the character of masons.

Let us leave the examples and turn to a quotation from a masonic book, which opens our eyes completely:

> A man commits some evil act. He confesses it to a priest. The priest—representing God—absolves the sinner from what he has done. How simple it is! How misleading for people! How comforting to let the evil deed be wiped out by an act of God, and to begin a new life! The power of forgiveness lies in ourselves. The possibility of starting a new life unburdened by the guilt of the past lies in our own soul. Or, what men have written and said is subsequently decreed to be the revelation of God.[24]

What are we as Christians to say to this? As far as the Bible is concerned, this is blasphemy. Should we then, when asked for advice, commend the membership of such lodges?

My experience is that when Freemasons come to faith in Christ, that is, when they experience conversion and a new birth, if they do not leave their lodge, they make no progress in their spiritual lives. On the other hand, I have often heard of men who, having turned to Christ, knew at once that they must break with the lodge.

An unusual lodge of a religious kind is the so-called spiritual lodge in Zürich. It has branches in Basle and Berlin. I do not know for certain whether this spiritual lodge is associated with the Swiss Grand Lodge in Alpina. This spiritual lodge conducts services in which the Bible is read and prayers are offered. But the sermon is not preached by a pastor. It comes from a spirit called *Joseph from the other side,* who makes himself known through the medium Beatrice. This is religious spiritism. When I have addressed meetings in Switzerland, I have often counseled people who had come under a ban as a result of this spiritual lodge. Despite its Christian appearance, I must issue a warning against this spiritist lodge.

We have no need of spirits from the world of the dead to tell us what to believe. We have the Bible, the Word of God inspired by the Holy Spirit. We have Jesus Christ, who said: "I am the light of the world: he that followeth me shall not walk in darkness, but shall have the light of life" (John 8:12).

22

GHOSTS

By ghosts we mean the shadowy reappearance of a deceased person in the place where he formerly lived. In the Bible, we have an experience of this sort in Matthew 17, where Moses and Elijah appear to the Son of God and prepare Him for His way of suffering. Naturally, I believe all the accounts recorded in the Bible are true.

There are some ghost experiences which can be attributed to a projection from the human subconscious. When, for example, a young wife loses her husband in a road accident, she may one day see her dead partner, either in a dream or a semiconscious state. This is a case of her wishes being projected. But in addition to these imminent ghosts, which can be explained in terms of the deeper levels of the human mind, there are also genuine ghosts. There are reports of these even in antiquity, though I shall not repeat them here. I will confine myself to examples from the present day.

Ex 66   A French minister's wife told the story of a ghost which
haunted her grandparents' house. In this house, a ghost had been
seen over many years, and, according to family chronicles, for several
centuries. The house was built in the thirteenth century. At one
time it had been a café known as Tannenzapfen. Some years ago,
the building became dangerous and was demolished. In the foundations, they found a skeleton which had been walled in. This was
probably connected with a crime. Here is another example which
suggests that houses, in which crimes have been committed, sometimes acquire spooky phenomena which disconcert the people who
live there.

Ex 67   Pastor Wirt of Hasle-Rüegsau in Switzerland told me
the following story. He was driving his horses into a nearby village.
At a certain point, a farmer shouted out a warning to him, "Hold
tight, pastor! The horses are going to shy." The pastor asked in
surprise what was going on. He was told that all the horses in the
neighborhood shied at this place. Many years ago, a crime had taken
place there. Popular rumor was that the criminal still haunted the
place.

I have many accounts of ghosts, but I will now relate one particularly serious one.

Ex 68   A Protestant minister had a remarkable experience, while
he was preparing his sermon, one Saturday evening. Suddenly the
door opened and his deceased predecessor, whom he was able to
recognize from a photograph, came into his study. The pastor was
startled by this extraordinary visitation and did not know if he was
suffering from a hallucination, or if the vision was something real.
The dead pastor spoke to him. He complained that he could find
no rest in the world beyond. The pastor asked him whether he could
help him in some way. The ghost replied that the reason he could
not find rest was because of a sordid matter concerning a bequest.
He would not be free from his torment until the wrong had been put
right. He told his amazed colleague that, together with his church
council, he had made an unjust decision about a will. As a result,
several of his church members had lost an inheritance they should
have received from America. The ghost asked the pastor to come
with him to take the relevant file from the filing cabinet. The ghost
led the way to the record office and found the relevant file among
a pile of papers. Taking the papers, the ghost explained the circumstances to the pastor. Then the phantom disappeared. The pastor
immediately took steps to put the matter right, and went to visit

the elderly former members of the church council. A meeting of the present council was called, and the decision in question was rescinded and the matter put right. From that time on, the ghost never again appeared in the minister's house, although for years strange footsteps and other phenomena had been observed there.

I realize this story raises difficult theological problems. Is it really possible at all that a man who is dead can come back from the life beyond to put right something he has done wrong here? Our understanding of the Bible's teaching would normally make us say *no*. On the other hand, this remarkable experience allowed a family to gain their rightful inheritance. A parapsychologist would say that the pastor had unconsciously become aware of the contents of the dubious papers in the file by means of a clairvoyance. Since he knew from a photograph what his predecessor looked like, he linked up the knowledge he had with a picture of the former pastor projected from his unconscious. This parapsychological explanation, however, is as incomprehensible and dubious as the story itself. I can only testify that the pastor had the experience, just as I have related it.

In the following example, another problem is raised.

Ex 69 A farmer went to his local minister for help. The farmer's family was being troubled by a ghost at night. The pastor advised the troubled man and his wife to pray for the ghost, that God might forgive him his sins. If he did so, the ghost would cease to appear. I must emphasize that I do not agree with this pastor's advice. We are not to pray for ghosts but to ask God to protect us from them. At most, we can do as Blumhardt did once and say to the ghost, "Go to Jesus Christ, if He will allow you into His presence." I would even go so far as to command ghosts in the name of Jesus Christ to appear no more.

Another situation is described in the next example.

Ex 70 For a long time, a deaconess was troubled by nightly visions of horrible looking ghosts. These visions led her to seek help from a minister, who began to pray for her. The pastor had never encountered anything like this before and was not able to give the sister the right advice in the circumstances. Not only that, but from that time onward, he began to have serious difficulties when he tried to pray for the sister. Every time he tried to pray for her, he felt as if someone were throttling him. As a result of this, I was called to help this sister.

This shows that ghost experiences also occur with people who are of psychic disposition, or who are oppressed as a result of sins of sorcery. This explains the fact that the pastor felt the hands around his throat and the violent attacks when he prayed for the sister. There is no doubt that this sister was under occult influence. Ghosts have a preference for manifesting themselves to people who have some psychic powers. It sometimes seems that ghosts from the world beyond use the psychic powers of a psychically oppressed person in order to make themselves visible. Such things are known to occur in spiritist séances, and that is why I mention this here.

I would add a piece of pastoral advice. One should be careful in dealing with ghosts. Do not ask them questions. In the name of Jesus Christ, one should forbid them to appear in one's home. We have the protection of the living God and need have no fear of these powers of darkness. Our eternal destiny is dependent on the life we lead here. We have no second chance of coming back from the other side to put things in order again and to make things good. In this connection, I reject the Catholic doctrine of purgatory as unscriptural. We are not to pray for the dead. They had time during their life here to make a decision for Jesus Christ. Even if pagans, who have never heard anything about Jesus, get this chance in eternity, that is the Lord's business and not a matter to be decided by our theology.

If there are some exceptional circumstances—and this I do not know—in which dead people are allowed to come back and put right something they have done wrong, that is again God's business. He is the Lord of His creation and His plan of salvation, and not a slave. If there are exceptions, we must not count on them. We must use every opportunity in this life to decide for Jesus Christ, the Redeemer of mankind, and to order our lives under His direction.

Additional Note:

This book was already prepared for publishing when another ghost experience worthy of publication came to my notice. I shall not mention names or places.

A woman's only son died. After the funeral she was often seen weeping by his grave. One day she felt someone's hand on her shoulder. Her dead son's voice addressed her. "Mother," it said, "do not weep. I am still living." The sad mother was overjoyed. She did not see her son; she only heard his voice.

This experience repeated itself several times. A few months later, the woman moved to another town. Shortly before she moved, her son spoke to her again and said reproachfully, "Are you going to leave me behind, then?" The mother decided to have her son's body exhumed and moved in a lead coffin.

The woman was in the process of unpacking in her new house

when she suddenly heard the voice of her dead son saying, "Mother, we have arrived." The woman looked out of the window and saw the van containing the lead coffin.

In the new home, a special room was furnished for the dead son, and in it the mother put all his possessions. She made his bed each day, although it was not used.

On one occasion when he came to her, she asked the dead young man, "Please tell me where you are." "Look up to the top of the hill," the voice replied. The mother looked, and saw a gate decorated with precious stones. "Are you well?" she asked. "Yes," came the reply, "I am well. You can see how nice it is behind that door."

Up to this point, one could argue that it was really the dead man who was appearing to the mother. The events that followed made her begin to doubt. Poltergeists began to appear in the house: knocking noises, scratching at the walls, footsteps, and other manifestations. When the voice spoke again, it said, "Watch out now, I am going into the drawer." The startled woman heard a terrible bang. This shattered her faith that it was her son who was visiting her, and for the first time, she sought pastoral help.

It is quite evident here that she had become the victim of a poltergeist. The story also reveals that this woman is psychic.

Ghost experiences cannot all be treated alike. I will distinguish several types.

1. I have heard reports from believing Christians of how, for instance, when they were in mortal danger a dead mother appeared and succeeded in warning them of the danger.

2. I have also many examples of old houses in which figures from former times appear. The so-called *Hambachgeist* was seen over a period of three hundred years, until the house was demolished and a cistern came to light in which were the skeletons of some women and children. The story was that the cistern had belonged to a monastery centuries ago.

3. Ghosts can also be materialization appearances of demons. Luther pointed out that demons and evil spirits take on the appearance of dead people to mislead the living.

4. Ghosts can also be products of a sick imagination or symptoms of a mental disorder.

5. Ghosts can be projected images from the minds of healthy people who have eidetic dispositions.

Let me repeat my warning that one should not have dealings with ghosts. Only in the first example quoted would it have been good for the person to check the accuracy of the information given and then to comply or refuse to follow the instructions. Even in cases like this, the devil sometimes acts under the camouflage of a good action.

23
GOBLINS AND ELVES

In my travels I have often gained valuable insights into the life and culture of primitive tribes and peoples. Some years ago, I gave twenty-nine lectures at the Bible school of the Swiss Indian Mission in Pucallpa, Peru. The missionaries took me to visit the various tribes. There I learned many interesting things.

Ex 71 A Christian believer among the Piro Indians told me, through an interpreter, of his encounter with a tiny dwarf who was only about two feet tall. This believer was hunting at the time, and was just about to kill a wild boar, when this tiny man stepped forward. He thought at first that it might be a pigmy, like those in South Africa. There are many such dwarfs in the Amazon area. This little fellow stopped him from shooting the boar. The hunter pushed him out of the way. The little fellow then showed an incredible strength and threw the hunter to the ground, where he lay unconscious for three days. Men from his village came out to search for him, and found him after three days. Experiences like this have led the Piros to believe that these little things are a kind of goblin. Missionaries see this as part of their pagan superstition. In this case, however, the man who had the experience was a Christian believer. Of course, it is true that in primitive tribes, even Christians can be influenced by their old pagan ideas. However, one ought not to dismiss an experience like this as a fairy tale.

Ex 72 In Africa, a missionary took me to visit the Xhosa tribe. This African tribe also believes that there are goblins and elves. These elves often appear to children and even play with them. The moment an adult comes on the scene, the elves disappear. The experience of these children could, of course, be regarded as the product of an eidetic disposition. *Eiditic* is a term used for the ability to project images of ideas or imagination outward, so that one can see the product of one's own imagination. This eidetic disposition is generally found in children under fourteen, especially those of primitive tribes.

I have often heard of experiences like this from missionaries. It is a different matter when one is told such things in highly civilized countries. I have travelled through Scandinavia several times and have visited every Scandinavian country, yes, even the North Pole. Particularly in Northern Sweden, one hears many stories of imps, pixies, elves, sprites, goblins and other remarkable creatures one associates with fairy tales. In Northern Sweden, I learned the names of several such little people. There are goblins about two feet tall, *gnomes, oeck,* and above all, *tomter,* which are widely believed in by the Swedes. Many elves are ready to play practical jokes. Goblins are regarded as useful spirits. If a person wants their help, he must apply to their chief, the devil himself. This, however, would cost a person his salvation.

The idea that these spirits are demonic in origin is in accordance with the Bible. I have observed furthermore that the elves, goblins, and all these little people appear especially to people who have a psychic disposition. This is another indirect confirmation that these little fairy-tale creatures are not ethically neutral. Rather, they correspond to the spirits and demons of the open places of which the Bible also speaks. Perhaps I should give an example which highlights two problems.

Ex 73 The authoress, Helga Braconnier, often foresaw disasters. She was psychic. On a pilot station north of the Baltic, she had a vision of a shipwreck. She warned the pilot, but he laughed at the idea. The next day an old Swede came to the authoress and said that a storm was coming, and the *tomter* who live in the cliffs were fleeing inland. That always meant there would be a flood. That evening the storm broke. A ship sent out an emergency signal. The pilot who had laughed at the woman who warned him had to go out with his pilot boat. The ship ran onto the cliffs and several people lost their lives. The warning of the old woman had come true.

One could write a book just about these little people like the *tomter,* but that is not my task.

The Swiss have also devoted themselves to investigating this problem of nature spirits. For example, Georg Sulzer, the former president of the Swiss Court of Appeal in Zürich, has written a book about the nature spirits. He distinguishes four types: gnomes, nymphs, sylphs or elves, and water sprites. This writer also states that these little people are about two feet tall. They are said to be grateful for help given to them, and to react to insults with practical jokes and acts of revenge.

Arthur Conan Doyle, author of the Sherlock Holmes stories, was a spiritualist. He published reports about nature spirits and the people who had seen them. Conan Doyle also possessed photographic negatives of nature spirits. The statement of one such spirit or demon of the open air is very informative. It said: "We demons are the remnants of a former creation which came into conflict with God. We have no hope of any kind. As far as humans are concerned, our activity consists of deceiving them and leading them astray. Originally, we were very wise, but because of our sin and our fall we have become considerably more stupid."

What does the Bible have to say on the subject of goblins, nature spirits, sprites, and demons of the open air? In Isaiah 13:21 satyrs are mentioned in connection with wild beasts. Their role is to destroy the land and make it unsafe. Isaiah 34:14 is an even clearer reference. "The wild beasts of the desert shall also meet with the wild beasts of the island, and the satyr shall cry to his fellow; the screech owl [night hag] shall also rest there, and find for herself a place of rest." Here we have the combination of wild animals, satyrs and night hag or screech owl, demons of the open places. Satyrs are mentioned again in 2 Chronicles 11:15, where King Rehoboam appoints priests to offer sacrifice to these demons.

Having looked at the Bible references, let us now glance at church history. Let us take what Martin Luther, the German reformer, thought about goblins. In his table talk he says on one occasion: "The goblin jolted me in bed. But I took little notice of him. When I was almost asleep, he began such a rumbling on the stairs that you would have thought someone was throwing three score barrels of wine down them. I stood up, went to the stairs, and called out 'If it is you, so be it.' Then I committed myself to the Lord, of whom it is written, 'Thou hast put all things under His feet,' and went back to bed. That is the best way to get rid of him: to scorn him and to call on Christ. That he cannot bear." Another time Luther is said to have thrown his inkpot after the devil.

In the face of all these powers of darkness, we may take heart from the message of the apostle Paul. Think for instance of Colossians 2:15. Freely translated this says, "Christ has unmasked the powers of darkness, He has disarmed the demons, and He draws along the mighty ones behind Him in His triumphal procession."

24
GROUP SUGGESTION

In my tours of East Asia, I have often come into contact with the problem of group suggestion. I will illustrate it by giving several examples.

Ex 74 The following story was told to me by a German doctor whom I know very well. Many years ago, he was a ship's doctor. One day his ship visited Hong Kong. Together with a lawyer and a naval officer, he went on a short excursion inland. While there, they came upon a large group of people. They stopped and watched a fakir demonstrating his abilities. Among other things, he performed the usual trick with the mango tree. The fakir put a mango seed into a bowl. Within a few minutes a little tree had grown there. The tree bloomed and produced fruit, and then the fakir offered the three foreign spectators a mango from the tree to eat. The doctor and his two companions ate the fruit. They were unable to explain what had happened. When the show was over, they discussed this "miracle." They asked one another, "Did we really eat a mango? Our hands are completely dry. Mangos are very juicy and sticky. Surely we would have traces of mango juice on our hands. Anyway, it is practically impossible to eat a mango without a knife. Has any of us a knife?" The naval officer had a pocketknife. They opened it. The knife, too, was clean. After they had returned to the ship, they even carried out a Nylander test to see if there were any traces of mango on the knife or on their hands. The test was negative. The three men concluded that they had been the victims of group suggestion. It is impossible for a tree to grow from a mango seed and to flower and produce fruit in a quarter of an hour.

I have heard similar stories in East Asia and know from experience that fakirs possess the power of inducing group suggestion. In the Western world I have not encountered such powers.

The problem, however, is more complex than appears from this example. Let us look at another case.

Ex 75 A Swiss pastor was visiting East Asia when he, similarly, came upon a fakir who was performing this mango tree miracle. The pastor photographed the various phases. He has shown me the pictures. In them, the fakir can be seen placing a seed in the bowl. The second picture shows the bowl several minutes later, with a little plant. A few minutes later, a little tree is to be seen, then the tree with flowers and fruit appears. The pastor had at first been of the opinion that this was a case of suggestion, but he was unable to account for the pictures. Cameras are not susceptible to suggestion.

This second example leads one to conclude that the fakir actually succeeded in causing a tree to grow from a seed in a short time. Yet this case also leaves certain questions unanswered. We must therefore go into further detail.

Ex 76   On almost every continent, I have encountered magicians who possess a kind of magnetic power which enables them to influence and accelerate the growth of plants. Even Watchman Nee, the Chinese Christian leader and writer, mentions this in his book, *The Latent Power of the Soul.* I have also read, in German books on parapsychology, that there are people who can magnetize plants and stimulate them to faster growth. I have not, however, heard that this magnetic power can enable someone to make a seed grow into a tree in a matter of minutes.

Ex 77   On the question of the photographs taken by the Swiss pastor, I have heard of similar phenomena both in East Asia and in Haiti. I have been told of spiritualists who are able to produce an image on a photographic plate or an x-ray screen by means of mental power. The person, who organized my lecture tour in Haiti, showed me the house of a magician, who is able to produce images on film, in a camera, even when it is not being used. This question is occasionally discussed in books on spiritism. I mention in this connection the book, *The World of Ted Serios,* published in the USA in 1967. Ted Serios, who came from Chicago, was able to project his ideas and thoughts on to a photographic plate. This process is called "psychokinetic photography." The author of the book is the Denver psychoanalyst, Jule Eisenbud.

A final example shows that what we have here are occult or demonic powers. It concerns a Swiss missionary who was working in East Asia.

Ex 78   The missionary was watching a fakir perform the famous rope trick. The fakir threw a rope into the air. The rope stood still and a young lad climbed up on it. Other tricks were performed. The missionary was surprised to see the trick with his own eyes. He took his camera and photographed it. In this case, the effect was different from that in the first example we mentioned. When the film was developed, he saw only the fakir sitting on the ground. The picture showed neither the rope nor the boy. The missionary realized that demonic powers were involved. The next time he saw a fakir, he challenged this illusion in the name of Jesus Christ. He saw it as an answer to prayer, when he found that he could no longer see the fakir's magic trick. The other spectators, however, watched the miracle with astonishment and puzzlement as before.

These few examples illustrate the complexity of this question. In any case, it is clear that the natural powers of a man are not sufficient to explain such tricks. We are faced here by powers from below. I advise Christians not to watch tricks performed by fakirs. If one unwittingly finds oneself among a crowd where such things are being performed, one must put oneself under God's protection. If necessary, we must also command the powers in the name of Jesus Christ. I found myself in the presence of fakirs several times in East Asia, and in such situations, I have called on the name of Jesus and put myself under His protection.

25
HALLOWE'EN

The article that follows will undoubtedly upset some religious people. The Catholic church in Europe keeps the Feast of All Saints each year on November 1. Devout people bring flowers and place them on the graves of their former relatives and friends. In some places they put lighted candles in their windows on the eve of November 1, to "help lost souls find their way" as they charmingly put it.

The same Festival is celebrated in the USA, but in a different way. Hallowe'en is more like a European carnival than an act of remembrance. The Americans hold Hallowe'en parties with fancy dress, masks, and plenty of alcohol. A little example will illustrate how seriously they take it.

Ex 79 I was giving a series of evangelistic talks in a church in Milwaukee. The pastor of the church had invited a colleague. The other pastor refused the invitation. He had been invited to a Hallowe'en party. The fancy dress party was more important to him than the gospel.

All Saints' Day and Hallowe'en originated in a pagan festival. Before the days of Christianity, the Druids in England (priests of a Celtic race) had the idea that people needed to be cleansed after they had died. The soul of the departed was transferred by magic to the body of an animal. During the night of October 31, the enchanted souls were freed by the Druid god, Samhain, and taken together into the Druid heaven.

This Druid festival was always accompanied by animal and sometimes human sacrifices and linked with all kinds of magic.

In spite of the coming of Christianity, this pagan festival continued to be kept in England until the sixth century. Gregory the Great (A.D. 540-604) advised the Archbishop of Canterbury to retain the hitherto Druid sacrifices and celebrate them in honor of the Christian saints.

This is one example of the Catholic policy of assimilation, and has parallels on many mission fields. In the summer of 1975, I was visiting a Catholic church in Bogota, Colombia, where I was astonished to find masks of Indian gods on the walls. The guide explained that the Spaniards had used these Indian gods to entice the Incas into the Christian church. In the light of Bible teaching, it is incredible that anyone should try to lead people to the living God with the aid of the demons.

To return to the Druid festival, English settlers brought these customs to America. There the festival enjoys widespread popularity, because it gives people an opportunity for a holiday.

In Germany, the association of All Saints' Day with the pagan Druid festival has long since disappeared. Only the religious custom has remained, and it is very popular among Catholic people. As long as the decoration of graves is only an expression of reverence for the departed, the custom can remain. The other custom of lighting candles to show lost souls the way is superstition. What counts in eternity is whether our lives have been lived for Christ or not. There is nothing we can do to alter the fate of the departed, however near and dear they are to us. Neither in the Old Testament nor the New is there any text which tells us to pray for the dead. In this connection, it may be added that masses for the dead, which were also introduced by Gregory the Great, are doctrinally wrong and superstitious.

26
HARI KRISHNA

Hari Krishna is an Eastern Indian sect which is collecting money in the Western world. I have come across them three times in the USA. On one occasion, I was strolling along a street in San Francisco. I noticed a group of young men. They were standing together, dressed in saffron yellow robes and singing an Eastern song. Their heads were shaved. Only one single tuft of hair remained, standing up vertically on top. They made a strange impression. When enough people had assembled, they began to take around the collection box.

Being familiar with their robes and their habits from my experience in East Asia, I did not give them a cent.

I came upon them a second time in Los Angeles. This Hari Krishna group is very active: for example, in this Californian metropolis they collect about a million dollars a year. No one knows what happens to the money.

The leader of this group is Tosan Krishna. He is twenty-three years old. He is at the same time the sect's administrative director. He insists that the money received is not used for the members of his church. He described its object like this: "Our task is to spread the Krishna consciousness, the Krishna message over the whole world."

I heard of this group for the third time in Manhattan, New York. They were in the process of buying a club house at the Columbia University for two and one-half million dollars. This action shows that the sect is extremely active and well-lined financially.

The sect has about two thousand members in the USA, and is said to have as many members in the other continents.

Let us now go over to Germany. In December 1974, an article entitled "Hari Krishna—the God Who Cashes in Many Millions From His Monks" appeared in a German magazine.

These bald-headed monks would have continued their shady business even longer in Germany, if the public prosecutor had not taken action against them. First of all, some of the ringleaders were imprisoned for illegal possession of firearms. Then 720,000 marks, which had been collected by begging, was confiscated by the authorities in Frankfurt. These sums of money, however, are not the aspect which should cause the most concern. Rather, it is the spiritual deceit carried out by these monks. Young people follow them with enthusiasm. Their parents are helpless to stop them. Their children usually disappear abroad, using false passports.

It is a question that many Christian parents ask themselves today: how do we protect our children from the spirit of the age? Young people are attracted by drugs and rock music, sex and alcohol, or become the victims of religious fanaticism. There is only one thing they are unwilling to do—to surrender their lives fully to Jesus Christ and become His disciples.

27
HEALING FANATICISM

In the last few decades there has been much discussion about miraculous healing. There are extremes on either side. I am convinced that God is able to help and to heal both with and without the aid of a doctor. There are many examples I could quote. I have also made it my practice for many years to obey the instructions in James 5:14, "Is any sick among you? Let him call for the elders of the church; and let them pray over him." But in spite of my positive attitude to faith healing, I am utterly opposed to healing fanaticism.

Ex 80   Near the entry to a highway, I saw a woman hitchhiker, whom I took on board. We were soon engaged in a religious discussion. The woman said she had toothache. It was because there was something wrong, she said, with her relationship with Jesus. She had not been to a dentist for years. She only got toothache when she had sinned. If the matter was put right, the toothache would disappear.

I replied that I did not share her conclusion. I go to the dentist when it is necessary. But I always pray when I go, for dental treatment can last six months and cause much pain.

Ex 81   In the USA, I have twice heard even more ridiculous views. Members of one extremist church claim that as a result of prayer, not only can they dispense with the services of a dentist, but that through faith, defective teeth can be fitted with gold fillings.

For me there is only one answer to this. I will trust the Lord for everything, but I am convinced that these stories are not true. The only possibility is that it might be a case of spiritistic apports.

I believe in a simple rule. God does not do for us what we can do for ourselves. I cannot sit back in an easy chair and ask God to dig my flower beds.

Ex 82   One of the followers of Osborn told me an equally ridiculous story. The report also appeared in a printed article. Osborn's sister is said to have prayed for a boy whose eye had been destroyed in an accident, with laying on of hands. As a result, the story went, the boy could see through his plastic eye. If he took the plastic eye out, he was still able to see through the empty socket. What have we here? Either the story is untrue, or it is a case of mediumistic sight such as is known to Tibetan sorcerers.

Ex 83   In 1963, I gave several addresses in a Canadian church. Several years later, the pastor, an easily influenced parson, fell victim to some extremists who overemphasized speaking in tongues, visions, and faith healing. The minister was no longer willing to be corrected.

We lost touch with one another. Eight years later when I was again in Canada, I heard a sad story. The minister's daughter-in-law had been very ill. The minister refused to bring in medical aid. His extremist friends gathered in the pastor's home and prayed for the healing of the young woman. She did not recover, but died. The minister would not allow the body to be taken to the mortuary. The group of extremists prayed in the pastor's home for the raising of the dead woman. This went on for three days. Then the body was collected by the police and buried. The church authorities removed the minister from office. Later, he was accepted for missionary service and sent to Jamaica. When I was speaking in Jamaica, I met him again. The good brother has become moderate once more in matters of faith.

Ex 84 A similar case was reported in a German church paper in the summer of 1975, under the heading *Dubious Substitute for Insulin*. It said:

> An American court is dealing at present with an unusual case of homicide. The parents of an eleven-year-old boy have been charged with stopping the doses of insulin which this child, who had suffered for years with diabetes, needed in order to live. The child died. The parents belong to a group associated with an extreme movement which has been steadily growing in the United States. Adherents of this group have so strong a faith in healing through prayer, that they refuse the use of medicines. According to the evidence given, the father and mother of the dead child did not even go to the burial; because they were of the firm belief, that their son would immediately rise again from the grave, to the glory of God.

Ex 85 On my lecturing tour of California in March 1975, I was given hospitality by a believing brother called W. T. in Santa Barbara. He told me of a sensational case. The famous leader of a sect in the USA advised the mother of a sick child not to go to the doctor but to trust God for healing. The woman followed his advice. The child died. The grief-stricken mother was so furious that she took the man to court who had advised her. This religious leader is a multi-millionaire, and so the court ordered him to make a payment of eleven million dollars to the mother. The California press made much of the case. The man will probably challenge the sentence; there is as little justification for that as there was for his unscriptural advice.

This list of unscriptural actions could be multiplied with many examples from both sides of the ocean.

The New Testament does not teach such extreme views. Paul says in Romans 13:14 "Care for your body" (Luther). Our body has been entrusted to us by God. We must use it according to God's instructions and give it the help and care which it needs. In 1 Corinthians 6:20 Paul says that we should serve and glorify God with our body and with our spirit. Healing fanaticism and extreme views do not come from the Spirit of the gospel.

28

HOMOSEXUALITY

During the sixties, a considerable storm of indignation arose in Christian circles in Europe over a statement of Dr. Theodor Bovet. This famous Swiss doctor spoke out at a church conference in favor of homosexuality.

Even more dust was raised by a report from Holland. A homosexual minister had married two homosexual men in his church. What was not clear to me was the legal status of this marriage. Official registry offices do not recognize couples of the same sex.

In the USA, I have been confronted with even more extreme cases. I will not recount my own experiences but rather record the words of a well-known American Baptist minister. He is the Rev. William W. Ayer, who for many years was pastor of the famous Calvary Baptist Church in New York. We met at Dr. Kenneth Moon's church in St. Petersburg, Florida, where I was giving several addresses. Ayer's article is entitled "Homosexualism in America—Will the Sodomites bring God's Judgment?" I can reproduce here only a shortened version of the original.

Ex 86 A series of lectures was being held at a university, and the subject for the first evening was homosexuality. The speaker was introduced as minister of a homosexual church. He declared quite openly: "I'm a gay person, and glad to be this way." What he said boiled down to this: "We are a minority group, and everyone else is picking on us. . . . Forty-five states outlaw private acts of homosexuality, and the police make the most of it. Society has criminalized us—apparently just because the book of Leviticus says we are an abomination. The police chase us down in our homosexual bars— the only places where we can go to meet other gays—and arrest us. They love to beat us up on the way to jail. . . . In most churches our situation is referred to as 'sin.' When we unite with a lover of our own sex, this is not celebrated by the church. . . . What are we doing about this? Well, we are organizing. We are fighting back. When the police raided a gay bar in New York City, we left by the back door, locked the cops in, set fire to the place. . . . They beat a hasty retreat."

These are some of the things which the pastor said. After him, a lesbian spoke.

Ex 87 "I'm a lesbian," she said. "That's a good thing for me and I'm happy about it. Last summer my lover and I had a wonderful experience. We went to a homosexual resort where we could walk around openly, holding hands in public. That evening, we necked openly. I had lived with my lover for seven years, but never in the past had we dared to show affection to one another openly in the presence of others. Well, as a result of being at that resort, I decided I would not play by the rules of society any more. From now on I make my own rules. I don't go by your rules. Homosexuality is no crime."

These public confessions represent only a fraction of what goes on. Let us give a few more short accounts.

Ex 88 In early September 1962, the District of Columbia licensed the Mattachine Society to solicit funds in Washington. The Mattachine Society is dedicated "to protect homosexuals from discrimination" and from violations of their civil rights (Dan Smoot Report, 10/26/64).

Ex 89 A United Church of Christ agency said in a recommendation to the denomination's executive council: "Homosexuality as such should not be an issue in considering qualifications for ordination" (New York—RNS).

Ex 90 The United Methodist Council of Youth Ministry announced in 1974 that it would ask the 1976 General Conference of that denomination to amend its *Book of Discipline* to read, "Sex, race, marital status, or sexual orientation shall not be a bar to the ordained ministry of the United Methodist Church."

Ex 91 An Anglican minister in England has expressed this view in blasphemous terms. He has openly suggested that Jesus was a homosexual, because He had only men as His disciples.

Ex 92 On August 9, 1963, the President of the Washington Chapter of the Homosexual International, testifying under oath before a Congressional committee, stated that there were between

200,000 and 250,000 deviates (Sodomites) who held positions in the Federal Government (Dan Smoot Report, 10/26/64).

Now we will move on from Ayer's report to a final example from my own experience.

Ex 93 I was invited to speak to two Protestant youth groups in West Germany. There were also some theology students there. Following my address there was a period of discussion. The leader of the opposition was a female theology student who had already passed her first exam in theology. We were talking about the divine sonship of Jesus, which is disputed by modern theologians. The student in question brought out her trump card: "Jesus was a man like ourselves. He was a homosexual." I jumped up and cried: "That is blasphemy. I cannot stay here any longer." I went to the door. Then another young person shouted after me: "And His mother Mary was a whore!"

What matters in making our assessment of homosexuality is not what the psychologists, the modern theologians, the doctors, or well-wishing philanthropists may say, but what the Bible says.

The expression *Sodomites* is derived from the account in Genesis 19:5. Many ordinary readers of the Bible do not understand the expression *to know*. The Hebrew word *yadah* means sexual union.

God condemned the inhabitants of Canaan to destruction because they were homosexuals. Several good kings of Israel were blessed by God, because they had the houses of the prostitutes pulled down and drove the Sodomites out of the land. We read about this in 1 Kings 14:24, 15:12, 22:46, and 2 Kings 23:7. The English translations of the Bible make it clear that male prostitutes are meant.

Clearest of all is the language of the New Testament. Paul writes in Romans 1:27 of "men, leaving the natural use of the woman, burned in their lust toward one another; men with men working that which is unseemly." Therefore, he says, God gave them up.

There are problems connected with homosexuality which have not been discussed here. Lack of space forbids that we do more than touch on them.

A distinction is drawn between people who have been born homosexual and those who have been perverted. From a medical point of view, the hereditary form is not curable. Perversion, on the other hand, can be overcome. Many believers will say, "God can do miracles." I believe so, too. But I have never yet met anyone who has been delivered from congenital homosexuality. Now, however, comes the decisive point. I know believing brethren who have a homosexual inclination, but who have not done anything wrong. In other words, by the power of God, they are able to control this unfortunate inclination. They are serving the Lord and know His blessing.

Those who became homosexual in early years as a result of being led astray by others can be set free. The perversion which they have developed disappears when they are truly converted and born again. "But as many as received him, to them he gave power to become the sons of God, even to them that believe on his name; which were born, not of blood, nor of the will of the flesh, but of God" (John 1:12-13).

29
HYPNOTISM

The word *hypnosis* is derived from the Greek word *hypnos*, meaning sleep. In laymen's language, one could say that hypnotism is a means of bringing on an artificial state of sleep. It would be more accurate to speak of a state of reduced consciousness.

Opinions on hypnosis differ widely even among experts. The well-known Genevan specialist, Dr. Paul Tournier, is opposed to hypnotism because it is an attack on the human psyche. Other specialists, like Dr. Lechler, say that they are prepared to use hypnosis for diagnosis but not for therapy. I have also met a number of specialists who use hypnosis both for diagnosis and therapy. In Winnipeg, Canada, I debated a Baptist missionary doctor who said he would be prepared to use all forms of hypnosis. In the course of the heated discussion, I noticed that this missionary was under bondage.

If asked for my opinion, I would have to admit that I have heard so many ill effects of hypnotism that I am opposed to it.

My chief area of experience with hypnotism has been East Asia. In the Western world, hypnotism was first developed in the time of Anton Mesmer (1778), together with mesmerism and animal magnetism. Hypnotism has been practiced in East Asia for thousands of years. My friends in East Asia have told me of examples of hypnosis and hypnotism of others which would be described in the West as improbable or as untrue.

I have observed examples of self-hypnosis. I have seen pilgrims in religious processions who, by means of self-hypnosis, which is similar to a trance, have made themselves insensitive to pain. I have seen them stick knives or bamboo sticks through their arms or parts of their faces without feeling pain. I have said something about this in another chapter, and also in other books.

The strongest form of self-hypnotism is the reduction of heart activity as practiced by yogis and fakirs. They have themselves put into a coffin and incarcerated in a stone vault for three to ten weeks. Their friends are told exactly when they must take them out again. Then the heart will resume its normal activity. There are examples of this in nature. In Switzerland, I read an article about the hibernation of marmots. The article said that marmots are able to reduce their pulse rate to one pulse per minute. This is similar to the auto-hypnosis of the yogis and fakirs of the Far East.

In the East, hypnosis is always associated with magic, spiritism, and similar twilight activities. This fact has strengthened my attitude of opposition to hypnotism.

I have often had discussions with Christian doctors, mainly in the Western world, about the value of hynosis.

Ex 94 One doctor in West Germany, for instance, maintains that he can sometimes cure migraine in one day by means of hypnotic treatment.

I had a very useful conversation about hypnosis with the chief consultant at the Sanatorio Cruz Blanca, Esquel, in Southern Argentina.

Ex 95 Now I want to recount an experience which the above-mentioned doctor had with hypnosis. A woman was brought to him suffering from a spider complex. Day and night, the woman was tormented by seeing spiders all over the house: on the floor, on the walls, on the ceiling. She suffered terribly. No amount of soothing words was of any use. The doctor hypnotized her. While she was in hypnosis he said to her: "When you awake, you will see no more spiders." The treatment was successful. When the woman awoke, she breathed a sigh of relief. All the spiders had gone. So far so good. But there was another side to the story. The doctor told me that from that day onwards the woman had become an extreme alcoholic. She was free from the spiders, but totally enslaved to alcohol. This experience and another similar one made the doctor resolve never to use hypnosis again. He said that in both cases it was a case of altered symptoms but not of deliverance.

Decisively to be rejected are all shows featuring magic tricks coupled with attempts at hypnotism. Even the experts in the field of hypnosis call such displays a nuisance, which ought to be prohibited. And yet many headmasters or principals allow such shows to take place in their schools, and so cause great harm to their children.

Ex 96   A girl in Tokyo was hypnotized at a school festival by a charlatan. He was not able to wake her from the hypnotic state. The girl emitted animal noises, developed a high temperature, and was only brought back to consciousness by medical specialists several days later.

Ex 97   A woman came to me for counseling and told me the following story. The head of the school had organized an evening entertainment. Various conjuring tricks were performed. The entertainer also made some experiments with hypnosis. In the case of this woman's thirteen-year-old son, the hypnotism was successful. From that day on, however, the boy had serious nightmares. In his sleep he would often cry out "The black man is coming, the black man is coming. Take the black man away from my throat." The boy's nightmares lasted for years. The mother was furious with this conjurer. The head of the school shares the blame for this unfortunate state of affairs. Entertainers who practice hypnotism ought never to be invited to take part in an entertainment.

Ex 98   My next example shows even more clearly the connection between hypnosis and occult powers. I was asked to speak at several meetings in a Baptist church in the state of Maine. The pastor of the church told me the story of his son while I was there.

His son had been converted to Christ at the age of sixteen. He was baptized and became a member of his father's church. He went to college about sixty miles away from his hometown.

At the end of the college year, an entertainment was held for the students and teachers. The president invited a certain entertainer, who performed all kinds of tricks and illusions. One thing he did was to pick out twenty-five students and bring them up to the platform to be hypnotized. One of them was given a big red potato, and it was suggested to him that it was a wonderful apple which he was now allowed to eat. The boy ate the red potato with great delight. To another boy, the entertainer suggested: "You are a baby, and here is your bottle of milk which you must drink." The boy drank the bottle of milk to the last drop. To a third, he said that it was very hot, that he was by a lake and could now bathe. The boy undressed and put on a pair of bathing trunks. All these tricks were greeted by laughter and applause from the audience. To the pastor's son he said, "You are in a horse race, and your horse has a chance of winning." The boy began to ride on a chair placed back to front as if he were sitting on a horse.

When the entertainment was over, the entertainer released them from the hypnosis: all except the pastor's son, whom he could not restore to consciousness. The president became angry. But try as he might, the man was unable to bring him back from this hypnotic state. There was nothing to do but to call the hospital.

An ambulance took the boy to the hospital, where five specialists tried to deal with the hypnotized boy. They were unable to. The father was not informed until six days later. He drove straight to the hospital by car and took his son home. Then he telephoned his local doctor who came immediately. The doctor was angry and said, "If he were my son, I would take the principal and the entertainer to court." The pastor and his wife prayed for the boy, who was still in a hypnotic state. They prayed for days, but nothing happened. Suddenly, the pastor came upon the idea of commanding in the name of Jesus. He looked in spirit to the cross of Christ on Calvary, and cried: "In the name of Jesus Christ, the Son of God, I command you dark powers to withdraw." At once the hypnotic spell was broken. The boy regained consciousness. At last the horse race ended.

This incident shows that the entertainer was a dabbler in the occult. His hypnosis was based upon magic. Such activity is criminal.

Of course I know that specialists totally reject this kind of hypnosis. I have already said so much. Thus we must distinguish between the hypnosis used by doctors for diagnosis and treatment and magically based hypnosis, which is clearly occult in character. But I must not neglect to add, that I reject even the kind of hypnosis used by doctors.

Ex 99 The following incident occurred in Eastern Switzerland some years ago. I was told about it by a Christian doctor. A demonstration of hypnotism was given by a healer in Appenzell. He was able to hypnotize certain people, especially those who were strongly psychic, in such a way that they became as stiff as a board. The doctor, who told me the story, heard about this and took three believers with him to the meeting. They agreed to pray during the demonstration, in order to discover the nature of this hypnosis. The hypnotist began, as usual, by choosing some suitable people from the audience. Then he began his experiment. That evening he was unsuccessful. Finally he said, "There are opposing forces present. We will stop the demonstration. Ask for your money back at the door."

The doctor and his friends knew then what kind of hypnosis this notorious healer had been using.

Ex 100 The most sensational example of hypnosis I know of comes from Zürich. It happened about fifteen years ago when I was lecturing for several weeks in Zürich. During this time, a Dutch hypnotist arrived in the city with his subject. The subject's name was Mirin Dajo. *Mirin Dajo* is Esperanto[25] for something wonderful. Both men belonged to spiritist circles in Holland.

The shows in Zürich drew large crowds. The reason was a unique sensation which had never been witnessed in Switzerland before. The hypnotist plunged a fencing foil through his victim's chest on the stage. At first, everyone thought it was a trick. In the circus, one sometimes sees tricks in which a person is sawn through, or put into a box and then stabbed from every side with a saber through gaps in the box. The explanation is that the saber folds up. The man in the box is unhurt.

In the case of Mirin Dajo, however, it was not a trick. Proof of this was given by Professor Brunner, then a professor at the University of Zürich. He asked the two men to repeat the performance in his clinic so he could take an x-ray photograph. The men were willing. The x-ray showed that the foil had indeed pierced the man's chest without going through vital organs like the heart and lungs. The point of the foil was nevertheless to be seen coming out at the front. The two Dutchmen had performed this feat some 500 times in various countries.

When they appeared in Zürich and repeated the experiment night after night, believers in Zürich began to feel very uncomfortable about it. Prayer groups began to meet and to pray to God to ask Him to end these gruesome displays. They suspected that behind them demonic forces were at work. The result? At the five hundred and first attempt, Mirin Dajo died. That was the end of these horrible demonstrations. Of course it would be possible to lay the blame for this man's death at the door of the believers in Zürich. I do not share this view. The believers did what they believed to be right. They were resisting the public display in their city of such occult, or even demonic, experiments.

It ought to be added that Mirin Dajo felt no pain as the foil was stuck into him. When the foil was removed, the two wounds did not bleed. They healed up within two hours. This is exactly like phenomena I observed in East Asia. The wounds which the East Asian pilgrims inflict upon themeslves likewise do not bleed, but they heal very quickly. Nor do they experience any pain. This shows that the experiment with Mirin Dajo is exactly like those in East Asia. This was not a case of fraud or deceit, for it was proved genuine by means of x-ray.

I must add a short concluding paragraph based on my counseling experience. I have often been asked whether a person can be hypnotized against his will. Experience shows that people who have a strong will cannot be hypnotized unless they consent. This is particularly true of believing Christians who arm themselves against hypnosis by prayer. Against this, the hypnotist has no power. If, however, a person has already been hypnotized, it is easier to hypnotize him again. Brennmann, a specialist in this field, has put it in these words, "No one comes unwillingly into a state of hypnosis. But it can be that he is himself unaware of his intention."

For the Christian, it is a good rule not to use any dubious forms of help. Perhaps we should remind ourselves of the words of the psalmist: "Our help is in the name of the LORD" (Psalm 124:8).

30
IRIS DIAGNOSIS

This expression is derived from two Greek words: *iris,* meaning rainbow; and *diagnosis,* meaning distinction. Iris diagnosis is the recognition or distinction of diseases by observation of the iris or rainbow membrane of the eye.

The principle of this method of diagnosis is the division of the iris into organic fields. These are arranged as on a clock face: sector twelve is supposed to correspond to the brain (cerebrum), sector six to the foot, knee, and leg. Every disease is said to cause an alteration in the corresponding organic field of the iris.

"There is nothing new under the sun." This proverbial saying from Ecclesiastes is certainly justified as far as iris diagnosis is concerned. Historically, iris diagnosis, like acupuncture, goes back to ancient Chinese methods of healing. Both methods are associated with astrology.

In the case of iris diagnosis, the eye was originally (in ancient China some three thousand years ago) divided into five concentric zones, alterations in which were evaluated in making the diagnosis. The later division into twelve fields corresponds to the astrological signs of the zodiac: aries, taurus, gemini, cancer, leo, virgo, libra, scorpio, sagittarius, capricorn, aquarius and pisces. In the last century new shoots began to sprout from the primitive, superstitious roots of iris diagnosis.

In 1836, an eleven-year-old Hungarian boy named Ignatz von Pézely was seized by an owl. He was only able to free himself from the bird's talons by breaking its leg. At the same moment, the boy noticed a black line in the owl's iris. It is almost unbelievable that this discovery, made by an eleven-year-old fighting for his life, formed the basis for renewed interest in iris diagnosis.

It would go beyond the limits of this book, if I were here to set out all the pros and cons of iris diagnosis. Anyone who wants to study the subject in depth will find hundreds of published examples available. Many of them are in Professor P. A. Jaensch's book, *Iris-diagnostick*. My own account is concerned only with cases which have come up in my counseling experience or of which I have heard in the course of my lecture tours.

Ex 101 In the spring of 1975, I was giving a series of lectures in a town in East Germany. Those who had invited me had asked me to speak, among other things, about acupuncture and iris diagnosis. Before I had begun to speak, five iris diagnosticians introduced themselves to me. They had come to hear my lecture. It looked as if what they meant was, "Watch what you say. We are here." In fact, I avoided any aggressive comment. Afterward, however, two of these men questioned me with hostility. There were also some further consequences of this encounter. I again looked at literature about iris diagnosis and then said to the one who had criticized me most severely, "I am willing to come and see you and learn more about it."

I took with me several other believers and went to see this famous iris diagnostician. Two things impressed me. First, he took time off to see us. Second, on the screen he showed us some excellent photographs of irises. This private session helped me and confirmed my experience over many years.

1. He showed pictures of left and right iris, with the sector divisions marked. My question was: "Medical science knows more than ten thousand different diseases. Your 'iris keys' (sectors) show only about thirty divisions. So, in every sector you are claiming to be able to distinguish 300 or 400 diseases. That is not possible." The iris diagnostician replied, "In the case of a disease, only the affected area, like the lung, the heart, or the stomach, shows up in an alteration of the iris."

My reply to this was, "Then iris diagnosis is unable to provide any accurate diagnosis, for there are countless diseases which may affect these organs."

2. I made the second observation when some of the visitors offered to undergo an iris check. The diagnostician named several diseases for each of them. This confirms what medical scientists say:

iris diagnosticians often give a list of diseases for a patient. One of them will turn out to be right. I know of one case in which an iris diagnostician named nineteen different areas of diseases in a single patient. Some of them, not surprisingly, were right.

3. One of the believers present was a young minister who retired at an early age because of serious liver trouble. He did not mention his disease. The iris diagnostician examined his eyes, but did not discover the severe damage to his liver.

I do not wish to be unjust. It is not unknown for professional doctors to give false diagnoses in many cases.

4. Another question touched on in the course of this visit was about the variety of systems. In my book *Aberglaube,* I have mentioned six types of iris keys. The expert we visited declared, "There are not six types, only one." This is simply not true. Karl Schulte, a very well-known iris diagnostician, mentions in his *Encyclopedia of Iris Diagnosis,* sixteen ways of dividing the iris. Another expert speaks of nineteen iris keys. The different systems cannot be harmonized. There is no room here to explain the differences. At the moment, an attempt is being made to harmonize the various systems.

Our visit to this iris diagnostician did not convince me that this type of diagnosis is scientific. Nevertheless, I am grateful to this man for the opportunity of seeing inside his workshop.

Iris diagnosticians defend their cause with great passion and vigor because their existence depends on it. Iris diagnosticians make their living by their diagnosis.

What I have said above by no means gives an exact analysis of the question of iris diagnosis. It is outside my competence to conduct a debate between scientific ophthalmology (the study of diseases of the eye, from Greek *ophthalmos,* eye) and iris diagnosis. I leave that to the experts.

What concerns me is the nature and the effects of iris diagnosis as they appear in counseling situations. I am dealing with the religious problem, not with the medical side.

In Professor Jaensch's book, *Irisdiagnostik,* I was surprised to find a chapter entitled, *Eye Diagnosis and Occultism.* I would hardly have expected to find such a subject being dealt with by a university lecturer. He writes facts which I have been trying for years to hammer into the readers of my books.[26]

First of all, he calls iris diagnosis an *Afterwissenschaft* (pseudo-science, or fantasy under a scientific guise). I quote: "Medieval ophthalmoscopy, or the prophesying of character from the appearance of a person's eyes, is on a level with chiromancy, the art of fortune-telling by means of the lines on the hand; metoposcopy, the art of interpreting the lines on the forehead; and physiognomy, the art of interpreting the features, warts, and spots on the face."[27]

What Professor Jaensch writes on the subject of occult diagnosis concurs with my book, *Christian Counselling and Occultism,* which appeared three years earlier.

There are psychic, occult methods of diagnosis. In order not to give rise to any misunderstandings, I must say that there are few occult iris diagnosticians. Many iris diagnosticians have nothing to do with the occult. The medical value of their diagnosis, however, is extraordinarily thin. In many cases it is meaningless.

It is a different case with those iris diagnosticians who work by occult means. They usually produce 100 percent accurate diagnoses.

How are their diagnoses made? There are some diagnosticians who are psychic and work with various forms of psychic power. The iris is just one *contact bridge* which can be used for the tapping of the conscious or subconscious mind through telepathy, clairvoyance, or trance. By this means, a psychometric diagnosis is produced (see the chapter on psychometry).

Psychic diagnosis is not always successful. Psychic powers cannot be employed in the case of every patient who enters the consulting room. Psychic diagnosis is also ineffective in the case of believing Christians who have a strong relationship with Jesus Christ.

It is easy for mistakes and confusion to arise surrounding this field. I must therefore mention that there are not only some iris diagnosticians, but also some fully-qualified members of the medical profession who use occult methods. I have counseled members of the medical profession who have confessed, and then given up their occult activities. It would be wrong to put all the blame on to the nonprofessional healers.

Some examples may clarify:

Ex 102   A father was ill and went to an iris diagnostician for advice. His family knew nothing about this method of therapy (treatment of disease). After several sessions with the eye diagnostician, the man's character began to change. His wife said, "He became a devil to his own family. He took to alcohol, bullied his wife and children, though until then he had been a friendly, peaceable man."

Over forty-four years I have collected thousands of examples which tell a similar story. Those who engage in occult activities undergo a change of character, feelings, and faith.

Ex 103 During a week of addresses in Gebweiler, Alsace, an elderly lady came to me and declared that her daughter was destined to die. I asked her to tell me more. She explained that E., an eye diagnostician in Strasbourg, had predicted that her daughter would die bearing her fifth child. Her fifth baby was now about to be born. The whole family was very anxious because of this sinister prophecy.

Here is a clear example of iris diagnosis connected with fortune-telling. Such activities should be forbidden.

Ex 104 A young man went to an iris diagnostician. Not only was he told what his illness was, but he was told the future. The young man recovered, but as far as his faith was concerned, he displayed remarkable changes. He began to feel physical pain when he went to church or when he wanted to read the Bible at home. He lost the ability and desire to pray or to sing Christian hymns. At the same time, personality defects appeared. He became an addict, a chain-smoker, and depressions set in which led to a complete emotional breakdown. His organic healing was dearly paid for in terms of emotional complications. This eye diagnostician works in an area known for its many occult healers.

I have been asked more than once whether all my examples concerning treatment by eye diagnosticians are negative. No, I have some which are without any apparent negative effects. I must say this for the sake of truthfulness, even if it does not suit radical critics in the Christian community.

My experience can be summed up in two observations:

1. Eye diagnosticians who are not occult cause no harmful effects on their patients. The medical value of their treatment, however, is very small.

2. Eye diagnosticians who work by occult means bring their patients under bondage. Their diagnoses are often accurate.

Every eye diagnostician will claim that he is one of the good sort. Under no circumstances, however, can the Bible text, "The light of the body is the eye" (Matthew 6:22), be used to justify eye diagnosis, as sometimes happens.

31

JEANE DIXON

Some years ago, the authoress Ruth Montgomery wrote a book called *Jeane Dixon, a Prophetess*.

Jeane Dixon can be described as a prophetess only by someone who is very spiritually confused.

Jeane Dixon and her predictions are being discussed all over the world. Some examples, which have been fully documented, have aroused widespread interest. Let us consider some political events she foresaw.

In 1944, she declared that China would become communistic. This prophecy was fulfilled in 1949.

In 1947, she prophesied the murder of Mahatma Gandhi. Six months later, he was shot by a fanatic.

In 1961, this woman predicted Marilyn Monroe's suicide. One year later, the famous filmstar committed suicide by an overdose of sleeping tablets.

Jeane Dixon predicted the murder of President John F. Kennedy. She prophesied the division of India and Pakistan and named the first president of Pakistan several months in advance. She also predicted the fall and reelection of Churchill, and the fall of Kruschev.

This account must now be critically examined. The first thing we notice is that *only* the great successes were documented and made known. This produces a distorted impression. How many false prophecies she made, no one knows. Jeane Dixon's answer is that ten percent of her predictions are wrong. I am skeptical about this claim. I think it probable that there are more. Honest fortunetellers have admitted that only fifty percent of their prophecies were right.

Several of her mistakes ought to be mentioned.

According to Dixon, the third world war was to have broken out in 1954.

Red China was to be received into the UN in 1958. It did not happen until 1971.

The Vietnam war was to end in 1966, but it lasted until 1975.

On October 19, 1968, she prophesied that Jacqueline Kennedy would not think of remarriage. The next day she married Onassis.

Do these critical objections mean that Jeane Dixon is a swindler? No! She has developed a great ability to tell the future. That became known throughout the world when she tried at all costs to stop John F. Kennedy from making his trip to Dallas.

What is the nature of Jeane Dixon's *prophecies?*

The first observation to make is that, as with all genuine fortunetellers, she foretells only tragic events like murder, fire, floods, and catastrophes: never anything good. This fact suggests a connection with the underworld and not with the realm of God.

Emil Krämer of Colmar, who is an old pastor with long experience of the occult, believes that the demonic world informs occult fortune-tellers of its plans. Since demons organize only murder, fires, and crimes, occult mediums who have connections with this lower world predict such events. This theory has more to be said for it than the far-fetched hypothesis of a tapping of the world consciousness or contact with timelessness, as maintained by Erich von Däniken.

Occult mediums get their powers from below and are oriented to the lower world. Such a view is allegedly in conflict with the religious habits of Jeane Dixon. Jeane Dixon regards her powers as a gift of God. She is a faithful Catholic and is said to go to mass every morning and to pray, using the Twenty-third Psalm.

We should not be misled by this religious attitude. We may compare the case of the soothsayer at Philippi mentioned in Acts 16: 16-18. During the apostle Paul's missionary journey, she appeared among the crowd and called out, "These men are the servants of the most high God, which shew unto us the way of salvation." She was providing a good advertisement for Paul's missionary work. Paul had the gift of discerning spirits. He turned to the woman and said: "I command thee in the name of Jesus Christ to come out of her." The soothsayer was delivered that very moment.

We must get used to the idea that fortunetellers often appear under a disguise of piety.

Despite her churchgoing habits Jeane Dixon is not a prophetess, but a soothsayer and a dangerous one at that. I have some examples from counseling in the USA. One woman, for example, told me that she had gone to Jeane Dixon for advice. Ever since then, her emotional and spiritual life had been adversely affected. She also experienced remarkable apparitions, which she never had before.

It should also make us pause to think, when we hear that even Catholic priests attack this devout Catholic in their books and sermons. They have become aware of something sinister about this woman.

Believing Christians ought not have a copy of the book about Jeane Dixon in their homes.

The best comment from a Biblical viewpoint about this soothsayer is to be found in the book, *Satan is Alive and Well on Planet Earth* by Hal Lindsey wth C. C. Carlson, on pages 114-128.

32
JEHOVAH'S WITNESSES

A full discussion of the sect called Jehovah's Witnesses would go beyond the limits of this book. In his book *Seher, Grübler, Enthusiasten,* Dr. Kurt Hutten has devoted fifty-five pages to this movement. In this chapter, some light will be thrown on this tenacious heresy in the form of a brief sketch.

1. *History.* In the nineteenth century, an American named William Miller became well-known for his calculations regarding the return of Christ. He named 1843 as the year in which the world would end. Miller was not the only man to make such calculations. In Germany, the well-known and respected theologian Bengel stated that Jesus would return in the year 1846. It was a very serious blow to believers in Germany that a theologian as Christ-centered and firm in the Bible as Bengel should have made such a mistake.

The Adventist movement in the USA, which had been encouraged by the speculations of Miller, a Baptist preacher, became the spiritual mother of the Jehovah's Witnesses. Today this has become what is probably the most strictly organized sect of our times.

The founder of the movement was Charles Taze Russell, who was born in 1852 at Pittsburgh, Pennsylvania. As a young businessman, he succeeded by his acumen in gathering what was, for those days, an enormous fortune. Yet his 300,000 dollars were less important to him than his unanswered religious questions. Not a bad attitude for a young businessman. He was repelled by the harsh legalism of the Calvinists. The threat of eternal punishment for the damned in hell left him no peace. He therefore devoted himself for five years to an extensive study of the Bible. The result was published in 1874 under the title, *The Object and Manner of Our Lord's Return.* His principal work was *Scripture Studies* in six volumes. (Rutherford later added a seventh volume.) His ideas were also spread through the magazine, *Zion's Watchtower,* which today is translated into all the major world languages and printed in millions.

In 1884, Russell founded the *Watch Tower Bible and Tract Society.* He died in 1916. His successor was the attorney, Joseph F. Rutherford. The movement was known by several names. Some called it the International Bible Students. Others called it Millenial Dawnists or Russellites. After Rutherford's death in 1942, Nathan Homer Knorr became leader of the movement.

The literature of the Jehovah's Witnesses is widely distributed throughout the world, as can be seen from some facts and figures. By 1932, Rutherford's writings had gone into 120 million copies. Watchtower publications are produced in 165 languages. The Jehovah's Witnesses have great printing works all over the world. What a blessing it would be if they were busy printing Biblical truth instead of false teaching.

2. *Eschatology*. One of the many reasons for rejecting the claim of the Jehovah's Witnesses to be witnessing to the truth is their fantastically distorted and confused eschatology (teaching about the end of the world).

Russell believed Adam and Eve were created in 4126 B.C. The week of years which the world was destined to last amounted to 6000 years. Christ would therefore come again in 1874. Russell and his followers waited in vain for this event to take place. When it did not, he added forty years of testing for God's people and arrived at the date of 1914. As luck would have it, he lived through a second disappointment; he did not die until 1916. Jehovah's Witnesses are, however, insensitive to ridicule. Many of them still believe that Christ appeared invisibly on earth in 1914.

Rutherford provided further tensions and expectations. In 1920 he wrote that Jesus would return in 1925. I well remember this date. In the village where I grew up, the Jehovah's Witnesses had some followers who told us what was to happen. I was still a small boy, and during 1925, I was frightened every time dark clouds appeared in the sky. I kept wondering: is Jesus coming? I knew, as a boy of twelve, that I was not ready to meet Jesus. The new date was wrong again. It did not result in many falling away from the movement. New explanations were continually found.

The leaders of the sect undertook a revision of their calculations. They made Adam and Eve 100 years younger and said that they had not been created until 4025 B.C. This would mean that Jesus should return in 1975. Wrong again! Yet they expect to be taken seriously as they continue to bother people on their doorsteps with their obstinate propaganda.

For the Jehovah's Witnesses, two future events are of outstanding importance: the final battle which will bring the world to an end, and the salvation of the theocratic organization.

Armageddon is the great judgment of all the opponents of the Jehovah's Witnesses. Christ will act as executioner and annihilate all who have not accepted the *truth* which the Witnesses proclaim.

They will themselves be divided into two classes. The first comprises the 144,000—the class of the Kingdom of Heaven, the consecrated ones who will reign with Christ. The second class will turn the earth into a wonderful paradise with every kind of happiness. They also believe that Beth-Sarim in California will be the official residence of the Old Testament men of God.

This division became necessary because the number of 144,000 elect was already full in the last century. It was necessary for the promises to extend to the six or seven million followers throughout the world.

Two ideas motivate the Jehovah's Witnesses: fear of annihilation at Armageddon, and hope of the unspeakable joys of paradise. With fear as a whip and blessedness as an overflowing cup, coupled with an extraordinary technique of salesmanship, the Jehovah's Witnesses are able to catch people who are not armed with a clear knowledge of the Scriptures.

3. *Christology.* What do the Witnesses believe about Jesus Christ?

Jesus is not God's executioner, but the Redeemer and Savior of the world. But the Bible says: "For God so loved the world that he gave his only begotten Son, that whosoever believeth in him should not perish, but have everlasting life" (John 3:16).

The Jehovah's Witnesses deny the Trinity. They say it is a pagan doctrine of three gods. Christ has been disempowered. In their view, He is not the Son of God, but merely the most perfect man whom God has made. The Bible says, however: "He that hath the Son hath life; and he that hath not the Son of God hath not life" (1 John 5:12).

In their book *The Truth Will Make You Free,* it is stated: "The designation of Jesus as Messiah or Christ proves that the main purpose of His coming was not to redeem or to save mankind." The Bible on the other hand says in Matthew 1:21: "He [Jesus] shall save his people from their sins." And again, in 1 Corinthians 15:22: "As in Adam all die, so also in Christ shall all be made alive."

The Jehovah's Witnesses maintain that human eyes cannot see Jesus at His coming.[28] The Bible says: "Behold, he cometh with the clouds; and every eye shall see him, and they also that pierced him" (Revelation 1:7).

Christ is the key who unlocks the Holy Scriptures. Anyone who tries to exclude Him will not get to the heart of the Bible. Anyone who denies the divinity of Christ cuts himself off from the community of the redeemed. The Jehovah's Witnesses, who call themselves the class of the Kingdom of Heaven, the privileged ones, are not within the kingdom.

Consequences. What consequences follow from the false teaching of the Jehovah's Witnesses? They say church leaders and political rulers are tools of Satan which must be resisted. For this reason, they speak evil of the existing churches and refuse to obey the state. They refuse to do military service and to take oaths. Thousands of them have gone to prison in various countries because of this. In Hitler's time, they were sent to concentration camps. Many paid for their beliefs with their lives.

Here we have an aspect which has elicited much respect. In the prisons and concentration camps, they showed a readiness to help and a humanity not found among the other prisoners. The blocks containing Jehovah's Witnesses were model blocks. They were honest, reliable, industrious, and never attempted to escape. Sometimes Himmler even held them up to his SS men as an example. We should recognize this human side of the movement with gratitude. But one cannot earn Heaven. There is only one gate into the kingdom of God: rebirth through the Holy Spirit, the acceptance of Jesus Christ as our personal Lord and Savior.

Occasionally people are freed from the slavery of the *Theocratic Organization.* They describe the days of their membership as brainwashing, as a spiritual or religious bondage, from which it is impossible for a person to free himself by his own strength. Here is revealed a diabolical captivity which can only be broken by Christ. Worth reading on this point is W. J. Schnell's *Thirty Years a Watchtower Slave.*

33
KATHRYN KUHLMAN

In these chaotic days, we have not only the right but the duty to test every movement by the standard of the Holy Scriptures. In particular, we must direct a Biblical test-lamp onto the paths of outstanding personalities who come up like comets on the spiritual horizon.

We have no right to judge:

"Judge not, that ye be not judged" (Matthew 7:1).

"Who art thou that judgest another man's servant?" (Romans 14:4).

"There is one lawgiver, who is able to save and to destroy: who art thou that judgest another?" (James 4:12).

But we have the duty to test:

"Prove all things, hold fast that which is good" (1 Thessalonians 5:21).

"Beloved, believe not every spirit, but try the spirits whether they are of God: because many false prophets are gone out into the world" (1 John 4:1).

Kathryn Kuhlman was a healer who drew large crowds to her meetings. Millions came to her for help. Her meetings were attended by up to ten thousand at a time.

Kathryn was born in Concordia, sixty miles from Kansas City. Her mother was a Methodist, her father a Baptist. As a young girl, she went to a Baptist seminary and was ordained as a Baptist preacher. Her first church was in Franklin, Pennsylvania. One day some people in her congregation said that they had been healed while she was preaching. Kathryn was astonished. When such occurrences became more frequent, she began to preach about faith healing, without ceasing to put the main emphasis on the salvation of the soul. Before long, she moved from Franklin to the great city of Pittsburgh, where ever-increasing crowds flocked to her services. From 1946, she conducted an average of 125 healing meetings per year. She used the largest halls in the USA, and her healing meetings were attended by about one and a half million people each year. This figure is given by a doctor named William Nolen.

In addition to the meetings, she appeared on many radio and TV programs. The huge sums of money given as offerings have been used for building twenty-five churches, many schools and homes, and for social projects of many kinds.

It is a thankless, but necessary, task to subject the healing work of this woman to the test of the Scriptures. I will do so in such a way as to allow as many other observers as possible to have their say.

The background of my views is the material I collected during many lecture tours in the USA. At the time of writing, I have been there thirty-four times for tours. I have read Miss Kuhlman's books, I have attended a four-hour healing meeting at the First Presbyterian Church in Pittsburgh; and I have had a personal conversation with her. I also have many verbal and written reports from people who attended her meetings.

At this point, I must thank most warmly my two principal informants. Mrs. H. Maynard Johnson, wife of the technical director of the Eitel Hospital in Minneapolis, collected twenty-eight cases of healing, with full addresses, from Minneapolis and the surrounding area for me. I also received an excellent, scientifically based article from Dr. H. H. Ehrenstein of Songtime Boston. Names of further assistants will appear in the course of the chapter.

First of all, I must give a brief sketch of the style of these healing meetings. After a fantastic organ prelude, Kathryn would appear on the stage dressed in a long blue or white robe. Everyone would stand up. She would say: "How glad I am to have you all here. The Holy Spirit will perform a great work among you." The atmosphere was heightened by an introductory hymn sung by thousands of expectant people. This was followed by prayer and a short sermon. Then Kathryn would suddenly announce, "Up there in the second row of the balcony a man has just been healed of cancer. Please come down to the platform," or "a girl in the seventeenth row has just been healed of a lung disease." It would continue in the same way for several hours. The people who had been healed came to the platform. Kathryn would hold her hands about six inches above the head of each and pray. They then would fall backwards to the floor. Two attendants would catch them as they fell, so they would not hurt themselves. The people who had been healed would lay for ten to thirty seconds unconscious on the floor. When they stood up, they would say that they had a wonderful feeling. While I was watching, I saw even ministers falling to the floor unconscious, one of them a Catholic priest.

Kathryn would then ask those who had been healed one or two questions, different every time. For instance, she asked a woman in her fifties, "Do you believe in Jesus?" "No, I am a Buddhist." A young man about twenty years old was asked: "Are you a Christian?" "No, I am an atheist." "Won't you believe in Jesus now that He has healed your wife?" Kathryn asked. A long silence passed. After much pressing on Kathryn's part, he finally said, "I will try."

Many people have tussled with the question of how it was that Kathryn could tell which person had been healed of which disease. Many doctors investigated this problem and came up with various answers. Was it clairvoyance or mediumistic contact?

The next question is, Did healing really take place, and did it last?

Another question relates to the spiritual aspect of these healings. Did the people who had been healed find the way to Jesus, and if they were Christians already, was any harm done to their faith?

A sensational aspect was the way those who had been healed fell backwards. What powers were involved? Was it hypnosis? Kathryn's friends called such people the *slain of the Lord*.

Let us now call some witnesses. Since I am one of them, I will first give three of my experiences.

Ex 105 At the healing meeting in Pittsburgh a woman doctor brought a woman on to the stage. The doctor gave the following report: "This woman had multiple sclerosis in an advanced stage. She used to wear two splints and was almost blind. Her abdomen was partially paralyzed. She had a permanent catheter for three years. Three months ago I went with the patient to one of Kathryn Kuhlman's meetings. The patient was healed. Since then she has needed neither splints nor catheter. The paralysis has disappeared. She is now a nurse in the hospital in which she used to be a patient."

There is no reason to doubt the truthfulness of this testimony. We know, of course, that the fact of healing gives us no indication of what power it was that brought it about.

Ex 106 My second example shows a spiritual situation. I met a man at the meeting who allowed me to ask him some questions. He was very willing to answer them.

"Have you experienced healing?"

"Yes, thirteen years ago I was healed at Kathryn's meeting."

"Do you belong to Jesus? Do you pray and read the Bible?"

"Yes, I follow Jesus and know Him as my Lord and Savior."

"Has your healing lasted?"

"Yes, for thirteen years."

This is another testimony that I cannot simply dismiss.

Ex 107 A third experience made me begin to have doubts. It was during a personal interview with Kathryn. She suddenly began to pray with me. She held her hands about six inches above my head. At once I began to pray in my heart, "Lord Jesus, if this woman gets her power from You, then bless both her and me. If she has gifts and power which do not come from You, protect me from them. I do not want to come under an alien influence." While Kathryn was praying, two ushers came and stood behind me to catch me as I fell. I felt nothing, however, and stood like a rock without losing my consciousness in the least. Then came a second surprise. Kathryn nudged me gently, probably in order to make me fall. She did not succeed. Then she asked me, "Do you have a healing ministry yourself?" I answered, "In my pastoral counseling it has happened occasionally, but that is not my calling: my task is to preach the Gospel and bring people to salvation."

Since this experience, I have for years kept my eyes and ears open to try to discover the truth behind these enormous healing demonstrations.

There is a problem about the experience of the man who was healed thirteen years ago and yet has suffered no ill effects in his spiritual life. On the assumption that Kathryn did not heal by divine power, as thousands of people believe, would it be possible for a person who had been healed in such a way to suffer no spiritual harm? I have enough examples from counseling people in similar situations to be able to say *yes.*

Ex 108   A German architect told me that he had found the way to Jesus through the preaching of a minister who was a drunkard. The minister was often drunk, but when he was sober, his preaching was sound. God can bring people to new life even by means of unworthy witnesses.

Ex 109   I have heard of several believers who have found the way of salvation through the ministry of a charlatan who taught unscriptural doctrines. I shall not mention this man by name, although he has done much harm.

The next witness we must call is Mrs. H. Maynard Johnson, whom I mentioned above, the lady from Minneapolis who has provided me with so much useful material. The reports she sent to me are of great evidential value, since they describe the *situation one year after* the healing took place. I will begin with Mrs. Johnson's own experience, in her own words, but shortened.

Ex 110   "My husband, daughter, and I went to see and hear Miss Kuhlman and pray that I might be healed of what my doctor had just told me could be the first stages of rheumatoid arthritis. I had been having pains in my joints, especially in my fingers and wrists. I have been forced to give up my hobbies of sewing and organ playing. Writing had become painful also. During Miss Kuhlman's healing service, she spoke from the stage saying that someone seated in our section was receiving a healing of arthritis. My arms went up over my head, and I began wiggling all my fingers and there was no pain. One of her helpers stopped at our row and told me to come with her to the front. As I approached Miss Kuhlman, she asked what I had been healed of; then she lightly touched my forehead with her finger tips, as she called out to God to remove the arthritis from my body. At that instant I was slain in the Spirit. I felt completely separated from my surroundings, as a beautiful peace went all through me. As we left the auditorium that day, I told my family, "If the physical healing wasn't meant to last, I know my spiritual healing will never leave me." A year later I can still make that statement: the physical healing has lasted, too. The day after the service, I was scheduled to go to the clinic to have extensive blood work done. My blood tests showed that I was not only normal, but better than normal. I have witnessed to many people regarding this marvelous healing of my body and spirit. My whole life direction has changed since this happened to me. My prayer life took on new meaning. My hunger for the Word has greatly increased. I continue to spread the word as to how great it is when we let God take complete control."

Because I am very grateful to Mrs. Johnson for the twenty-eight case histories she has so carefully reported for me, I might be tempted to keep my own views to myself. But this case also raises a number of questions.

1. In cases of arthritis, the psyche and psychosomatic connections often play a part. Healings from arthritis head the list of all healings by suggestion.

2. I cannot accept this phenomenon of being *slain in the Spirit* as a work of the Holy Spirit. When people fall to the ground in the course of a spiritual revival, in repentance and sorrow for sin, weeping over their sins and asking for God for forgiveness, it is quite a different matter.

3. What are we to make of Mrs. Johnson's reference to a spiritual healing which would still be there even if the physical healing should disappear? The expression *spiritual healing* is used by many spiritist healers. The only kind of spiritual healing the Bible knows is the process of conversion and regeneration. Mrs. Johnson was already a believing Christian when she went to the meeting. There is no such thing as a second rebirth. This so-called spiritual healing does not make sense and could be compared with what is known in extreme circles as the baptism of the Holy Spirit.

Lack of space unfortunately forbids me to discuss all twenty-eight healings in detail, interesting as that would be. I will here record the general conclusion.

One year after meeting with Kathryn, the state of all twenty-eight people said by her to have been healed was as follows: Ten had not been healed, seven had experienced an improvement in their condition, eleven had diseases in which the mind can play an important part. In the whole of this extensive report, there is *not one clear case of healing from an organic disease.* So for all the trouble taken by Mrs. Johnson, for which I thank her again, *nothing has been proved.*

A further witness is a woman who worked for two years as secretary to Kathryn Kuhlman. She followed me and caught up with me at the airport of a great American city. In a conversation, she told me that for two years she had recorded the addresses of those who had been healed, and had later made enquiries as to their condition. Seventy-five percent of those on the register had remained well.

What value can we place on these figures?

1. In the first place, it is her job as secretary to represent her employer. Does this not prejudice objectivity?

2. Her journey after me was quite clearly undertaken with the object of conveying a good impression of the healings.

3. It is obvious that this woman does not possess the necessary knowledge of medicine and psychology to enable her to assess the nature of the healings.

4. Healing is a field in which it is hard to get a clear, overall view. It may occur as a result of suggestion, hypnosis, mediumistic, or occult powers, but it can also have a sound medical or Biblical basis.

This assessment of the figures she gave me is not an attack on the integrity of the lady in question. I formed a very good impression of her as I did of Mrs. Johnson.

In the spring of 1974, there was a "charismatic" congress in Jerusalem under the title of *The Holy Spirit.* Kathryn Kuhlman took part. Six months after this world conference of Pentecostal churches, I received a letter from a lady working with the Finnish Missionary Society in Jerusalem. It was about Kathryn Kuhlman.

Ex 111   Jerusalem   Sept. 17, 1974

Dear Dr. Koch,

I write because I don't know anybody else who could answer my questions.

I have read Kathryn Kuhlman's book, *God Can Do It Again* and was positively impressed. When K. K. came to Jerusalem last spring (1974), I went to her miracle-service with great expectation. At the first meeting I felt happy, but afterwards I started to doubt.

1. How could she know when a person was healed?

2. With whose power was the healing done?

3. Why did the healed people fall on the floor, when she prayed for them?

I went to a second meeting and tried to pray the whole time, but also to watch carefully. After the healing service, K. K. left the platform, and went through the crowd standing in the big hall. Suddenly I felt an oppression and a fear that she should touch me. I closed my eyes, lifted my arms and prayed in Jesus' name that God would help me. When K. K. passed in the place where I stood, she gripped my right arm very strongly for a moment. Nothing happened. After a while, I felt strong power, like electricity, above me. I felt like I was going to die. My arms were paralyzed and I couldn't take them down immediately. Since then I have felt a big difficulty to believe that her power is from God. I have just finished K. K.'s second book, *I Believe in Miracles*. It seems to me very good and I can not understand why she gave me another impression.

I can't get rid of my doubts alone, and they have not ceased to disturb me spiritually.

If you understand this and could answer me in spite of your huge burden of work, I would be extremely thankful.

This Finnish missionary is not alone in her experience. Others, myself included, have noticed the difference between the books and the person. Often people have told me that, by praying continuously through a meeting, they have become aware of an unscriptural atmosphere. It is possible even then for subjective elements to become mixed with objective assessment.

Vim Malgo goes into the question of the World Congress on the Holy Spirit in Jerusalem. Four unscriptural points come out in this report.

1. The Holy Spirit was the central theme. The Holy Spirit does not allow himself to be given a central place; the Holy Spirit makes Jesus central (John 16:13).

2. The baptism of the Holy Spirit is identical with regeneration. A child of God is filled (Ephesians 5:18) ever more deeply with the Holy Spirit, according to his faithful obedience.

3. The Holy Spirit does not allow himself to be the main person. Jesus says in John 16:14, "He will glorify me."

4. Finally, it was an ecumenical congress at which all shades of opinion were represented.[29]

Vim Malgo's conclusion is that it was not the Holy Spirit who was at work, but other spirits. The so-called *baptism of the Spirit* is usually a baptism with spirits.

Malgo says: "The spirits find one another." In English we have the saying, "Birds of a feather flock together." It is therefore characteristic that Kathryn Kuhlman was one of the main speakers and drew the largest number of hearers. This point has troubled me more and more over the years: Kathryn accepted invitations from wild extremists and stood on the same platform with them.

There is a long report about Kathryn Kuhlman's appearances in Vancouver and Seattle. Lack of space again compels me to mention only the main points. This observer writes, "Kathryn Kuhlman calls herself an instrument of the Lord. In reality, she is a medium of the lord of this world. A person cannot receive a second birth from the Holy Spirit when someone touches his face and says a few words to him. I believe in the charismata [gifts of the Spirit]. But what Kathryn Kuhlman displays is not a gift of the Holy Spirit of God, but a gift of the spirits who rule in the air. These spirits make use of her, herself deceived and deceiving others. . . . She is a medium of Satan."

Another who writes in similar vein is a well-known professor of theology at the University of Tübingen who has the reputation among believers of being a born-again Christian. This professor wrote to me, "Kathryn Kuhlman is a spiritist. Twenty years ago you would have said so yourself."

Certainly I would never make such a harsh judgment without careful investigation. We must think and speak well of a person, as long as he has not shown himself to be evil.

The most scientific assessment is the report Dr. Ehrenstein of the USA has sent me. The article, which appeared in a Christian magazine, is entitled "In Search of a Miracle." It is written by a doctor and surgeon from Minneapolis, Dr. Nolen, who also has a good name as a Christian.

Dr. Nolen had the addresses and telephone numbers of eighty-two people in Minneapolis sent to him. These people had been to the Kuhlman meeting and had been said to be healed. Some of them were sufferers from cancer, multiple sclerosis, and other diseases. Dr. Nolen followed up those who had been *healed* in order to get an accurate picture of the whole story.

Ex 112 Before the beginning of a meeting, the doctor was standing near the elevator in which about 100 patients in wheelchairs were being taken up in turns. Among them was a man without a wheelchair who was limping very badly. The doctor asked him, "You find it painful to walk?"

"Yes, I had an operation two years ago. But it did not heal. So now I am hoping that Kathryn Kuhlman will heal me."

"Shall I get you a wheelchair?"

"Yes, that would be nice of you."

The doctor brought the lame man a wheelchair, in which he was taken into the auditorium. During the meeting Kathryn called out into the hall, "There's a man here with cancer in his hip. You're cured. Your pain is gone. Come down and claim your cure."

The man in the wheelchair was embarrassed at the idea of being pushed forward to the platform in a wheelchair. So he stood up and walked slowly down the aisle. Behind him came one of the ushers, pushing his wheelchair. The doctor watched carefully. It was the man for whom he had borrowed the chair. When he reached the stage, Kathryn Kuhlman asked him,

"Whose wheelchair is that? Not yours surely?"

"Yes, it is," said the man. He did not want to give a long explanation. Kathryn continued,

"You've had cancer in the hip and now your pain is gone. Is that right?"

"Yes," he answered.

"Bend over so everyone can see." He bent over. "Walk around." He walked around. "Isn't the Holy Spirit wonderful?" she cried. A sound of rejoicing went round the hall.

Afterward, the doctor inquired of this man. Nothing had changed in his condition. But in Christian circles, the news was spread everywhere that a man in a wheelchair had been healed.

Ex 113 Another case, that Dr. Nolen followed up, was that of a woman who was said to have been cured of lung cancer. In his own words, "When I contacted her, Leona told me that she had not had lung cancer at all. 'I have Hodgkin's disease,' she said, 'and some of the glands in my chest are involved. But since no one else got up when Miss Kuhlman said that someone with lung cancer is being cured, I figured it had to be me. I've been back to my doctor and he says he can't see any change in my x-ray. I think I breathe better, but it's hard to tell, since I never had much trouble breathing anyway.' "

Dr. Nolen also obtained from Kathryn Kuhlman a list of eight people who were alleged to have been cured of cancer. Again the result of his investigations was completely negative.

Dr. Nolen comments,

> The more I learned of the results of Kathryn Kuhlman's miracle service, the more doubtful I became that any good she was doing could possibly outweigh the misery she was causing. . . . I don't believe she is a liar or a charlatan or that she is, consciously, dishonest. . . . I think she sincerely believes that the thousands of sick people who come to her services and claim cures are, through her ministrations, being cured of organic diseases. . . . The problem is—and I'm sorry this has to be so blunt—one of ignorance. Miss Kuhlman doesn't know the difference between psychogenic and organic diseases. Though she uses hypnotic techniques, she doesn't *know* anything about hypnotism and the power of suggestion. She doesn't know anything about the autonomic nervous system. Or, if she does know something about these things, she has certainly learned to hide her knowledge.

Dr. Nolen's report, which I have reproduced here in a shortened form, does not answer all the questions raised by these strange healings. In particular, he does not deal with the falling backwards of the patients—or he simply calls it hypnosis. Such an explanation is inadequate. Doctors, ministers, and strong-willed people cannot be laid out on the floor, as if they had been knocked out by hypnosis. Here other powers are involved. Again, the sometimes accurate indication of the place where the patients are sitting and of the nature of their diseases sounds remarkably like psychic contact.

It will be held against me that at first I spoke favorably of her. I have already answered this objection. We ought to maintain a positive judgment about a person until he has given proof to the contrary. During the four years since that first meeting, I have received a great deal of material. This has resulted in a different impression from the one which I formed at first.

In any case, Kathryn Kuhlman stands or falls before her Lord. Jesus has the last word about her and her work, and not we shortsighted men. We have the duty to test her work and to keep the Church of Christ informed. Let us take care that *our* work is able to stand in the eyes of the Lord. When King David saw his own guilt in the light of God, he sighed: "For mine iniquities are gone over my head: as an heavy burden they are too heavy for me" (Psalms 38:4). When we recognize our own guilt, the desire to cast stones goes away. Nevertheless, we are not spared the necessary duty of acting as signposts to the Church of Christ, even when this means great heartache.

And it should be obvious from this chapter that it gives me no joy to have to write about Kathryn Kuhlman. We might add this biographical note: Kathryn Kuhlman died on Februray 20, 1976.

34
LEGALISM

Legalism creates a stiff, hard spirit, mentioned in the Bible: "Ministers of the new testament; not of the letter, but of the spirit: for the letter killeth, but the spirit giveth life" (2 Corinthians 3:6).

This chapter does not belong in a collection of occult movements, but it nevertheless reveals a great need. My experience in counseling for over forty-five years has shown me the disastrous effect which legalistic Christians can have. What area of life is not subject to the disapproval of cold and loveless Christians?

Ex 114 In 1962, I spoke at the First Presbyterian Church of Hollywood and there met Miss Henrietta Mears. She is one of the most unusual Christians I have ever met. Billy Graham once called her his spiritual mother. Miss Mears began a Sunday school class in her church for girls in trouble. After twelve years, this Sunday school had no less than 6,000 members. Several hundred Sunday school teachers, who had been trained by Miss Mears, were responsible for the many groups and classes. The teachers' lesson books were soon being used all over the English-speaking world. For many years, I have been in the habit of keeping a written record of everything, and I therefore published a biography of Miss Mears, complete with a photograph. And what happened? A Swiss brother, who read the biography, wrote to me and said that he had cut the photograph out of the book, because Miss Mears had short hair.

A Christian woman, who also has short hair, commented, "I would love to have long hair. But I have a skin disease which makes my hair fall out if it is long, so I have had to keep it cut short."

Even if there is no disease requiring a person to have short hair, I do not share the legalistic views of this brother, although I am familiar with 1 Corinthians 11:6.

Legalistic Christians, who have never succeeded in leading a single person to Christ, criticize a woman, as a result of whose ministry 600 missionaries are working on every continent today.

What I think about the ministry of Christian women I have already made known in my book, *Charismatic Gifts.* I will not repeat myself here.

Since we are talking of spiritual yardsticks, I will give another example.

Ex 115   When my book, *Wine of God,* was published in the USA, the esteemed editor of an evangelical publication felt moved to criticize it. He based his criticism on 2 Corinthians 6:14, "Be ye not unequally yoked with unbelievers." Then he cast his stones against a much-used man of God, Father Daniel of Madras. The Lord has used Father Daniel, and through his ministry, thousands have been converted. Spiritual experiences of that sort are always a work of God's grace and not the work of man. Many believers, however, allow their pride and disobedience to stand in the Lord's way. Father Daniel has been allowed to see professional men and beggars, high-ranking Hindus and criminals turning to Christ under his ministry. As a young man, he was prayed for and blessed by Sadhu Sundar Singh. He was still unmarried. One day, the Lord gave him the instruction to marry a certain Hindu girl. Daniel resisted, saying: "Lord, do You want to test me? I will not marry any pagan girl." The Lord gave him no peace. After several signs, he had to acknowledge that it was the will of the Lord, and he obeyed. Shortly after the wedding, his young wife became a convinced Christian.

This is, of course, an unusual course of events. On the basis of 2 Corinthians 6:14, I have never advised a Christian man to marry an unbeliever. But the Bible is not a casuistic law book. If this union was the will of God, even the editor of a Christian magazine cannot alter it. God has richly blessed this union, as may be read in the biography of Father Daniel. In German, it is contained in my book *Jesus auf allen Kontinenten* and in English, it can be found in *Wine of God.* To say not a word about the richly blest work of a man of God, but instead to try and kill it stone dead with a single argument, represents an insufferable degree of legalism.

I often pray for you my brother editor. In the spirit and in the love of Christ, let us look at this matter sincerely. Shall we suppose that in your life, your addresses, your articles, and your conduct ninety-nine percent was good and one percent unscriptural. And then a biographer came along, telling the story of your life, but saying nothing about all the work that God had blessed, just publishing and broadcasting to all the world the one percent which was unscriptural. How would you feel about that? It would be a gross distortion of the facts, an appalling injustice: it would be murder of your reputation. That is exactly what you have done to brother Daniel. God has used Father Daniel in a mighty way. He has seen more blessing, conversions, and cases of deliverance from the power of evil forces than you and I put together. Yet you pass over in silence all the work of this man whom God has blessed, fish out one point which does not fit into the narrow limits of your legalistic theology, and publish this widely among the American public. Is that not murder of a reputation, for which you will one day be called to account?

Similar in character is the verdict of the same publication on the revival in the Solomon Islands. Muri Thompson, the New Zealand evangelist, had the experience of seeing the Spirit of God moving over a great mass of people at the same time. There were about three thousand people there, including a few Australian and American missionaries. The Holy Spirit broke in upon the whole gathering in power, leading them to repentance and to salvation. Your comment, in your book review, was: "We know that God can do this, but He does not do it. We know that the Holy Spirit can carry it out, but He does not do so."

I must ask you if you sit on God's committee that you know so exactly what God is and is not doing? Is the testimony of responsible Christians not enough for you? Have you never visited a revival area like Korea, Indonesia, Uganda, or Taiwan and noticed, that in revival areas, events frequently occur which remind us of the Acts of the Apostles? I am familiar with the thinking behind this criticism. Exaggerated dispensationalism declares that all charismatic gifts and powers ceased with the close of the apostolic age, or, at the latest, with the closing of the canon at the synods of Jamnia and Joppa (A.D. 201).

Dispensational theology has been taught in Europe since the time of Luther. As far as prophecy is concerned, in view of the events of the last days, I agree with it. In the case of revivals, however, it is evident that charismatic powers sometimes come to life. This is to be observed, particularly, in areas where most people are illiterate. Because these people can neither read nor write, they are unable to study the Bible. God has sometimes revealed Himself to these people by means of miracles. The period of miracles usually comes to an end when the illiterate have learned to read the Bible. There are, moreover, a number of charismatic gifts which have not died out. I know of many men in the history of the church who have possessed the gift of healing. There is not space to mention all their names here nor to describe their work.

It is another evidence of legalistic and self-opinionated arrogance, when the above publication simply dismisses the account of the revival on the Solomon Islands as untrue. I suggest that people read the reports of the Australian South Sea Mission, which maintains a Biblical moderation and has no tendencies to extremism.

I realize that the outpouring of the Holy Spirit at the first Pentecost is not something which can be repeated. The Holy Spirit has been poured out, He is present in the church. But He has still to come to pagan and spiritually-dead communities. He must also come to us, whether it be that we have not yet been spiritually born again, or whether we have not yet submitted to His lordship. There are many believers who quench the Holy Spirit, grieve Him, disobey Him, and constantly oppose Him. That was the accusation Jesus made against the legalistic Pharisees. He would also have to make it today against many present-day Christians.

In Jesus' day the Pharisees, the scribes, and the priests—the theologians—accused Jesus of blasphemy and had Him condemned by the Roman authorities. Throughout church history, men of God, who have been used in a special way, have suffered similar persecution. For example, Ludwig Harms, founder of the Hermannsburger Mission in Germany, was brought before the church authorities by his brother clergy sixty-two times. In no case were they able to substantiate any charge against him. In the Old Testament, the true prophets were persecuted. In the New Testament period, the disciples and apostles of Jesus were persecuted. During church history, men of God have been persecuted by church leaders and nominal Christians. It is the same today. All this and still more is contained in the warning: "The letter killeth, but the Spirit giveth life."

To believe in salvation or to be faithful to orthodoxy without the Holy Spirit is to miss the reality and the dynamic of the Bible.

The law brings death. The Spirit brings life. Let us not meddle constantly in God's handiwork with our well-intentioned theology!

One final point: The thrust of that publication is evangelism. I, too, have always striven to be an evangelist after the Bible pattern. I'm sure that you know of my fight against everything that is unscriptural; extremist views, the so-called charismatic movement, which is not charismatic, and many other distortions and extreme movements of our day. Have you ever wondered what impression the world receives when an editor of an evangelistic magazine attacks a fellow worker in evangelism? The Holy Spirit leads us together, unites and binds believers together in the love of Christ. Legalism divides, cuts brothers off from each other, breaks the bonds that Christ has tied by His redeeming work on Calvary. Behind this division, this tearing asunder, behind this disunity is the enemy from below, who rejoices in and capitalizes on it.

The Holy Spirit builds up the Church of Christ. Theology in every age has been in danger of destroying the Church of Christ. This is true also of exaggerated forms of dispensational theology. The fact that I am making an attack on the abuse of theology is not the result of the well-known envy of those who have nothing. I have myself attained the doctorate of theology at the University of Tübingen.

As fellow Christians and as fellow servants of Christ, let us respect one another's calling and our varied ministries. But as the French say, *noblesse oblige!*

35
LEVITATION

Levitation is one of the accomplishments of spiritist mediums. Levitation is the free floating in air of the human body. It is perhaps a demonic imitation of what happened to certain people as recorded in the Scriptures. For example, we read in Acts 8:39: "the Spirit of the Lord caught away Philip."

The practice of levitation is rare in civilized countries, but is common in pagan lands and those where spiritism is practiced widely. One or two examples will illustrate levitation.

Ex 116 Two Lutheran ministers took part in a levitation session in Wels, Austria. They were curious and wanted to study the subject. Both saw the spiritist medium achieve levitation and float in a horizontal position up to the ceiling of the room. I must issue a warning against taking part in experiments of this sort. The devil attacks not only the curious, but also those who think they can safely participate in spiritist experiments to study them.

As I write this chapter on levitation, I am on my thirty-third lecture tour of the USA and Canada. In the course of counseling people during this tour, I have heard of two more cases of levitation.

Ex 117 A seventeen-year-old girl, who is definitely a Christian, went into a certain room in her school. Without realizing it, she had come upon a spiritist séance in full swing. When the girl entered the room, a medium was floating up to the ceiling. The girl was able just to breathe a prayer. The medium fell to the floor and was hurt. The presence of the believing girl disturbed the sinister work of the spirits.

Ex 118 A missionary working in Africa with the Sudan Interior Mission had his first experience of a levitation in the open air. He regarded it as his duty to stop this spiritistic phenomenon. He laid his hand on the one who was floating in air and tried to pray. At that moment, he was thrown to the ground by an electric shock. That taught him the lesson that one must not lay hands on a practicing medium. Jesus laid hands only on the sick. In cases of possession, He simply commanded the spirits.

The Africans who were present at this outdoor incident laughed at the missionary. Where the occult is concerned, pagans are usually better informed than missionaries.

Ex 119 At the annual Umbanda festival of religious spiritism in Bahia, Brazil, levitations are nearly always performed. Here again a missionary had the same experience as the SIM missionary in Africa. He laid his hand on the head of a girl who was floating in the air in an attempt to free her from the demonic power which enslaved her. He, too, received an electric shock which threw him to the ground.

It is the privilege of puffed-up, empty-headed rationalists to laugh at things they do not understand. We must take Satan seriously— but still more so the One who, on the cross of Calvary, won the victory over the power of darkness.

In connection with this chapter on levitation, the section on *translocation* also should be read.

36
MAGIC

People's opinions about magic depend on their intellectual and spiritual position. The occult addict thinks differently from the arrogant rationalist. To begin with, therefore, some preliminary questions must be answered.

1. The term *magic* is one which has a wide range of uses. Let us consider some of these.

a. There is magic in the broadest sense of the word. Everything that fascinates people, and also everything which cannot be explained—the numinous, an atmosphere, can be described as magic.

The magic leather draws millions to the football stadiums. One can speak of the magic of sport.

A connoisseur of Greek art once said, "A single statue of Phidias outweighs the poverty of millions of people." Here we have the magic of art, which puts its devotees under a spell.

A positivist philosopher has said: "The highest form of happiness here on earth is the union of man and woman. For that I gladly forgo Heaven." This is the idolizing—the magic of erotic love.

There is also a religious magic, when church ceremonies, candles, incense, beautiful figures of saints, and sacred art are more important to someone than a personal relationship with God. Impressive worship can draw us away from what really matters.

b. There is also the magic which is simply a form of entertainment. In various countries, there is even a magic circle, an association of people or groups who perform for entertainment. Conjuring tricks are not magic. I have often noticed, however, that conjurers also make occasional use of genuine magic. This book contains some examples of this.

c. A third form of magic is quackery. Here again, this is no genuine magic, but simply deception. Every now and then one of these quacks is taken to court by someone he has swindled. Some years ago, for example, the *Bauerschen Zelemente* were forbidden on the ground that people were being deceitfully manipulated. A length of copper wire worth one mark was sold to patients for large sums. The sick people were told to wear the wire around their bodies, and that they would then get better. At the time of writing this book, a similar court action involving a healer is taking place. A crafty healing practitioner has been trying to cure his patients with a glass ball and a little capsule of salt.

Well, there will always be people who are easily fooled. Sometimes healing or improvement of the patient's condition results through suggestion or selfsuggestion.

Quackery is widespread in the USA. I have collected many examples there.

A chemical firm in Chicago produces no less than sixteen hundred antidotes to magic. A Kansas newspaper reports that a woman quack doctor charged between one hundred and eight hundred dollars for each course of treatment. Another quack in Washington, D.C., earned five hundred dollars a day from his customers. When a quack in New York was prosecuted, he was able to produce in his defense many letters of thanks from rich people in high offices.

Even intelligence and education are no protection against the advertising tricks of these *ratcatchers*. This kind of magic is a matter of playing on the superstition and stupidity of contemporary man. It must be added, however, that some quacks also engage in occult practices.

Another important point is that one sometimes comes across genuine healing practitioners who are neither quacks nor charlatans nor occultists. I even know some such healers who are believing Christians. One of them is among my personal friends.

d. We know of yet another form of magic. Ethnologists, who study the folklore, the magical customs of primitive tribes, racial characteristics and a thousand other things, contrast primitives, with their magical view of life, and the civilized peoples with their rational and scientific view.

e. Distinct from all these subdivisions and parallel forms of magic, there is what we may call genuine magic. This is the form of magic condemned in the Bible, the art of casting spells, of sorcery: the devil's art. Let us listen first to some warnings from Scripture:

"Thou shalt not suffer a witch to live" (Exodus 22:18).

"Therefore hearken not to your . . . diviners, . . . enchanters, . . . nor to your sorcerers" (Jeremiah 27:9).

"And I will cut off witchcrafts out of thine hand, and thou shalt have no more soothsayers" (Micah 5:12).

"And I will come near to you to judgment; and I will be a swift witness against the sorcerers" (Malachi 3:5).

I have come to know the sinister practices of genuine magic through my ministry of counseling and by visiting more than four hundred mission fields.

2. From my counseling experience with people on every continent, I have met the following main forms of magic:

Healing and making ill by magic
Magic ban and loosing of bans
Magic curses and magic persecutions
Love and hate magic
Protective magic and death magic.

Note these few examples from my missionary journeys:

Ex 120 Curses. A certain magician was at odds with his son. The quarrels had begun over the question of an inheritance. His daughter and son-in-law understood that they had inherited the farm belonging to her father. One day, the old farmer went to church. His son-in-law came along the same road with a horse and cart. The old farmer asked him to give him a ride. Instead of answering him, the son-in-law took out his whip and hit the old father-in-law. The farmer went into a terrible rage and shouted after him, "May the lightning strike you!" While the old farmer was sitting in church, listening to the sermon, a storm came up. One single flash of lightning struck. Not long afterward the fire alarm was heard. The service was interrupted, and the people rushed back home. One farmhouse had been set afire by the lightning. It was that belonging to the son-in-law who had been cursed by the old man. The house was burned to its foundations.

A story like this raises many problems. Was it simply a coincidence, or did the curse work? Experience shows that curses normally function only when the person who utters them is psychic. A second observation is that genuine, born-again Christians are not affected by a curse of this sort, if they have placed themselves under the protection of Jesus.

Ex 121 I have visited Mexico three times and have given several talks in the German church in Mexico City. While on such a visit I heard a strange story of magical persecution. If a person who practices black magic wishes to harm someone or make him ill, he places a doll daubed with blood in front of that person's door. Before doing so, he sticks thorns or a needle into the doll. In addition to this symbolic, or analogical magic, magic words are then recited. The strange thing is that the victim becomes ill in the part of the body that was pierced in the doll. Such things are practiced by voodoo magicians in Haiti and by the Macumba cult in Brazil.

Ex 122 During my lecture tours in India, I heard of the practices of Hindu magicians. When they wish to persecute someone, they obtain some of the enemy's hair and nail it to a tree, reciting magic words as they do so. The victim then becomes ill or has an accident.

Ex 123 It was a strange thing to me when I heard something similar in Switzerland, in the region of Staad and Saanen. While I was preaching in this area, a certain preacher informed me of an unusual custom among the local farmers. If they wanted to bring harm to somebody, they would try to obtain some of his hair. They can do this, for instance, through the barber, whom they tip and swear to silence. They take their enemy's hair, bore a hole in one of the beams of their house, put the hair in it, knock a peg in, recite a spell from the *Sixth and Seventh Book of Moses,* and wish ill on their enemy. Surprisingly, these imprecations are fulfilled. Magic persecution is known not only in India and in Mexico, but also in Switzerland.

Ex 124 I heard of more examples of hair magic in Argentina, not only from a native pastor but also from Dr. Winter, head of the Cruz Blanca Sanatorium in Esquel, Chubuts province. If a death magician wants to kill an enemy, he obtains several of his victim's hairs, and then, while the moon is on the wane, he concentrates on his victim. He uses magic spells and his psychic powers, and kills his enemy.

Ex 125 Dr. Winter told me an example from his own circle of friends. A young man wanted to marry a girl. They were already engaged. His sister did not like the fiancée and succeeded in splitting up the young couple. The young man, however, had sent his fiancée a lock of his hair cut many years before. After the engagement had been broken off, he married another girl. One year after the marriage, he died. His former fiancée had gone to a powerful magician and asked him to cast a death spell. After the funeral, the disappointed girl brought back the lock of hair to the spiteful sister and said, "Do you want it? It belonged to your dead brother." The grief stricken woman took her brother's lock of hair. Soon she became seriously ill. She went to many doctors, but none was able to help her. Then it was pointed out to her by a gypsy that she was under a magical death spell. The gypsy also offered to help her in her trouble. She provided a protective spell. As a result the sick woman recovered. But she also developed a serious neurosis. She had one illness after another. When she married and had children, her children were also mentally and nervously affected.

Ex 126 Now for some examples of magic bans. A woman told me the story of her family. At the age of seven, her mother had looked after the geese. A man who was known to practice black magic came by and asked, "Little Marie, how many geese have you?" The child told him the number. The man went on. Suddenly the geese began to fall down, one after another, and die. The girl ran home and told what had happened. Her father hurried to the water and murmured a spell that he had learned from the *Sixth and Seventh Book of Moses.* The geese stopped dying at once.

What is now the situation in this family? The little girl who looked after the geese suffered from depressions her whole life. The woman who told me about it, the granddaughter of the magic charmer, sees visions and has great inhibitions in her spiritual life. Her son, the great grandchild, is mentally ill, suffers from delusions, and is now in a mental home for the third time. Magic always demands it price.

Ex 127 The wife of a teacher in Holstein, North Germany, told me the following story. The men of her family had been teachers of religion for seven generations. They followed the superstitious custom of bringing water during Easter night each year and sprinkling it on the children.

On one occasion, a horse was stolen from the parents. They put a spell on the horse. They took a leather lappet from the horse's harness and nailed it to a post, using a magical formula. This was supposed to make the horse stand still under a ban. They were actually able to find the horse by this means. The whole family, right down to the grandchildren and great grandchildren, are opposed to God, although the forefathers were all teachers of religion. There is, moreover, continual quarrelling, discord, and afflictions of every kind in the family.

The question arises for Christian believers—are we powerless in the face of magical attacks from these occultists? Nominal and careless Christians can indeed be in danger. This example is from Japan. My informant is Joe Carroll, a missionary in whose house I stayed in Tokyo.

Ex 128 A young American missionary, who had worked in Japan a short time, thought he was called to go and pray in a Buddhist temple and to command the powers of darkness in the name of Jesus. In other words, he wanted, as it were, to mount a spiritual offensive against this Buddhist temple. In his naivete, he imagined that it was part of his duty as a missionary. The result was rather different. After he prayed in the Buddhist temple, the missionary went out of his mind. He was sent back to the USA in a straitjacket. It is not enough to say "He who is in us is stronger than he who is in the world." I have complete confidence in this word of the Scriptures, but I would still not be fool-hardy. Those who expose themselves to unnecessary danger are destroyed. I have heard of several cases on mission fields where good missionaries have suffered injury through the attacks of magicians.

Satanic attacks, however, teach us to pray. When we surround ourselves with the wall of fire of which Zechariah 2:5 speaks, no occultist, sorcerer, or demon can harm us.

Ex 129   An Englishwoman travelled to South Africa and worked there for a year. She fell in love with a Bantu, a black man. They became engaged. When the year was over, the English girl returned home. The couple made wedding plans. The English girl was not a Christian, but her mother prayed faithfully. Now came a clash between the spiritual forces of this home. The mother prayed for the salvation of her daughter. The daughter, however, had, through the Bantu come under a magic ban. The Bantu was a magician. Soon noises were heard in the house. Poltergeists manifested themselves. An unpleasant smell, as of a rotting corpse, was noticed in various rooms, especially in that of the girl. They could smell sulphur. The girl was unable to understand it and went to an Anglican priest to ask for advice. When she had told the whole story, the Anglican priest advised her to destroy all the objects she had received from her fiancé in South Africa. This would remove all the means of contact and influence through which this African could use his magic. The girl followed this advice. The decisive point, however, was that the mother faithfully prayed for her and asked other Christians to pray also. The house was freed from these ghostly manifestations.

It would be possible to be frightened by these magical, dark arts. Yet we have no reason to be frightened, if we belong to Jesus Christ and follow Him faithfully. I will give some examples to show how faithful Christians are protected by their Lord.

Ex 130   One of my friends is Werner Ambühl of St. Gallen. He runs the telephone counseling ministry there. One day a dentist telephoned him and said: "You are stronger than I am. I must do the logical thing."

Ambühl asked him: "What do you mean?"

"I have been annoyed by you and your Christian nonsense," replied the dentist. "I have tried to attack you with magic and to kill you by magic. I have not succeeded. You are stronger than I am. Therefore I must now bear the consequences."

Ambühl tried to lead him to Christ. It was of no use. Several days later, he read in the newspaper that this dentist had taken his own life. Such things are also known on the mission fields.

Ex 131   My friend, John Ballantyne, in England wrote to me in January, 1976, about an English teacher who had given a radio talk which aroused much interest. She was protesting about religious instruction by unbelieving teachers. She said she had withdrawn her four children from religious instruction at the schools they attended, because the time was being used to teach spiritism and witchcraft. Such teaching is a crime against children.

Ex 132 Years ago I gave some lectures at the Chungchow Bible School on the Chinese border. I met there a missionary called Griebenow. As a young man he had been a missionary in Tibet. He had learned the Tibetan language from a Tibetan lama. One day the Tibetan said, "Mr. Griebenow, now I know what the Christian faith means. Your God is more powerful than my god." Griebenow replied, "Your god is the devil. Do you know that?"

"Yes, I know," answered the lama.

The missionary continued: "How do you know now that my God is more powerful?"

"When I noticed that you were a missionary," answered the man, "I tried to make you ill with the help of magic. I was unable to. Then I tried to send you a fire devil to burn your house. He did not obey. Then I used the most powerful death magic that we have in Tibet to try and kill you. Again, no success. You have a wall around you which I cannot penetrate."

Griebenow replied: "If you have already discovered that my God is more powerful than your demons, why do you not accept my God?" The lama said, "The demons would kill me that same day. He who has signed himself over to the devil and then tries to shake him off is killed by him." The missionary did not succeed in winning the lama for Christ. Later he heard that this lama had died in despair.

It is a wonderful message that we Christians have. The Old Testament tells us, "For I, saith the LORD, will be unto her a wall of fire round about, and will be the glory in the midst of her" (Zechariah 2:5). And in the New Testament, Jesus says: "Neither shall any man pluck them out of my hand" (John 10:28). What is of vital importance is whether we have entrusted ourselves completely to Jesus— not like the Christians of Laodicea who were neither hot nor cold.

37
MAGIC CHARMS

Charming belongs to the section on magical healing. In Germany there are various expressions for it. In South Germany it is called *Brauchen* (using), in Hamburg *Bepusten* or *Beblasen* (blowing), on the Lüneburg Heath *Wegversetzen* (shifting away). Other terms are *Beschreien* (to decry, bewitch), and *Bespeien* (to spit on). There are some dreadful cases on record.

Ex 133   A woman came to me for counseling. She explained that as a little girl she had been sent by her mother to a charmer when she was ill. The old charmer said to the girl, "Open your mouth a moment." When the girl opened her mouth, the old witch spat a juicy mouthful right inside. The girl shuddered with nausea, and this feeling of disgust troubled her, not just for weeks afterwards, but for years. But the drastic treatment, horrible as it was, did work and she was healed.

Ex 134   A mother was unwilling to allow her daughter to get married. She would have nothing to do with her future son-in-law. The girl resolved to marry him notwithstanding. When she left her parents' home with her husband, her mother let out a scream like an animal's cry. The daughter's marriage was marked by many problems and difficulties. Even the grandchildren were pursued by the curse of this grandmother who had decried her daughter.

I have come across yet other expressions abroad. In Austria, charming is called *Wenden* (turning away), in Switzerland *mit Worten heilen* (healing with words), in Poland *measuring the soul,* and in France *practicing sympathy.*

In Alsace there is a book of magic which is called the *Sympathetic Family Scrap-book.* This book contains magic charms and information on how to practice charming or *sympathy.* In the United States, I have heard in Pennsylvania the expression *powwow.* This term probably comes from the Indians. In South America, I have heard the term *Brucho.* This word probably originated with the German settlers who came from South Germany. The South German word for charming is *Brauchen,* which in the Alemannic dialect becomes *bruche.* From the word *bruche,* the South American word *Brucho* has then developed. In Argentina, I found again the Polish expression *measuring the soul.* It was probably brought to Argentina by Polish settlers. I will give an example of a *Brucho.*

Ex 135   A man's riding horse became ill. He sought advice from a Brucho and carried out what he was told to do with successful results. He pulled three hairs from the horse's tail and stretched them three times between his chest and the horse's nostrils. He then recited one of the charms from the *Sixth and Seventh Book of Moses,* which is also found in South America, and added the three highest names. The horse was healed. But since that time, the man's family has suffered from mental and nervous disorders. In this case, the charming was carried out in the form of white magic, using the three highest names.

Black magic is distinguished from white magic by its form. In the worldwide literature of magic, it is maintained that black magic is done by the help of the devil and white magic with the help of God. This definition is false. White magic is just as dependent on the powers from below as is black magic. The evidence is not difficult to find. The effects of white magic are the same as those of black magic. In white magic the three highest names are used for these evil ends. Usually a magic charm is added to the three highest names, taken from the *Six and Seventh Books of Moses* or from another book of magic.

Magical charming is practiced throughout the whole world. Taking examples from every continent, I could produce about fifteen hundred cases of charming.

In the course of my many series of lectures in Switzerland, I have often heard the names of notorious charmers mentioned by people whom I have counseled. I will mention a few, although doing so puts me in some danger. The names which cropped up most frequently in Switzerland were Hermano, Schneider, Hugendobler Gräzer, Grünefelder, Kern, as well as many others. In Germany, I was surprised to find that in Schleswig-Holstein even doctors send patients with erysipelas or shingles to charmers. Indeed, I even discovered elders of the church, a Protestant clergyman, and several Catholic priests who act as charmers themselves. These men are probably unaware of the tragedies they bring about.

Families in which charming is practiced, whether actively or as a patient, are literally pursued by misfortune. Suicide, murder, serious and incurable diseases, and many other troubles abound in such families.

One of the most dangerous and well-known charmers of the Lüneburg Heath was Shepherd Ast.

Ex 136 Heinrich Ast was born on April 4, 1848, in Gronau on the Leine. He later moved to Radbruch on the Lüneburg Heath. His healing work began about 1894. In the beginning, he had about ten patients a day. After a few months, the number of visitors rose to six hundred each day. By 1895, a daily stream of almost one thousand people were coming to Radbruch to see him. This charmer's methods of diagnosis and cure were extremely simple. He cut three hairs from the neck of each patient, held them up to the light, examined them with a magnifying glass, and gave his diagnosis. These diagnoses were on several occasions checked by doctors. Strangely enough they were correct. After the diagnosis, he handed the patient a mixture that he had prepared. Often it happened that patients received the same mixture for quite different diseases. Nonetheless, thousands maintained that they had been cured by Shepherd Ast.

The healing method of Shepherd Ast was never recognized by medical science, and rightly so. It was an occult method. To judge by the technique, the diagnosis made use of psychometry. The healer takes some object belonging to the patient, and for one or two seconds concentrates on the person seeking healing. Some healers do this by going into a trance, some in a semi-trance. In the case of Shepherd Ast, a normal process of mental concentration on the patient sufficed. I know that thousands of people were cured by Shepherd Ast: that is, that they found physical healing. But at the same time they came under terrible oppression. I shall have more to say about this later.

Shepherd Ast, who had come to Radbruch as poor as a beggar, died, in 1921, as a very rich man. He left a great estate: five houses, five large farms, an enormous sum of money. Heinrich, Ast's biographer, declares that he treated and healed hundreds of thousands of people. The other side of the story has become known to me during my many lecture tours all round the Lüneburg Heath.

Ex 137   Since we are talking about the Lüneburg Heath, I must also mention another problem. In that area, I have again and again come across pyromaniacs. Pyromaniacs are people who, from time to time, are seized with a desire to burn things. For example, in the Lüneburg district, several historic buildings were burned down by a youth. After his arrest, he declared in court that this craving for fire came upon him sometimes, and then he just had to set fire to something. In the late summer of 1975, there was a large fire on the Lüneburg Heath which destroyed thousands of acres of forest. Again it was the problem of pyromania. It means that people find pleasure and satisfaction in making a fire. Several times when I have been counseling people, I have discovered the origin of such pyromania. Normally it occurs in people whose forebears, whether parents or grandparents, were magic charmers—or who were themselves charmed in their youth. Naturally our psychiatrists and psychotherapists are unaware of this. If you tell them, they attach no importance to this observation.

Let us now leave Germany and go to a very different corner of the world.

Ex 138   Some years ago, I gave several lectures in Gambell on St. Lawrence Island. I was staying with a missionary named Shinen.

The next-door neighbor was Allen Walunga. His father had become a Christian some years before. It was a radical change for the whole family, since the father had for many years actively engaged in the pernicious art of Shamanism. Shamans are the practitioners of black magic among the Eskimos of North Alaska, as well as in Siberia, and the various islands of the Bering Straits.

The son, Allen, grew up as a perfectly normal boy. After his father became a Christian, it was as if a dark spell had been cast on the lad. At times he was no longer his own master. It could almost be described as a state of demon possession. It was as if the dark powers that had such hold of the father had transferred themselves now to the son. Allen was a gifted boy and went to college at Fairbanks. One day this dark, demonic power came over Allen again. He broke into the girls' dorm, raped a girl in his sexual frenzy, and killed her. Then he attacked a second girl who cried loudly for help. Her cries were heard. Some of the staff arrived in time to prevent Allen from carrying out a second atrocity.

Allen was arrested. A long enquiry and a still longer court trial followed. Several psychiatrists presented their reports. Some assessed him as normal, others declared him to be of limited accountability. Some even maintained that he was a schizophrenic type. The judge was in a very difficult position. Finally, Allen Walunga was found guilty of murder and sentenced.

One psychiatrist's report was interesting. He thought that the conversion of the family from Shamanism to Christianity had brought Allen into a terrible conflict. The change of faith had been responsible for his explosive outbursts and sadistic acts.

It is absurd to hold the Christian faith responsible for such crimes. One cannot expect anything different from an unbelieving psychiatrist. But a grain of truth is concealed in this misleading report. In counseling I have occasionally found the following pattern. When one member of a family has been delivered from demon possession or a serious occult oppression, another member of the family sometimes comes under the power of the same spirit. This only happens in those cases where the whole family does not place itself under the protection of Jesus Christ. Some further examples will illustrate the effects of magic charming.

Ex 139   A girl was charmed at the age of three. As far back as she can remember, she has suffered from depression, suicidal thoughts, self-tormenting ideas, and numerous accidents. In one year, she had three concussions. Her brother, who was also subjected to a magic charm, suffers from the same mental disorders. He is unruly and afflicted with suicidal thoughts. He has finally developed a compulsion to kill children in the name of God.

Not all compulsions, of course, have an occult background. But in about one-half of the compulsive neurotics I have counseled, I was able to detect occult activity in the past.

Ex 140 A man went to an occult charmer in Herisau, Switzerland. The treatment he received led to the cure of his organic symptoms. But since then the patient has suffered from depression. At night he hears knockings and rattlings and sees faces and mutilated figures.

Sometimes charmers work under a mask of Christianity. The two examples which follow will illustrate.

Ex 141 An evangelist became ill and went to two healers who were reputed to be Christian men. After the treatment, he was afflicted with strong depressive and sexual temptations, which led him to seek my advice. These men were thus not Christian healers and charmers, but occult charmers working under a Christian disguise.

Ex 142 While this book was being written, a Christian woman told me the following story. A lady missionary belonging to a German society opened her home to a healer who was in the habit of going to Bible studies of a Christian Fellowship group,[30] and was therefore regarded as a believer. From near and far, members of the Christian Fellowship came to be treated by this Christian healer. My informant herself took several people from her Fellowship in her car to see this brother. On the way she prayed somewhat like this, "Lord Jesus, if this man does not work by Thy power, protect me from him." They all came in turn to be treated in the man's consulting room. When my informant entered the room, the healer looked at her and ordered her to leave his consulting room at once, with the comment, "I cannot do anything for you." That was the answer to her prayer. She warned the missionary that she was harboring an ungodly man in her house. The missionary was very angry at first, but then agreed to pray about it. The effect of intensive prayer was that, without having to be given notice, this healer and charmer left the house; because he could no longer stand the spiritual atmosphere.

Ex 143 A young man went to a charmer to be treated for infantile paralysis. The cultist gave him an amulet to put round his neck and advised him to put a pair of scissors and a Bible under his pillow. The charmer also wrote him out a magic charm and instructed the boy to place it in his Bible. The paralysis was cured, but the boy hanged himself at the age of sixteen.

Ex 144   A woman had been to see Hugentobler in Switzerland, when she was a girl, to be treated by magic. Hugentobler wrote out a pact in which she sold herself to the devil. The woman had to sign it, then tear the paper up and drink it with water. The result was that she was healed. But ever since she has suffered from anxiety, nervousness, depression, and suicidal thoughts.

Ex 145   A man practiced magic charming in a village. The outward success of his cures was even recognized by the local doctor. Even the local minister kept sending people who had serious illnesses to see this charmer, who was a regular church attendant. When the minister retired, the new pastor began to attack magic and occult activity in his sermons. The whole community was amazed by the way these two pastors contradicted one another. The new minister was a man blessed by God. The whole church came during his time to a change of outlook on many subjects. The magic charmer was himself convinced of the wrongness of his activities. He gave up charming and experienced a complete inner renewal. The second minister was soon transferred, because he had developed special gifts in the work of the Kingdom and was therefore marked out for a new position.

A third minister had the same attitude as the first one. One day a member of the community, who was seriously ill, was advised by the doctor to consult the former charmer. The doctor explained to the patient, "I can do no more for you, but go and see if the old shepherd will heal you. He can do things which ordinary people cannot." The patient asked the pastor and the doctor to use their influence in trying to persuade the shepherd. Both men visited the old shepherd and talked to him. The pastor said, "If God has given you this gift of healing, you must put it to use for the benefit of your neighbor."

He replied, "Pastor, by God's grace I have come to realize that magic charming is the work of Satan. I will never again do it so long as I live."

And so it was. There was disastrous confusion in the church because the first and third ministers had been in favor of magic charming, while the second had taken the opposite view. The first and third ministers were blind leaders of the blind. The second minister, who took his stand in opposition to charming, was a man whom God blest.

Ex 146   It seems as if while I write this book, the Lord is constantly supplying new material. While I was writing this chapter, a German brought up in Russia came to me and laid his heart bare. He said that his parents had been Christian people. They had no church in the village where they lived in Russia, but his father used to hold home Bible studies, to which many Volksdeutsche came. One day the son got sick. There was no doctor for miles in any direction. So his mother got him to kneel down. She placed her hands on his head, recited a magic charm and the three highest names, and he was healed. It was not until long afterwards that he discovered that it had been a charm from the *Sixth and Seventh Book of Moses.*

What the mother had done was not a Biblical prayer, as laid down in James 5:14, but magic. She had misused the three highest names as a magic charm on her own son. Now the man had come to me for counseling. He told me that his whole life was suffering as a result of this charm. Although his father had been a believer who held fast to the Bible, he, the son, could not come to terms with the Word of God and with Christ. Every area of his life became disordered. He had no control over himself where alcohol was concerned, and he did other things which cannot be mentioned here. It was only when he encountered my lectures and my books, that he realized he had been under severe occult influence, as a result of the magical cure. He repented, confessed all his sins, and in the name of Jesus Christ declared himself free from this spell cast by his own mother.

There is often but a narrow thread between the divine and the demonic. The natural man has not the gift of distinguishing between them. However, when the Holy Spirit has been able to open our eyes, and when we have sufficient counseling experience; we are in a position to distinguish these two areas from one another.

38
MAOISM

The word *Maoism* sums up the view of life which looks to Mao, the founder and dictator of modern China.

In the USA and in Germany, particularly in Heidelberg, I have met students and other young people demonstrating and parading through the streets with red flags and the booklet *Thoughts of Mao* in their hands.

Mao started an ideological movement whose ripples have touched the entire globe. What worries many Christians is the way in which the Mao movement has penetrated the churches.

Ex 147 Let us hear first what Dr. Bennet, a member of the Executive Committee of the World Council of Churches, wrote about Red China:

> We cannot use our usual moral standards in assessing Red China. It deserves our reverence rather than our condemnation. Communism is to be seen as an instrument of modernization of national unification and increasing social welfare. Red China is the new savior for the poor nations of the earth.

Mao, the new savior from the East! A man on whose hands was the blood of millions. A revolutionary who, in the opinion of those who have a good knowledge of the cultural revolution, allowed more than a million Christians to be killed!

Let us look at another situation. The World Council of Churches held a conference of one of its subdivisions in Bangkok, Thailand. I was invited by Charoon Waichudist, bishop of the Thai church, to take part in this ten-day event. Various speakers condemned the presence of the Americans in Vietnam at that time. No one mentioned that Chinese troops had entered North Korea, with no respect for demarcation lines or treaties. The world was silent about the fact that the Vietcong were constantly making new attacks and overrunning the whole of Vietnam. The Americans answered a cry of help from the East, and then all the nations cried in protest, together with the ecclesiastical leaders in Geneva, Washington, and elsewhere. This is a sign of the progress communist subversion has made even in church leadership.

Excellent testimony on the subject of Maoism is to be found in the news sheet of the German Ministers' Prayer Fellowship of December 1974. One of the articles is entitled, "Salvation by Mao." At an ecumenical conference on China, to which people had been invited by the Lutheran World Federation, one of the five study groups came to the conclusion that "the Chinese revolution must be regarded as part of God's work of salvation." Heinz Beckmann wrote concerning this totally absurd thesis, "Up till now it has not been known in the Church that God has decided to base His work of redemption on a revolution in which millions lost their lives."

According to conservative estimates, Mao's *work of redemption* murdered 22 million people. Others speak of 50 million victims.

The cultural revolution was an orgy of bloody violence.

Christ did not murder anyone. He died for others. The theologians who write good things about Maoism are not only stone deaf to the Gospel but are inspired by Satan.

Since then many more instances have appeared of ministers adding fuel to the flames of red terrorism.

Ex 148   Pastorin Edda Groth of Hamburg-Bramfeld, who has since been deprived of her office, declared, "Mao is nearer to God than all the popes and bishops of the last one thousand years. Mao's kingdom is part of the realization of the kingdom of God."

Ex 149   Cornelius Burghardt, a curate who has since been arrested, said, "We must use every means in our fight for places of freedom—even bombs." Burghardt is the man who hid Ulrike Meinhof, procured false passports for her, and drove her to her destination in his car.

It is extraordinary that the Church opens its pulpits to red ideologists. Is it surprising that, for example, in Berlin, thousands leave the Church every month?

In the Hamburg area, thirty communists pastors have formed a communist cell. Hessen has twelve ministers who are members of the Communist Party. In the whole of West Germany, there are nearly sixty ministers who belong to the DKP (German Communist Party). The Church seminary in Berlin has been exposed as a center of communism. Lothar Münn, president of the Berlin police court, has written to Bishop Scharf: "Out of sixteen ministers, fifteen are atheists. God grant that our church is not destroyed by this evil."

We live in the evil days of which Paul speaks: "Now the Spirit speaketh expressly, that in the latter times some shall depart from the faith, giving heed to seducing spirits, and doctrines of devils" (1 Timothy 4:1).

People with theological training, who have the right to preach and who should be proclaiming the good news of Jesus Christ, are being governed not only by the spirit of the age but by the devil.

The German national church is powerless in opposition to this state of affairs. The way is being prepared for the coming church of the Antichrist, the lying church. The ecumenical movement, with certain notable exceptions, is steering in the same perilous waters.

39
MEDITATION

An informative book about meditation is that by Dr. Friso Melzer, called *Concentration, Meditation, Contemplation.* The first part leads the reader to become a centered person by means of collecting himself inwardly. The second part deals with a great number of exercises in meditation. The third is a "meditation on death" *(meditatio mortis).*

There is not space here to discuss Melzer's book. At the present time a so-called *wave of meditation* may be observed. One may compare also the chapter in this book on transcendental meditation.

Indicative of this trend is the fact that, for example, the conferences on meditation at Bad Boll are well-attended and generally over booked.

In Bad Boll, we are also introduced to the sources from which meditation is derived, or at least gains new impulses. Hans Heinz Pollack has written about the conference in Bad Boll: "College chaplain, Albrecht Strebel, has no intention of joining the present-day craze for yoga. But that does not prevent this minister, who is himself an expert on Far Eastern Zen, from using elements of yoga in the meditations he conducts."

Some students of meditation say, "We only want to learn from the technique of yoga, not from its philosophical content."

A novel form of meditation is to be seen in the graphotherapy of Dr. Hippius, of the Free Clinic, Todtmoos. Here meditative drawing is used as a special exercise in meditation. The drawings or paintings are said not to be done consciously, using the intellect, but rather to unlock the unconscious and so relax the whole person. The works which result "remind us again of the painting of Zen," writes H. Pollack.

We have twice used the word *Zen.* We must explain in one sentence what it means. Zen is a Japanese form of Buddhism, which aims to lead to personal liberation by means of mental concentration and meditation.

It is, then, a matter of self-help. No one will want to prevent man from trying to find a solution to his own problems. But in the Far Eastern systems of meditation the temptation has never successfully been overcome to practice self-deliverance in the religious sphere also.

This attempt to bring about one's own salvation often finds its way into the practice of meditation in the West as well. Let us look at the practical effects. My counseling work in East and West has given me insight into the nature and practice of meditation.

Ex 150   In 1969, I stayed with Pastor Tharchin in Kalimpong for two weeks, on the Tibetan frontier. Tharchin is the only Tibetan who has been ordained as a Christian minister. The most wonderful baptism Pastor Tharchin ever performed was that of David Tenzing in 1963. David had been chief priest of no less than twenty-two monasteries in Eastern Tibet. In 1962, Tharchin gave him a New Testament and led him to Christ. Tenzing made a radical decision. As an intellectual Buddhist, he had studied philosophy and logic and had made it his regular habit to practice various forms of meditation. The missionary Margarete Urban asked him once, "Do you still meditate?" "No," replied Tenzing.

When someone comes to Christ in East Asia and experiences a transformation of life, he gives up Buddhist meditation. Yet in the West, many accept it quite uncritically.

I quote now from two letters I have received.

Ex 151   Valter Öhman, a Christian brother in Stockholm, wrote to me, "Far Eastern meditation is at present gaining ground in Sweden. Many think that it is stimulating and edifying to meditate, and yet it is evident that meditation can mislead. If meditation is not thoroughly Christian in content, it leads to pagan communion with spirits. Meditation based on a false ideology brings people into contact with false spirits and a false god. The result is not liberation but oppression and possession."

Ex 152   The news sheet of the Blue Cross, "Bla Korset," has published a thrilling testimony in this connection. It concerns a Swede named Kjell Wallgren, whose search for the truth led him as far away as the Himalayas. There a Buddhist monk, who was a master of meditation, introduced him to the art. By means of the exercises he learned, the Swede developed such a degree of self-control that he was able to separate his soul from his body and send it out.

His meditation ended in spiritism. In his excursion of the soul, he travelled through the unseen world. There he met souls, who like him, had reached this state by means of meditation. The effort to find liberation by meditating had brought them into contact with the world of lost spirits. In his hopelessness, the Swede suddenly became aware of a power, which he later recognized as the power of Jesus. This power drew him back to his body again.

Frightened by his experience, the man stopped meditating and tried to return to Sweden. Since he had no money, he had great difficulties in reaching his homeland. Totally disillusioned with Buddhism, he was now ready to listen to the Christian message. He attended an evangelistic meeting, which was addressed by an African Christian, who was working in Sweden. From the preaching of this man, he learned the great message against meditation in John 14:6, "I am the way, the truth, and the life; no one cometh unto the Father but by me."

There is only one way to the Father, only one way to heaven, only one way to salvation: Jesus Christ. The disappointed traveller of Asia received this truth in his own life, and everything changed.

Ex 153   A Mrs. R. Gerlich, Stuttgart, one of those who receives my newsletter, wrote: "Recently on the radio there was a lecture lasting for hours, with exercises in meditation. The speaker said that yoga should be seen not only as a physical exercise, but also as a mental and spiritual one. This spirit would gain control of a person. There was a worldwide unity reaching from the Western mystics to the Eastern religions. The whole lecture was peppered with Biblical quotations, preceded and followed by practical exercises. A demonic thing! Believers must be warned!"

The example which follows illustrates that even believers can sometimes be led astray by the movements of our day.

Ex 154   A civil servant with university training suffered from depressions. Being a churchman, he went to see a minister. This minister is known even in the Christian Fellowship movement and in free church circles as a believer. He advised the man suffering from depression to do some yoga exercises. For one exercise, the pastor told the man to look at a burning candle and meditate. The man followed the advice, but his depression did not cease. Then he decided to come to see me. He was surprised when I advised him to stop his yoga exercises at once, indeed, to renounce yoga completely and to give his life to Christ. I am surprised that a believing minister could advise a depressed person to practice meditation and yoga as a cure.

I was shocked to hear of another negative example of meditation in connection with believing ministers and evangelists.

Ex 155   Someone I knew well was a minister and evangelist. He has since died. One day we both went to a conference where the subject of meditation was under discussion. After the speaker had finished, my friend and I began talking with one of those who had been listening. My friend said he had been practicing meditation for many years. He had even developed a special skill of meditating about people. If he concentrated on a person for three days, he would know all that person's secrets, his plans and intentions, his past, his sins, his present difficulties, and much besides. I was troubled by this confession. Just like the Swede of whom we read earlier, this minister's meditation had landed him in occultism and demonic clairvoyance. Perhaps it was because of this that God suddenly removed this minister and evangelist from his work, although he was only fifty years of age.

It may be objected that I have only mentioned negative examples. That is true. I am totally opposed to meditation in the Far Eastern pattern. Compare also the chapter on yoga in this book.

Is there such a thing as positive meditation? Yes, there is a kind of meditation which is legitimate for Christians, for which we must be open:

> Faithful Bible reading accompanied by believing prayer,
> Thinking over the word of truth,
> Searching one's conscience in the light of God,
> All, and more besides, under the guidance of the Holy Spirit,
> who leads us into all truth.

We do not need to search deeply into ourselves, but rather into Him who died for us on the cross. We have no need to discover the deep self, but rather to discover our Lord and Savior. We cannot empty ourselves by means of techniques and postures—then other powers flood in. We must be filled with the Spirit of the Father and the Son, who would come to us and make their home with us (John 14:23).

40
METAMORPHOSIS

The term *metamorphosis,* is derived from the Greek verb *metamorphoomai,* to change form. The question to be discussed in this chapter is this: Is it possible for people to change into animals?

It is certainly possible in fairy tales. The prince changes into a frog. A beautiful princess is transformed into a deer by a wicked witch. We, however, are not concerned here with fairy tales and myths. Instances of actual metamorphosis have been reported to me in many countries. Occasionally, the question has come up in the course of my counseling work.

I have come across three forms of animal metamorphosis.

1. There are some hysterical people who can become prone to epidemic possession and imagine that they are animals. This happened in the last century in a convent in South France. The nuns imagined that they were cats and ran around on all fours meowing.

I heard of another example in the USA. There a group of hippies likewise took to imitating four-legged animals and to barking like dogs. As a result they became known as yippies.

This is of course not an animal metamorphosis at all. It is a case of delusion.

2. The second form is connected with the ability of some strong spiritist mediums to split off some of their energy. This energy can then be materialized in the form of an animal. There are examples of this in literature, in the history of missions, and in counseling.

One may think for instance of the German stories of the Werewolf. Switzerland has about thirty stories about cats which come into the same category. What does this mean? There are some powerful mediums, capable of materialization, who can split off energy when in a state of trance, and transfer this energy over to a cat which they then send out to annoy one of their neighbors. Milk and butter can disappear. Cows can be milked dry, and other things. If someone catches the cat and beats it, the blows affect the medium. I was asked years ago to publish the story of these Swiss cats. I dared not. Why? For two reasons.

First, nothing is achieved by broadcasting sensational stories of this kind. My concern is with the pastoral aspect of the problem.

Second, one only encourages ridicule. I remember a large conference of ministers in Männedorf, Switzerland. I had been invited by my friend, Pastor Fritz Eichin. About two hundred ministers had gathered. There were some excellent speakers, including Professor Blanke of Zurich University and Professor Carl Gustav Jung, the most famous of all depth psychologists. In the course of a private conversation, Jung recalled some spiritist experiences from his own childhood. He dared not speak publicly of his spiritist theories. He did nonetheless write an introduction to Fanny Moser's book *Spuk*.

I will only say, as far as this second form of metamorphosis is concerned, that I have heard three confessions from mediums who were capable of transfiguration. These three confessions may be taken as honest, in that the mediums concerned were seeking help to become free. In one case, the medium, who was a man, did become free. His wife had formed a circle of praying friends who prayed for him for years, until the Lord Jesus freed this man from his heavy bondage.

3. The third form is the transformation of a whole medium into an animal. This is the most sinister form of metamorphosis. I have heard of it in Tibet and in Africa.

Ex 156   I will start with an example of a *hyena man*. Near to a mission station lived a pagan whose neighbors said he turned himself into a hyena at night and fed himself while in that form. During the day, he needed no ordinary human food.

I heard an even stranger story in Liberia, this time with some evidence to back it up. I was staying with a district governor who had been educated in Europe. He is a believing Christian. After dinner he told me something about his district. One story about a hunter was of particular interest to me, because I had heard similar things in other African countries.

Ex 157   A hunter had gone out hunting. His boy was carrying his gun for him. In the jungle they both caught sight of a leopard. The boy silently handed the hunter his gun. He raised it, took aim, and fired. At once he heard a woman's voice crying, "You are a murderer. You have shot me." Both hurried over to the wounded woman. The hunter asked the boy, "Did you not see a leopard?"

"Yes, certainly."

"I'm sure I did too. How can one explain this?"

They gave the screaming woman first aid and took her back to the village. The relatives of the wounded woman took the hunter to court. The judge listened to the whole story, and then, to everyone's amazement, acquitted the hunter. As the reason for his verdict he said, "I know that the hunter is telling the truth. This woman was my first wife. I divorced her when I discovered that she could turn herself into a leopard."

That is African justice. The governor finished the story by saying, "We in our government know that there are leopard people. So we have a law which prescribes the death penalty for such offences."

To a man of Western education, the idea that a human can transform himself into an animal seems incompatible with reason. But anyone who has spent many years travelling from one mission field to another finds that he must change his thinking about many things. The power of Satan becomes especially evident on the mission field. Correspondingly, one comes to value all the more Jesus' victory over the power of darkness.

41
NEO-RATIONALISM

Martin Luther made Germany the leading country of the Reformation. Bultmann and his followers have caused Germany to lose this leading position in theology.

Professor Hermann Sasse said the same thing to me when I was in Australia. He added, "Theological leadership has passed over to the USA."

What do the neo-rationalists seek to do? To fit the Bible and its statements to the pattern of human reason. They are not the first to attempt this. Marcion tried to do it in the second century. The liberal theologians of the nineteenth century likewise steered their ship into these shallow and perilous waters. It has been left to the neo-rationalists of the twentieth century to carry this atheism in disguise to its extreme limit.

This is not the place for conducting a theological discussion. Respected brethren like Bergmann, Beyerhaus, Deitenbeck, Künneth, Rodenberg, and many others have been doing that for years.

I will mention just one book written in laymen's language, *Alarm um die Bibel* by Dr. Bergmann. This book has been so widely read that one hundred thousand copies have been printed.

This book is not a scholarly debate. It is based on counseling experience and is written for everyday Christians. Here are some of my experiences.

Ex 158 One of my friends was an elder in a suburban church in Frankfurt. The young minister used to serve up a confusion of ideas to his congregation every Sunday. The recipe was like this: take a little ethics, add two pinches of social activity, garnish with some titillating facts from the news of the moment, and the church will soon have had enough. For several Sundays, the elder listened to this *sermon salad*. Then he went to the vestry and had a talk with the young minister about spiritual things. It was, of course, to no avail. He talked to him again, and finally resigned his office as elder. He said, "I cannot be responsible to the congregation for such unscriptural preaching." His next step, taken after much prayer and heartsearching, was to leave that church.

Ex 159 During a lecture tour in North Germany, I stayed with a believing minister. He told me of something which had happened in his own district. A young minister had said, in the course of a Christmas sermon, that the child in the crib at Bethlehem was not the Son of God. After the service, the church elders met together without the minister. Then they went to the minister's house and said to the startled minister, "That is the last time you will preach in our pulpit." They informed the superintendent and the church authorities immediately, who agreed. The minister was moved at once. In his next parish, he was more cautious, though he did not change his views.

We need more stalwart church elders grounded in the Bible like these. This kind of church discipline from below is a healthy thing.

Ex 160 My friend, Heinz Plaum in Chicago, told me the following story. He was talking to a Lutheran pastor, and said, "Luther would turn in his grave if he could hear pastors like that preaching." The Lutheran pastor replied, "Do you seriously believe that Luther would be allowed to preach in our pulpits today?"

The effect of the neo-rationalist teachers and pastors on young people today is catastrophic.

Ex 161 One of my friends, who is minister of a large church in Münster, had a promising son. This son had been converted in early years and wanted to study theology. In the sixth form, the class was given a modernist to teach them religion. This teacher proceeded to destroy everything the believing parents had sown in the hearts of their children. The boy began to have doubts. Nevertheless, after passing his examinations brilliantly, he resolved to study theology. The lecturers worked along the same lines as the religious education teacher at school. The boy's parents were no longer able to halt the decline in their son's faith. He continued his course in theology, but he did not go into the ministry.

It is a matter of concern and sorrow to all believing parents when their own influence is not strong enough to build a dam against the tide of this Satan-inspired theology.

Ex 162 Professor Braun, who was for some years lecturer at the theological seminary in Berlin and then at the University of Mainz, followed the same course of development. It is said that at the age of sixteen he was converted in the Christian Endeavor movement. Later he threw it all overboard and became one of the leading modernist theologians. He became particularly well known for saying that he could not believe in a personal God.

Ex 163 A Christian brother wrote and told me the tragic story of his eldest son. The boy had been moved to accept Christ during an evangelistic campaign. Since then he had faithfully read his Bible and prayed. He made good progress at school. For seven years, he was top of the class. Then a new minister came to their small town. His credentials included a doctor of theology, and soon he took over the teaching of R. E. in the sixth form. The parents were deeply concerned to hear what the son brought home from these lessons: the Bible is not God's word, but the work of men. The Bethlehem story and the story of the Cross were not important in themselves but only for the spiritual truth they contained. There was no point in prayer, for there was no one to whom we could pray. Prayer was only a means of calming oneself. This work of destruction bore its own fruit. The young man gave up the idea of studying theology. He no longer read the Bible. Prayer became superfluous.

In view of all this, the boy's father asked me, "Must we allow our children to come under the influence of ministers like this, who destroy everything that their believing parents and evangelists have planted?"

My reply was that the father should take a stand and withdraw his son from religious instruction. Today I would be still more radical. I should not be prepared to remain the member of a church that destroyed the faith and despised the Bible.

It would be interesting to study the attitudes of neo-rationalist bishops. I know of many individual examples, but I cannot record them all here. I will restrict myself to two examples.

Ex 164   Bishop Lilje has the reputation in Germany of being a believing Christian. This made it all the harder to understand why for years he had a modernist, Heinz Zahrnt, as the editor of his Sunday newspaper. Well-known men endeavored to point out to Lilje the inconsistency of his attitude, but in vain. Lilje remained loyal to Zahrnt. Then Zahrnt was elected as president of the Kirchentag.

Under Zahrnt's leadership, the Kirchentag went further and further in the perilous direction of modernism. It became a serious question for many ministers who were believers, whether they could any longer invite their congregations to the Kirchentag. The Confessional Movement then decided to hold its own Gemeindetag, which took place in Stuttgart. This conference was richly blessed by God.

I was also faced with the question of whether I should take part in the Kirchentag. Wilhelm Horkel wrote to me, asking if I would lead a discussion group at the Kirchentag on the subject of Christian counseling and occultism. I declined, telling him that I would not cooperate with an organization run by modernists.

Ex 165   There are bishops who take a different line. H. H.

Harms, the former chief pastor of the Michaelis Church in Hamburg, became bishop of Oldenburg. He is not known worldwide like Lilje, but he maintains a clear witness. After visiting a certain church, his closing words to the minister were, "You have kept back the Gospel from your people." We need more bishops of this caliber, who do not allow their judgment to be clouded by the mirage of modern theology.

Neo-rationalism spells the death of the Christian Church. In the New Testament, an end is made of all the cleverness of the demythologizers.

"God made foolish the wisdom of this world" (1 Corinthians 1:20).

"He taketh the wise in their own craftiness" (1 Corinthians 3:19).

Holy Scripture's answer to the neo-rationalist theology is "Christ; in whom are hid all the treasures of wisdom and knowledge" (Colossians 2:2-3).

42

OUIJA BOARD

"Ouija Board" is the English name for a spiritualistic fortune-telling game, known in France as *planchette* and in Germany as *Psychograph*. In the English-speaking world, use of the ouija board has reached epidemic proportions. In 1967 in North America alone, four million of these devilish boards were produced and sold. It is a master stroke of Satan's strategy of deception, that this form of fortunetelling has found its way even into Christian homes.

I deliberately refrain from describing the ouija board. I would not want this book to help curious people to try it out.

American psychologists would have us believe that the game is harmless. They hold that it is only a matter of bringing to light things hidden in our subconscious minds. This view can swiftly be refuted. With the ouija board, revelations from the hidden past and predictions about the future are made. These things could not possibly be stored in our subconscious minds.

Ex 166   One of my friends is Mr. Ehret of Nappanee, Indiana. One day he went into a public building and saw several students playing with an ouija board. Not knowing what it was, he asked them. He was told that it was a means of revealing hidden things. "Good, I will test it out then. When was the house built in which we are now?" The ouija board gave the date: 1894. Mr. Ehret found the caretaker and he confirmed the date.

Ex 167 In North America and in Europe, many healing practitioners make their diagnosis by means of the ouija board. The method varies. Some lay their left hand on the patient's arm and use their right hand to guide a pendulum or glass over the letter board, which then spells out the disease. If the healer is strongly psychic, it is not even necessary for the patient to be present. It suffices for the healer to concentrate his mind on the patient.

The fact that there are demonic forces at work behind the ouija board is easily demonstrated by some examples on a spiritual level.

Ex 168 I have several times visited Kelowna, B.C., and have spoken in four different churches there. One of my friends told me about the following incident. In the Okanagan valley, about seventy pastors had been touched by the Saskatoon revival. One of the blessings of the revival was that, from Pendikton to Vernon, warnings were given from the pulpits abouts the sins of sorcery. One Mennonite pastor warned his children, too. His eleven-year-old son went into a room at school one day where some children were playing silly games with an ouija board. The pastor's son heard the following conversation, "Who is behind your power?"

"Hitler," replied the ouija board.

The children laughed and said, "Stop trying to pull the wool over our eyes. Tell us the truth."

The board then spelled out, "Lucifer."

The young lads did not know this name. (What sort of religious instruction had they been given?)

They asked again: "Who is Lucifer?" Then came the clear reply: "Satan."

At this, the eleven-year-old son of the Mennonite pastor stepped forward and called out, "If your power comes from the devil, then I command you in the name of Jesus Christ to stop." And that is what happened. The ouija board gave no more answers.

Ex 169 A teacher, who is also the minister of a church, was walking along a school corridor. Some children came running out of a room shouting, "We have seen a devil's face."

"What were you doing?" inquired the pastor.

"We were playing with an ouija board."

"Let me see it." He entered the room, saw the board lying there and thought to himself, perhaps too confidently, *We will soon deal with you!* He kneeled down in the presence of several of the children and prayed. At once he had the feeling that two invisible hands were round his throat, trying to throttle him. Only then did he

realize the danger of his position. He committed himself to the protection of Jesus Christ and commanded these powers in the name
of the Lord. Thereupon the hands released his neck.

These examples are enough to show that demonic power lies
behind the ouija board. I will close with the words of a Christian
psychiatrist in New York, "The ouija board is filling our psychiatric
clinics in New York."

The devil continues to pretend that he is harmless and to convince those who think they are wise that the whole thing is humbug.
In this way, he wins round after round and continues to entrap his
victims.

Additional note:

While I was writing this chapter, another report about ouija boards
reached me. The manager of the firm in Massachusetts that produces
these spiritistic boards says, "The film 'The Exorcist' has caused the
sales of ouija boards to grow again. It is chiefly girls between the
ages of eleven and eighteen who seek to satisfy their curiosity in
this way."

Clay Atkinson, the manager in question, speaks of the many letters of thanks received by the firm. It is no wonder that this devil's
factory sold over six million of the boards by 1974. Many letters
confirm that people made contact with the dead by means of the
ouija board. In doing so, they have fallen victim to a great and
sinister deception. It is not the dead who answer them, but demons,
who have sometimes appropriated dead people's knowledge in order
to give an impression of authenticity. Bishop Pike, who also took part
in this unseemly game of contacting the departed, did not receive a
reply from his son who had committed suicide, but from his son's
demon.

If the American government knew how much evil this one firm
in Massachusetts has brought on the American people, they would
prohibit the production of these devilish boards at once.

43

PARAPSYCHOLOGY

Parapsychology is the science of occult phenomena. This is the
definition given by Hans Driesch, the philosopher of Leipzig, in
his book *Methodenlehre* published in 1932. Professor Hans Bender
of Freiburg University, who is regarded as the world's leading parapsychologist, has this to say: "Parapsychology attempts to carry out
factual, unprejudiced research in the controversial area where be-

lievers in the occult and their opponents stand in irreconcilable opposition."[31] By *believers in the occult,* he means spiritists, witches, and all who engage in occult activities. By *their opponents,* he means rationalists who dismiss as make-believe and charlatanry everything which does not fit in within the narrow limits of their horizon. I belong to neither group. I investigate the problems on the basis of a wide experience of counseling. I have observed for many years how people suffer damage as a result of occult activity. My task is to make these things known, to warn, and to give pastoral advice as widely as I can.

1. *History*

As a science, parapsychology has a history of about one hundred years, although occult activities have been going on for thousands of years. In about 1850, the spiritists became prominent in the USA. The spiritist séance movement spread around the world. Out of desire to conduct a thorough investigation of the phenomena, the English Society for Psychical Research was formed in 1882. From the outset, the parapsychologists made efforts to have their subject recognized by the universities. They were not successful in this until about fifty years later. Then in 1934, a laboratory for parapsychological research was opened at Duke University, USA, under the leadership of Professor J. B. Rhine (author of *The Reach of the Mind*). In the same year, a Dutchman named W. H. C. Tenhaeff was given a lectureship in parapsychology at the University of Utrecht. In 1954, a chair of limited areas of psychology was set up at the University of Freiburg under Dr. Hans Bender. In 1960, Leningrad University followed suit with the establishment of an institute for research into paranormal remote influence, under Professor L. L. Vassiliev. In 1964, Professor Onetto was given a lectureship in parapsychology at the University of Santiago. In 1975, Dr. M. Johnson became Professor of Parapsychology at Utrecht University.

2. *Hypotheses*

Since experts have been studying para-normal phenomena. their opinions about these have varied. One may distinguish three basic points of view.

a. Animists say that the powers within the human mind are strong enough to bring about parapsychological effects. Nearly all the professors who teach at universities share this view. If they did not, they would not be able to hold their own at a university. I must refer again to the conversation which took place at the end of a great conference in Switzerland, already mentioned in the chapter on "Metamorphosis." Speakers at the conference included the famous depth psychologist, Professor Carl Gustav Jung, and Professor Fritz Blanke, a church historian from the University of Zurich. After a lecture, a private conversation took place among a small group of people. My friend, Pastor Fritz Eichin, was one of them. Professor Jung spoke very positively of the so-called spiritistic hypothesis. One of those present then asked him, "Professor, why do you not state that publicly in your lectures or in your books?" Professor Jung replied, "My colleagues would regard me as mentally unbalanced." Those who hold a chair in a university are compelled to reject the idea of influence from superhuman powers, lest their authority as scientists be impugned.

In my books and lectures, I have often pointed out to supporters of the animist theory that they ought to study the background of those who engage in the occult. If they did so, they would discover that occultists, witches, spiritists, and mediums usually come from families where sorcery has been practiced. Magic activities in forebears produces psychic powers which become hereditary. One who has acknowledged this is Professor Siebeck, former head of the Medical Clinic of Heidelberg University. He acknowledged this after I had given him a list of such instances. I have often been surprised that Professor Bender has taken no notice of this well-documented observation.

b. Spiritists maintain that the para-normal manifestations are brought about by the help of their friends on the other side, the so-called *operators*. In other words, they say that powers, or spirits from the other world, interfere with our lives and bring about these occult phenomena. This is the view held by all spiritists.

c. The third view is not found in the literature of parapsychology because it comes from Christian faith. In this connection, I mention two English books: *Soul and Spirit* by Jessie Penn Lewis, and *The Latent Power of the Soul* by Watchman Nee. Both writers maintain that Adam had considerably greater powers in Paradise than he did after the Fall. It was as if when he fell his original powers were locked up in the depths of his mind. In the case of occult manifestations, these powers, locked up and hidden in fallen man, are released by Satan and made available for his purposes. If we omit the religious angle, this theory appears similar to the animist theory. Yet it is quite different. According to the animist theory, the factor causing the para-normal powers is the unconscious. Both Professor Driesch and Professor Bender speak frequently of the standpipes of the unconscious. Lewis and Watchman Nee, on the other hand, say that the causative factor is Satan and the demons the nonhuman agents. Here Lewis and Nee are nearer to the spiritists, with the important difference: that while spiritists call these demons their good helpers, Lewis and Nee describe these activities as devilish.

3. *Comment*

Concerning the animist views, I have a number of reservations.

a. Professor Bender described the poltergeist of Rosenheim. Here many poltergeist manifestations appear in the presence of a nineteen-year-old girl. Among other things, a filing cabinet weighing 3½ cwt. twice moved a foot from its place. This was witnessed by the physicist Professor Büchels and other observers. Professor Bender holds, as we have already said, the animist theory. He calls the poltergeist phenomenon *psychokinesis*. This means that the causative powers originate in the human psyche. This would mean in the case of the heavy filing cabinet that the psychic powers of the girl were stronger than her natural physical powers. I discussed cases of this sort with a theoretical physicist from the University of Mainz. He said, "The psychic powers of thousands of people would not be sufficient to bring about such phenomena." Whence then is this nineteen-year-old girl supposed to derive psychic powers equal to those of thousands upon thousands of men? Professor Bender suggests in his book that people with these mediumistic powers are able to organize the energy of others as well.[32] That is, incidentally, a suggestion I have made in a number of my books. A spiritist medium uses not only his own mediumistic power, but also releases the mediumistic power of those who are present. That is also the secret of the Uri Geller effect, when Uri mobilizes the mediumistic powers of his audience even over the television. In the homes of mediumistic viewers, knives and forks were bent in the same way as by Uri Geller in his television show.

In the case of the Rosenheim poltergeist, however, there were not thousands of people present whose psychic power could be organized by the girl. The animist explanation lets us down not only in the case of the poltergeist of Rosenheim, but in nearly all cases of poltergeist activity. Professor Bender, however, has to maintain his animist view for the reason already mentioned, in order not to appear ridiculous among his colleagues at the university, as intimated by Professor Jung.

b. It is easy enough for the spiritists. They explain the psychokinesis by reference to the operators on the other side, their helpers, who bring their influence to bear from that other world on our material world. To me these good, other-worldly friends of the spiritists are demons.

For several decades I have been collecting thousands of examples of the dreadful effects of spiritism. These effects are usually not evident until a spiritist tries to free himself from the net of spiritism and to come to faith in Christ. As long as a spiritist serves the devil, he is left in peace.

These religious comments are ridiculous in the eyes of our scientists. I am well aware of that. But I am not afraid of it. In Genesis 19, we are told how the inhabitants of Sodom thought it ridiculous when they were warned by Lot. Their fate is related in Genesis 19.

At the present time we have statements by two very good mediums in support of the spiritist theory. The first is Uri Geller, who says that during his experiments forces from outside are at work in him.

Matthew Manning is perhaps an even stronger medium. In 1967, poltergeists made their appearance in Manning's house in England. Objects moved inexplicably at their own volition. A Professor Owen investigated the poltergeist manifestations and declared that it was not a trick. To begin with, Matthew Manning believed that these phenomena had originated in his own psyche. Later he abandoned this view.

His reason was as follows. Matthew was writing an article about an architect of the eighteenth century who had built his parents' house. As he was writing, some old-fashioned signatures and dates suddenly appeared on the wall of the room. They all had some connection with the architect. When checked in the church register, these dates and names were found to be correct. Parapsychological experts were called in. No one actually saw the names and figures being written, but sounds of writing were heard. Afterwards, used pencils were found in the room. Apports of objects from the eighteenth century also took place. The knowledge and information communicated to the young man by the writing on the wall cannot have originated in his own psyche. They were completely unknown to him. Since then Matthew has given up the animist theory, and now believes in external influence from the spirits of the departed. Manning has experienced many other manifestations. They cannot all be recorded here in detail. Professor Bender spent three days investigating this new and well-known medium, in his institute, but he remains as convinced as ever of his animist hypothesis.

c.   I do not need to say anything further about the thesis of Lewis and Nee. As far as counseling is concerned, it makes no difference whether the demons release and use hidden powers in the soul of man, or whether they transfer their own personal powers. The effect is the same from a pastoral point of view.

4. *Summary*

Counseling does not concern itself with the animist or spiritist theories. The problems of the Christian pastor lie on a higher plane. Thousands of cases reveal that occultism in any form, even in a scientific form, harms people. This applies even to scientific parapsychologists who attend spiritist séances in order to study the activity of the mediums. The Scriptural command to have nothing to do with spiritists applies, not only to ordinary people, but also to parapsychologists who work by scientific methods. In fact, we know of no parapsychologist who is a convinced Christian. It will be objected that Professor Rhine, for instance, was a churchgoer. To be a Christian and to be a churchgoer are normally two different things. It is possible to be both, but usually it is not so. The word of God says: "Except a man be born again, he cannot see the kingdom of God" (John 3:3). "Now if any man have not the Spirit of Christ, he is none of his" (Romans 8:9b). "No man can say that Jesus is the Lord, but by the Holy Ghost" (1 Corinthians 12:3b). To be a Christian for tradition's sake is to be a nominal Christian, unless a personal decision for Christ has been made. I cannot believe that a Christian, who has really given his life to Christ, would be able to take part in parapsychological experiments involving the use of mediums.

These words will perhaps be thought hard and arrogant. I believe, however, that the time has come for plain speaking about these facts. Even in Christian circles today, we have books about occult phenomena which make the whole problem seem harmless. For example, Dr. Kurt Hutten's *Seher, Grübler, Enthusiasten* is an excellent source of information. What is absent from the book is any warning against many occult movements. That was not, of course, Dr. Hutten's intention. A reader, however, would refer to this book and then say that things are not nearly as bad as the evangelists say.

44
PEDITHERAPY

Peditherapy could be described almost as a technical parallel to iris diagnosis. The term is compounded from the Latin *pes,* foot, and the Greek *therapeuō,* to heal. Peditherapy is the art of healing by means of the foot. The foot is divided into thirty-eight zones, which are said to correspond to certain parts of the body. One is reminded of the so-called head zones, although the reflex zones on the sole of the foot have nothing to do with those.

Proponents of this new healing method believe that certain organs can be influenced by massaging the reflex zones.

The merits or demerits of such massage are matters for doctors to discuss. That is not my province. What I am concerned about in this section is the occult use of the reflex zones. This has come to my notice in counseling. Occult peditherapists believe they can diagnose disease by touching the reflex zones. If a slight pain is caused by touching a certain zone, the corresponding organ is said to be diseased.

The medical profession calls this quackery. The problem, however, is not as simple as that. Occult therapists can use the reflex zones as contact bridges and so produce diagnoses which stand up to scientific examination. What we have here is a form of extrasensory diagnosis which brings occult oppression upon the patient.

45
POLTERGEISTS

From the morass of stories about poltergeists, which must run into millions, four particular areas of interest may be picked out.

1. *Hallucinations*

People with mental disorders can experience illusions of all five senses; sight, hearing, touch, taste, and smell. These sensory illusions are found especially in connection with schizophrenic conditions. Old people in a state of senile degeneration are also frequently plagued by such hallucinations, which seem very real to them. Sick people who suffer from them will not allow themselves to be convinced that their experiences are not real. Schizophrenic symptoms are often coupled with paranoiac delusions. Patients of this sort will not let their fantasies be corrected.

2. *Poltergeists associated with a person*

In this connection, I refer the reader to the book *Spuk* by Fanni Moser, with an introduction by Carl Gustav Jung.

I have records of many cases of people in whose vicinity poltergeist activity is continually taking place. Often they are young people who produce poltergeists unconsciously at the age of puberty. Some examples follow.

Ex 170 A minister's son came to me for counseling. His father taught religion at a high school and used a copy of the *Sixth and Seventh Book of Moses* which he kept for use in his teaching. He carefully locked it away in his bookcase. His twelve-year-old son was watching. His curiosity was greatly roused because his father always locked it away so carefully. When his father was not there, he took a key, brought the book out, read it, and wrote down some of the spells. Then he tried out these spells. He was surprised to find that they worked. That was the beginning of great trouble in the boy's life. Sometimes when he was sitting in a room with the doors closed, the door would unlock, swing open, swing back, and shut again, all of its own accord. Sometimes he saw a chair slide across the floor of the room as if pushed along by invisible hands. His emotional life was also greatly disturbed and strong addictive tendencies developed.

The young man grew up, got married, but his poltergeists followed him. When he was on vacation with his young wife, the same phenomena occurred as in his own home. Finally, he came to the point where he was afraid he would go mad and have to be committed to an institution. He came to me for pastoral help. I showed him the reason for his troubles and tried to show him, also, the way to find deliverance through Christ. He was a sincere young man. He confessed all his sin, renounced the power of sorcery, and gave his life to Christ. After this, the poltergeists troubled him no more.

This poltergeist was attached to a particular person. It had begun with the reading of the *Sixth and Seventh Book of Moses*, or more particularly with the practical use of the magic spells contained in that book.

Professor Hans Bender has often pointed out the connection between poltergeists and young people at the age of puberty. I would remind the reader of the Rosenheim poltergeist, which was active only in the presence of the nineteen-year-old secretary. Or I can repeat the story of a poltergeist which has been investigated by both Professor Bender and myself.

Ex 171 Poltergeists were manifesting themselves in the house of a West German burgomaster. The newspaper reported the case. Professor Bender went to the village and asked the burgomaster about all the details. In the burgomaster's house there were, among other things, objects appearing and disappearing in rooms with shut doors. Sometimes these objects were hot: a glass marble flew into the kitchen while the door was shut; and when it was picked up, it was hot. Professor

Bender measured the temperature. He established that the decrease in the temperature of the kitchen was equivalent to the increase in temperature of the marble. In other words, the energy balance was what one might expect. But this did not explain the cause of these poltergeist phenomena.

Professor Bender also established that the poltergeist was only active when the burgomaster's fourteen-year-old son was in the house or in the yard outside. There was no question of fraud. In the course of six weeks, the burgomaster recorded 136 flying objects. The professor did not succeed in solving the mystery.

When I spoke to the burgomaster, I asked him if his parents, grandparents, or members of his family, had ever practiced spiritism or magic. The burgomaster admitted that from time immemorial the cows and horses on his estate had been charmed when they were sick. He had also had this done himself. The boy had been present on nearly every occasion when the animals were charmed.

I have recorded thousands of instances like this. In every case, some occult connection is found, and it is, therefore, legitimate to conclude that the poltergeist has something to do with the sorcery practiced by the forebears or during the life of the present occupants of the house. Deliverance of a house means that the people who are the cause of these poltergeist manifestations must come to Christ to be freed from occult oppression.

I have many examples of flying objects behind closed doors.

Ex 172   In the Philippines, an evangelist came to me for counseling. He had heard my lectures both at the Theological Seminary and at the University of Manila. He thought that I might be able to help him. He told me that every time his sister was in the house, hot stones would fly down from the ceiling. Sometimes his small children had picked up the stones and burned their fingers. The stones fell even when the doors and windows were closed. When the sister was not there, the shower of stones did not take place. He wanted to know what he could do about it. I asked him to send his sister to me for counseling. I further advised him, when the stones began to fall, to place himself and his family under the protection of Jesus Christ and to forbid the stones to fall, in the name of Jesus. The evangelist did as I suggested. Not long afterward, he told me the stones were not as bad as they had been. His sister, however, did not come for counseling.

Ex 173   This example is taken from a daily newspaper, although I have a record of many similar incidents.

Parapsychological phenomenon or bad joke? This is the question which faces the inhabitants of the little Belgian village of Wilsele near Louvain. Four houses in the village have been suffering from a daily shower of stones, but it has not been possible to find out who is responsible. "The stones appear to come from nowhere," said one of the victims, who, like several other families, has had to put up wire netting to protect his windows.

The police at first suspected hooligans, but they made no progress toward solving the mystery. Neither continuous patrols on the beat, nor the offer of a reward for the identification of suspects, has led to a solution. Several parapsychologists, among them scientists from the University of Utrecht, are at present studying the phenomenon. The mysterious incidents always take place in the presence of the fourteen-year-old son of the Corda family.

The father, Alfons Corda, has already filled several sacks with the stones he has collected, some of which are 8 inches in diameter. His son has been hit several times by falling stones, in the face and other parts of his body. "Life has become impossible for us here," says Alfons Corda. According to him the stones fall only in the afternoon, usually when the weather is fine, on his house and those of his neighbors.

The parapsychologists, who are always very cautious and skeptical in their attitude, point out that such phenomena are not unknown; and that it is particularly common for adolescent children to possess the hitherto unexplained power of telekinesis, although they are unable to control it.

Dr. Frieso Melser mentions in one of his books an incident of this kind from his missionary experience. I have been telephoned and asked for help by owners of houses where such poltergeists manifest themselves. If, however, I wanted to visit every house in Germany which has poltergeists, I should have to travel to a different house every day, and I do not have time enough for that.

Ex 174 One day I received a telephone call from a village in the vicinity of Pirmasens. They wanted me to come at once to help the owner of a farmhouse. There were hot stones falling both on the house and on the barn. I told them that I did not have time to come. Several days later there was a report in the paper to the effect that this farm had been set on fire by the hot stones.

The so-called *spirit stones* are a poltergeist phenomenon which occurs only in connection with a person under mediumistic oppression. It can also happen that a sorcerer with strong psychic powers can bring a shower of stones like this upon an enemy. The incident reported by Frieso Melser is in this category. We will return to this subject in section 4 of this chapter on poltergeists.

The difference between the parapsychologist and the Christian counselor is that the parapsychologist is only able to study the phenomena but not to give help. The counselor, who is a disciple of Jesus Christ, equipped with His power, can show a person who is endangered by these things the way to deliverance. Sorcery, oppression, and poltergeists can be brought to an end by spiritual authority. This authority does not however derive from the personality of the counselor, but from Jesus Christ alone.

3. *Poltergeists associated with a place*

There are in Europe some old castles and houses which have been haunted for centuries. Sometimes the manifestations are so harrassing to the occupants, that the house has to be sealed up by the police. This happened with a house in the Jungferngasse in Berne. I have read that the same was done with a house in Bavaria. In old castles, in particular, the ghost of an old woman ancestor is said to wander around. Sometimes these poltergeists or ghosts are associated in popular opinion with crimes that have taken place in the castles or houses concerned. Some psychologists, especially those who are rationalists, try to explain away these manifestations on psychological grounds. There are, however, some manifestations associated with particular places which occur even when the occupants have had no prior knowledge of them. I know of one parsonage in which such things took place for generations. No minister stayed long in this parish. They asked to be moved on. No one family that left gave any information to their successors, so as not to cause them disquiet. And yet every time a new minister and his family moved in, they had the same experiences, which they too kept to themselves.

Ex 175 I was told of the following incident by a very well-known Christian worker in Germany. Years ago he lived in a house in which a terrible din was heard during the night. It sounded as if all the crockery and glass were being smashed together. Heavy footsteps were heard, scratching noises on the walls, and a whistling of wind as if there was a great storm raging even when the air outside was still. All the people in the house could hear the din. The same phenomena were observed in the house next door. There, too, the occupants heard this dreadful din in the middle of the night. The person who told me of this was a Christian, and he and his whole family prayed about it. As they prayed, they consciously placed themselves, in faith, under the protection of Jesus' blood. From that day on, there was complete peace in both houses.

In this case, the cause of the manifestations was not discovered, but the Christian worker did the right thing. He claimed the victory of Christ over these dark powers. This act is unknown to parapsychology, and indeed unacceptable. My father's friend, Dr. Alfred Lechler, who died some years ago, once said: "There is not only such a thing as possession of people, there is also possession of houses; and it is much easier to cleanse a house which has come under occult oppression than it is to free a possessed person." I would point out that Dr. Lechler was well known in Germany, both as a psychiatrist and as a Christian of clear convictions.

Finally an example from England.

Ex 176 While I was on a lecture tour in England, a young married couple came to me for counseling. They had bought a house which had previously housed the well-known English spiritist, Harry Edwards. As soon as they moved in, the couple noticed something uncanny about the house. During the night they heard all sorts of rumbling, banging, rattling of chains, heavy footsteps, and so on. They had sadly resolved to sell the house. They advertised it. A South African came to look at it. He looked the house over and cried enthusiastically: "Yes, I will buy this house. The heavenly beings, the ones from the other side, live here!" The couple saw that this South African was a spiritist and refused to sell it to him. They sold it to someone else.

Harry Edwards had practiced his spiritism in this house for years, and that was the reason for the poltergeists. The problem could have been solved in a different way. If this young couple had formed a prayer group in the house, and if possible met together with them for one-half hour every evening, they would have been able to drive the spirit out. Unfortunately, the fact is that among Christians there are so few men and women with strong faith in the power of prayer. There are many Christian churches which have no real prayer meeting at all. Of course the minister would say that they meet once a week or once a month for prayer. I have sometimes been present at such prayer meetings and have been shocked at the sleepiness and lukewarm prayer life of these so-called prayer groups. Prayer is not always a quiet matter. Prayer can also mean a battle. By this I do not mean that we should shout, go wild, scream, and clap our hands, as is done in some extreme circles, but that in all soberness, under the control of the Holy Spirit, we should claim the promises we are given in the Bible and drive out these powers of darkness.

4. *Poltergeists controlled by sorcerers with strong psychic powers*

We come now to the most controversial area of poltergeist manifestations. Let me begin with an example which is thoroughly documented.

Ex 177   One day I received a letter from a minister in a North German city. He asked me to come and see him because a house in his parish had suddenly become haunted. It was a pretty house with a lovely garden. The owner had one day received a letter from a neighbor, requesting that the house be put up for sale. This she refused to do. Then the neighbor warned that she would have her way in the end. Ever since then, poltergeists had appeared in this lady's beautiful home. Four loud sounds, like claps of thunder, were heard in the house. The owner could not understand what had caused the noise, nor could she find out from whence it came. She went to her minister. He came to the house with his curate. While they were there, the loud thunderclaps were heard, although nothing that might have caused them was found in the house. It was not a matter of steam in the heating system or an airlock in the waterpipes, for the sounds came from the direction of the doors. The minister, not knowing how he could help, reported the matter to the police. A police officer came around. He also heard the noises. It was a mystery to him, so he reported it to the chief of police, who sent a whole patrol of police to investigate. More than ten policemen came to the house. All stood at the doors, some inside and some outside. When the dreadful noise came again, they pulled the doors open. Each policeman said the noise was on the opposite side. Not even all these policemen were able to discover the cause of the noise.

Then the owner of the house began legal proceedings against her neighbor at the local court. The case came up for trial. The judge who had studied the statements declared in court: "We are not living in the Middle Ages. I will not preside over a trial like this." He refused to hear the case.

As I did not wish to go to the town myself, the minister sent me a report of how the affair ended. The owner of the house was so tormented by these poltergeist manifestations, day and night, that she finally could see no other way out than to sell the house to the highest bidder. That was the neighbor who had threatened her earlier and had said that she would get the house in the end. As soon as this neighbor, who had very strong psychic powers, moved into the house, the noise ceased.

Our parapsychologists will perhaps say that this story is rather far-fetched, and one should not take it seriously. I would point out that, in this case, two ministers and more than ten police officers were witnesses of these events. If a parapsychologist accepts such a story as genuine, he will speak of psychokinesis, powers of the psyche. I am becoming almost deaf to this continual appeal on the part of parapsychologists to adolescent young people and to psychokinesis. This appears in all their reports. None of them takes the trouble to discover the underlying causes.

In this case of a poltergeist caused by psychic influence from another person, a spiritual solution could have been found. The city in which it took place, however, is renowned for the weak church and the lack of believing Christians. If a prayer meeting had been set up in this house, attended not by nominal or traditional Christians, but by faithful men and women of prayer, strong in faith, they would have been able to master this sorcerer oppression in the name of Jesus.

Here is another example for which no explanation was found.

Ex 178 The episode which follows was told to me by a lawyer who describes himself as a rationalist who does not believe in anything supernatural. This lawyer had built himself a bungalow in a beautiful district. The day he and his family moved into the new house, they had a strange experience. On the hall floor stood a coffin, which they were able to see for two or three minutes. Then the coffin disappeared. On the floor, however, was a water stain the same size as the coffin. The lawyer was disconcerted. He put his hand to his head, wondering whether the strains of the last few days had caused him to have an hallucination. Yet there was the rectangular stain on the floor, and when he touched it, it felt damp. So it was no hallucination. For the next few days, the lawyer was quite beside himself. It was the first time in his life he had ever experienced anything like this. It was a significant blow to his rationalist views.

The experience led him to seek advice. It proved impossible to discover the origin of this poltergeist phenomenon.

Sometimes incidents of this sort may be explained in the following way. Perhaps there is in the neighborhood a person of strongly psychic disposition, who envies the lawyer's lovely house and therefore tries to turn him against it. Or perhaps the bungalow obstructs some neighbor's view, and the neighbor seeks vengeance.

It is not my intention that this section on controlled poltergeists should cause anyone to develop a persecution complex. I advise anyone who has to do with such things to review his whole life, give himself to Christ, and place himself under Christ's protection. I do this whenever I write books like this. I pray daily for the Lord's protection, remembering verses like Hebrews 1:14, which says of the angels: "Are they not all ministering spirits, sent forth to minister for them who shall be heirs of salvation?" I pray daily for my family and myself that we may have the Lord's protection against all the powers of darkness. He who stands under the protection of Jesus need fear none of these things. He will soon become free of them, if he deals with them in a spiritual manner and with the support of other believers. Read Psalm 91. I have often been wonderfully strengthened by the words of this Psalm:

> He that dwelleth in the secret place of the most High shall abide under the shadow of the Almighty. I will say of the LORD, He is my refuge and my fortress; my God; in Him will I trust. Surely he shall deliver thee from the snare of the fowler, and from the noisome pestilence. He shall cover thee with his feathers, and under his wings shalt thou trust: his truth shall be thy shield and buckler. Thou shalt not be afraid for the terror by night; nor for the arrow that flieth by day; nor for the pestilence that walketh in darkness; nor for the destruction that wasteth at noonday. A thousand shall fall at thy right side, and ten thousand at thy right hand; but it shall not come nigh thee.

46
PORNOGRAPHY

The word *pornography* is made up of two Greek words: *porneia,* immorality, prostitution, and *graphō,* to write. The term *pornography* as generally used today means the publication of immoral literature and obscene pictures. Only three aspects of this horrible evil will be mentioned here.

1. *The lust for profits*

A German newspaper reported that in one year, pornographic literature worth DM.1,600 million had been brought into Germany from Denmark. How expensive these products often are is shown by the experience of a certain pastor in North Germany. This pastor felt called to discover who were the sellers of pornographic picture books. He went to a dirty-looking bookstall on the Reeperbahn in Hamburg (the red-light zone) and asked for something "tasty." The clerk brought out a book from under the counter containing pictures of all kinds of sexual activities. The *client* asked the price. The answer was DM.600 ($240, £120). The *client* thanked the man and went off. Half an hour later he returned with a police officer and began proceedings against this sex shop.

Another example was told to me when I was in the USA. A publisher of communist leanings confessed at the end of his life that during his lifetime he had published several billion dollars' worth of pornographic literature in the USA, with the object of ruining the nation.

2. *Corruption of the young*

For several years now Christian parents have been watching, with great alarm, the development of so-called sex education in the schools. All protests made to teachers and school authorities have been fruitless. Sex education, often of a most offensive nature, is compulsory even in the lower classes of our schools. One father said to me: "My eight-year-old son knows more about these things than I did when I was married."

What effects this mandatory instruction can have is illustrated by the example which follows, which could be multiplied a hundred times. An eight-year-old boy came home and said to his little sister: "Get undressed. I want to try something. The teacher told us some interesting things today." The parents of this boy registered a strong objection with the teacher—unsuccessfully, of course.

At the end of 1975, there was a scandal in the province of Hessen. A prison inmate had written a pornographic book about sexual activities behind bars. At one time such a book would have been prohibited and its author punished. But today? The book was examined by an official expert at the Education Department in Hessen, who recommended it to the minister of education for experimental introduction in the high schools. Most schools refused to have it because it was too dirty. The head of one gymnasium (equivalent of English grammar school) introduced it in the higher classes as part of their general reading. A storm resulted. A woman teacher made a strong protest to the head. The latter parried the attack by saying: "The Bible also contains disgusting stories. What do you really want?" The teacher was furious. "The Bible condemns such disgusting practices, but this filthy book recommends them. The Bible does not revel in all kinds of degenerate perversions, but pronounces God's judgment upon them." The parents joined the Christian teacher in opposition to this book. Again the response of the school authorities was a shrug of the shoulders. Finally some of the pupils had to resort to strike action, refusing to read any more of the book. They preferred to get a bad grade than to let this filth be emptied over them.

What a judgment will one day hang over these ministries of education, school authorities, and teachers who poison our young people and tear down all the barriers of decency and good morals!

3. *Eschatological development.*

A saying of Lenin is often to be heard: "Interest the young in sex, and you will have them in your power." The communists put this advice into practice to effectively undermine the Western world. They are aiming at the schoolchildren and their teachers.

In the USA I read a report in which it was claimed that a list of six thousand teachers who are communists had been drawn up. In West Europe a similar alarming development may be observed. There may well be thousands of teachers in Italy, France, England and West Germany who take their red ideology with them into the classroom. I have many individual examples of this.

Undermining society or flooding it with sex is not, however, merely a ploy of the communists. Behind it stands the evil manipulator, Satan, whose aim is universal moral, physical, and intellectual world revolution.

He will not have the last word! Of that we can be sure.

47
PREDICTIVE DREAMS

The question of predictive dreams is one that must be handled with care. To avoid any misunderstanding, I will say at the outset that I believe all the dreams recorded in the Bible. These Biblical dreams, however, occurred in a different age from our own. In the days when Joseph dreamed and interpreted dreams in Egypt, there was as yet no written Word of God—apart from isolated records like the Book of Jashar. Again, the appearance of angels to Elizabeth, Mary, Joseph, and the three Wise Men was conditioned by the special saving events of their time.

Today we have the written Word of God, the Bible, as the guideline for our faith. The Bible contains all that we need for our salvation. We have no need of additional dreams, visions, or appearances.

This does not mean that God cannot reveal Himself by dreams to people in special situations today. This is true especially for primitive people who cannot read or write and are therefore unable to find guidance from the Bible. In the revivals of Indonesia, the Solomon Islands, Korea, and Formosa, dreams have sometimes been genuine revelations of God.

In other situations God sometimes shows people the way, or prepares them for important events ahead by means of dreams. I will give two examples.

Ex 179 Pastor Müller had invited me to preach the Gospel in Pelotas, Brazil. On the first evening there was a certain Catholic man in the congregation, who continued to come each day. On the Wednesday this man came to me for counseling and told me the following story:

Three weeks before these evangelistic meetings began, this gentleman had a dream. He saw a cross. Under it was a man who was preaching the Gospel in a foreign language. Then the man disappeared, and he heard the voice of Jesus saying: "I am the way, the truth, and the life." The dream ended there. During the next few days he forgot about the dream. Then, a week before the meetings were to start, someone pressed a handbill into his hand, inviting him to come.

The first evening, which was a Sunday, I spoke about spiritism. As he was not only a Catholic but also a spiritist, the subject interested him, and he came to listen. At the meeting his interest was further awakened, and he came again on the second and third evenings. Then he suddenly remembered his dream. "Of course—this is what I saw in my dream. A man preaching the Gospel in another language." On the morning he came to see me, he confessed his sins and gave his life over to Jesus.

Ex 180 When I was on a speaking tour in Quebec, I heard of another incident from my friend, Gottfried Amend. A thirteen-year-old boy named Roy was already a follower of Jesus. He was generally liked because of his happy personality. One morning he told his mother, "Last night I dreamed that I swam across a river and saw the Lord Jesus." The dream made a very deep impression on Roy, and he also told it to his pastor. "My heart was wide open for the Lord," he wrote, "and my tears flowed in streams. I looked again at Jesus, and as I did so I had the feeling that He had come to call me." Two weeks later, Roy drowned in a lake during a young people's outing from his church. Hardly anyone was able to feel sad about his death, which had been so clearly announced beforehand. The pastor read the boy's letter at the funeral. "Roy is much happier now," said his friends, "for he is with the Lord."

I have intentionally begun with two positive examples. Now we must say something against predictive dreams. Professor Carl Jung says that the great majority of our dreams are rooted in the collective unconscious, the family unconscious, and the individual unconscious. Further factors involved in the origin of dreams are childhood experiences, memories of the day, unfulfilled wishes, and so on.

I am sorry that Jung omits one important area, although he was familiar with it. I refer to dreams which are occult in origin. People who are under occult influence as a result of occult activities engaged in either by their forebears or themselves, often have dreams which are fulfilled a few days later. The dreams are often negative: disasters, deaths, train accidents, car accidents, fires, and visits of which they are afraid. Sometimes dreams of this sort provide a clue that a person is suffering from occult oppression. Anyone who has such experiences ought to ask God to take away this psychic gift of predictive dreams. This ability is a hindrance to the life of faith.

My only plea is that these psychic dreams are not confused with those which Jesus sometimes sends, as in the case of Roy, who was prepared for his death in this way by the Lord. Psychic dreams result in fear. Dreams sent by the Lord produce joy.

48
PROCESSEANS

This word means the people of progress. It is an English sect. Since this book will have a wider circulation in its English translation than in the original German, it is necessary to deal with the English sects. It is, in any case, a matter of experience that spiritual movements from England and America find their way into Europe also. Let us begin with an example from Germany.

Ex 181 Some years ago, I held two evangelistic campaigns in collaboration with my friend, Pastor Wilhelm Brauer, in Lübeck. I stayed at his home. One evening he told me the following story.

His sons had seen two men on Lübeck railway station dressed in long black robes. They thought the men must be Anglican priests or American Lutherans. So they said:

"Are you looking for somewhere to stay?"

"Yes, we are."

"Our father is a minister. We have open house. Come with us. We live quite near here."

The two men in black robes accepted the invitation gratefully. They were made welcome by brother Brauer. At the evening meal, however, Pastor Brauer was shocked. The two foreigners were both wearing a silver chain with a cross. But on their arms, each had a devil's symbol. Brauer asked his guests quite openly, "What is the meaning of those? Are you not pastors?"

"We are Processeans."

"What are they?" asked Pastor Brauer.

"We believe that Christ and the devil will be reconciled."

Brother Brauer became uneasy when he heard this. And rightly so. He resolved not to take in any more strangers without enquiry.

Let us look at how this sect operates. My information comes from England and Canada.

The Process Church was founded in London in 1963 by Robert de Grimston. Grimston travels all over the world teaching his doctrines. Wherever he goes, he founds groups. His teachings are to be found in the "Brethren Informations" (B.I.'s). The sect exists from donations. In 1966, a group of Process people arrived in Mexico. They had to leave the country because they ran out of money.

Today the sect has followers in Turkey, Israel, and Greece. The largest groups are found in England, the USA, and Canada. In Toronto, the Process people live at 99 Gloucester Street, in a commune which has strict rules. Their leader is brother Malachi.

The house and community rules of this commune include the following prohibitions: no alcohol, no drugs, no premarital sex, no possessions. These are rules similar to those in the old monastic orders. The highest rule of life is the so-called Golden Rule from Matthew 7:12, "Therefore all things whatsoever ye would that men should do to you, do ye even so to them." This rule given to us by Jesus is distorted, however, by what is added to it. They say: "If you want love, then first give love." This is quite acceptable. But they continue: "If you want hate, then you must hate." That is quite out of keeping with Biblical thought. Jesus said: "Bless those who curse you."

The movement is still further unmasked when one investigates the theology and practices of this sect.

The Processeans believe in three gods: Jehovah, Lucifer, and Satan. They ascribe to these gods the following attributes:

Jehovah is a self-righteous god, who thirsts for vengeance and demands only obedience, fulfilment of duty, and self-denial.

Lucifer is the god of joyful living. He allows men to enjoy life in all its aspects. He demands peace and harmony among men. *Satan* instigates all that is negative: orgies of cruelty and violence, intolerance, and excess. He wants to drive men to madness.

These doctrines mark out the Process Church as a church of Satan. The insignia and rites point in the same direction. I have already mentioned the silver pectoral cross. On the upper arm or on the collar, they wear the "Goat of Mendes," a symbol of Satan. On their altar they have two silver chalices, one for Christ and the other for Satan. The preacher always preaches his sermons under the symbol of Satan. He uses a substitute bible, which is full of sayings which are either distortions of Biblical texts or invented texts of their own.

In this counterfeit bible it says, for instance, Christ said, "Love your enemies." Satan is Jesus' worst enemy. In fulfilment of this love commandment, Jesus has become reconciled with Satan. At the last day they will appear together. Christ will pronounce the judgment. Satan will carry it out. The judgment will be made with wisdom. The carrying out of the sentence will be in love. Other strange statements are made about the activity of Jesus; for example, Jesus is the transcendent bringer of unity between the three gods. Thus, in the final consummation of human history, the end will be the harmony of all that happens and all that has been created. This idea is to be found in the cult of Mithras, three hundred years before Christ, and in Gnosticism, the heresy of the second century, and yet again in the teaching of universalism *(apokatastasis hapantōn).*

There is a grain of truth in the claim of the Processeans to be a church of the last days. The appearance of cults of Satan is indeed a prelude to the second coming of our Lord Jesus Christ. The Process Church also says that the end of the world will come in about the year 2000 A.D., amid massive catastrophes. But the Processeans have a certain fatalism in their approach to this expectation. When they meet, they greet one another with the words, "As it is." The answer is, "So be it."

We must not fail to add that this church engages in occult practices such as telepathy. All in all, the Process church is a church of Satan, but not one which has orgies like the satanic church of Anton la Vey, the black pope in San Francisco.

49
QUEEN OF DARKNESS—QUEEN OF BLACK WITCHES

On my missionary journeys, I have several times come into contact with former magicians and even their leaders in the course of counseling. I have told their stories in various books about my missionary travels. I will mention the relevant passages for the sake of those who would like to read them.

A report about the Sauguma cult in New Guinea is to be found in my book *Unter der Führung Jesu,* on page 224. The leaders of this cult still practice child sacrifice, and occasionally even sacrifice adults, in connection with cannibalism. The last example of this terrible practice known to me was the murder of fourteen people in West Irian, near Djajapura, in the autumn of 1974. Those willing to testify to the truth of this are Dr. Jackson, psychiatrist and theologian from Milwaukee, and Dr. Kenneth Moon of St. Petersburg, Florida.

My encounter with the chief magician, the so-called Country Devil of Liberia, turned into an experience of the triumph of Jesus over all dark powers. This chief magician confessed all his terrible sins and accepted Christ. The missionaries in that area had prepared the ground well.[33]

In Rio de Janeiro, I heard the story of a cult mother of the spiritist Macumba cult. Her name is Ottilia de Pontes. She has allowed me to publish her story.[34] Mrs. Pontes is today an evangelist who is richly blessed by the Lord in Brazil. Her photograph is to be seen in my missionary book *Jesus auf allen Kontinenten.*[35] The wonderful story of her salvation is recorded in the same book.[36]

In 1973 I gave a series of lectures on Haiti. This former French colony is the home of voodoo, a mixture of black magic and criminal spiritism. Here a Queen of Darkness is chosen each year, one of whose duties is to perform the fourteen-day child sacrifice. The missionaries gave me information of grisly details.

Now I want to give an example in detail from England. I should like to say at the outset that I have heard all the details contained in this dreadful report several times in other countries—in East Asia, Africa, and South America. If I had not, I should not believe this English account. The writer is Doreen Irvine, who has published her life story under the title *From Witchcraft to Christ.*[37] What we read in this book is so incredible that one can hardly grasp it, and yet it is fact.

What I shall do here is to present a shortened version of part of

Mrs. Irvine's story. She wrote:

> The practice of devil worship and my role as high priestess
> were the most important things in my life.
> Black witches have great power and arc not to be taken lightly.
> They are able to call up, or call down, powers of darkness to
> aid them.
> Very often they exhume fresh graves and offer the bodies in
> sacrifice to Satan. They break into churches, burn Bibles and
> prayer books. Wherever holy ground is desecrated, an emblem
> of witchcraft is left behind.
> Black witches and Satanists believe . . . that Lucifer will one
> day conquer Christ.
> Be warned: those who walk down the dark road of witchcraft
> lose their reason, often going completely insane.[38]

And she goes on to describe how witches and Satanists do unnatural
things. They dance in the nude, and indulge in sex orgies, lesbianism,
homosexuality, and sadistic and masochistic excesses. The more a member of a witches' coven gives herself to the devil, the more her occult
powers increase.

Doreen Irvine continues:

> My powers as a black witch were great, and I added to my
> knowledge of evil every day. My ability to levitate four or five
> feet was very real. It was not a hoax. Demons aided me.
> Killing birds in flight after they had been let loose from a cage
> was another act I performed as a witch. I could also make ob-
> jects appear and disappear. I also mastered apport, which is
> often used when witches demonstrate their powers before others.
> I was not surprised when the chief Satanist suggested that I
> advance in witchcraft. "You might even be queen of black witches
> one day, Diana." (Diana was her stage name.)
> "What, I?"
> "Yes! I'll submit your name. But keep practicing your powers
> so that you will be ready for the test."

The test of power to which the chief Satanist referred was to be
held on Dartmoor in Devon, the center of two large and active
covens.[39]

Mrs. Irvine met with her coven one clear, moonlit night at exactly

12 P.M. A coven consists of thirteen witches, including their leader. During their naked dance, three men suddenly appeared on the scene. The dancing women were frightened. There were no trees or rocks nearby behind which they could hide.

> "What shall we do?" asked the witches anxiously. "There's no place to hide!"
> "Don't worry," said Doreen, "I can make myself invisible."
> 'What about us?"
> 'If you put yourselves in my hands, I'll make you invisible, too."[40]
> There was no time to lose. Hastily, the others did as I told them. Standing perfectly still in a circle, we raised our hands so that they touched.
> I called up powers of darkness from demons and Satan himself. Within seconds, a green swirling mist enveloped us. We could scarcely see each other. As the three men passed us, I could easily have reached out my hand and touched them, one of whom had walked under our raised hands into the center of our circle.
> "Let's go home," we heard one of the men say "There are no witches here. We're wasting our time."
> The reason the three men appeared was explained when I read the local newspaper the next day. An article in the center pages was headlined: "No Witches on Dartmoor." It related that a local preacher had taken two reporters onto Dartmoor the previous evening to investigate a rumor that witches would be present there. The search had been fruitless, by all accounts. The local preacher, however, was not convinced that witches had not been on the moor. He was right, of course. Unawares, he had been within inches of them.[41]

We should take warning from this story that even believers can be deceived by the enemy. It is more probable in this instance, however, that the Lord was protecting the believing preacher in spite of the immediate presence of dark powers.

After this experience on Dartmoor, Doreen Irvine faced her greatest test. Together with six other witches she was told to demonstrate her occult powers. The one who was most successful of the seven would be Queen of Darkness. All seven were known for their great magical powers.

The competition began with the usual ceremonies, during which the demons and Lucifer were invoked.

The first test began when a bird was set free from its cage. Doreen was the only one who was able to kill the bird in the air.

One test followed another. Finally came the most difficult test of all: fire walking. I will again give the story in Doreen's own words:

> The test was to walk through a great bonfire [not a ring of fire, please note, but a great blaze]. The successful candidate would meet Lucifer in the center of the blaze, and Lucifer would be *seen* by the assembly to take the hand of the witch and guide her through the flames so that she would emerge completely unscathed.
>
> I walked confidently into the flames of seven feet or more, all the time calling on my great master, Diablos. Suddenly I saw him materialize before me—a great black figure. I took his hand and walked with him to the center of the great blaze. There I paused, the great flames leaping around me.
>
> Only when I emerged at the other side of the blaze did my master Diablos disappear. Not even the smell of burning was upon my loose witch's robe or my long, flowing hair.
>
> Everyone was prostrated on the ground.
>
> "Hail, Diana, queen of the black witches!" rose the loud cry of over a thousand witches.
>
> A crown of pure gold was placed on my head, a cloak beautifully embroidered with gold was thrown around my shoulders, and an orb of gold placed in my left hand. I took my seat on the throne, which had been prepared before the ceremony.
>
> One can laugh at legends of witchcraft when evidences of evil are not at hand or ever witnessed, yet had anyone been on the moor that night, he would not have laughed.[42]

The report would be incomplete if we were to mention only the dark side of Doreen's life. We are interested more in what Christ can do than in how Satan destroys people's lives.

The Lord had His eye on this woman, caught as she was in the bonds of witchcraft.

It was spring 1964. Doreen was walking the notorious streets of Bristol one night. She was pursuing the oldest profession in the world and waiting for customers. Then she read, on a church bulletin board, the Bible text "Blessed are the pure in heart, for they shall see God."

Pure in heart? See God? She tried to forget the impression these words had made. She could not. In a rage, she pulled the poster down. She went on to another street. The words she had read continued to come to her mind. There is no God, she tried to tell herself. A few days later, she had gotten over the shock.

Three months later the same thing happened again. Once more there were Christian posters on the church bulletin-boards, inviting people to meetings where Eric Hutchings was to speak.

Doreen asked a passer-by, "Who is this Eric Hutchings?" The woman had no idea. Then she saw some people going into a large hall, with Bibles in their hands. Doreen concluded that Eric Hutchings must be some sort of religious hyprocrite. She flew into a rage. *I will go and punch him on the nose,* she thought to herself. "Don't go. You belong to me," said another voice within her.

Yet she was strongly drawn to go into this hall, which was already packed with people. The usher found her a seat in the middle of the back row. She felt embarrassed, for all the people in the row had to stand up to let her in.

The meeting began with a lovely solo which captured Doreen's attention. She remembered her childhood, the time when she had learned children's prayers. She felt so dirty now.

Eric Hutchings began his sermon with the words: "If you do not know the Lord Jesus Christ as your personal Savior, you are lost. You are dead in trespasses and sins. The Bible says you are BOUND." Doreen jumped to her feet, forgetting all around her, and shouted: "He's right. I AM bound!" The crowd turned around to look at her. Even Hutchings was unable to speak for a moment. Then he continued: "If you go to church Sunday after Sunday and do not know the Lord Jesus Christ as your personal Savior, you too are lost." Doreen wanted to shout out again, but she was afraid to, because of all the people around her. Hutchings concluded his sermon with an appeal. "Come to Jesus tonight. Come out to the front." As people started coming forward, the choir sang "Just as I am, without one plea." Doreen trembled all over. She was resolved to go forward but was unable to. It was as if another power was tying her to the seat. Again she heard the voice, "You belong to me. You cannot go forward. It is too late for you. You belong to me."

A terrible struggle took place, a struggle with Satan. He tried to stop his victim. In this struggle Doreen suddenly became aware that another power was helping her, a power which was stronger than Satan's bonds. She jumped up and went forward. Satan lost the battle.

Doreen prayed: "I'm coming, Jesus. Please take the darkness away."
She could say no more. Prayer was so foreign to her.

Several counselors, among them Mrs. Hutchings, tried to help her.
After she had spoken with them, she left the hall with the Gospel of
John and a little book about the way of salvation.

On the next street corner she met her colleagues.

> "Hello, Diana," they chorused. "Where have you been? We've
> been looking for you."
>
> "I just was saved at Colston Hall," I answered them simply.
> They thought I was leading them on. They roared with laughter.
>
> "I'm not joking. I gave my heart to Jesus at Colston Hall."
>
> They stared in unbelief. "Come off it, Diana. It's us—your
> friends."
>
> "I'm perfectly well aware of that. But it's true. I'm going home
> now to read my Bible."[43]

It was extremely helpful to Doreen that she confessed her decision
to follow Jesus to her old friends immediately. It is very important
that after conversion we make our position clear at once. Those who
are afraid make a false start.

That, in short, is the story of Doreen's conversion. A woman who
had been bound to Satan by a thousand ties became a witness for
Jesus Christ.

No one need lose hope. Doreen was Queen of Black Witches and
a prostitute. She was freed from this hell by Jesus Christ, the Son
of God.

"He that committeth sin is of the devil; for the devil sinneth from
the beginning. For this purpose the Son of God was manifested, that
he might destroy the works of the devil" (1 John 3:8).

50
ROCK MUSIC

"What do you think of rock music?" I have often been asked this
question. I am always embarrassed by it, for I just do not understand
this music at all. If I accidentally come to hear it, I run, for this
music makes me feel ill.

I know from my travels in Africa and South America that this
kind of music is used in cultic dances. Primitive people dance themselves into a frenzy to such music, often ending in sexual orgies.

There is a kind of music which uplifts. Think for instance of the music of Johann Sebastian Bach. There is also a kind of music which destroys all that is good and drags people down. There is music which has divine inspiration, and music which has demonic inspiration. But that is a subjective judgment, as I said already. Everyone has the right to his own opinion.

Let us hear what an expert in this controversial subject has to say.

In the autumn of 1971, conferences took place in the states of Massachusetts, Maine, and New Hampshire. There were much-sought-after men addressing these gatherings. One of them was Jack Wyrtzen, who sometimes has as many as five thousand people in his congregation. My own addresses in twenty-three churches were given before and after these conference weeks.

During this time I met Bob Larsen. He was one of the speakers, probably the youngest and also one of the most popular. Let us consider his life.

Ex 182   Bob was a rock musician who later became an evangelist. He is a professional when it comes to discussing rock.

At the age of thirteen, Bob already had his own band. He became a young rock star. Rock radio stations constantly invited him to sing. Popularity and wealth came to this celebrated young musician in floods.

Then it all suddenly stopped. One evening the young man was free —not a frequent occurrence—and did not know what to do.

He felt sad; his conscience began to trouble him. In his loneliness and emptiness, he felt drawn to go into a small church. A psychologist would say: a typical adolescent mood which almost everyone experiences.

It was more than that. Bob's parents were Christians and prayed much for their *prodigal son*.

During the service, the Holy Spirit touched this young man. The poverty of his young life was brought before his eyes. Guilt, sin, and lack of peace weighed him down.

He gave his life to Jesus that same night. He made a radical break with his past. He dismissed his band. He put away the instrument of his success, his electric guitar. He did not even want to use it to sing spiritual songs. It did not seem appropriate. He wanted to have the chance to get away from it all.

In prayer Bob asked the Lord, "What shall I do now?" The way became plain. The next step was to study the Bible. In doing so, he came to see clearly what his next task was. He became a witness for Jesus, a preacher of the Gospel.

Having come to Christ from a life devoted to rock music, he felt led to try and reach the young rock fans for Christ. The radio stations were still open to him. He used these open doors. Right across the country, Bob Larsen spoke on all the radio networks about his conversion from rock music to Jesus Christ.

He made a most interesting discovery, which is really a sign of the times in which we live.

If Bob Larsen spoke in churches, he was attacked. People said, "You are exaggerating. Rock music can be used for the gospel, too."

"No," said Bob, "this music has a spirit which comes from dark and muddy waters. It can not be cleansed and used for the Holy Spirit."

When Bob Larsen spoke to the rock fans, he found that they agreed. They said, "You are on the right track. Go on as you are. We all feel something of the demonism of this music."

The discovery, in short, is that where the truth ought to be found, it is rejected. Where it is not expected, it is accepted.

This means nothing less than that a rock fan is nearer to the kingdom of God than some elders of the church. That is a present-day version of the words of Jesus, "The tax-gatherers and prostitutes go into the kingdom of God sooner than the hypocritical Pharisees."

So a former rock musician has set up a witness for the prodigal sons and daughters. None is too bad for Jesus. It is not too late for any of them. Jesus' mercy is open to all who seek him.

When I have been collecting material for my books, I have very often found that exactly the right information has come into my hands at the right time. This happened again as I have been writing this chapter. A brother from California has sent me some very enlightening information about rock music and has asked me to make use of his observations in this book. I will give the most important parts of his letter.

EX 183   The Bible tells us that, in the latter days, people will give heed to seducing spirits and the doctrines of demons. These demons are capable of finding people to speak through. Many rock musicians have allowed themselves to be used as the mouthpieces of demons.

In the popular music field, satanic influence is very strong. Some spirit-filled Christian scholars should look into the wording of these songs. These are not harmless love songs. They have subtle twists and turns that work death to the hearer of them. This is the music that turned a generation of teen-agers to drugs and sex.

1. *Titles and themes*

Even in the songs released for popular consumption over the air, one can see the following concepts:

> "falling into a burning ring of fire"
> "making a pact with the devil"
> "people with smiling faces that hide the evil that dwells within"
> "lost my soul in '68"
> "call on my name and I'll be there and grant your wish"
> Constant harping on the power of witchcraft, selling one's soul, that Jesus will torture "us when the time has come," that spells and incantations work;
> bragging that the Beatles are more popular than Jesus and that Christianity will melt into obscurity;
> "working towards a world with no religion";
> million dollar groups calling themselves by names such as *Black Sabbath* or *Covenant;*
> "the black snake that lives in a black hole, hiding from the sun—until the night comes"
> "we are our own saviors"
> "witches in the woods"
> "God of the morning"
> "we are coming up from below"
> "that the children are all out to get what they can, while their parents are home sleeping—they lost what they thought they were keeping."
> The word Heaven is always used sarcastically as a place where no one wants to go.

2. *Words with special meanings*

The inspiration behind the above wording is obvious, but also there are sets of words in which the meaning is far different from the commonly accepted meaning. It is as if these words constitute a code that is hidden to keep the real meaning from the uninitiated.

Rain—they seem terrified by it, they want someone to stop it. Some of the songs speak of drowning in it. Only the rock musicians understand what is meant by it.

Rainbow—promised to those who "hold out to the end," a rainbow at the end of the rain. They do not only sing about it. Rainbows are now popular hippie insignia and prominent on posters. Several huge groups of drug cultists, satanists, and a communist society in Wisconsin call themselves rainbow (people, family, tribe).

Sun—they hide from it, say that it can burn their eyes out, is something that is coming soon.

Mountain, California, car, winter, dark or shadow, thirty-eight pistol, door, and time are also words, that, if you look closely into the context in which they are used, you will see they don't even come close to the English meaning.

3. *Knowledge of facts in the Bible*

Rock music often displays recognition of Bible teachings, or distorts these into their opposites.

They speak of the impassible gulf fixed between Heaven and Hell as the ocean, a canyon, or wall, or a river wider than a mile (Luke 16:26). All of the songs infer that some day they hope to cross this barrier.

These songs infer that Hell is a place of torment and that soon they are "going home" if the "rain doesn't stop" (Matthew 13:40).

Following the father of lies, they openly deny that Christ is divine, saying "Jesus Christ, Superstar, are you really who you say you are?" This results in the destroying of the faith of millions of gullible people.

Bob Dylan, a major multi-millionaire musician, wrote a book called *Tarantula* that symbolically describes the destruction of hell (Revelation 20:10). He wrote it in the first person with himself in the role of Satan. The words in the book such as rain, sun, car, mountain, and all the rest have exactly the same meaning as they do in his songs.

Demons are very profitable to their holders (Acts 16:19). The amount of money gained is in the billions. The people deluded by them run into millions.

So much for this letter, which I have edited slightly and which told me things I had not known in detail.

In the meantime, rock music has already passed its peak. But the devil continues to produce new records in order to remain in business.

The "pop festivals" have pushed the rockers somewhat into the background. According to an English newspaper report, one pop festival drew about 270,000 young people. The police were unable to cope with the congestion and lawbreaking which took place.

In Ludwigsburg, it was quieter. I give the report as it appeared in the *Rhein-Neckar Zeitung* of August 16, 1975.

Ex 184 Twenty-five thousand pop music fans came. The great

Open Air Festival went off relatively quietly. One hundred-sixty people were engaged by the authorities to keep order. So, without violence and without excesses, the Ludwigsburg Open Air Festival went on stage at the weekend. These thousands of young pop fans came to the baroque town from every part of the Federal Republic. The invasion of young people was awaited by the town authorities with mixed feelings. Experience of similar spectacles elsewhere fully justified this skepticism: fights between spectators and attendants, orgies of drugs and alcohol, all these things had already caused some festivals to end in confusion. The concert organizers brought in attendants who had to be checked by the Ludwigsburg police to satisfy the local authority. "Rockers were not accepted," a public spokesman stated.

The effects of a festival which went off *quietly* are described in the same paper. One hundred and seventy-four people had to be helped because they had used too much alcohol or drugs, thirteen young people were admitted to hospital and twenty-five visitors to the Festival were taken into custody for offenses against the drug laws.

What must it be like at other festivals if this was a quiet one?

51
ROD AND PENDULUM

The material I have collected about the rod and the pendulum over the last forty-five years is so extensive that I could write a large volume of sensational stories involving them. Here I can only outline some of the problems.

1. *The instrument used*

Diviners normally use a forked willow twig, although some use a rod of fishbone or one of steel. There are some diviners who use no instrument at all, but simply spread out their fingers to detect the *earth rays*. Others use a pendulum, that is, a metal weight attached to a thread. Since the rod and pendulum belong to the same sphere of operations, the societies of water diviners and pendulum users have been emalgamated to form the Society of Radiaesthesia. Years ago I met the president of this society. He comes from Hamburg and works not only with rod and pendulum, but also approves of and does magic charming. He told me this, when we met at a conference.

2. *The confusion of spirits*

Even believing Christians are divided on the question of what they should think of rod and pendulum. I have met doctors, pastors, missionaries, and even evangelists who use the rod or pendulum and believe they have received this gift from God. Satan's cunning is very evident here, when even believing Christians are deceived by him. I will give an example.

Ex 185 While I was taking part in an evangelistic campaign in France, the local pastor asked me to talk on the subject of rod and pendulum. Many of his church members practiced these occult area arts. After my address, one of the pastors who had been listening asked if he might speak. I first asked the local pastor if he would agree to this; for I have often found that, those who practice the occult will come up on to the platform and say exactly the opposite to what I have been saying. "You must let him speak," whispered the pastor to me. "He is our dean; he is over me." The dean turned to the congregation and said: "You all know me. I have to confess that for twenty-five years I have used the pendulum to find out hidden things. Whenever I had questions I could not answer, I consulted the pendulum. I have used it to serve my church. Now I have come to see that the use of the pendulum is *not* a gift of God but is a gift from below. I must repent of it, and I ask you all to forgive me."

This example shows that a minister who was regarded in the whole surrounding area as a believer, in fact, practiced magic for twenty-five years, and so brought occult influence upon his church. He experienced more serious consequences in his own life, which I will not detail here.

3. *History*

After this short introduction, an equally brief look at the use of rod and pendulum in the history of mankind. Some of the oldest findings of this magic are probably the cave drawings in the Orange Free State, South Africa. The archaeologists reckon these cave drawings, which feature the so-called wishing wand, to be more than six thousand years old.

We also find the rod in the Chinese culture of over four thousand years ago. In those days, the rod was used to look for water and also to check building sites to make sure they were not over underground watercourses. The rod is also found among the ancient Greeks. The poet, Homer, mentioned it. The Romans, too, used rod and pendulum. The entire history of Europe over the last two thousand years indicates a widespread use of rod and pendulum. It is a depressing thing for me to hear that a theologian who has the reputation of being a believer approves the use of rod and pendulum and believes that it is a gift of God. Such an opinion can only be formed out of a lack of pastoral experience and ignorance of the serious consequences.

4. *Geophysics*

Rod diviners and pendulum users maintain that the reaction of the rod or pendulum is caused by what they call earth rays. Earth rays of this sort are not known to science. There are, however, other physical factors which could be adduced in explanation of the earth rays. Our earth possesses an electromagnetic field; hence the compass needles will point towards the magnetic North Pole. The earth's magnetic field is not uniform: that is, it is not equally strong everywhere, but has fields of interference. These fields of interference are caused by geological faults, caves, underground streams, mineral deposits, salt, oil, iron, and the like. They can be measured. There is a whole range of instruments which can be used to measure these interference centers: the magnetometer, the double compass, the Askania scales, the VHF probe, the gerameter. The best instrument is the proton resonance magnetometer. Experiments have already been conducted with experienced diviners to see whether they can locate these fields of interference with the rod or pendulum. Some of the diviners were able to do so. This result, however, does not mean that, from a Christian point of view, one can accept the activity of the rod and pendulum practitioners. This will become even clearer from the next section.

5. *The psychic factor*

Rod diviners maintain that people are in danger if their place of work or their bed is situated in a spot where there are earth rays. They usually advise people to move their desk or bed to another place, or to ward off the danger by means of a *de-radiation box*. I have been able to examine a large number of these de-radiation boxes. The whole thing is a colossal humbug. I have not the time to describe this de-radiation apparatus here.

If the interference centers of the earth's magnetic field can have a negative influence on people, the use of precise measuring instruments is not out of place. But under no circumstances should psychic powers be used to test such centers of interference.

The question arises as to whether these fields of interference really do have an influence on people. Animal experiments have shown that ants, cats, and bees seek out these centers and like them. Domestic animals avoid them if possible. In the case of human beings, it is only those who are of psychic disposition or who have a weak and sensitive nervous system who react to them. If such a sensitivity to interference fields is found in a person, it is proper to use one of the above-mentioned scientific instruments to measure the power of the field. The use of rod or pendulum in this connection is something I totally reject.

It may be held against me that years ago I was not so radical in my views as I am now. There is a reason for this. In 1953, my first book, *Christian Counselling and Occultism,* was published. When I wrote it, I had only six hundred examples of occult experiences. Over the years, more and more of my books attacking occultism have been published. The result is that I have been much in demand for counseling all over the world. In the twenty-four years since, I have advised about twenty thousand people, either in personal conversation or by mail. Among these there were perhaps ten or eleven thousand who have had dealings with the occult.

We still do not know what we should understand by the psychic factor. There is not sufficient space here for an exhaustive discussion. I will make only some marginal comments. Psychic powers are mostly found in proximity to sins of sorcery. If the forefathers up to the third or even fourth generation were spiritists or if they practiced magic and other forms of occult activity, the descendants are usually psychic. Psychic powers may be either conscious or unknown. Some people are psychic without realizing it. Others come to realize that they are psychic through some particular experience. Sensitivity to the rod and ability to make a pendulum react are psychic powers. I have investigated the family histories of many people who have a psychic disposition. The gift of using the rod or discovering secret things by means of the pendulum can be acquired in three ways: by heredity, by transference from a powerful worker with the occult, or by experimenting with magic formulas as described in occult books. The question of whether there is such a thing as psychic powers which are neutral has often been discussed. If a Christian discovers he has a psychic disposition, he should ask God to take it away. The idea of some theologians that psychic powers can be purified and then used in the service of God's kingdom is unscriptural. This is shown by the story of the fortuneteller of Philippi in Acts 16:16-18. If a Christian uses psychic powers, he is committing sin and is in need of forgiveness.

6. *Counseling*

I will give two examples concerning doctors, which demonstrate that one cannot play with psychic powers.

Ex 186   A doctor came to me for pastoral advice. He said he had been using the pendulum in his work for two years. He was able to find out many hidden things with its aid. If someone gave him a photo of a person, he was able with the pendulum to give precise details as to the person's name, address, occupation and all other data about his life. He could even predict future events precisely with his pendulum. The doctor was troubled about these powers. He also noticed some character changes for the worse taking place in himself. He became a strong alcoholic and a chain smoker, smoking up to eighty cigarettes each day. He also went off the rails in other respects and became totally degenerate. He was afraid that he might end up in a mental institution. He came to me for counseling and confessed all the evils of his life. I showed him the way to Jesus. It was very hard for him to become free of his psychic gift. We had four sessions together. A prayer group was formed, which prayed for him for about four months, until he became completely free. Such a strong psychic disposition is, of course, rare. But here one can see the gift in its mature form, where the consequences can be clearly studied and seen.

Ex 187 During a series of talks I was giving in a certain town, I became ill and asked for the name of a Christian doctor. One was recommended with whom I made an appointment. When I entered his consulting room, I saw a pendulum hanging on the wall. When I asked him if he used this pendulum in his work, he replied that he used it to give an additional diagnosis. I ought to mention that this was not a mere healer, but a properly qualified doctor. After he had said this, I told him that I could not use his services as a doctor, since I would have nothing to do with pendulum practice. He was astonished. I explained why I felt this way. At the same time, I prayed inwardly that God would open his eyes. Then I had the idea of seeking God's judgment on the matter. I must emphasize that this is the only occasion in my life that I have done this. I said to him: "You may use your pendulum on me." He took the instrument in his hand, but it would not work. He looked at me in amazement and said: "You are the first person with whom the pendulum has not worked." I prayed on, rejoicing that God was at work already. He made me stand in two other parts of his consulting room. The pendulum did not move. The doctor asked me: "What have you done? What sort of a person are you?" "I believe in Jesus Christ," I replied, "and I am convinced that psychic powers come from below, and that we should not make use of them. That includes the use of the pendulum." I admitted that I had prayed for God to make His

will known and for God to open his eyes. The doctor replied that
he accepted this. "If you can stop the pendulum by prayer, then
it is not natural power that lies behind the pendulum; it must be a
power opposed to God." The doctor kept his promise. He has never
since used the pendulum.

I advise no one to do as I did. I have only done it once in my
life, and then because the Lord gave me an inner peace about it, in
order to open the eyes of this doctor.

Powers that can be disturbed by prayer are not physical powers.
Perhaps that may be underlined by reference to another example.

Ex 188   This is the experience of a friend of mine in France,
whom I've known for many years. He happened to go into the house
of a friend just as a water-diviner was there looking for water. My
friend was troubled by this, and he went into a room in the house,
threw himself down on his knees and cried to God: "Lord, if these
powers are not from You, then stop them." Suddenly he heard the
dowser outside cursing and swearing. "I had just found a strong
watercourse here," he said. "Why can't I find it any longer?" To
the man praying inside this was God's answer.

In the final chapter of this book, *In the Conqueror's Train*, another
account is given of how a missionary was freed from the gifts and
the evil influence of dowsing.

7. *Dowsing unmasked*

The occult character of rod and pendulum divining is revealed
quite plainly by the following incident. I was present as an observer
and critical participant at a conference attended by some sixty dowsers
from various countries. A Swiss pendulum user said he did not need
to go over the area itself with a rod or pendulum in order to find
water or underground treasures. It was enough for him to be given
a map: he would then locate the treasures on the map. He even gave
us an example: he was able to use his pendulum on a map of Japan
to locate water, oil, salt, and other minerals. This map of Japan was
perhaps printed in Switzerland, with paper and printing ink also
produced in Switzerland. The map of Japan could never reproduce
earth impulses from Japan. Here the map is merely a kind of contact bridge the dowser uses to feel his way into the nature of the
earth's surface in Japan. This is, in other words, quite clearly an
instance of occult activity. Dowsers call it *telesthesia*, perception at
a distance. They distinguish physical dowsing, in which the dowser
must walk over the ground himself, from mental dowsing, in which
the rod or pendulum diviner requires only a sketch or map of the

area in question. It is almost unbelievable that the theologian who chaired this conference regarded all these powers as natural gifts of God. He was quite sure, of course, of the approbation of the dowsers. Only two of those present protested: the French doctor, Arthur Bach, from Nancy, and myself. To cheers from the rod and pendulum dowsers we were reproved with angry words by the presiding Professor of Theology.

To conclude the whole chapter, I include an excellent report which I found in the *San Francisco Chronicle* of January 6, 1976. The article, which is a kind of confession, is signed by a believing man called John Price. I take this opportunity of thanking him for his clear and courageous testimony. These are his words:

> I was a dowser. This gift is passed on in families by the laws of genetics. Edgard Cayce's grandfather was an old magician, who had the power to make a broom dance around his room. He was often travelling to search for water with his rod.
>
> The ability to work with a rod or pendulum can also be easily passed on. An old dowser who guides the hand of a young, psychic person can pass on this gift. The effect is seen immediately, and a new magician is born. That is the way that I got involved in these things. My own father passed the ability on to me. Since then I have travelled much, searching for water and passing on my ability to others.
>
> Divining with the rod is mentioned in the Bible also, in Hosea 4:12. The Hebrew word for *staff* in the King James Version means a wandering rod cut out of a forked branch. The prophet Hosea warned the people of Israel against this magical practice.
>
> Five years ago I began to read the Bible with my wife, who is a Christian. The result was that I was converted and found Christ. I submitted to believers' baptism by total immersion. From that day onward, my various divining rods have been dumb. They do not work any more.

I am extremely grateful for this report, because it confirms my own observations: sensitivity to the rod by heredity and transference, liberation by turning to Christ. The mention of Cayce's grandfather, who was a sorcerer, also sheds further light on Cayce, whose story is also in this book.

52
ROSICRUCIANS

The Rosicrucians call themselves a brotherhood order. The full name of this order is *Antiquus Mysticus Ordo Rosae Crucis*. This Latin name means "ancient mystic order of the rose-cross." The headquarters of the International Brotherhood is in San Jose, California.

A colorful, glittering picture is presented of the Rosicrucians by their own account of the movement. The order claims to have its roots in the mystical schools of Egypt at the time of Pharaoh Amenophis IV (1350 B.C.). They also claim to have been active in Israel at the time of Moses. They say that they helped with the construction of Solomon's temple.

The symbol of the Rosicrucians is a cross with a rose. The significance of these is explained in *Essay 17,* published by the German Grand Lodge in Baden-Baden: "The cross symbolizes the human body with arms outstretched in greeting to the rising sun. The rose in the middle of the cross signifies the soul of man. Rosicrucians attach this leitmotiv to the symbol: *Ad rosam per crucem, ad crucem per rosam* (To the rose through the cross, to the cross through the rose)."

In their doctrines, the Rosicrucians are eager to keep themselves free from all racial, political, or religious attachment.

What does the order teach? A pamphlet published in Baden-Baden gives the following answer. "The order teaches a system of metaphysical and scientific philosophy aimed at awaking the latent powers of man, so that a person can make better use of his natural talents and lead a happier and more useful life."

An illuminating introduction to the order is given in the brochure *Meisterung des Lebens* (Mastery of Life). This booklet is published by the Grand Lodge and naturally does not provide an objective picture.

What do unbiased historians have to say about the Rosicrucians? The alleged connection with the Egyptian secret societies has yet to be proved, let alone that with Moses and Solomon.

The earliest evidence we have of the order is the appearance of two writings at the beginning of the seventeenth century. These are the *Fama Fraternitatis* (1604) and the *Confessio Fraternitatis* (1614), or *Tradition of the Brotherhood,* and *Confession of the Brotherhood.* These publications are ascribed by Rosicrucians to Francis Bacon.

There is no evidence for this. Historians have other opinions about the authorship.

The *Reader's Digest Encyclopaedia* briefly describes the Rosicrucians as a secret theosophical society from the sixteenth century.

The shorter *Brockhaus* dictionary calls the Rosicrucians "members of secret societies of the seventeenth and eighteenth centuries. The order of German Gold- and Rosicrucians, founded about 1760 in South Germany, was a masonic order."

The RGG, *Religion in Geschichte und Gegenwart,* has the following comment, "The Gold- and Rosicrucians can be traced as a mystic federation, with a basis in magic, cabbalism, and alchemy, from 1757. Newly organized in 1767 and 1777, they developed effective propaganda in the masonic movement."[44]

For the Christian who would order his life in accordance with the Bible, these comments speak for themselves. The brochure *Meisterung des Lebens* gives us further information as well. The following quotation is given from Albert Magnus: "Do not seek too eagerly for the grace of surrender or for tearful endurance. Let it rather be your first duty to remain inwardly united with God by good will in the thinking part of your soul."[45]

Before we can remain united with God, the bond of unity must first be established. That has been done by Jesus Christ on the cross. We experience it when we accept Jesus Christ as our Savior and Lord. By our own good will we can neither become united with God nor remain united with Him.

Things are made even clearer elsewhere in the booklet. The page is entitled: "The secret world within us. Abilities which we know of and ought to use."[46]

What abilities are these?

1. "By touching letters and other objects we can become the recipients of painful messages." This is psychometry, a form of extrasensory perception.

2. "Thoughts or sense-impressions can be transmitted at a distance." This is an occult form of mental suggestion.

3. "Our consciousness can suddenly see far-off places and events." This is clairvoyance by means of psychic powers.

4. "Some people reveal their true character by magnetic radiation." This is the spiritists' idea of the so-called "aura."

In this booklet *Meisterung des Lebens,* therefore, the order of Rosicrucians encourages its members to take up psychic and occult practices. This makes the situation clear.

A Christian who has experienced a new birth through the Holy Spirit will suffer spiritual harm if he belongs to this order. It will not harm a nominal Christian. He will not notice the bondage he is under until he wants to give his life to Christ.

53
SATAN WORSHIP

The liberal theologian Röhr (1777-1848) described belief in the devil as a pitiful delusion belonging to an unenlightened era. Adolf Schlatter, a theologian who based his views on the Bible and whom I had the privilege of hearing while I was at Tübingen, declared that the message of the Bible includes belief in the devil. Here we see both an unscriptural and a Scriptural doctrine.

Let us look at another starting point for the discussion of belief in Satan and Satan worship.

In October 1975, I read in a Bavarian Catholic newspaper a statement of Pope Paul VI, which made my hackles rise. According to this newspaper report, the Pope had declared that Lutheranism was responsible for the tragic state of Europe. It is easy to prove the contrary. We only need look at Italy, where Lutheranism was unable to gain a foothold. If the Pope is right, Italy ought to be the best developed country in Europe. In fact she is economically the weakest country in Europe, torn apart by many strikes and political struggles. On the other hand, the countries which since the Reformation have adopted Protestantism like Sweden, Germany, Switzerland, and England have a much more stable economy. Part of the taxes of Lutherans in Germany flow into Italy as EEC subsidies, and not vice versa.

Another report from the Vatican has reconciled me to at least a small degree with the Pope. This report, dated November 15, 1972, describes how, for the first time, the Pope devoted an entire address to the subject of Satanic cults. He mentioned that even in Italy, Satanists were celebrating the black mass and breaking into churches. For example, they ransacked the cathedral of Turin where the so-called shroud of Jesus is kept. The Pope then said, "We are all standing under a dark lordship, the lordship of the devil, who is the prince of this world." In the same address he took the problem a step further, saying, "I regret the fact that other Christian theologians show little interest in the study of Satanic movements. Many seek an alternative in the study of psychoanalysis and psychiatry, and even spiritism, studies which sadly are widespread in every country, near and far, today." Later in the same talk the Pope exclaimed: "The devil lives."

In the Bible and in the history of religions, Satan worship is often identified with the snake cult. This goes back to the original temptation in Paradise, where the devil appeared to the first man and woman in the form of a snake. The inhabitants of the land of Canaan worshipped Satan in the form of a snake. We find the same thing in Egypt. The magicians who withstood Moses belonged to the snake cult. They were able to hypnotize snakes so that they became stiff like a stick. These sorcerers were able to do the opposite miracle to that of Moses. Moses could, by God's power, change his rod into a snake. The sorcerers could, by Satan's power, turn snakes into rods, and then bring them back out of the hypnotic state.

Several centuries before Christ, the Ophite cult began in Syria. The Ophites were snake and Satan worshippers. They called themselves Gnostics, possessors of a higher wisdom. In some points, the Gnostics held the same views as those held today by universalists. The Ophites believed that after death, man has the chance of developing upward over long periods of time, until he reaches complete salvation. In holding this conviction, they are following the prophecy of Satan, when he said to Eve: "You will not die, but your eyes will be opened."

Another snake cult is mentioned in the Old Testament, in the form of the brazen serpent. In Numbers 21, Moses is commanded by God to set up a brazen serpent. The Israelites, who had been bitten by poisonous snakes, were to look toward the brazen serpent in faith, and those who did so remained alive. This brazen serpent was given, then, by God as a symbol of salvation. We may compare John 3, where the crucifixion of Jesus is likewise said to be a sign of salvation lifted high. But what God gave the people of Israel in those days as a symbol of salvation became, in later centuries, a form of idolatry. The snake was called Nehushtan, and was used by the Israelites some four to five hundred years after the time of Moses for magic and idolatry.

The history of the Christian church is full of Satanic and snake cults. It would take too long to go through them all. I refer the reader to a helpful English book on the subject by Tatford, called *Satan, the Prince of Darkness*.[55] The book is recommended because it is written from a good, Scriptural standpoint, but also because it contains a good knowledge of the history of religion.

Now I will give some examples.

Ex 189   It has been said of the Knights Templar that they were the founders of a regular church of Satan. Those who wished to join this order were required to tread underfoot a cross lying on the ground and to spit on it. Not only this, but they had to sign themselves over to the devil with their blood. The King of France ordered the Templars to be pursued and arrested in 1307 and 1311. Under torture there were of course some confessions made which did not correspond remotely to the truth. French historians like Abbé Barnuel maintain that the French revolution was carefully and methodically prepared by these Templars.

In the circles of the Templars, the black mass was celebrated. Everything which we hold holy on Biblical grounds was dragged in the dirt by them. On the altar they had a naked woman. They mixed the communion wine with the blood of a slaughtered child. They altered the prayers, substituting the name of Satan for that of God. All these are things which we know also in the present-day churches of Satan. The rites of the Satan worshippers were carried by some of them from Paris to the USA, and thence to Rome and other lands.

There is not only a French line of devil cults, there is also a German line.

Ex 190   In the thirteenth century, a Friesian clan with the name of Stedinger was notorious for its Satanic ceremonies. The Stedingers were renowned for every form of sorcery and ungodliness. They plundered churches, desecrated the sacraments and crucifixes. They shed innocent blood. They killed, and indulged in all manner of orgies. They even rebelled against the authorities, so that in 1234, the Duke of Brabant had to go to war against them. He killed 8,000 of them, and the rest were scattered. The surviving members of this clan took their occult arts with them all over the country, and the problem became even worse than before.

A third type of Satanic cult was found in Great Britain. The Druids, priests of an ancient Celtic tribe, were highly renowned for their knowledge of astronomy. Besides this, they practiced human and animal sacrifice in order to reconcile sinful man to God. I have already mentioned this in the section on Halloween. The history of the Druids is reckoned to have extended from 1900 B.C. to about A.D. 500 or 600. Some scholars connect the great ruined monument at Stonehenge with the Druids. Stonehenge is in the south of England, north of Salisbury. I heard from an English friend that groups of devil worshippers have continued in Cornwall to this day.

On the mission field I have again met various kinds of snake cult. Two examples follow:

Ex 191   In Nigeria there is the cobra cult. I was told about this by a missionary. People who join the cobra cult must sign their soul over to the devil. As a reward, they receive power over cobras. The cobras obey the members of the cult. On one occasion a sorcerer, who was my informant's bitterest enemy, sent a cobra to this missionary with the commission to kill him. The missionary realized the danger, put himself under the protection of Jesus, and commanded the snake in the name of the Lord. The snake could do nothing to harm him. This is another example of how God protects His children.

Ex 192   While I was staying with a Christian district governor, who had been educated in Europe, he told me of a similar snake cult in Liberia. The members have to sign themselves over to the devil, and then they receive power over all snakes, not just one sort. If a member of the cult wishes to kill an enemy, he sends a dangerous, poisonous snake with the commission to bite that person.

A young man who belonged to this snake cult found Christ through the ministry of missionaries of the Sudan Interior Mission. The young man renounced the cult in the name of Jesus and became free from this Satanic bondage. One day, just as he was entering a house, he saw a large black snake in the room. He cried out, for he knew that as a result of his conversion he had lost his power over the snakes. He remembered Christ's gift of power over snakes promised in Mark 16 and commanded the snake in the name of Jesus. The snake was unable to harm him.

Here we see again that Satan's power is kept within bounds by the faith of disciples of Jesus Christ and by the exalted Lord himself.

Ex 193   In the USA, I have several times encountered a snake cult of a different kind. During a lecture tour in Colorado, I heard of a tragic incident in a Pentecostal church. Two young preachers had brought poisonous snakes with them into a service. They read verses from Mark 16, where it says that by faith they will pick up serpents, and if they drink any deadly thing, it will not hurt them. Then they put the poisonous snakes around their necks, played with them, and were bitten by them. In spite of their sincere faith, both pastors died. The police heard of the incident and removed the poisonous snakes from the church.

I heard of the same thing again while touring the states of New England in the Northeast of the USA. Here too a pastor, acting on the basis of Mark 16:18, put a poisonous snake around his neck. He also died from the poisonous bite.

I heard a similar story once again in the state of Illinois. These last three examples have of course nothing to do with the snake cults and cults of Satan. They are merely the expression of a religious fanaticism and a false interpretation of the Bible. In a similar situation Jesus said: "Thou shalt not tempt the Lord thy God" (Matthew 4:7).

I return now to the subject of real Satan worship. Human and animal sacrifices, which were practiced by the ancient pagan peoples, are being practiced today by those who worship Satan.

Ex 194   I have already mentioned in another context the story of seventeen-year-old Ross Cochran. He was originally a member of a church of Satan. He found Christ and left the church of Satan. Subsequently he was tortured to death by his former friends. The chief instigator of his murder was another seventeen-year-old, Otis Hester. When he was arrested, he showed the policeman a tattoo on his left hand which depicted a cross upside down with the words "His Majesty the Devil."

Ex 195   Another example is even more horrifying. A young couple was asked by an American family to come and baby-sit. When the parents came home, they found that the young couple, who belonged to a Satanic cult, had roasted the baby on a gridiron. The horrified parents had entrusted their child to two "young devils."

Some dreadful developments have taken place in America. About twelve years ago, the Bible and prayers were banned in the public schools. Instead, teaching about spiritism, the occult, and Satanic cults have crept into the school curriculum. Recently there has been discussion in one or two of the states as to whether it is sufficient to have teaching about Satanic things, and whether one ought not to include the practice of them as well.

I was present when a discussion of this sort was taking place in New Hampshire. I was invited by a senator to say something about my experiences in the USA. The senators had met to discuss whether, in addition to the already existing teaching about Satanic practices, actual experiments in spiritism and magic ought not to be conducted in school. I told them some terrible examples from my own experience involving American seminaries and colleges, which so impressed the senators that they refused this application for the introduction of practical experiments.

Tanat Cult

When visiting England: Cornwall, Devon, Somerset, and Dorset, in this itinerant ministry I heard of the Tanat cult. This has its origin in a pre-Christian fertility cult. The sun was regarded as male, the moon as female. The cult symbols were accordingly a penis (for the sun) and a vagina (for the moon). The signs are bread and salt. In the ceremonies of the Tanat cult, bread and salt are placed on the body of a woman. The woman lies on the table clad in a red robe. She is only partially dressed. Behind the altar are again the symbols of the male and female principles.

When the first Christian missionaries came to England, and the people had only been partly Christianized; the Tanat cult developed into what is known as the black mass. This is celebrated to this day, not only in England but all over the world. The black mass is conducted in a form similar to that of the pre-Christian Tanat cult. The Lord's Supper is enacted in a manner too horrible to be described here. The black mass is, needless to say, accompanied by sexual orgies.

In these four counties there are still many Tanatists. The Christian mission has never reached the whole population.

Horned God Cult

The Horned God Cult has its headquarters in London and is a splinter group of the Satan cult. Every member has a horned god at home. This horned god has its arms outstretched, like Jesus on the cross. The feet are fashioned like a snake. In another chapter, mention has been made of the "goat of Mendes." This goat's head is the symbol of Satan. The Horned God Cult is thus a form of Satan worship.

In the museum of magical objects, in Boughton-on-the-Water, one can see not only the symbols of the Horned God Cult but also a reconstructed altar of the Tanat cult.

On the question of *deliverance* from Satanic cults, I would refer the reader to the testimony of David Hansen in the final chapter. I also recommend the book *Satan's Seller* by Mike Warnke. The author was himself a high priest in the church of Satan and was freed by Christ. He has written his testimony in this book.

A wonderful example of deliverance from the power of Satan is given by Ernest H. Nickerson in his excellent paper "The Path of Life." His article is entitled "A Former Satanist Is Now a Preacher of the Gospel."

Hershel Smith joined the Satanists as a schoolboy. At the age of thirteen he skinned a small dog alive and drank its blood. Later, he developed a sadistic penchant for eating skin peeled off from the

fingers and feet of other people who would let him. He became known
as the *skin eater*. He did many other absurd things out of his love
for Satan. This made him a marked man in Satanist circles, and Hershel
had a successful career in such circles. Finally he became high priest,
practicing everything that goes with the worship and veneration of
Satan.

Yet this man, bound to Satan by a thousand chains, was rescued
from his downward path by the victor of Calvary. Hershel Smith became a disciple of Christ. Today he feels a special responsibility
towards young people who have gone astray as he did. He supports
and runs a youth center in California, where he shows young people
the way to Jesus, who can free them.

54
SCIENTOLOGY

Scientology is a movement of American origin that has spread to
English-speaking areas of every continent. It is difficult to define what
this word is supposed to mean: literally it is *the knowledge of sciences*.
It does not appear in the dictionary.

The founder of this strange movement is Dr. Ronald Hubbard,
who was born in Tidden, Nebraska, USA, in 1911. He holds a doctor
of philosophy degree from Lafayette, a dubious center of learning
which is recognized by no college. He has written a very great deal.
He claims to have written about ten million words. That would mean
one hundred books of three hundred pages each.

Hubbard has been married three times, has seven children, and now
lives about thirty miles south of London, at Saint Hill Manor.

His movement has grown rapidly. It can be found in the great
cities of Europe. Scientists take no notice of Hubbard.

Hubbard has twice come into the limelight. In 1950 he published
a book entitled *Dianetics: The Modern Science of Mental Health*. Hubbard's system is reminiscent of psychoanalysis, although specialists in
psychotherapy do not even take the trouble to try out his methods.
The key word used by Hubbard in his healing practice is *reliving*. The
treatment takes this form. The patient takes two electrodes in his
hands. A meter, which Hubbard calls an *E-meter*, is connected between them. Then a question and answer session begins. If the therapist
finds a problem which the patient has not yet mastered, the meter
needle jumps, due to the increase in mental tension. The therapist then
continues to talk about this difficult subject until the meter returns to

normal. The patient is then regarded as cured. This is a method which in some ways resembles that used in electro-acupuncture.

The book *Dianetics* became a best seller in 1950 and earned Hubbard a lot of money. His short courses of treatment are also a gold mine. A course of twenty-five sessions brings in $800. A millionaire in Florida even paid $28,000 for his course of treatment, according to a police report.

Not only the general public, but also the authorities have been taking an increasing interest in him. In 1963 the police, acting on a court order, searched his headquarters in Washington. One hundred E-meters and various books of his were confiscated. The investigation revealed that Hubbard treated every kind of disease: mental disorders, neuroses, cancer, polio, and many others. Another discovery was that even the diagnoses were not true. These painful investigations were no doubt the reason Hubbard left the USA and moved to England. Since then Hubbard has changed the name of his movement. He gave up the name *Dianetics* and now calls it *Scientology*. In order to make a greater impact and to create open doors, he declared that Scientology is a religion. This gave his *ministers* entry to hospitals, prisons, and public institutions.

The sort of people the Scientologists are is clear from a letter which has been published. The history of the letter is as follows. A young man was being treated by a Scientologist in New York. The bill came to $350. The young man refused to pay because the treatment had been unsuccessful. He then received a letter headed The Founding Church of Scientology and bearing the signature of a Rev. S. Andrew Bagley, Organization Secretary. "If you want to start a donnybrook, buddy, wail away," the letter said. "To use the argot of the streets, I'll just start my people to work on you, and then before long you will be broke and out of a job, and broken in health. Then I can have my nasty little chuckle about you. . . . You won't take long to finish off. I would estimate three weeks. Remember: I am not a mealy-mouthed, psalm-canting preacher. I am a minister of the Church of Scientology! I am able to heal the sick and I do. But I have other abilities, which include a knowledge of men's minds, that I will use to crush you to your knees."

After receiving this letter the young man paid his bill at once. One cannot help being reminded by this letter of what Mary Baker Eddy called *malpractice*. It is a case of occult powers being employed to bring harm to people.

I am well aware that this organization could take me to court, and I therefore look after this letter very carefully.

What has this brutality to do with the spirit of Jesus Christ? Is it not a strategem of the archenemy, that people would rather be deceived than receive through Christ a peace which passes all understanding?

On December 15, 1975, the West German Third Television program carried a feature on Scientology. In this program it was stated that the movement has ten million followers altogether in the world. There are ten thousand in Germany. Scientologists believe in the excursion of the soul. Their aim here on earth is a life without mental illness and without war. With good will, all denominations can find unity. A preliminary stage in the purification process, leading up to the excursion of the soul, is the earthly aim of becoming a person free of complexes. Their program to achieve this can be carried out by a correspondence course. All courses together cost $6,000.

In this television program, a young man appeared who had belonged to the scientologists and had then left the movement. His reason: "They did not keep their promises, therefore I left them." After leaving the movement, he received a letter informing him that if he came back he would have to go through all the courses again, at a cost of $4,000. If he did not come back, he owed $1,900 for services rendered.

After him came a *priest* of Scientology, who said: "We receive no church tax, so we have to ask for payment for our services."

It is a matter of concern that young people are strongly attracted by this movement. The fascination of something new entices them. The television reporter gave a warning that the leaders of Scientology prosecute private individuals who say anything negative about their movement.

I wrote earlier in this book that American movements generally appear in Europe or Germany ten years later. This time it did not take so long.

55
SENSITIVITY TRAINING

Sensitivity training is a method used in the USA for solving problems. It is a kind of group therapy. The members of the group sit together and discuss the question of their lives, their jobs, their marriages, and all the things they cannot master. The lights are turned out, and the members of the group touch one another's bodies. One man who told me about this kind of group therapy said that in touching one another sexual stimulation is also involved. The same informant told me that this form of group therapy is particularly suitable for dealing with severe marital problems. From a psychological point of view this is not surprising, for a man or woman who finds no fulfilment in marriage can find it by means of the touching which goes on in this group therapy.

56
SIXTH AND SEVENTH BOOK OF MOSES

The *Sixth and Seventh Book of Moses* has nothing to do with Moses, the man of God in the Bible. The sorcerers of the middle ages only chose Moses as their patron saint, because he outdid the ancient Egyptian sorcerers by the power of God.

In counseling people, I have on several occasions been handed copies of their book. I have always burned them. The oldest copy was produced in 1503. In the preface, it said that the original was in the Vatican at Rome, and that the book had been printed under the protection of the Pope. These doubtful claims would first need to be checked to see if they are true. Another edition had a note in the preface to the effect that these magic spells had been collected by a monk from Erfurt. The editions which have come out over the last four-hundred years vary considerably in content.

In the nineteenth century, the *Sixth and Seventh Book of Moses* was combined with parts of a French book of magic called *The Fiery Dragon*. This was printed, according to one manuscript, in 1522. I have found three publishers in Germany who have reproduced this awful book. In one German town, the attorney-general indicted a firm that had published this book. I wrote the report for this indictment, because I have in my files several hundred instances of the terrible effects of this book of magic.

It seems that Germany is the land where the *Sixth and Seventh Book of Moses* originated. The book, however, is found in other lands, in various translations. The title varies, too. In Germany, we call it the *Sixth and Seventh Book of Moses*. In other countries, the title is simply *The Devil's Bible*. There are now fifteen books of Moses, none of which have anything to do with the Biblical Moses.

Anyone who possesses such a book should burn it at once. I do not believe that the very possession of the book brings a person under the devil's power, but I have evidence that houses in which this book is kept are accident and disaster prone.

Ex 196   A minister's wife told me that her husband is also teacher of religious education at a high school. The pupils asked the minister to give them a lesson about the occult and about the *Sixth and Seventh Book of Moses*. The minister knew little about it, and therefore ordered a copy from a German publisher. He studied it so as to inform himself. His wife told me, "Ever since we have had that book in the house we have had trouble. We have constant illness and accidents, and continual strife and quarreling."

Ex 197   I know a Christian couple who have three sons. Two of these sons are in Christian work and their work is being blessed by God. The third has also a strong desire for the Word of God and for Christian fellowship. He goes to church, but he cannot find peace. He told me that he had carefully studied the *Sixth and Seventh Book of Moses* years ago. It may be dismissed as a funny superstition, but I know from long experience that the study of this book brings the reader under a ban. So it was with this young man from a Christian family. He simply cannot come through to faith, although it is his desire to get right with God. The *Sixth and Seventh Book of Moses* brings its possessors, their homes, and their families under a ban.

Ex 198   A person who owned the *Sixth and Seventh Book of Moses* learned from it how to practice black magic. He memorized the spells which would harm his enemies. He tried them out and was amazed to find that they worked. He would concentrate at midnight on an enemy. He would take a rag doll, stick several needles into it, name his enemies, and then add a magic formula from the *Sixth and Seventh Book of Moses*. He was surprised when his enemy actually became seriously ill. Over the years he developed strong magical powers. Those who knew him were afraid of him.

Ex 199   The minister of a certain Christian group is a very hard worker. He is well known for the way he ministers to a group which is weak and spiritually dead. After hearing an address in which light was thrown upon the occult, this preacher confessed that for years he had taken an interest in occult literature and that he possessed copies of all the magic books, including the *Sixth and Seventh Book of Moses*.

Ex 200   In connection with the *Sixth and Seventh Book of Moses*, I also know of cases where those who have read the book have learned how to kill small animals by magical power. Others even specialize in larger farm animals like pigs, calves, cows, and horses, which they can kill by supernatural means. I will not give any examples here because I am often ridiculed when I do so.

Anyone who wants examples should consult my booklet *Wider das 6.und7.Buch Moses,* published by Brunnenverlag, Basle.

If the devil were only a ridiculous, powerless, harmless figure, Christ would not have had to die to free us from his power. For those who surrender themselves to Jesus, 1 John 3:8, paraphrased here, applies: "The reason the Son of God appeared was to destroy the works of the devil."

57
SOUL FORCE

When you read this title, you probably have no idea what it could mean. There are two excellent books which explain the meaning of the term. The most important work is Jessie Penn-Lewis's *Soul and Spirit.* The other is Watchman Nee's *The Latent Power of the Soul.* But we still have not explained what *soul force* is.

In the USA, I have several times come upon a movement within the Christian churches which calls itself Soul Force. When I asked what it meant, I was given the following explanation. If some members of a church become lukewarm and no longer attend the services, other members who have remained faithful sit together and try to bring the backsliders back to church by means of mental powers at a distance.

When I heard this, I was shocked. This is nothing less than the use of remote mental suggestion, which is basically a subdivision of magic. So here are Christian churches using magic and sorcery to bring lukewarm Christians back to church. To put it plainly, they are trying to bring these Christians back to Christ with the aid of the devil. The church members who practice this Soul Force are unaware that in doing so, they come under a Satanic ban.

This strange form of mission reminds me of similar procedures elsewhere. I have heard several accounts in pastoral conversations of how former Christian Scientists who have left that church have been persecuted and made ill by mental suggestion. I have mentioned this *malpractice* in the chapter on Christian Science.

I was also reminded of the use of Soul Force in Germany and Switzerland. There, again in the course of pastoral counseling, I

have heard how representatives of firms use Soul Force when visiting
people in their homes or businesses, in order to talk their clients into
making a purchase or placing an order. We have here a dishonest
kind of salesmanship technique, based on magic, which is gaining
ground today.

The total picture of the use of Soul Force—mental powers used
in a magical way—is much more complex than has been described
here. In 1 Corinthians 2:14-15 we read: "For the natural man re-
ceiveth not the things of the Spirit of God . . . he that is spiritual
judgeth all things." We can apply these words to this short chapter.
The unspiritual man has nothing to do with the Spirit of God. Only
the spiritual, Spirit-filled man has an understanding of the things
of God.

58
SPEAKING IN TONGUES

I am not concerned in this book with authentic experiences, but with
the occult and demonic perversions of this phenomenon. I have met
some Christians who occasionally pray quietly in tongues in their
own private prayers. No one except their pastor knows about it. It
is not even known in the church. I have no intention of devaluing
the experiences of these loyal Christians, whose own life of faith and
willingness-for-sacrifice puts their critics in the shade. But no one
should therefore excuse himself with the familiar attitude, "Even if
it is unauthentic with everyone else, it is genuine with me." I have
to say a decisive *no* to the tongues movement itself. Every year the
number of negative experiences of which I hear grows.

Over a hundred books could be mentioned which deal with this
subject. I cannot list them here. The most scholarly is the book *The
Psychology of Speaking in Tongues* by John P. Kildahl. The tongues
movement has brought about such confusion and division in the
churches of the USA that the American Lutheran Church felt compelled to set up a commission to study the phenomenon. The commission consisted of Dr. Qualben, a psychiatrist, Dr. Satre, a theologian, and Dr. Kildahl, a psychologist. Their report makes some excellent comments on the question of speaking in tongues, but I find
it somewhat lacking on the spiritual side.

In Germany, the publishing house of Hänssler has brought out
Francis Schaeffer's book *Die neue Welle*. Hubmer's book I have al-

ready mentioned in an earlier chapter. Two of my books, *The Strife of Tongues* and *Charismatic Gifts,* deal with this subject.[47]

It looks almost as if the tongues and the so-called charismatic movements are the most dangerous weapon Satan uses against the Christian camp. It must, however, be clearly emphasized that within these two movements there are many true Christians who remain there because they lack the gift of discerning spirit.

In this book I shall deal with only the demonic side. Let us begin with a quotation from Hubmer. "In cases where men like Johannes Seitz prayed with people who claimed to have been baptized in the Spirit, it often became clear through the frightful scenes which resulted that this baptism had a demonic origin."[48] Some examples follow.

Ex 201 In March 1975 I gave several addresses in Dr. Kenneth Moon's church in St. Petersburg, Florida. A missionary came to see me. He told me of a difficult pastoral situation. He was ministering in Orlando, Florida, to a woman who spoke in tongues. He pointed out to her that there are often spiritistic spirits hiding behind this gift of tongues. When she started to pray in tongues, the missionary asked her, "You spirit speaking in tongues, do you confess that Christ has come in the flesh?" At first there was no answer. He then commanded the spirit in the name of Jesus to reveal itself. Finally, the spirit said, while the woman was not fully conscious, "I belong to a church."

The missionary did not leave it at that. "Which church?" he asked. "The church of Satan," came the astonishing reply. Then the pastor commanded these powers in the name of Jesus Christ to depart. The woman became free by the power of God. To God be the glory!

Ex 202 I learned of a similar incident in a report from the Canadian revival preacher Bill McLeod. Rosteck, an American evangelist, carries on a pastoral ministry similar to mine. In Toccoa in the state of Georgia, there was a woman who continually started speaking in tongues at the prayer meeting. There was no interpreter there. According to the instructions given in 1 Corinthians 14:28, she should have remained silent. The brethren asked her, "Please pray in English, so that we can understand you and pray with you." "I cannot pray in English," answered the woman, "I keep speaking in tongues." The brethren decided to carry out the test mentioned in 1 John 4. The brethren asked: "Do you confess that Christ has come in the flesh?" They received no answer. They therefore commanded the spirit which was speaking in tongues, "In the name of

Jesus Christ we command you to answer us. Do you confess Christ?"
Then came the amazing reaction. "No, I hate him," cried the woman.
The nature of her tongues speaking was revealed.

Similar things have been experienced by a Canadian missionary
who worked in Borneo for ten years. He is the Rev. George A. Birch,
whom I first met at a missionary conference in Java. We soon became
friends, finding we were on the same spiritual "wavelength." We
met again when I was speaking in Vancouver, B.C., Canada. I have
also received several letters from brother Birch, in which he has encouraged me to continue my work. Those who are called to fight
against occultism and to attack fanatical, extremist practices find
that they are open to many attacks. What I like about brother Birch
is that he accepts genuine gifts of the Spirit and at the same time
opposes human or demonic imitations.

Brother Birch has investigated twenty cases of tongues in Canada,
nineteen were demonic in nature. In one case, the person speaking in
tongues said, "You don't need to test my spirit; I bring about the
speaking in tongues myself." One of the nineteen cases may be re-
counted.

Ex 203   Shirley came from a Christian family. As a young girl
she came to faith in Christ, and a few years later joined a youth
group called "Youth with a Mission." All the members of this group,
who belonged to a Pentecostal church, spoke in tongues—all, that
is, except Shirley. Her friends told her, "As long as you have not
received the baptism of the Spirit, you will have no power for witness."

Shirley prayed much for the gift of tongues. Then one day at a
meeting of the Pentecostal church she went forward to the platform,
holding her hands in the air. She received the gift of speaking in
tongues. "Praise the Lord!" everyone shouted in joy, "Shirley got
the baptism of the Holy Spirit."

Some time later, she heard about demonic imitations of the gift
of tongues. At the same time she noticed that most of the members
of the "Youth with a Mission" group were falling away. Some became
drug addicts; one was sent to prison. None of them continued to
follow Jesus. This made her doubts increase. She agreed to let brother
Birch test the spirit that was speaking in tongues according to I John
4:2. As Shirley was praying in tongues, brother Birch asked, "You
spirit speaking in tongues, do you confess that Jesus Christ has come
in the flesh?" After he had repeated the question, the demon cried

out, "No! No!" Thereupon brother Birch commanded it, in the name of Jesus Christ, to reveal its name.

"Lucifer with three of his comrades," came the reply. "Saul, Demetrius, Judas." Then the voices cried out from the girl. "I hate you, I hate you." The girl at once jumped up and tried to strangle brother Birch. This man of God put himself under the protection of Jesus Christ (Luke 10:19) and bound the demons in the name of the Lord. Then he commanded them,

"In the name of Jesus Christ, tell us when you entered this girl."

"At that meeting of the Pentecostal church," they replied, "on August 17."

"What do you intend to do with her?"

"We want to keep her back from the truth. That is why we took control of her tongue." Brother Birch then instructed Shirley to declare herself free from these demons in the name of Jesus Christ. She did so. Then brother Birch commanded the demons to leave the girl, because she belonged to Jesus Christ. The girl was freed, and she gave God thanks and praise for her salvation and deliverance.

Several facts become evident from this story. Demons speak in the first person. When they talk about the person whom they have possessed, they speak in the third person.

Those who try to gain spiritual gifts, e.g., the gift of speaking in tongues by force, come into the hands of other spirits. 1 Corinthians 12:11 tells us that the Spirit of God gives gifts to those whom He will.

Paul also shows us in 1 Corinthians 12:29-30 that not everyone receives all the gifts. The gifts vary.

There are several points I regard as having great importance in brother Birch's report.

It sometimes happens that demons claim to be the Holy Spirit or Jesus. Thus they occasionally utter the name of Jesus. If one then commands them in the name of *Jesus Christ* to reveal themselves, they are forced to declare: "I am the unholy Jesus." Another confession we have mentioned elsewhere, "I am the Jesus of Satan." The name *Jesus* is not restricted to Jesus Christ. It is an ordinary person's name, as we can see from Colossians 4:11, for instance.

A feature that causes both brother Birch and me grave concern is that demons will occasionally answer the test question of 1 John 4:2 in the affirmative. In this way they sometimes lead whole groups of Christians astray. This is the most devilish misuse of the word of God which Satan allows himself. I have discussed this with several experienced men of God. We know no answer, but we can see from the consequences that there are satanic counterfeits even taking this form.

I will close by mentioning another of my friends, V. Raymond Edman, formerly president of Wheaton College. He wrote the preface to my book *Christian Counseling and Occultism,* and invited me to speak at Wheaton College on a number of occasions. He divided speaking in tongues into three types: the gift of God, speaking in tongues as a result of suggestion or autosuggestion, and demonic speaking in tongues. This is the same division that I have set out in my booklet *The Strife of Tongues.* This makes it clear on the one hand that we do not, like some extreme theologians, confine all gifts of the Spirit to the first century. The Holy Spirit did not go out of business in the first century. But on the other hand, there are more cases of human or demonic imitation. That is the business of Satan.

Do not quench the Holy Spirit
Do not grieve the Holy Spirit
Do not imitate the Holy Spirit
Do not force the Holy Spirit, but
Be *filled* with the Holy Spirit as commanded in Ephesians 5:18.

59
SPIRIT OF THE AGE

We are surrounded by a sea of confusion. Many and various are the intellectual movements which are popular today. When we speak of the spirit of the age, we are not referring to the complaints made by the older generation, against the present day or about the departure of the good old days. The spirit of the age is a complex matter.

On the Christian front, one may note the de-Christianization of the Western world and the reduction of missionary activity in the former colonial areas. Just one small example. In the years 1967 to 1974, nine thousand Catholic priests resigned from the priesthood in France. Moreover, between 1970 and 1974, the number of Catholic theology students declined by sixty-eight percent. In the United States, two hundred priests resigned in 1973, and in the last seven years, the number of those studying theology decreased from forty-nine thousand to seventeen thousand. The same trend may be observed in almost every country of the West.

Until a few years ago, only fifteen out of every hundred students of Protestant theology in Germany became pastors. The others either changed their majors or took up other careers. Recently this situation has changed. Because of the *numerus clausus* rule in Germany, which means that only a certain fixed number of students are admitted to each faculty, many students have taken up theology, because they were not allowed to study anything else. In these cases it is not a matter of an inward calling, or of being a convinced follower of Jesus Christ; instead the shortage of places at universities has driven young people into the arms of the church. Can one suppose that they will later turn into Spirit-filled, powerful witnesses of Christ in the pulpit? No answer is needed to that question.

On the mission field depressing things are also happening. A missionary in East Asia, who has been working there for many years, told me that his society had sent them a young missionary, who had been completely ruined by modern theology. They could not find a use for this young man, and so sent him home again. On several mission fields I have been told that mission stations have had to close because the society at home could not find young missionaries to send out. This state of affairs may be blamed on modern theology, the ecumenical movement and secularization: the growing worldliness of the Christian churches.

While we observe these signs of weariness and decay, we find also, running parallel, a new activeness among occult groups and movements. Note these examples:

Ex 204 I have already mentioned that in October 1970, the American student, Isaac Bonewits of Berkeley University, California, attained the degree of Doctor of Magic Arts. Bonewits is the first person in the world to be given such a title. On attaining the degree, he received congratulatory telegrams from several African witch doctors.

Ex 205 In the summer of 1975, I stayed in Bogotá, Colombia. At almost the same time there was a World Congress of Witchcraft taking place in Colombia. Three thousand sorcerers, spiritists, and witches assembled in this Colombian metropolis. The conference included lectures and practical experiments in the field of black magic, spiritism, and other occult arts. Since there was no common language at the conference, those taking part were asked to communicate with each other by telepathy and mental suggestion. During the conference, magical healings also took place. At spiritist séances, the spirits of dead tyrants like Nero, Napoleon, Hitler, Perón, and other historical personalities were called up. There were group discussions on parapsychology, alchemy, astrology, divination, exorcism, and also on macumba and voodoo. During the nights, black mass was celebrated.

At the same time, reports of attacks on the Christian churches began to appear in the daily papers. The Christians asked for intercession and circulated the houses with Christian literature warning people against these occult practices. This conference has made Bogotá into one of the most important centers of satanic cults and black magic in the world.

Ex 206   As I was writing this book, I received a letter from a missionary friend of mine in South Africa. He told me the following story. Where this missionary lives there is a college where two to three hundred students are being trained to lead satanic and magical groups. In view of these disgraceful studies, my friend decided that he must give the students copies of my English books which warn against occultism.

South Africa is not the only country where courses of study are offered in sorcery and magic. There are similar institutions in England, Canada, USA, Brazil, Haiti, and in other countries.

Even more mischievous than openly occult movements are those in which magic is mixed with religious fanaticism.

Ex 207   In the USA, a movement has started which calls itself the Arcane School. There are centers of this school in New York, Geneva, Tokyo, and other world cities. The founder and director is Alice Bailey. She has written thirty books, which she claims were dictated to her by spirits. This cult encourages its followers to meditate and pray for peace every afternoon at 5 P.M. This peace will come about through the help of Buddha and the return of our Lord. Jesus will return in 1984.

Here we see a mixture of spiritism, Christianity, and Buddhism. There is no doubt that hundreds, perhaps thousands, of people are deceived by this pseudo-religious, occult swindle.

There are many movements like this in the USA, which try to combine spiritism and Christianity. They include the Inner Peace Movement, the Spiritual Frontiers Fellowship, the Churches' Fellowship for Psychic Studies, and the Church of Divine Science. The character of these "churches" may be seen by considering one example of the many detailed accounts which I have.

Ex 208   A man went home after attending a service in one of these spiritist churches. He demanded that his wife, who was a believing Christian, destroy all the Bibles and religious papers in the house. Some time later this man went to a meeting at his spiritist church. After the meeting he went home, murdered his wife, and cut her body into small pieces.

People will try to make those who hear of this atrocity believe that the man was mentally ill. But this does not fit the facts. I have many examples to confirm the observation that participation in spiritist meetings or membership of a spiritist church brings dreadful consequences.

Ex 209 Another group which claims to be Christian is known in the USA as the New Testament Missionary Fellowship. This name leads one automatically to conclude that it is a Christian organization. But the facts are otherwise. The aim of this group is to "deprogram" young people who have been given a Christian upbringing at home. In other words, the aim is to rid them of their Christian ideas. In order to achieve this, they take young people off to an unknown destination and brainwash them to free these victims of Christian education from their religious ideas. A case of this was brought to court in New York in May 1973. Some members of this so-called Christian church were charged with religious kidnapping. They were convicted.

Ex 210 One of my friends sent me a report of a church conference in Trinidad. This report is contained in the *Trinidad Guardian* of September 10, 1975. During the conference, the delegates in Group 10 suggested that the Christian churches should study ancient Caribbean sorcery, so that there may be more enlightened understanding of its attraction. The inhabitants of the Caribbean islands would far sooner go to a Caribbean sorcerer than to a Christian pastor. The sorcerer would speedily give them help, but the Christian pastor would only have comforting words to offer.

The Caribbean sorcery is called Obeah. It originated with the slaves who were brought in former days from West Africa to the Caribbean islands. The delegates declared that it was the fault of the missionaries that this African sorcery had acquired a derogatory connotation. The same Group 10 suggested that voodoo and modern Pentecostalism were closely related. The two movements had similar characteristics. Followers of voodoo, like Pentecostals, would sing and dance and clap their hands. The messages often were non-intellectual in character. Both groups believed that God was directly present in their midst. Active members of both groups had the ability to speak in foreign languages and to see visions. The neo-charismatic movement must also be included along with the other two. These observations are of great interest to sober, Bible-believing Christians who are opposed to the new charismatic and the tongues movements. Needless to say, the proposals of Group 10 were not adopted by the other delegates. Many others spoke out against them. It is, however, significant that at a church conference of believers who call themselves Christians such proposals could be made at all.

Ex 211   During my speaking tour in Jamaica in 1973 at the Theological Seminary in Kingston, I learned about the chief form of sorcery practiced in Jamaica. It is called Pocomania. Pocomania is a mixture of religious ideas and African sorcery. It would take a whole book to describe Pocomania in detail. The movement, however, is little known in North America and Europe, and I shall make only a few comments about it here.

Experts on Pocomania say that this form of sorcery is a mixture of the Methodist revival movement and African sorcery. The Bible is used as a book of white magic. The *Sixth and Seventh Book of Moses* is given equal status. I was surprised to find this book, which originates in Germany, in Jamaica also.

Everything that is practiced in spiritist circles is practiced in Pocomania—cult of the dead, table lifting, demon cult—also speaking in tongues, mind healing, exorcism: in short everything associated with extreme Christian groups. Even death magic is practiced. The three- or four-week trance, which can be found among the yogis of East Asia, is also practiced in Pocomania. Anyone who has become gripped by this movement is in the hands of Satan and has only a slim chance of becoming free, unless he experiences complete deliverance through Christ.

The trend of our times becomes evident in all these syncretistic movements. Behind them is a definite strategy controlled from below. The devil mixes occult and religious elements together; he obscures clear distinctions, and millions of victims fall into his trap. The spirit of the age is controlled from below. This control from the abyss or spirit world is clear in the following example.

Ex 212   In summer of 1974 a remarkable trial took place in Tanzania. Omar Mustalla had been happily married for four years. One evening he came home, took his revolver, and shot his wife. The doctors were unable to save her. Before she died she said: "I do not understand why my husband acted in this way. We were very happy together." The murderer was given psychiatric tests. One of the doctors was an Indian called Shandra Bhava. He formed a remarkable theory. He declared that Omar had received the command to murder his wife from the other world, from his former fiancée who had died of an incurable disease. Omar had promised his former fiancée on her deathbed that he would never marry another woman. When he broke this promise, the former fiancée gave him the command from the other side to kill his present wife. The court ruled that the Indian doctor's explanation was right, and acquitted Omar Mustalla.

The trial would not have ended in that way in Germany or in America. This example shows, however, that this Indian believed that people can be influenced from the world beyond. This is also the view of nearly all spiritists.

We would reject such a belief and say it is absurd. We, however, know from the prophetic parts of the Bible that in the last days Satan will try to obscure men's powers of judgment. He will try to confuse the mind, destroy people's sense of truth, and create uncontrollable intellectual chaos. This is the great strategy of the world below, which forms and controls the spirit of the age.

These few comments on the subject in its religious and occult aspect will suffice. One could trace a similar process in politics, philosophy, law and other areas as well. But there is not sufficient space for that here.

60
SPIRITISM

The word *spiritism* is derived from the Latin *spiritus,* spirit. It can be defined as the doctrine or cult of spirits.

Before we go into the chaos of the spirit cults, I must make two preliminary observations:

1. I have never taken part in a spiritist séance and never will. I must make this clear, since certain slanderers have spread the rumor that I have joined in spiritist groups.

2. This chapter on spiritism should only be read after one has consciously, by faith, put oneself under the protection of Jesus Christ. Since Jesus' victory on the cross we have no need to fear these demonic powers, but neither ought we to take lightly the study of such material.

Spiritism has become a worldwide movement and is on the increase in every country. During my eight visits to Brazil, it has been confirmed for me by missionaries that spiritism is rapidly gaining ground in Brazil. Twenty years ago there were reckoned to be 10 million spiritists. Today this number has increased almost fivefold.

In Brazil we find criminal spiritism, Macumba; spiritism in a more or less religious form, Umbanda; and the so-called Kardec spiritism, which has a social aspect. It is in the great cities, particularly, that centers of spiritist cults are to be found. The city of Rio, for instance, is said to have seven thousand groups of spiritists.

Spiritism is found not only in Brazil, but in every land. Haiti is another great center of spiritism. Voodoo is a combination of magic and spiritism. In the USA, California is a witches' cauldron of spiritist activities. Los Angeles is said to have six thousand spiritist groups and forty spiritist churches. In Europe, England heads the spiritist movement. England has about one-hundred-two spiritist churches. Also found in England is the spiritist healing organization of Harry Edwards, to which some two thousand spiritist healers belong. Other demonic playgrounds in Europe are Paris and Lyons, where not only spiritism flourishes, but the black mass is celebrated often. In Germany there are some two hundred groups in Hamburg, and a similar number in Frankfurt. According to the late Professor Blanke, Basle has about four hundred groups and Zurich has about six hundred groups.

African paganism is also spiritist. Finally, in East Asia spiritism is a great power. Here live more than a billion people who are influenced directly or indirectly by the ancestor cult. The ancestor cult is not simply a form of piety involving the veneration of deceased relatives, but is a demonic cult. The members of the ancestor cult pray to their ancestors; they ask them for advice and bring them sacrifices. In Red China, Mao tried to abolish not only Christianity but also the ancestor cult. He did not succeed. If the ancestor cult be included in the spiritist movement, it can be said that one third of mankind is involved in spiritism today.

My knowledge of spiritism is not derived from books. Counseling is the only starting point for my experience. As I write this book, I have been dealing with these problems in counseling for forty-five years. There are fake manifestations by spiritist mediums. Some mediums use deceitful manipulations when their psychic powers are not strong enough for an experiment. I am not concerned with fake spiritism. I am only interested in describing genuine phenomena.

The material is so extensive that one could write a large book about it. I am therefore compelled to restrict myself here to a thorough analysis. In order to reduce the material to some kind of order, we divide spiritist phenomena into four main types: extrasensory perception, extrasensory influence, extrasensory apparitions, and spiritist cults.

EXTRASENSORY PERCEPTION

a) *Spiritist Visions*

Spiritist visions are sometimes similar to Biblical visions, but they have a totally different origin. Biblical visions come from the sphere of God, the sphere of the Holy Spirit. Spiritist visions are satanic in inspiration. An example follows.

Ex 213 In Porto Alegre, Brazil, a seventeen-year-old girl came to me for counseling. A large arsenal of weapons had been burned down, and she had foreseen the event in a dream. She had seen the great buildings being burned down to the foundations. The same day, pictures appeared in the paper showing the scene just as she had dreamed it.

A parapsychologist would say that the girl had received a telepathic communication of the fire. I have no quarrel with this explanation; but it does not explain the reason why she has this gift. Both of the girl's grandfathers were active spiritists in Brazil. Where spiritism has been practiced by forebears, the children up to the third and fourth generation possess psychic powers. A person is freed from these psychic powers when he surrenders his life to Christ and declares himself free from these powers and from the sins of his ancestors.

b) *Spiritist Prophecy*

During my preaching tours in Los Angeles, I collected nearly a hundred examples in my file. On the subject of spiritist prophecy, let me recount the following experience which was told to me by a former spiritist.

Ex 214 A man who had belonged to an extreme Pentecostal group broke with the group and formed his own. In their meetings, they allowed the spirits to dictate to them what they were to do. Thus, one spirit guide instructed the men and women to have intimate relations with each other in order that further spirits might be begotten and born. Nine months later these women gave birth to the young spirits in the meeting. They received a terrible blow on the head from the unseen powers and then the new spirit was born. The new spirits were not visible.

Here we have a complete suspension of human thought processes and intelligence. A psychiatrist would consider all the members of such a spiritist group as mentally ill. In fact, many of the members do end up with a mental disorder or a similar kind of disorder known as mediumistic psychosis.

c)   *Table Lifting*

Ex 215   At a technical college in London, table lifting was being practiced by a group of teachers and students. Those taking part sat around a circular table and joined hands. The medium tried to communicate with the spirits of the departed. The students and teachers asked questions which were answered by tapping signals from the table. On one occasion, information was given by the table that during the next hour a young man in the city would have a car accident. The young man's name, age, and description were also given. The students did not believe it. The next day they read of an accident involving someone of that name in the newspaper. This incident naturally gave a great impetus to spiritism in the college. It is really criminal that in many colleges in the USA, Canada, and England, teachers and students are allowed to practice table lifting during teaching time or breaks.

A similar practice is that of glass moving. An example follows.

Ex 216   A Lutheran minister was invited to dinner by a doctor friend. After the meal, the doctor invited his guest to join him in a party game. They sat down at a table. On the table was an alphabet arranged in a circle, with a glass plate on top of it, and a liquor glass on the glass plate. The doctor said, "I will now call up the spirit of someone who is dead, who will answer our questions." The questions were answered by means of the glass, which moved round the alphabet. The minister regarded this as a clever trick and tried every possible means of discovering the source of the energy. He could not. He was invited several times more by the doctor. After this, the minister's spiritual attitude began to change. He was no longer able to pray or to read the Bible. When he stood in the pulpit, he had unbearable pains. These attacks of pain came only in connection with the exercise of his office or with private Bible reading. It came to the point where he had to hand in his resignation to the church authorities. I counseled both the minister and the doctor. The doctor made a general confession and renounced spiritism. He became a believer. The minister, however, was completely ruined by spiritism.

d)   *The Ouija Board*

Use of the ouija board is widespread in North America and in England. It is a wooden board with the alphabet on the outer ring and figures on the inner ring. The ouija board is similar to glass moving in operation, either a glass or a pendulum being used. Naive people regard it as a party game. American psychologists believe that the ouija board can be used to bring out things hidden in the subconscious. That is true up to a point, but it is not an adequate explanation, since future events also can be found out by using the ouija board.

Ex 217   In Singapore I heard a story which shows the background of the ouija board. I was lecturing at a Bible school in Singapore. During a discussion, a girl student told the following story: "I have only been a Christian for a few months. Shortly after I had come to Christ, I was invited by three girl friends to join them in a game. I accepted the invitation, and saw in front of me a round board with letters and numbers. One of my friends said that she would conjure up the spirit of a dead person, who would answer their questions. I felt very uneasy and began to pray in my heart. The one in charge of the game placed two fingers on a little glass which was standing in the middle of the board. It did not respond to any of her questions. Then she asked,

'Is someone disturbing you?'

'Yes,' came the prompt reply. I could not bear my uneasy feelings any longer and left the room. Later my friends told me the end of the story. When I had gone, the one in charge asked, 'Who is disturbing you?' The answer was spelled out: 'The girl who has left the room.'

'Why did she disturb you?' asked the other girl.

'Because God is with her,' came the reply."

We see from this experience that faith in Jesus Christ and the spiritist ouija board game are totally opposed to one another. Here the power of God strikes against the power of Satan.

e)   *Speaking in a Trance*

Speaking in a trance is a practice of mediums. It only takes place when a medium is present who has mastered this form of spiritism. The medium puts himself into a trance, a kind of deep sleep, and the spirits are then said to be able to speak through the medium to the people present.

Ex 218   I had been asked to preach in a Lutheran church in South Africa. The last minister had allowed himself to be led astray by spiritists. When he hesitated, he had been told by the spiritists that Luther spoke at their meetings. What Lutheran minister would not be eager to hear Martin Luther speak? The Lutheran minister therefore went to the séance, with his wife and daughter. The pastor quickly observed that what was going on was a piece of shameless deceit on the part of the demons: Martin Luther certainly never preached in so primitive and unspiritual a manner as through this spiritist medium. After a terrible struggle, he renounced spiritism. But a short time later he died. His wife and daughter were unable to free themselves but remained caught in the spiritists' coils.

f) *Automatic Writing*

In spiritist automatic writing, the medium must achieve complete inner quietness and must not concentrate on anything. Suddenly, the compulsion to write comes over the medium. One of the most versatile and powerful mediums of our day is Matthew Manning, whom we have already mentioned in another connection. A number of parapsychologists have studied Manning. Here is an example that illustrates automatic writing.

Ex 219 A parapsychologist visited Manning to check out some of his experiments. Manning offered to give the parapsychologist a diagnosis of his state of health. Manning took a sheet of paper and wrote the parapsychologist's date of birth at the top of the page. Then Manning waited. After a minute, his hand began to write in a quite different style of handwriting. The writing was signed at the bottom, Thomas Penn. The diagnosis that this Thomas Penn from the other side gave was also interesting. It was, "A malfunction in the epigastric region."

The parapsychologist asked Manning, "Do you know what is meant by 'the epigastric region'?" "No," said Manning, "I don't know." "It isn't altogether clear to me either," said the parapsychologist. When checked by a doctor, the diagnosis proved to be correct. This knowledge cannot therefore have come from Manning's subconscious. This is a case where extra-human forces are at work.

Automatic drawing is on the same level. Manning takes a crayon in his hand, waits, and then suddenly starts to draw quickly. After a few minutes his style changes. He draws in the style of well-known artists. When the parapsychologist was there, Manning drew a reproduction of the rhinoceros which Albrecht Dürer drew in 1515, and which is hanging in the British Museum in London. A few minutes later, Manning drew a picture of Salome with the head of John the Baptist on a table before her. The original is by Aubrey Beardsley. I have seen both drawings and know that Manning has certainly not the artistic ability to copy the drawing of Albrecht Dürer or the painting of Beardsley from memory.

Manning originally believed that his subconscious mind was responsible for all these powers. He has long since given up that view. He now believes that he receives his impulses and abilities from the unseen world.

g) *Spiritist Soothsaying*

In 1962 and 1964, I had long lecture tours in Australia. I gathered many examples of spiritism in Brisbane, Sydney, Wollongong, Newcastle, Melbourne, and other cities. An example from Sydney follows.

Ex 220 In a Women's Fellowship group, a woman openly told me that she had taken part in a spiritist séance. During the séance, a woman asked whether her husband, who had been missing for years, was still alive. The questioner was asked to give the medium a piece of her husband's clothing. The medium then shut his eyes for a few seconds, and said, "Your husband is living in Italy." This later turned out to be true. What we have here is a combination of psychometry and spiritist soothsaying. People who make use of such help come under a ban.

h) *Conversation with Spirits*

Strong mediums with well-developed powers need no special means of contact in order to speak with the spirits. They can see the spirits, speak to them, and receive answers. An example of this from Lismore in Australia, which I also heard when touring Australia.

Ex 221 A woman came to me for counseling and told me of the severe attacks to which she was subjected. Her uncle had been a spiritist. Before he died, he transferred his psychic powers to the niece. This is something often done by charmers, who are not able to die until they have transferred their magical powers to someone else. Ever since this young woman had taken over the psychic powers of her dying uncle, she had undergone terrible anxiety states. She saw demons, heard knocking, experienced poltergeists, and other disturbances. In her need, she went to a doctor instead of an experienced pastor. The doctor thought she was suffering from a form of schizophrenia and sent her to a hospital. There she received further psychiatric treatment, with no effect. She was sent home, and had the same experiences as before. She could not only see the spirits, but could speak to them, ask questions, and receive answers. The result was that her nerves became more and more unsettled.

Ex 222 After I spoke in Frankfurt, a spiritist girl came to me, admitting that she had been conversing with spirits for years. She had started with table-tapping and glass-moving. Later she no longer needed these aids, but was able to put questions to the spirits directly. They answered her. When I pointed out to her that these spirits would destroy her life, she acknowledged it frankly.

i)   *Excursion of the Soul*

There are some spiritist mediums who possess the ability to detach their souls from their body, and send them out to discover hidden things. This is a spiritist form of clairvoyance. An example follows.

Ex 223   In London I gave a lecture in All Saints Hall. Many Anglican priests were present. A discussion followed the lecture. One Anglican minister declared that he had the power to detach his soul from his body and send it off to find our hidden things. This state of separation took place without his willing it. He thought that it was like the gift of the apostle Paul, who says in 2 Corinthians 12:3 "whether in the body or out of the body I do not know." The minister said further that he could only stop this process by thinking about the cross of Jesus Christ. He regarded his ability as a gift of God. He said he also had the gift of second sight.

I pointed out to this minister that I had observed that excursion of the soul is a phenomenon in spiritist families. Normally, the parents or grandparents have been spiritists and these abilities appear in their descendants. The minister questioned this. Then I suddenly found I had a supporter. A man stood up at the back whom I did not know. He said, "I used to have the same ability, but I was delivered from it by Christ. Simply call on Jesus Christ, for he who calls on the name of the Lord Jesus will be saved."

One or two days later I received a telephone call from this Anglican priest, asking if I had time to see him. He confessed that he had had dealings with spiritists. He renounced spiritism, accepted Jesus Christ and invited me to speak in his church. The church was packed.

j)   *Astral Traveling (Astroprojection)*

Spiritists who practice the excursion of the soul send their souls on journeys around this world only. Strong mediums who have mastered astral traveling claim that they can send their soul to the moon or the planets to discover things there. Some are even so bold that they claim to have penetrated the sphere of God. This is completely absurd. God does not let spiritists interfere with His doings. I will give an example to illustrate.

Ex 224a   AM Shaman (witchdoctor) in Alaska claims that he was often on the moon before the American astronauts. Of course, that is a lie. This is more evident in the next example.

Ex 224b   A woman spiritualistic medium holds that on several trips to the moon she saw forest and water on the backside of the moon. Again, this cannot be true.

Ex 224c Another lady believes she is able to send her soul to Paradise to speak with Jesus. It is not true. Why? She also believes she is a re-incarnation of Mary Magdalene. Reincarnation belief is a heresy. Nor is anyone able to force an encounter with Jesus in Paradise.

EXTRASENSORY INFLUENCE

The first section was concerned with spiritistic knowledge, or perception. In this section we come to spiritistic manifestations of power.

k) *Materialization*

The term *materialization* is used to describe the production of phantom figures by mediums. The departed are alleged to become visible. I have dealt with this subject already in my book *Between Christ and Satan*, and also in the more technical book *Christian Counselling and Occultism*. I cannot repeat here everything said in these books. I will give just one example.

Ex 225 One of my friends is a Lutheran minister. One day he went, together with a young professor of theology in Berlin, to a "materialization session." The leader of the group promised that he could bring back any dead person from the place of the departed. The theology professor accordingly asked if he could see Philipp Melanchthon, the friend of Martin Luther. At once a white phantom appeared, which did in fact look similar to Philipp Melanchthon. The theology professor took a snapshot with his camera. He was amazed to find that a poor picture of Philipp Melanchthon actually appeared on the film. This shows that phantoms of this kind can be photographed. Schrenck-Notzing also conducted some successful experiments of this sort. In order to avoid misunderstanding, I must state here that this phantom in the séance in Berlin was not Philipp Melanchthon. It is impossible for a medium to recall a man of God from the other side.

It will be objected that in 1 Samuel 28 it is recorded that the medium at Endor called up the prophet Samuel from the realm of the dead. But with regard to this difficult chapter, I must once again say that the witch of Endor did not have the power to call up Samuel. An unexpected turn is clearly to be seen in this Bible narrative. The medium would probably have deceived the disguised king Saul, as she had deceived many others over the years. But suddenly she cried out. God had stepped in and taken over. Samuel appeared, sent by God to pronounce the death sentence on King Saul. A detailed exposition, however, I have given in other books.

Mediums who can materialize are people under powerful bondage. In Berne, the beautiful capital city of Switzerland, a medium who practiced materialization came to me for counseling. She cried out: "Dr. Koch, I am in the devil's talons. Please help me!" I showed her the way to Jesus, and she said with me a prayer of renunciation. I do not know, however, what has become of her since.

l)   *Transfiguration*

Transfiguration occurs when a spiritist medium changes his facial appearance into that of another person. For example:

Ex 226   In London I met Mr. Millen. For years he was a highly-qualified medium. His wife and a prayer group began to intercede for him. After fierce struggles he was finally able to become free through Christ. This former spiritist told me something of his mediumistic powers. He had, for example, mastered transfiguration. When he sat in a trance, it was as though an invisible substance clothed him. This was probably what spiritists call ectoplasm, or teleplasm. His face then took on the appearance of a dead person whom someone wanted to see. For example, a woman asked to see her grandmother and recognized her in the transformation. She embraced her grandmother and cried.

m)   *Translocation*

There are some spiritist mediums who can dematerialize. In other words, they suddenly become invisible and reappear in another place: they translocate. This phenomenon has various names in the different continents. In Japan and South America it is called "riding on the wind." I have written a separate chapter about translocation, so will give no examples here.

n)   *Apports*

This word is derived from the Latin *apportare,* to bring near. It is used to describe the sudden appearance of objects in rooms with closed doors. There are two kinds. Either the objects disappear or they remain. Two examples:

Ex 227   A minister told me of a visit he had received from three spiritists. One of the spiritists held out his open hand toward the minister and said, "Now, look carefully." The same moment, several red, precious stones appeared in the spiritist's open hand. It was not a trick. The stones did not come from his sleeve. The spiritist said, "These are gifts from our friends on the other side. In a few minutes they will disappear again." The minister watched carefully. Several minutes later the stones disappeared.

Ex 228 In the second example the apport remained. The house of a farmer, whom I knew, was burned down. He had to put his tractor in his neighbor's barn. When the farmer whose house burned down went to collect the tractor, the engine would not start. The tractor was towed to a repair garage. The cylinder block was opened up. Inside the cylinder was an iron object. The mechanic wrote to the tractor's manufacturers and said there must have been a fault in the construction, since the block of the new tractor had not been opened before. A fitter from the factory came and said that it could not have been a fault at the factory. There were no objects like the one found in the block in the factory.

An argument ensued about the object. The cylinder block had not been opened either by the owner or by his neighbor. The farmers would not have been able to do so. No one at the garage had opened it, for the tractor had been bought only a short time previously. Where had this object come from? The owner informed me and asked my advice. It turned out that in the house in which this remarkable apport had taken place spiritism had been practiced for generations.

Further examples could be cited concerning Matthew Manning, who is also able to produce apports.

o) *Deports*

Deports are the opposite of apports. The word deport is derived from the Latin *deportare,* to carry away, make disappear.

Ex 229 For years a Frenchman repeatedly came to me for counseling. He had originally been a magician and spiritist, and possessed strong psychic powers. Little by little he was freed from spiritism. He confessed all his sins, surrendered his life to Jesus, and in my presence renounced the powers of darkness. Yet he did not become completely free through his conversion. Remarkable deports manifested themselves. Money disappeared from a locked cashbox to which no one had a second key.

From the other end, strong spiritists have admitted that they are able to steal money. I have examples of this from Switzerland and from England.

p) *Levitation*

Levitation is practiced by spiritists on every continent. The word is derived from the Latin *levitas,* light weight, mobility, and the verb *levare,* to make lighter, raise up.

In spiritist levitation, the earth's gravity appears to be suspended.

People float up to the ceiling. This devilish practice also includes
the phenomenon of "sledging." I must explain this briefly. In a farmhouse in the Alps, poltergeists manifested themselves, but only
when the fourteen-year-old son of the house was present. If the
boy lay down in his bed, it was lifted up by an invisible force and
pushed along like a sled. The phenomenon was investigated several
times by a professor, an electrical engineer, and a parapsychologist,
but they were unable to discover the cause. The only thing that
emerged later under pastoral examination was that spiritism had
been practiced in the house for decades.

q)   *Telekinesis*

The word *telekinesis* comes from two Greek roots. The first is
teleō, to bring to an end, or *to telos,* end, distance, boundary. The
second is the verb *kineō,* to move forward. The term could therefore be rendered "moving at a distance." Professor Bender calls it
psychokinesis. This implies that the explanation for this ability to
move things at a distance is to be sought in the powers of the
psyche. I have already pointed out that for a 3½ cwt. oak wardrobe
to be moved by the powers of the psyche, it would require the energy
of 10,000 or 100,000 men. It would be a good thing to allow a
physicist to inform us on this point. Work which our bodies are
unable to achieve by physical effort cannot be taken over by the
mind. Another example concerning Manning:

Ex 230 Matthew Manning was put into a pair of steel handcuffs. He then conversed quietly with the parapsychologist who was
there to observe the experiment, without moving his hands. Suddenly
the steel handcuffs were bent completely out of shape. The handcuffs were examined by experts. They could not explain the occurrence. This shows that Matthew Manning is an even stronger medium
than Uri Geller.

r)   *Spiritistic Aggressive Magic*

Ex 231 One day a minister and his wife came to see me. A
twenty-year-old spiritist was bombarding another girl with her magic.
She had already twice given her a copy of the *Sixth and Seventh Book
of Moses.* The girl had thrown them straight into the Rhine River.
Now the spiritist threatened her. "I will make sure," she said, "that
you also fall into the Rhine." The spiritist, whose name was Iris, was
now in a state institution for drug addiction. Her victim sought refuge
with the minister. The minister at once informed the doctor in charge
of the spiritist and then came to me. The doctor regarded it as untrue that one could bring trouble on others by means of the *Sixth*

and Seventh Book of Moses. She described it as superstition. Then they all had it proved to them.

The doctor used the institution's bugging device to listen in to a conversation between the spiritist and another inmate. It revealed that the spiritist was planning to bring her victim to ruin. The attack was planned for Monday evening at eight o'clock. The doctor informed the minister. On the Monday evening, the minister and his wife went to see the girl against whom the attack was planned, without saying anything to her about it. They wanted to see if the attack would have an objective effect. At eight o'clock the girl went pale and began to tremble. When the minister tried to pray with her, the girl was unable to put her hands together. Her knees knocked. A fear of death came over her. The minister reported back to the doctor that the attack was very evident, although the girl knew nothing about it. In other words, this was not a case of suggestion. The doctor had for her part been observing the spiritist during the time of the attack. The spiritist was in a trance and did not react to the words of the doctor. Even when pinched or pricked with a needle there was no reaction.

We have here an example which is attested and confirmed unexceptionably by all four participants When the spiritist came out of her trance she was in a rage. She was furious because her attack had been beaten back. She therefore planned another attack for a week later. The minister came to see me a second time and asked for my advice as to how to ward off such an attack. I advised him first of all to talk with the victim and tell her to entrust her life completely to Jesus Christ. She must also learn to put herself in faith under the protection of Jesus. I also asked the minister to form a prayer group to pray at the time of the attack that the victim might be preserved from the attacks of darkness. And that is what happened!

s) *Spiritistic Defensive Magic*

A person may be protected from magical attacks by the power of Jesus Christ. This is the Biblical way. But there is also a satanic method of defense. I will not go into satanic forms of defense, involving open scissors or knives, for I do not want any reader to get the idea of trying it out for himself.

t) *Spiritist Operations*

There is a special chapter on this subject later in this book. I will give here only one interesting example.

Ex 232 I was told this story by a missionary while I was on a lecture tour in Africa. This man had gone to a spirit healer when he was ill, because he was unaware of the nature of these healing powers. This spiritist carried out operations on the so-called astral body, which were supposed to take effect on the natural body of the patient. For instance, he healed gall stones by placing a glass upside down on the patient's navel. In the glass there was a small candle. The candle used up the oxygen and then slowly went out. While this was happening the spirit healer lay in a trance. When the light had gone out, the gall stones also disappeared. An x-ray photograph showed that the stones had gone.

u) *Spiritist Miracles*

The devil is always trying to imitate the miracles of the Bible. Twice on my tours I have heard of the dead being raised by the power of sorcery. I am not in a position to verify these two cases, because I do not know whether the people concerned were actually dead or only in a cataleptic state.

Ex 233   In the Middle East I heard of a Moslem sorcerer who raised a man to life again after he had been dead for several days. The man who had been raised fell at the sorcerer's feet and begged him not to send him back to the place where he had been.

Ex 234   The second example I heard about in Barrow, at the northernmost extremity of the American continent. At a service in Barrow I spoke to an Eskimo congregation of nineteen hundred. It was a wonderful spiritual experience. At the same time I heard from the Eskimos of the reality of the Shamans, who still exist and who have not given up their devilish practices in spite of the work of Christian missions. The Shaman Alualuk was a strong spiritist and used to converse with the spirits. One day another pagan Eskimo died, whose name was Taiakpama. The relatives asked Alualuk to raise him from the dead. The Shaman succeeded in bringing the dead man back to life. Taiakpama lived another ten years. Then came the time when Alualuk recognized the devilish nature of his sorcery. He accepted the message of the missionary and surrendered his life to Christ. From that time on he lost his power as a Shaman.

One occasionally hears reports from the mission fields of people being raised from the dead, but only by the power of faith in Christ. And even in these cases one never knows whether the dead person was really physically dead or only in a completely rigid state. Clinical death is only evidenced by symptoms of decomposition. I have some examples where these were present.

In reporting such things one exposes oneself to attack from believing Christians. There are theologians and Bible school lecturers who recognize the miracles in the Bible only theoretically. When God does something of the same sort today, doubt and criticism are used to explain it away.

v) *Dematerialization*

Dematerialization is the ability to make one's body disappear. We shall consider it again under the heading of translocation, in connection with riding on the wind. It is also a familiar motif in fairy tales. One thinks for example of Siegfried's cloak of invisibility in the saga of the Niebelungen. In the chapter on the "Queen of Darkness," the example of the English spiritist who made herself and her friends disappear was given. She wrote the book *From Witchcraft to Christ.* Following is an example from the mission field.

Ex 235 On an island renowned for black magic and spiritism, I met a young man who possessed very strong psychic powers. At a missionary conference, he came to faith in Christ. He confessed that he had three murders on his conscience. The police had been after him for years. They had never been able to find him, however, because he was able to make himself invisible when pursued. Of course people may have their doubts about such a story. But two points may be mentioned which indicate that the statement was true. When people have been convicted of sin by the Holy Spirit and have received Jesus Christ as their Lord, they generally speak the truth. The second indication is the similarity of cases on various mission fields on every continent.

w) *Teleplasm*

Teleplasm is another term derived from two Greek roots. The first is *telos,* end; and second *plasma,* imitation. Literally translated, therefore, teleplasm means imitation at a distance. This is another activity of which I have often been told in counseling sessions.

Ex 236 The first product of teleplasm, or ectoplasm, I came across was one shown to me by a missionary called Margrit Häusner in France. It was a "feather duster" made out of feathers which had been extracted from a pillow. Feather dusters are regarded in France as products of spiritist persecution.

Ex 237 I heard of another example from the Island of Man on the Ivory Coast. I was told of it by a woman missionary. While she was still a small child, she had been taken away by a spiritist and charmed. After this, she began crying out in the night and became severely ill. Five bones appeared in her knee, which were later found not to be lacking in the bone structure of the knee. The mother asked the spiritist why she had brought this on them. "I must do it to a certain number of people," replied the spiritist, "then I shall be free myself." This, then, is a process similar to apports.

Ex 238   In Paris I gave several lectures at various seminaries: in Vaux, then at the Bible School of Nogent sur Marne, and in the Tabernacle (Pastor Blocher's church). During this time, a Jew came to me for counseling. He was a painter by profession. He had worked for several years in Italy. There he began his search for the truth, because his life did not satisfy him. At first he tried some false movements. He progressed from Jewish cabbalism to yoga, to spiritism, and to many other occult movements. He did not find the truth there; instead he came into one form of severe bondage after another.

His desire to find the truth became even stronger. He came into contact with Christians; first of all Catholics, who were his first pointers to the truth. They, however, were unable to lead him to Jesus, but only to Mary, the mother of Jesus.

Finally he found some people, evangelical Christians, who were disciples of Jesus Christ. They were able to show him the way of salvation.

Today he is at Bible school in Paris and wants to become a missionary. The bondage has not yet been fully overcome. He experiences attacks which have their origin in spiritism. At night he feels as if a veil, like ectoplasm, is being drawn over his head. Then he is unable to pray, and doubts come into his mind. A voice says to him, "You are not free at all. You will still come to a bad end."

He confessed all his sins in my presence, and I showed him anew the way to Jesus. We said together a prayer of renunciation. He was willing to hand over his life completely to Jesus and to become a preacher of the gospel.

EXTRASENSORY APPARITIONS

x)   *Spiritist Apparitions*
The wide field of spiritist apparitions which are known as poltergeists would furnish enough material for a weighty volume.

Ex 239   When I was preaching in Edmonton, Canada, á twenty-one-year-old girl came to me for counseling. She said that at night the doors in her house would open. The radio turned itself on. She could hear footsteps, scratching and knocking noises, see gleams of light and faces, hear voices and transparent people walking back and forth, even though all the doors were locked. She was not suffering from a mental disorder. I told her that there were spiritists either in the house or among her ancestors. She admitted this. Her grandmother had been a charmer and a spiritist and had died in terrible circumstances.

Ex 240 One example which greatly shocked me happened in my immediate neighborhood. A man of the Christian Fellowship movement, whom I had known very well for many years, was on his deathbed. While he was dying, poltergeists appeared throughout the house. The windows rattled, although there was no wind outside. The family heard scratching noises on the walls, the rattle of chains and heavy footsteps. The wife, who was sitting by the dying man's bedside, could no longer bear to stay in the room. She telephoned a Christian hospital and asked for a nurse to be sent. The hospital made an exception to its general rule and sent a night nurse, because the man had been a well-known member of the Fellowship for many years. The nurse had only been in the room for a few hours when she began to hear the same noises. She also found it impossible to pray with the dying man. Someone was holding her throat and preventing her from speaking. She hurried back to the hospital and told the matron: "The devil is loose in that man's house. I cannot stay there for the night. It is impossible. The atmosphere oppresses me."

Finally the local minister was called. He was a believer and a friend of mine. He has since died. The minister wanted to give the Communion to the dying man, but he experienced the same poltergeists as the night nurse and the man's wife. He too found that he could not stay in this demonic atmosphere. He was scarcely able to utter a prayer.

After terrible struggles, the man finally died. After the funeral the minister said to me, "There you can see that the devil is allowed to attack even men of God in their last struggle with death." "I will be quite honest with you," I replied, "I know that this man has for many years not only attended a spiritist meeting, but also led it." On Saturday evenings he would have in his house a number of teachers and other professional men and practice table tapping. On Sundays he held a Bible meeting. He was spiritually cold and dead. He was driving in two directions at once. That was the reason the devil tried to make it clear as he was dying, "I have a certain right to this man and to be in his house."

y) *Spiritist Cults*

Spiritist cults are to be found all over the world. The background of nearly all pagan religions is influenced by spiritism. The East Asian ancestor cult would be the first to mention, because it is followed by about one billion people. Reference to it has already been made in another chapter.

I discovered specialized spiritist cults on my two visits to New Guinea. There are four main cults there: the Saugumma cult, the Tambaram cult, the Cargo cult, and the Bembe cult. All four have associations with the dead and the spirits.

Particularly horrible is the Alaut cult on the island of Timor, as I have mentioned elsewhere.

z) *Spiritist Lodges*

Spiritist lodges are to be found predominantly in the Western world. They are the intellectuals' equivalent of the low-level cults of the primitive peoples.

It is worth mentioning that in some masonic lodges, the eighteenth degree is spiritistic.

Lodges of a religious character have appeared in large numbers in recent years. Mention has already been made of the "spiritual" lodge in Zurich, which has various daughter institutions. There is a great number of religious lodges in Brazil, California and England. London alone is said to have thirty religious lodges. If one points out to members the devilish activities that go on, they reply, "We invoke only the good spirits. We keep the evil ones away." As if that lay within the power of man!

aa) *Spiritistic Churches*

Spiritistic churches are to be found chiefly in the English speaking world. England has over one hundred of these churches, and in Los Angeles, California, there are about forty. I was surprised some years ago to discover in Glasgow that there is a "spiritist" church close to the Bible Training Institute.

Ex 241 I heard an amusing story in Kitchener, Canada. Many years ago I conducted a number of evangelistic campaigns in Kitchener. There I met Dr. Jantzen, for whom I have an extremely high regard. He later moved from Kitchener to Clearbrook, Abbotsford, sixty miles from Vancouver. There I met him again when I was giving some lectures at the Mennonite Bible School.

In Kitchener, Dr. Jantzen had no church building of his own. He hired a hall for the meetings of the growing church. The room was divided in the middle by a folding screen. After the service was over one Sunday, the elders came to Dr. Jantzen in dismay. "Brother Jantzen," they said, "the spiritists, of all people, have rented the other half of the hall. We must move out and look for another meeting place."

Dr. Jantzen laughed and said emphatically: "We must move? No, they must move! We will pray them out of here!"

And that is what happened. The spiritists, who had started by holding their meeting every Sunday in the other half of the hall, began after a few weeks to come only once a fortnight.

Dr. Jantzen and his elders continued to pray. After a few months, the spiritists came only once a month. Even that was not the end. Finally they stopped coming altogether. The Christians had prayed them out of the hall.

Nominal Christians without a clear understanding might be inclined to rebuke me and to say: "That was not a very Christian attitude to take!" Do such short-sighted critics know the real nature and effects of spiritism?

Spiritism is a cult of spirits and demons and brings everyone who takes part under a terrible ban. Christian churches have become lukewarm and lax, and there is far too little teaching about the devilishness of this movement.

Ex 242 Another example takes us into the realm of the Greek Orthodox Church. Twenty-five years ago I held some international youth camps in Saloniki, Athens, and Corinth. In Saloniki, a young man who was seeking for salvation asked a priest, "How can I get nearer to God? The liturgy of our Orthodox Church does not satisfy my spiritually hungry heart." The priest replied: "I will introduce you to an esoteric group. There you will find more than our church has to offer."

During the weeks that followed, the young Greek went with this priest to a little meeting in which contact was made with the dead. It was a spiritist meeting. He did not escape the evil effects of this. In addition to his spiritual hunger, he began to suffer from depression and nightmares. The young man stopped going to the spiritist meetings, and continued his search. He met me in connection with an evangelistic campaign. We talked together. Another brother led him to a decision after he had prayed earnestly for him for a time. It was not a quick conversion. The young Greek was too strongly tied to the Orthodox Church, and too strongly bound by spiritism. It was several months before this young man became free from all bondage through Christ.

Spiritism Among Believing Christians

Spiritism among believing Christians is the most horrible form of the spirit cult. First an example from Zurich.

Ex 243   A Christian family, who would appear to the outside world to belong not to the spiritists but to a circle of believers, holds an unusual form of family prayers each day. Each day an aunt makes contact with a departed man of God, who brings them a word. Stockmaier, Hauser, Blumhardt, Spurgeon, and Wesley are some of the men of God who are mentioned. When I pointed out that this was spiritism with a mask of Christianity, they were most indignant.

It is a painful and shattering fact that in extreme circles, spirits from below are more in evidence than the Holy Spirit. Hundreds of thousands of people are misled by the pious camouflage and go astray.

The prophet Jeremiah would weep again today in the words of long ago: "Oh that my head were waters, and mine eyes a fountain of tears, that I might weep day and night for the slain of the daughter of my people!" (Jeremiah 9:1). The slain of the Lord, as the charismatics call them, are indeed slain, but not by the Holy Spirit. They have been slain by the spirits from the abyss.

We have reached the end of this tour of the satanic labyrinth of spiritism.   In the Old Testament,   God commanded that the spiritists be rooted out of the land. Today we no longer burn witches. But we must issue a warning so loud that the furthermost corner of the earth will hear it.

He who can pray, let him join in prayer. This book is being published simultaneously in German, English, and French.   A worldwide warning must be given.

61
SPIRITIST HEALING

It is chiefly spiritism under a religious disguise which we find active in the field of healing.   There are also so-called faith healers who work not by the power of the Holy Spirit, but by religious spiritism or by white magic.

The USA had a well-known spiritist healer in Edgar Cayce, who made his diagnosis and exercised his healing powers in a trance.

There is at present a widespread spiritist healing organization in England.   The president is Harry Edwards, who has within his organization some two thousand healers. He boasts of having between one hundred twenty and two hundred Anglican priests among his clients. His book, *Spiritual Healing,* has been translated into several languages.

It would be a mistake to dismiss these healing methods as a pure swindle. Successful cures do take place. But at what cost! For many years I have been observing the serious negative effects of such healing on people's mental and spiritual health.

Edwards has made the spiritistic character of his activity clear by saying, "When my angels are not present, I cannot heal." Here an interesting parallel to the healing work of William Branham may be seen. Years ago he told his interpreter, Pastor Ruff, "If my angel does not give the sign, I cannot heal." Ruff noticed several features of spiritism in the work of Branham, and therefore stopped working with him. These "angels" of whom Edwards and Branham spoke are evil spirits masquerading as angels of light. As in many areas of the occult, we are here reminded again that the devil appears as an angel of light (2 Corinthians 11:14).

Another evidence is the fact that neither Edwards nor Branham were able to perform cures when faced with born-again Christians who had committed themselves to the protection of Christ. In the case of Branham, I have experienced this myself. When he spoke in Karlsruhe and Lausanne, there were several believers among the audience—including myself—who prayed along these lines: "Lord, if this man's powers are from You, then bless and use him, but if the healing gifts are not from You, then hinder him." The result? On both occasions Branham said from the platform, "There are disturbing powers here. I can do nothing."

People have often told me of similar experiences. Another spiritist healer was Dr. Trampler in Munich. Two women sat praying in his consulting room. Both of them were told, "I can do nothing for you. Go back home."

A more drastic incident occurred in connection with the spiritist healer Seiler of Ottenheim, near Lahr. A Christian woman from Freiburg sat praying in his waiting room, when suddenly the healer came out of his consulting room in a rage and shouted "Get out of here and go home, you old cow! I can't help you."

Christians who are already aware of the spiritist nature of such dubious healers should under no circumstances go to them for treatment. The Lord will not help those who do that.

An even more sinister area of healing is described in the chapter which follows.

62
SPIRITIST OPERATIONS

Even more catastrophic than spiritist healing under a camouflage of religion are the effects of spiritist operations.

In the last few years a certain Filipino has been making a name for himself. He carries out pseudo-operations, without using any surgical instruments. He puts himself into a semi-trance, and then moves his hands over the patient as if he were performing a real operation. Those who have been healed maintain that he is able to remove an appendix or a gall bladder without opening the abdomen. Before I am prepared to believe that, I should want to see an x-ray, to make sure it was true. Nevertheless, the fact is that people travel from as far away as Europe and America to see this spiritist healer. What amazes me is that a European doctor even organizes such trips.

If this Filipino is actually able to operate on or remove diseased organs without instruments, it is a case of dematerialization, a phenomenon which has often been mentioned to me in counseling. I have never taken part in any spiritist practices myself, and will never do so. I must repeat this again, because some people slanderously accuse me of participating in séances.

Two people I have counseled have mentioned the activities of this Filipino. A student who underwent a "spirit operation" of this kind returned home suffering from severe depressions. He had suicidal thoughts, was totally apathetic, and was unable to continue his studies. He first went to see a psychotherapist, who was unable to understand him. The psychotherapist sent the student to me. I tried to show him the way to Jesus and deliverance. I was not successful. It was as if his soul was ossified.

The other patient of this Filipino who came to me was a Swiss Christian woman. She had been ill for many years and was persuaded by the reports of miraculous healings to travel to the Philippines. Both she and her relatives were much in prayer for her during this journey and the treatment. The Filipino was not able to do anything for her. He had been blocked by prayer.

The most successful spiritist surgeon was a Brazilian named Arigo. The things which he has done are simply a chain of miracles—demonic miracles. The Catholic church has named him as a spiritist healer.

I have been to Brazil eight times for various tours. I have also been to Belo Horizonte. In this little town, an incredible surgical miracle was performed by Arigo. Senator Lucio Bittencourt had been holding an election meeting to which Arigo and his friends from Cogonhas had travelled. Bittencourt was suffering from lung cancer and planned to go to the USA for an operation when the election campaign was over.

The Senator and Arigo were staying at the same hotel. During the night Bittencourt suddenly saw Arigo in his room, with a razor in his hand. He heard Arigo say, "You are in great danger." Then he lost consciousness. When he woke up again he felt different in himself. He turned the light on and found that there were clots of blood on his pajama jacket. He took the jacket off and looked at his chest in the mirror. On his chest was a fine cut. Knowing what he did of Arigo's healing skills, he hurried to Arigo's room and asked him: "Have you operated on me?"

"No, you must have drunk too much."

"I must know exactly what happened," said the Senator. "I will take the next plane and go to see my doctor in Rio."

Bittencourt told the doctor that he had had his operation. The specialist took some x-ray pictures and confirmed it. "Yes. You have been operated on according to American surgical methods. We have not yet gotten so far in Brazil." Then the Senator explained what had taken place. This story caused a great sensation in the papers, and brought a flood of visitors to Arigo's clinic.

American doctors, journalists, and camera men went to Arigo's clinic. They carried out all manner of tests, but were unable to discover any deception. Arigo was willing for any test to be carried out. He even allowed his operations to be filmed. An American doctor, Dr. Puharich, even had a lipoma removed. The operation was performed with a rusty knife, without any local anaesthetic or antiseptic materials. Dr. Puharich felt no pain. This operation was also filmed.

What is the character of these remarkable operations? First, a word about Arigo himself. He had only four years' basic schooling and no medical education. By profession he was a miner; later he was employed by the public authorities. He performed his operations in a trance. He claimed to be "possessed" by the spirit of a German doctor, Dr. Adolph Fritz. This is however a mis-

leading claim, for no German doctor would carry out such
operations without anaesthetics or antiseptics, or with a rusty knife,
nor could anyone perform something like a lung operation under
such conditions. Arigo's surgical incisions also healed very rapidly,
without stitches. Moreover, there is no doctor in the world who
can make an exact diagnosis at a distance without any examination.
When Arigo was in a trance, he could give any client a precise
diagnosis at once. What we have here is a case of clairsentient
diagnosis, which only the strongest spiritist mediums can produce.

Arigo was simply possessed. The smokescreen of piety can do
nothing to invalidate that fact. Over the door of his house, Arigo
had a notice saying, "Here in this house we are all Catholics."
When he performed an operation in his own house, he would
make the patient lie below a picture of Jesus with the words "Pense
em Jesus" (Think of Jesus) written on it. Before he began work
in the morning he would say the Lord's prayer.

Visitors were deceived by this seemingly Christian setting. The
devil has in his repertoire even Christian-looking notices which he
uses to catch souls. For it is men's souls which are in danger.
These "miracle cures" are paid for with the loss of the soul's
salvation.

This all sounds hard, malicious, bigoted, fanatical, and anything
else naive and innocent people like to call it. But anyone who has
had to observe for forty-five years the effects of spiritism can only
warn people with all the strength at his disposal.

Let us be quite clear about this: Arigo's cures were not a trick
or a swindle. They were real operations. This is the reason people
even in high positions in the government came to him secretly for
treatment. He was sentenced by the courts to sixteen months'
imprisonment for unauthorized healing. The president, whose own
daughter had been treated by Arigo, reduced the sentence to two
months.

It is because of the devastating side effects that I feel impelled
to issue the strongest warning. Healing of the body at the cost of
the soul's salvation is not worth it.

The senator mentioned above was killed later in an air crash,
and Arigo in a car accident. This is another thing I have often
observed; people who are under occult subjection, or even demon-
ized, frequently are in fatal accidents. I have many examples of
this in my files. William Branham, who was another religious
spiritist, also died in a car crash.

A German miracle healer suffered the same fate, as have many others. Are we not willing finally to take warning?

63
SUPERSTITION

Luther said that what does not center on Christ is superstition. In the jungle of superstition there are thousands of varieties. This book stems from practical experience, and some examples will introduce us to the maze.

Ex 244 The following story appeared in a Hamburg newspaper. A farmer in Holstein (a province of North Germany) had sick cattle. He brought a spellbinder from the next village and had the cattleshed fumigated with devil's dung. The charmer said, "The first person to enter the farmyard tomorrow or the person who in the next three days wants to borrow something is the one who has put a spell on the cattle." The next morning, the first person to set foot in the yard was a seventy-year-old woman farmhand. The farmer accused her of witchcraft and beat her.

Fear of witchcraft has brought trouble to many innocent people. In this example we find another kind of superstition as well. It is hard to believe, but a fact nonetheless, that many chemists in Holstein still sell "asa foetida," or devil's dung. But if anyone should think that such things are confined to Germany, he is wrong. In Chicago there are about sixteen hundred magical and countermagical substances for sale in drugstores, according to a report I read in an American newspaper.

Another kind of superstition is the fear of and faith in numbers. Of course there are in the Bible, numbers which have a certain meaning. In Revelation, for example, the number seven occurs frequently. The Antichrist will have the number 666. But everything in the Bible can, of course, be distorted into a superstition. Here is an example.

Ex 245 In Ireland it is held that the seventh child in a family possesses special powers. If a father and his son are both seventh children, then the result is a child with great abilities. This is the case with Finbarr Nolan, an Irish teenager. When Finbarr was only three months old, his first patient arrived. Word of the double seven had got around. The mother allowed healings to be performed as soon as the little boy was two years old and able to make the sign of the cross. The family is Catholic.

As the child grew, his healing powers became more and more well-known. Stories of miracles multiplied: arthritis, worms, skin diseases, paralysis, and blindness had all been cured.

Several hundred patients gathered daily at his door. His daily routine is like this. At midday, Finbarr rises. His mother explains that he goes every night to a night-club and does not get back until 4 a.m. In the afternoon, the first to come in are the women and girls, in a large group session. They take some of their clothes off. The treatment takes only five seconds. Finbarr dips his finger in a vessel of holy water which is held before him, and touches the diseased parts. He does not speak to the patients. The organization is in the hands of his brother.

The same pattern is followed in the group session for men. In about four hours, two to three hundred people are treated. At the end, the healer stands in the middle of the large room. He bows his head. Everyone stands up and joins in prayer. When Finbarr crosses himself, they all know that the session has ended. Finbarr has been asked whether there is any significance in the use of the holy water. He says there is not. He does it only because another healer advised him to do so. His feeling is that in the process of healing, power goes out of his body into that of the patient. Neither the holy water nor the sign of the cross have anything to do with it. Those who have been healed sometimes make generous donations. The income tax authorities are constantly on his trail. As far as the Catholic church is concerned, relations at first were good. But the church demanded a share of the income. When Finbarr refused, the church began to issue warnings. They said, "Trust the Virgin Mary and not Finbarr."

Incidentally, where are we told in the Bible to trust the Virgin Mary? Why this monstrous shift of emphasis from Jesus to His mother? Paul writes "For there is one God, and one mediator between God and men, the man Christ Jesus" (1 Timothy 2:5).

The question of how Finbarr's healing powers are to be explained will be considered in the chapter on magic. Here we are concerned only with superstition about numbers.

One superstition which has reached chronic proportions is the fear of Friday the thirteenth. Psychologists call this superstition "triskedecaphobia", from the Greek *triskaideka,* thirteen, and *phobos,* fear. One or two examples:

Ex 246   A London housewife named Joyce Ratcliffe refuses to leave her house several days each year. These are the Fridays which fall on the 13th of the month. On these days, her husband has to take time off work to do the shopping.

Ex 247 Psychological surveys have shown that in the USA at least a million women are glad when Friday the 13th is past.

Ex 248 In England, some local authorities omit the number 13 when numbering the houses in a street. Many hotels have no room with this number. Occasionally ships' captains refuse to set sail on Friday the 13th.

Whence this fear of Friday the 13th? One fanciful explanation is that Eve led Adam astray on a Friday. But who really knowns that?

Others refer to a Scandinavian saga. The Nordic gods invited twelve people to a banquet. Loki was not invited because he was a known troublemaker. But he came, uninvited, as the thirteenth, and brought ill-fortune with him. Baldur, the favorite of the gods, had to die. Thus even our pagan forefathers regarded thirteen as an unlucky number.

In Christian tradition, the unlucky number is associated with Judas, who was the thirteenth person present at the Last Supper.

These explanations, whether with pagan or Christian associations, are simply superstition. All forms of superstition show that the creature has lost his ties with the Creator. He who knows that his life is in the hand of God has no fear of Friday 13th or any "unlucky number."

In Matthew 10:30 Jesus says: "But the very hairs of your head are all numbered." Are we not prepared to entrust ourselves to the one to whom all authority and power in Heaven and on earth has been given?

As the hymn writer puts it:

> From Him, who loves me now so well,
> What power my soul can sever?
> Shall life? or death? or earth? or hell?
> No! I am His for ever.

64
SYMBOLS OF PEACE

The so-called peace movement uses the Teutonic rune of death as its symbol. All over the world there are sisters and ministers of both Catholic and Protestant persuasion who wear the peace symbol or display it at Christian meetings. This hideous practice ought to be discontinued as soon as possible. Let us hear a little of the history of the peace symbol.

1.   At the time of the first-century persecution of Christians, the symbol now used as a symbol of peace was called the Neronic cross. Tradition tells that Nero, the hater of Christians, had Peter crucified head downwards. The *symbol of peace* thus signifies an inverted cross and is a symbol of hatred against Christians.

2.   In the eighth century, the Saracens fought in Spain against the Catholic church.   Their warriors had the Neronic cross on their shields when, in 711, they began their march of conquest over the Iberian peninsula.   The same symbol of hatred against Christians was used again by the Saracens when they fought against the Crusaders in A.D. 1099.

2.   Throughout the Middle Ages, the Neronic cross—known in many places as the pentagram—served as the symbol of the black mass, satanic cults, and blasphemy. In the gruesome ceremonies of the secret cults, use was also made of an image of the devil carved out of wood, with eyes in exactly the shape of the Neronic cross. One of these wooden images may still be seen in the museum of sorcery and satanic cults in Bayonne, France.

4.   It is in the twentieth century that the peace symbol has had its most varied history. The arch-communist Bertrand Russell designed a symbol for a peace march by leftist groups in 1958. He used the historic Neronic cross, because he himself was a determined opponent of Christianity.   One single sentence from his essay "The Will to Doubt" makes his position clear. He writes, "I hope that every form of religious faith will die."   In the Communist newspaper *The Daily Worker,* he spelled out his political creed in the following words, "Apart from the Soviet way there exists no more hope for anything." The attitude of this "apostle of peace" ought to open the eyes of all who blindly wear the symbol of peace.

5.   The situation becomes clearer still when we look around the ranks of those who wear the symbol. The symbol is worn by leaders of the communist student movement in the USA. Red radicals have the peace symbol on their flags. The Arab guerrillas who fight against Israel with Russian weapons have this symbol on their arms. The black pope Anton La Vey in San Francisco displays the symbol of peace on a great screen before the com-

mencement of black masses and orgies which he and his followers celebrate.

It is horrible that Christians should be so blind that they dare to wear this symbol, which stands for the murder of millions of Christians.

The communists want to establish "peace." But what kind of peace is it when people of differing political and religious views are placed in psychiatric hospitals and given injections until they become vegetables?

Genuine peace is found in only one place in all the world: at the foot of the cross of Calvary. There died a man who did not murder others in order to bring peace to the world, but rather allowed himself to be murdered without resistance in order to break the principle of violence and murder. One died for our guilt; through Him our conscience can find peace. He is truly our peace (Ephesians 2:14).

65
TELEVISION

It is well known that on both sides of the Atlantic there are many earnest Christians who will not have a television set in their homes. In many cases they have a low opinion of those Christians who possess one.

Cultural and technological progress has in every age been regarded by conservative Christians as the work of the devil. I will give several examples:

Ex 249 When the first bicycles appeared in the nineteenth century, the famous Miss Trudel declared that she could not imagine the Chrischona brethren ever riding such a thing. Today the Chrischona brethren have graduated from using bicycles to driving cars.

Ex 250 In the USA and Canada there are many Mennonites who are renowned for keeping old traditions. When cars appeared, they stuck to their carriages. They declared that car driving had been invented by the devil. Similarly they refused to install electricity and continued to light their homes with oil lamps. The most conservative Mennonites are the Amish people. Needless to say, there were some of them who disapproved of driving cars. After a struggle, they finally brought themselves to buy cars. But in order not to appear too sinful, they painted the chrome parts black.

Ex 251   Pastor Modersohn, who was one of Germany's best-known evangelists in the first half of this century, said in 1912: "Flesh-colored stockings are of the devil." But today, every Christian woman wears flesh-colored stockings.

Every technical advance has shared this fate, from the first railway engine to the radio. I wonder how many elderly Christians who travel by express train to Hamburg to visit their sons realize that when the railway first appeared, it was known for years by Christians as the "devil's coach" or "devil's carriage"?

It is not a sign of deep spirituality to ascribe all technical inventions to the devil. In His creation ordinance God said, "Fill the earth and subdue it" (Genesis 1:28).

I do not regard television as neutral, although I know of good uses to which it can be put. When Billy Graham came to England some years ago, he could reach the whole country with his messages by means of television. And it pleased God to bring many to Christ by this means. Similarly, during Eurovision 70, Billy Graham was heard and seen in seventy German towns at the same time.

Similarly, when I was conducting a campaign in Pelotas, South Brazil, my addresses were relayed to another hall in sound and vision. In Australia one of my addresses was actually broadcast over the whole continent on national television. In the USA and Canada, I have also appeared in various regional programs.

Why should the use of such technical aids be left to the devil? Satan uses the best equipment. We are not called to enter into the contest against him armed like Stone-Age men with stone axes and wooden clubs.

Apart from the possibility of reaching millions of people with the Gospel, television has other good sides to it. Tens of thousands enjoy the nature programs. Many documentary films and classical music programs are greatly appreciated.

That, however, is only one side of the matter. From a Christian viewpoint, it may be reckoned that for every five or ten good programs, there are a hundred where television is misused.

There is no end to the catalog of horrors which have resulted from television.

Ex 252   In September 1975, the *Rhein-Neckar Zeitung* carried a report about two girls aged thirteen and fourteen who had murdered an eight-year-old boy. When they were interrogated and asked why they had done it, they said: "We have seen so many murders on television that we wanted to find out for ourselves what it's like to kill someone."

Ex 253 Another newspaper told of some boys who had been watching a film about American Indians. Afterward, they tied one of their friends to a stake, "Indian fashion." They disappeared and left their victim to his fate. When the boy's parents returned they found their little son dead. He had been strangled by a cord around his neck.

Television has a dangerous power of suggestion. A picture can penetrate the subconscious mind and take control of a person. Psychologists call this an *imago* (from Latin *imago,* picture).

The second negative effect of television is the theft of time. Detective films rob believers of time for Bible reading and prayer. Every evangelist knows that when there is a mystery on, fewer people will come to the meeting. We shall one day be called to account to God for what we have done with our time.

The third and most serious effect is that of the very nature of some programs.

Ex 254 When the American astronauts made their first landing on the moon, I was sitting in front of a TV screen in the USA. I switched on the TV a few minutes early and was shocked to discover that the program just before featured a spiritist séance. I looked away until the actual moon landing began. For some years now, television program directors have included occult activities in their program. My experience leads me to regard that as a crime against the people.

Ex 255 In California, a high school teacher came to me for counseling. He had been listening to a satanist on television who said something like this, "The God of the Christians has long since gone out of business. If you are looking for realities and evidences of power, then come to us. We will give them to you." The teacher accordingly joined a satanist group and came under a terrible bondage. By the power of God he has since become free from the bonds of Satan.

Ex 256 Occult programs have also been shown in Germany. Remember Uri Geller? He is neither a liar nor a charlatan as hard-boiled rationalists like to maintain. Uri has psychic powers. When he conducted his experiments on television, the same powers were released in some viewers who were psychic. Spoons and other objects were bent. Only the ignorant make fun of these things. Anyone who is familiar with the subject knows that satanic realities underlie these activities.

Ex 257   On August 30, 1975 the chief television station in West Germany broadcasted a program called Hypnoland. The subtitle was "A journey into the land of hypnosis." I did not watch the program. I did hear of the effects of the show, which featured the Australian hypnotist, Martin St. James. Many viewers fell into a hypnotic state during the broadcast and recovered their full consciousness only when it was over. Some people suffered from disordered consciousness for several days or weeks.

During the Therapy Week at Karlsruhe at the end of August 1975, Professor Dieter Langen, an expert from the University of Mainz, commented on shows of this sort. He dismissed the shallow criticism that it had been the greatest bluff of the year. He affirmed that hypnosis is possible even through an interpreter. Professor Langen said he would press for legislation to prevent such broadcasts. In Sweden they have been forbidden for a long time already.

Behind the scenes there is an awareness of the damage television can do. In Flensburg, for instance, a TV clinic has been opened for the treatment of children who have been harmed. Will our legislators do nothing until the minds and nerves of countless thousands have been ruined for the sake of this Molech, television?

In this context I would mention the article by Gottfried Eisenhut in his missionary broadsheet "Central", July 1975. This report, which includes many scientific details, is headed "Magic Through Television." Here is one example mentioned in the article:

Ex 258   "A six-year-old child sat on his father's knee. On the television there was a 'relaxing program.' A young girl was stabbed. At the same moment this child cried out, 'The knife's in my tummy!' The child was taken to a doctor and kept crying every thirty seconds. It was taken to the TV clinic at Flensburg. Many months later the mental disturbance had still not been cured."

Only the future will tell how much harm television has done, particularly to children and young people whose nervous conditions have not yet been firmly established. Although most people do not realize it, television brings about a weakening of the human will, a disintegration of the mental powers of resistance, and a uniformity of thought. TV also tends to control decision-making and to obscure our powers of judgment.

Let us remember the words of Goethe, "The people never notice the devil, even when he has them by the throat." And he has the people by the throat.

66

TRANSCENDENTAL MEDITATION

This Eastern method of meditation was introduced into the United States in 1965 by Maharishi Mahesh Yogi. *Maharishi* means teacher, learned man, and guide and is a title used in India for Christian, Buddhist, and Hindu leaders. *Mahesh* is a surname. The addition of *Yogi* indicates that this Hindu monk has his background in yoga. Transcendental meditation (TM for short) is derived from the teachings of yoga, although it represents only a part of stage one of yoga.

The word *transcendental* is misleading. In theological language, it is used to describe that which belongs to the realm of the divine. Transcendence, the realm of the Trinity, is not accessible to human beings.

Within transcendental meditation, according to Maharishi Mahesh Yogi, *transcendental* means no more than crossing from conscious to unconscious activity. The nature of the system can best be explained by a description of the exercises in meditation.

There are at present in the United States about two hundred-fifty centers at which TM is taught. Some four-thousand teachers are scattered across the country. There are also about one-thousand teachers working in sixty other countries. From the USA, teachers have gone to Germany and Switzerland to teach this new form of meditation. It is significant that among the earliest disciples of TM were the Beatles. Up to two thirds of the followers of this movement are still recruited from aimless young people, many of whom are on drugs. Some hope to become free from their drug addiction through this meditation. According to Lindsey and Carlson, the movement has thirty-thousand members in the universities of North America.[49]

The introductory course in the USA is four evening sessions long and costs $100. Participants are taught to sit down for twenty minutes each day, relax, shut their eyes, and meditate. Each one is given his own special *mantra* as an aid to meditation. The word *mantra* is from the Sanskrit and means something like password, motto, or giver of power, bearer of mysteries. The mantra must be kept secret. No one is allowed to reveal his mantra to another, or it will lose its power.

During the meditation exercises, the mantra has to be repeated for twenty minutes. If one's thoughts wander, one should not force oneself to use the mantra. That would mean that the conscious mind was checking and controlling the subconscious. Meditation is intended to open the gate of the unconscious and mobilize its powers.

TM claims it is not a philosophy, a religion, or autosuggestion, but simply a technique to liberate the powers locked in the unconscious.

What results are expected from this meditation? Some participants give up TM after a few exercises, having found it no help. The majority, however, swear by TM and practice it successfully.

What is achieved? Those who practice it claim to find relaxation; stress is relieved, tensions disappear. Some even claim that after some time they can feel their blood circulate. In addition to such passive experiences, there is also an active side. A reservoir of unbounded energy is discovered. People become creative, capable of greater achievement. They become better able to cope with everyday life. They are no longer "lived," driven and controlled by the unconscious. They begin to live themselves, to be master of the situation.

On the medical side, it has been confirmed that the physical and psychological condition of patients who practice TM is visibly improved. Blood pressure becomes normal, circulation more stable. The mental state becomes more relaxed.

This all sounds very good. What is there to be said from a Biblical and Christian point of view?

What would happen if people spent the forty minutes or sixty (where it is practiced three times a day) in Bible study and prayer? Would the results not be even more evident?

What is the significance of the mystery? At the beginning of the meditation, the person has to produce and use three fruits, six flowers, and a new, white handkerchief as initiatory offerings. As we have already said, no one is allowed to reveal his mantra. Such mysterious rites are also to be found in freemasonry and certain kinds of magic.

Another thing that does not conform to the Christian faith is the many hundredfold repetition of the mantra. This leads inevitably to the assumption that results will automatically follow, such as is frequently found in non-Christian religions. The thoughtless droning of prayers corresponds to this automatic repetition of the mantra. Psychologically, it is a method by which the consciousness is by-passed and the unconscious given free play. This is in contradiction to the Bible plan of salvation. Our conscious mind must be submitted to the control of the Holy Spirit.

Something which I regard as greatly significant is the fact that this kind of meditation works best for people with a psychic disposition. That alone is sufficient ground for warning Christians against it.

Last but not least, do we need a Hindu monk to teach us how to relax? We have Jesus, the Son of God, who has brought us not just relaxation but redemption, deliverance from our "deep self," and peace.

67
TRANSLOCATION

Translocation is an even more remarkable phenomenon than levitation. Translocation is a change of place by means of demonic powers. This idea is found in popular myths and folklore. Among the Muslims there are stories about flying carpets. In Germany we have tales of witches who ride on a broomstick on the witches' sabbath, and the tale of the seven-league boots.

On the mission field, however, I have heard accounts from missionaries which have nothing to do with such fantasies.

Ex 259 In Japan I was told that there are a few Shintoist priests who possess demonic powers. They have the power, given them by Satan, to dematerialize on the top of one mountain and to reappear a few minutes later on the top of another mountain. When one hears such a story for the first time, one dismisses it as pure fantasy. I, however, have heard such stories on every continent except Europe and North America. Civilization does indeed drive out things of this sort. Satan's intrigues are broken still more by the preaching of the gospel.

Ex 260 In India I have heard stories about translocation from reliable and responsible witnesses. Indian sorcerers can cross rivers by means of spiritist translocation.

This is a demonic counterfeit of the miracle which took place when Jesus walked on the Sea of Galilee. There is no miracle in the Bible which the devil does not try to imitate.

Ex 261 I was told by a missionary in Ecuador that his cook possessed the powers of translocation. One day the missionary noticed that there was no flour, although this was needed for the midday meal that day. The cook said, "That is no problem. I will soon bring some!"

"How will you manage to do that?" asked the amazed missionary, "It is about ten miles to the town."

"Just leave it to me. I know about these things." A few minutes later the cook had returned with the flour he needed. After much questioning, he explained to the missionary the phenomenon of "riding on the wind," another name for translocation.

Ex 262   The most impressive and best attested example I have is from Haiti. This island is well known as a stronghold of Satan, being renowned for voodoo. When I was lecturing in Haiti, I heard some most remarkable things. An American missionary, who had been working in Haiti for fourteen years, told me some of his experiences. I will recount one example of riding on the wind.

A voodoo sorcerer wished to send a letter to a colleague, who lived some one hundred-fifty miles away. He sent his boy off with the letter. When he had gone about a hundred yards from the house, the boy became invisible. About one half an hour later, he had reached the colleague's house. The sorcerer wrote a reply. About two hours later, the boy had returned with this reply. He had covered about three-hundred miles without using any means of transportation. The letter of reply was the evidence that the boy had been there.

Missionaries who have to do with such sorcerers know that such things truly take place. It would be wrong, however, to jump to any conclusions. Sorcerers with powers like these are very rare, even in pagan areas.

As in the case of levitation, we are reminded of the story of Philip in Acts 8, when he was caught up by the Spirit of the Lord. On the question of becoming invisible, the section called "Queen of Darkness" should also be read.

68

URI GELLER

This young Israeli has roused great interest and controversy throughout the world by his experiments. On every continent there has been a conflict of views, ranging from believing acceptance to extreme rejection.

What is it all about? When Uri appears on the television or demonstrates his inexplicable abilities in a public hall, forks and spoons are bent. Old clocks which have not worked for years begin to tick again.

Let us consider one well-documented example. On Sunday, January 19, 1975 a German television station broadcast a program of entertainment.

During this show Uri Geller appeared, resting his finger on a fork. Without becoming hot, the fork slowly bent. Members of the audience examined the fork. It had become soft like plastic. Uri was asked what power it was that caused this. "Power from outside," he replied.

Uri also made the remarkable statement, "I should not be surprised if during this program, thousands of families find that their cutlery is bent."

That is exactly what happened. Professor Bender, who had been invited to take part in this show as an expert, has reported that after it nineteen-thousand telephone calls were received. The *Bildzeitung* (popular daily paper) received fourteen-hundred-fifty letters from "victims." Professor Bender received nine-hundred letters from Germany and three hundred from Switzerland.

One convincing example was mentioned in the course of the program. A Mrs. S. had had pieces of cutlery bent during and following Uri Geller's show. She called in her neighbor, and finally the police. Two officers examined the cutlery in her house. A spoon even bent in the presence of one of them. Cutlery in the open drawer kept bending, although no one went near it. There was no question of a trick or a secret source of power. One of the policemen said that he was ready to testify to the incident on oath.

After the people concerned had given their accounts of what happened, the panel were asked to give their opinions. The panel consisted of Professor Bender, a lawyer, and a journalist.

The lawyer said that in such a case he would have called in Professor Bender as an expert.

The journalist, 100 percent rationalist, threw doubt on the whole story.

Professor Bender answered this newsman, so convinced by his own skepticism, by citing an apt quotation from Freud, "He who regards himself as a skeptic should be honest enough to begin by doubting his own skepticism." In my opinion, Professor Bender should have described the journalist's attitude as the arrogance of ignorance.

I believe the most important thing in the program was Professor Bender's verdict. He spoke of the possibility of psychokinesis. This expression was coined by Professor Rhine of Duke University, USA. Other parapsychologists speak of telekinesis. Psychokinesis is a word which implies an explanation. Those who hold this view are of the opinion that these inexplicable phenomena are evidences of power in the psyche. This theory is in contradiction to other hypotheses according to which the mind can have a direct influence upon matter.

Those who hold either view agree that these powers come from the person himself, that it is an immanent rather than a transcendent factor which is responsible. The power is something within man, not something superhuman.

In common with thousands of mediums, Uri Geller has a different view. They attribute their gifts to power from outside. The animist and the spiritist explanations conflict on this point.

As far as Christian counseling is concerned, it does not matter which view is held. The counselor is concerned with the effect and the possibility of healing. This question will be dealt with in the final chapters of this book.

This is not all that must be said about the Uri Geller question. Since my first book on the occult appeared in 1952, I have counseled about twenty-thousand people in conversations and by mail. More than ten-thousand of these concerned occult experiences which had had negative effects. This large number of spontaneous cases enable one to form a truer overall impression than can be gained from experiments.

How does one explain the fact that during Uri Geller's show thousands of viewers experienced similar effects? From one point of view, the problem is simpler than the parapsychologists think. There are hundreds of thousands of psychic people who are quite ignorant of the fact that they are psychic. Uri is a strong medium. Strong psychic powers like these appear when both sets of parents and grandparents have been psychic and have passed their psychic powers in dominance to their son and grandson, in this case Uri. There are also other ways in which such psychic powers can arise. Double or fourfold hereditary mediumship is extremely strong. It enables the medium to make contact with other people present who are psychic, or even with psychic people who are a great distance away.

All the people who found that their cutlery was bent during the Uri Geller show are either unconsciously or consciously psychic. Uri cannot bend a fork at distance of 500 kilometers (311 miles) unless there is in that place a psychic person whose mediumistic powers he can use.

Uri is only a catalyst. A question which must be asked on Biblical and ethical grounds is that of the character of these psychic powers. What we have here is not a gift of God, nor is it a natural gift. Psychic powers as strong as those possessed by Uri Geller come from the sins of sorcery committed by one's ancestors. It would be better if he did not use them, but rather, if he would ask God for deliverance.

As far as the origin is concerned, the judgment of the parapsychologists is not correct. These powers are not psychogenic, but heterogenic: they do not originate in one's mental powers, but in powers from outside. Uri's own explanation is nearer the truth than is the opinion of the panel.

69
VAMPIRES

Two experiences will introduce us to the meaning of this word.

Ex 263 During my missionary journeys in South America, I encountered six different Indian tribes in Peru. For example, I gave twenty-nine lectures at the Indian Bible School of the Swiss Indian Mission. The missionaries also took me on excursions from the school to the various mission areas.

Mr. Sachtler took me to see the Aguaruna, and Mr. Zehnder took me to the Shipibos and Conibos.

One of the places where I spent the night will remain in my memory until my dying day. We were shown to the hut in which we were to sleep, which consisted of eight poles and a roof of palm leaves. The sides were open, and the floor was of beaten clay.

When I looked up to the ridge piece of the roof, I saw many animals standing side by side, with their heads hanging down. "Are they flying dogs?" I asked the missionary. "No," he informed me, "they are vampire bats, that suck the blood of animals and humans by night. Hens and babies die from it. Cattle and adults survive."

"That sounds like a good prospect for a night's sleep! Is there nothing we can do to stop them?"

"Yes," replied the missionary, "We can look for somewhere else to sleep, where there are no vampires."

"Will that do any good? Jungle creatures have a good sense of smell. They will find us."

In the meantime, I had thought of a solution. It was not for nothing that I had been a rascal in my younger days and had learned all the tricks that boys know. On the clay floor of the hut I built a fire, and on it I put several large leaves from a banana tree. After a few minutes a yellowish-green smoke was rising to the roof. The vampires quickly went off to find another perch. Now I saw for the first time how large these creatures were. They had a wing span of 50 centimeters (19 inches) or more. The missionary told me further:

"They have teeth as sharp as knives. You hardly notice their bite."

I had chased away the vampires. I brought in a sufficient supply of green leaves to keep the fire going all night as a protection against the vampires return. I had also chased away Mr. Sachtler. He said:

"If I sleep here, I shall be like a smoked ham by the morning." He found somewhere else to sleep.

There is another type of vampire. The word is used in connection with the popular belief that the dead can come out of their graves at night to drink the blood of the living.

Vampirism is practiced by Satanists and those who have sold themselves to the devil with their blood, by the Macumba people, and by those who practice voodoo. These people torture their fellow humans, especially children, sucking their blood or drinking it as part of a ritual, or in the celebration of the black mass. I have reports of dreadful incidences of this sort in my files. I will give two examples here, though these are not the worst ones I have on record.

Ex 264   In the summer of 1974, there was a gruesome trial in Nuremberg. The defendant was a forty-one-year-old man named Karl Hofmann, who confessed in court that he had broken into thirty-five mortuaries in order to suck the blood of people who had recently died. In the course of the trial, the defendant admitted further atrocities. In May 1972, he had surprised a courting couple in their car. He had shot the young couple and then drunk their blood.

Hofmann also confessed to a third crime, that of shooting the night-watchman at a mortuary. The man did not die, but was severely injured.

The psychiatrist's report said that Hofmann was mentally ill and recommended that he be admitted to a mental institution.

It is not surprising that while both judges and psychiatrists are appalled by such behavior, they are ignorant as to the causes of such crimes.

If one were to investigate this man's past or the history of his forebears, one would discover the roots of such abnormal behavior.

Ex 265   Here is another example from the mission field. An attractive, twenty-five-year-old woman in Sumatra had five husbands who all died, one after another. In each case she had married shortly after the death of the previous one. All five husbands died of the same disease, acute anemia (shortage of blood).

Following this tragedy, the young woman's parents sought out a witch doctor who gave the following explanation: "The young woman is possessed by a Nagasjatingarong (vampire) who sucks the blood of every husband that this beautiful woman has, because he wants to possess her alone."

According to this sorcerer, the five men had all had a rival from the other side. In other words, this was a case of spiritism, demon cult, incubus, succuba (demon marriage).

There is no end to the cunning tricks of the archenemy. It makes us treasure still more the song of triumph in Psalm 118:15-16: "The voice of rejoicing and salvation is in the tabernacles of the righteous: the right hand of the Lord doeth valiantly. The right hand of the LORD is exalted: the right hand of the LORD doeth valiantly." If we did not have this sure confidence, the power of darkness would weigh us down.

70
WELEDA MEDICINES AND HERBAL REMEDIES

I often receive letters asking me if it is true that Weleda medicines are magically charmed. The question of magic charming is dealt with in another chapter of this book. Here I need only say that charming is an occult, magical practice.

To give an open answer to this question is not without its dangers. I could be sued by the firm for damaging their trade.

One of my old friends, the Chrischona preacher Herrmann of Colmar, had an altercation years ago with the Weleda works in Alsace. It was about a booklet that Herrmann had written, in which there was a warning against the Weleda medicines. The Weleda firm obtained a ruling that Herrmann must either not publish the booklet or cut out the offending pages. That was the end of that booklet.

In order to learn more, I bought a book from the Weleda firm. The title is *Grundlagen der Potenzierungsforschung (Principles of Involution Research)*. It is clear to me from reading it that the Weleda medicines are not subjected to magic charms. They are, however, pre-treated biorhythmically. This process consists of taking some of the constituents of the Weleda medicines and, at the full moon, setting them in motion of biorhythmic frequency. They are moved round at various angles to the moon, twelve times in twelve fixed circles.

This information was enough to show me the nature of these medicines. I am familiar with moon magic both among primitive peoples and in the civilized western world. I hope it will not be taken amiss that I cannot approve of this kind of pre-treatment.

These biorhythmic ideas go back to Rudolf Steiner. He used theosophy, spiritism, and magic in constructing his philosophical system. Years ago I saw a newsletter from Steiner in which he gave instructions for the conduct of spiritist table-tapping. This is enough to make me reject anything that comes from Rudolf Steiner.

While we are on the subject of medicines, I must touch on another question. I have often been asked whether it is right for Christians to use the herbal remedies of Pastor Künzli and Pastor Emmenegger. There is no doubt that these herbs, the natural produce of our earth, can have healing properties if taken in the right quantities. The problem is that both Pastor Künzli and Pastor Emmenegger made use of the pendulum to test the herbs for their healing properties.

Pendulum dowsing is neither a gift of God nor a natural power, but an occult practice. Things which have been produced or selected by an occult method should not be accepted by Christians.

But I must issue a warning about going to the other extreme. It is wrong to have an exaggerated fear of the occult. Those who when ill use herbal remedies which are incidentally mentioned in Pastor Künzli's book of herbal medicine need not worry about this. Herbal remedies can be misused, but there is a right place for them also.

My grandmother knew nothing of Pastor Künzli or his book, but she taught me the use of many kinds of herbal tea, St. John's wort for kidney trouble, coltsfoot for bronchitis, a weed called *Bettellaus* for diabetes, centaury for stomach upsets, and many others. The Creator has given us in nature many things to help us, and we should use them gratefully. It might be mentioned that the prophet Isaiah recommended King Hezekiah to make a cake of figs and put it on his boil. And it worked (Isaiah 38:21). Let us be on guard against sorcery and idolatry, but do not let us call everything we do not understand occult.

71
YOGA

The word *yoga* is derived from Sanskrit and is possibly the root underlying the Greek word *iōgē*, shelter, and the Latin *jugum*, yoke. If these linguistic associations are anything to go by, to practice yoga is to put oneself under a yoke, or to seek shelter from a protective power.

It is impossible to present yoga fully in a short chapter. To begin with, there are many forms of Indian and Tibetan yoga, so many that it would take more than one large volume to list them all. It would take up too much space here even to describe one single form.

For a good introduction to yoga, Maurice Ray's book *Joga, ja oder nein?* is recommended. This book describes Hatha Yoga and Raja (Royal) Yoga from the standpoint of the Christian faith. It is the best discussion of yoga from a Christian point of view known to me.

In this brief account I can only give a very limited part of the whole. I have used the following sources:

1. Pastoral counseling in the West and the East, especially in East Asia, where I have traveled extensively eight times.
2. Information given me by the Indian professor de Roy, who has studied the yoga practice in his country.
3. The definitive work by Mishra on Patanjali Yoga: *The Textbook of Yoga Psychology.*

Several key sentences from Mishra's work will introduce us to the spiritual atmosphere of yoga:

a. The higher ego of man is transcendent and immanent, without beginning and without end, it has no birth and no death.

b. *Yoga* means the synthesis of the physical and metaphysical universe.

c. Heaven and hell are only products of the human mind.

d. Behind magic, mysticism and also behind the occult the yoga system is present.[50]

These four sentences show clearly that yoga and the Bible cannot be harmonized in the remotest way. The systems of the Far East and the Christian faith are irreconcilable opposites.

If we take a cross section of the most well-known forms of yoga, we can recognize four stages.

The *first* stage has the aim of helping the student of yoga to gain control of his consciousness and his body. This goal is achieved by means of mental and physical exercises.

The mental exercises include meditation, autogenic training, concentration, and "koan," a litany involving the continuous repetition of a mantra (secret word).

The physical exercises include breathing exercises and various bodily postures like the lotus position, the cobra position, and the headstand.

This first stage is thus psychosomatic in nature, producing unity of body and mind.

There are many Christians who believe that it is possible to participate in this first stage of yoga without harm. It is merely a matter of relaxation exercises. If only this were true! Counseling experience tells otherwise. This technique of relaxation and these "emptying exercises" so highly spoken of by the yogis lead to the inflowing of another spirit—other spirits. The students of yoga do not notice it.

Ex 266   G.C., a Christian teacher, told me that during an evangelistic campaign, a certain man and his daughter had wished to surrender their lives to Christ. But they found themselves unable to do so. Only after they had renounced their yoga exercises and repented of them did they succeed in coming through to Christ.

Ex 267   In Johannesburg, South Africa, I counseled a theology student. He was a young man who had been converted to Christ some years before. Hearing about a yoga course which had been announced in church, he applied to join. After a few months, he noticed a change in his spiritual life. His desire to read the Bible disappeared. He also became tired of prayer. I advised him very strongly to give up his yoga exercises at once and to renounce the whole thing.

The *second* stage of yoga involves the control of the unconscious mind. When a person has mastered the second stage, he can control and guide, for instance, his visceral nerves. I have met masters of the second stage who can perform astonishing feats.

Ex 268   In a Western university town, I met a theology student who practiced the second stage of yoga. He was able to increase or decrease his circulation of blood. Being inclined to be humorous, he used to entertain his fellow students by showing off his abilities. He could make one of his ears red and the other one white at the same time. He could also cause red spots to appear on his skin by suggestion.

I could only wonder what kind of gospel this young man will one day preach to his parishioners.

Ex 269   In a great metropolis, I heard of a police officer who is likewise a master of the second stage. He was able to produce stigmata (wound marks) on the palms of his hands, by suggestion. He is certainly not a saint: he is an atheist. Incidentally, we may note in passing that wound marks on the palms are not necessarily a religious phenomenon. There are unconscious and conscious, religious and non-religious stigmata; in other words, four types of wound marks which have absolutely nothing to do with Christ. As to whether imitation stigmata appear also as a result of mystical meditation on the wounds of Christ, I can only say that it is possible. It is certainly not necessary for faith or for salvation. We have Jesus, and we have no need of people who bear the stigmata, whether saints or otherwise, to give us salvation.

Ex 270   In Southeast Asia, I have often seen yogis who are able to reduce their breathing, pulse-rate, and circulation to a minimum.

They then go into a trance-like sleep, which can last between two and four weeks. During this time they take neither food nor fluids.

Ex 271   The most enlightening experience I have had of this sort was in California. A young woman came to me for counseling. She told me that she had been a master of the second stage of yoga. In the course of her yoga exercises, she had actually chosen Jesus as her guru. Note this, not Jesus as her Savior and Redeemer, but only as her example, her great master. During her yoga exercises, she developed occult powers. She became unhappy about it, and tried to free herself. It was then that she first realized what a power yoga had over her. She began to seek Christ. Several of her friends prayed for her. After terrible struggles she became free. She wrote an account of her experiences entitled "From Yoga to Christ." She gave me permission to publish it.

Yoga does not liberate; it enslaves. Yoga does not free; it binds. Yoga does not enlighten; it brings confusion. Yoga does not prepare the way for Christ, as Father J. M. Déchanet (Cahier du Val) claims, but makes people immune to redemption through Christ. Yoga does not open the door for the Holy Spirit, but for spiritist spirits.

This will become even plainer when we describe briefly stages three and four.

The *third* stage of yoga is concerned with the mastery of the natural powers. I have found very few examples of this in the West, but very many in the East. It is the speciality of Tibetan yogis to combine magic and yoga. After three years of apprenticeship under a lama, who is the master of this art, the adept (apprentice) has to be able to produce energy in the form of heat in natural objects, such as melting ice by means of mental concentration.

I have still more frequently come across the converse of this, where yogis are able to produce heat and even flames. We find this among the fire worshippers, who also practice fire magic.

Ex 272   In Port Elizabeth, one of these fire masters, who had emigrated from India to South Africa, came to me for counseling. He made a confession and asked for my help. I showed him the way to Jesus. He was willing to accept Jesus as his Lord. I do not know if he has continued in the faith. Occultists often fall back into their old ways.

Those who are still in doubt as to whether stage one or two of yoga results in occult processes must admit that when it comes to stage three, yoga leads to the powers of the abyss.

Maurice Ray writes, "Everyone who seriously engages in Hatha

Yoga gains new powers. These include telepathy, presentiments, second sight and all the powers of a supernatural order which are indispensable for occult activities."[51] Perhaps we ought to have this in mind when we read the example of the pastor who was able to discover hidden things by meditation.

At the *fourth* stage, the yogi gains the mastery of the dark arts. The Lamas of Tibet are particularly well known for this. I have collected very many examples of stage four yoga. In Kalimpong on the Tibetan border, I came into contact with many Tibetans. I have also received reports from former missionaries in Tibet. Especially enlightening was the confession of a man who has given me permission to publish his story.

Ex 273 My informant had studied yoga, magic and spiritism for ten years with the Lamas. He had heard of my lectures in Sydney and followed me on to Newcastle, Australia. He made a full confession and named his specific sins. He said, "What the Lamas teach is the cult of spirits, the cult of demons. Please help me to become free." We had a long talk together. From this man I learned that the Tibetan yogis are masters of the trance, materialization, excursion of the soul, telekinesis, levitation, perfectly controlled telepathy, and all the arts of spiritism. At stage four, which I have met in this intensity only with Tibetans, Zombis, Alauts, Maccumbas, and voodooists, yoga can no longer, with the best will in the world, disguise its true character. Here yoga reaches its ultimate master — Satan, whose desire it is with his promises and his wiles to snatch people away into the abyss.

There is no need for further comment on the religious side of yoga. Yoga ends not only in self-redemption and atheism, but in the cult of demons. Those who undertake to take part in yoga exercises enter a force field by which they are unwittingly directed towards the origin of these powers. These are the powers of which Paul speaks in his epistles, (see Colossians 2:15). Christ has freed us from the spirits, demons, and powers. The chief of these powers is Lucifer, who is seeking to win back those he has lost. And what successes he has gained, for yoga has become the fashion in the West!

A quotation from a book published overseas confirms my own view. In the book *Satan kämpft um diese Welt,* by Lindsey and Carlson, we read, "Chris Pike (a son of Bishop Pike) told me in a personal interview that he previously practiced yoga and meditation. As a result he had become controlled by spirit beings which had nearly destroyed his life. He then renounced these powers in the name of

Jesus, and today he is a witness to the transforming power of Jesus Christ. His life was completely changed."[52]

All Christians who are allowing themselves unsuspectingly to be led astray into yoga should take note of Galatians 5:1, "Stand fast therefore in the liberty wherewith Christ hath made us free, and be not entangled again with the yoke of bondage."

B. EFFECTS OF OCCULT MOVEMENTS AND DEVICES

It requires knowledge and experience in many areas to be able to distinguish the effects of sins of sorcery from medical and particularly psychiatric syndromes.

As I was writing this chapter, a friend told me of a psychiatrist who had spoken out against my books. This man had said he would read not a single line of them, because I rejected psychiatry. But how does this doctor know that I reject his disciplines if he has never read a line I have written? Anyone who has read my books *Christian Counselling and Occultism* or *Demonism Past and Present* will know that I have always maintained that a counselor who has studied psychiatry will find it helpful in dealing with the occult.

I resist only the encroachments of those psychiatrists who think they can master religious problems also. Obviously in a case of religious delusions and suchlike, psychiatric treatment is indicated. If, however, there is oppression resulting from occult activities, an experienced counselor is needed.

There are, of course, borderline cases where it is desirable that both a psychiatrist and a counselor should be involved, if possible together.

I have used the term *counselor*. Who is fitted to give counseling advice on the subject of occult oppression?

Not a modern theologian, to whom the irrational and the supernatural are foreign and unacceptable.

Not a believing pastor who has his mind closed to such counseling on *a priori* grounds.

Not an experienced counselor even, who thinks that he can do without the help of medical science.

The number of counselors fitted for this task is very small. As a result, those few who do exist find that they are so besieged by people seeking help that they do not know what to do. All those friends of mine who engage in counseling those who are occultly oppressed groan under the burden of these demands for help.

Who then is qualified to work in this field?

1. Only a person who has experienced a genuine rebirth through the power of the Holy Spirit.

2. Only a Christian who has gained wide experience through much counseling. It may be objected that everyone has to begin without experience. That is true. Beginners should be accompanied for a year or more by an older Christian, in order that they may grow and feel their way into this difficult area.

3. I have often been asked if every Christian should venture into the area of occult counseling. I would reply that no one ought to seek this ministry. If circumstances throw him into such a situation, he should form a prayer group of brethren around him, in order that he may not be shot down by the devil.

4. Among my closest friends, I have six times had the sad experience of seeing believing counselors who have engaged in counseling those bound by occult powers themselves broken in the process. I have frequently felt that a call is needed before engaging in this difficult ministry. One who is involved in counseling the occult-bound is usually not understood and indeed opposed even by well-meaning Christians. Without a divine commission, it is almost impossible to bear the weight of this onerous ministry.

5. It is very helpful for a counselor in this field to have medical, or even better, a psychiatric training. The study of theology is not as important as a medical training. Theological study is full of historical, philological, and philosophical ballast and often neglects the practical problems of life. I still have notes of the lectures on counseling I received at the University of Heidelberg. These lectures were so thin and empty that they cried out to heaven. But how are theology professors to know otherwise, if they have had neither a second birth nor any pastoral experience? Men of God are extremely rare as university lecturers. Many universities have not so much as one man with that training.

These words are not written in spiritual pride. One must, however, have the courage to call a spade a spade. I dare to do so in the name of God.

The effects of occult activity are many-sided, and I must confine myself here to the most important types so as to keep the book within bounds.

1
MEDIUMISTIC AFFINITY

Definition: The term *mediumistic affinity* is derived from two Latin words. The first is *medius, media, medium,* a word which has many meanings. Here just one is meant: mediator. A medium is a contact person between the known and the unknown, between the natural and the supernatural, between inquisitive people and evil spirits.

The second word is *affinitas,* close connection, contact, relation. Another way of expressing the idea of mediumistic affinity would be to talk of "ability to make psychic contact." Forty-five years of observation in this field has made it clear to me that, in most cases, mediumistic affinity is unconscious. This has something to do with the fact that psychic powers do not lie in the conscious mind, but in the unconscious. Hundreds of thousands of people are mediumistic, or psychic, without realizing it.

As I have already said in another chapter, mediumship can have any of three roots: heredity, transference, and magical experimentation.

1. *The extent of mediumship*

Mediumship covers a very wide area. When forks were bent in the homes of viewers during the Uri Geller show, the unconscious mediumship of the viewers was being tapped and used by the equally unconscious (or conscious?) powers of Uri Geller.

If phantoms of the "departed" are made to appear by a medium at a spiritist séance and the medium's own powers are not strong enough, the psychic participants are tapped and their mediumistic powers are used to assist.

People of psychic disposition are attracted by groups in which mediumistic powers are active, like mystic cults, spiritist groups, extreme and fanatical groups, unscriptural sects and movements. There are some extreme Pentecostal groups which are a regular Eldorado for psychic people. In many cases mediumship has a covering layer of religion, as for example in the neo-charismatic movement. Even if it seems wearisome to repeat, let it be said that there are in these groups also genuine, faithful children of God, for whom I have the greatest respect. But they do not really belong in these extreme groups.

2. *The ethical character of mediumship*

Because mediumship has its place in the unconscious mind, it is always in opposition to a conscious decision to follow Christ. Psychic people find it extraordinarily difficult to accept Jesus Christ as their Lord.

Psychic powers originate in the sorcery of a person's forebears or in his own. These powers are oppressive. *Affinity* means not only an ability to make contact, but also adhesion. A psychic person adheres unconsciously, or sometimes consciously, to the abominable sins of his forefathers, or to his own sins of sorcery, or he is linked unconsciously to a psychic circle of all those of psychic disposition.

This adhesion to the occult is a great problem on the mission field and in counseling in connection with evangelism. In areas like Los Angeles, Haiti, Rio de Janeiro, the Lüneburg Heath, and a thousand others that are similarly infested with occult activities, counseling is so difficult that evangelists shudder.

Mediumistic affinity is the breeding ground of the most crazy sects, cults, and lodges. This is why Los Angeles is so rich in these monstrosities from the swamp of Satan.

3. *Becoming conscious of a psychic disposition*

Unconscious mediumship can occasionally come to light as a result of certain experiences and so become conscious. An example from my counseling will serve to make clear what I mean.

Ex 274 A young woman came to me for counseling. She complained that every time a member of her family or close relative was about to die, she would see a shadowy figure in her room at night. She was afraid of these visions. Two or three days later she would hear of the person's death.

A parapsychologist would perhaps point to telepathy as the explanation of these experiences. Severe illnesses can sometimes be sensed by telepathy. This explanation, however, does not suffice in this case, for fatal accidents cannot be communicated by telepathy, three days before they happen.

The experiences of this young woman present us with the so-called "gift of second sight." Those who have this disposition frequently foresee deaths, fires, and catastrophies. What is the origin of this disposition?

After she had told me all about her visions, I asked her if her parents or grandparents had engaged in spiritism. She affirmed at once that they had. "In our family," she said, "table tapping has been practiced as a party game for at least three generations." She took part in this game herself as a child.

As a result of this spiritistic game, the young woman became psychic. Her mediumship manifested itself in the experiences she had at night.

4. *Forms of mediumship and strength of these powers*

Mediumship has many ways of expressing itself. It may be predictive dreams, which are fulfilled some days later. It may be sensitivity to the rod or pendulum. If a person who has never in his life had anything to do with the occult takes a rod or pendulum in his hand and the thing functions without any conscious impulsion, that person is psychic.

Mediumship varies in strength. A person with a low degree of mediumship may go through his whole life without being aware of it. On the other hand, a very strong degree of mediumship will make itself known even in childhood.

We know, for instance, of certain healing mediums who were able to heal people when the mediums were only ages 4 to 7. I have given some examples earlier in this book.

From a Biblical viewpoint, psychic gifts are the satanic counterpart of the gifts of the Holy Spirit. Satan's counterfeit gifts are mostly exercised under a religious front, and therefore their demonic character goes unrecognized. Indeed these counterfeit gifts are sometimes even declared to be gifts of the Holy Spirit.

The most well-known psychic gifts include many forms already mentioned in this book; clairvoyance, telesthesia, clairaudience, ability to go into trance, automatic writing, telekinesis, excursion of the soul, apports, causation of poltergeist phenomena, sensitivity to rod and pendulum, and many other such things.

Anyone who suffers from such troubles — for they cannot be called gifts — should not regard himself as important, but should rather be concerned to find deliverance. The parapsychologists, of course, are very pleased when they find a highly qualified medium for their experiments. It furthers their "science" and brings them more fame.

The devil's strategy is many-sided. To occultists he represents his intrigues as "new knowledge," while he convinces the rationalists that it is all a matter of tricks, swindle, and superstition.

5. *Genuine experiences of God*

In contrast to psychic experiences are genuine experiences of God. God can forewarn and protect His children in various ways. I will give an example. My informant is a long-standing friend of mine in England, Paul Hunt of Englefield Green.

Ex 275 Paul's friend Richard and his wife are believing Christians. One day they were riding a tandem down a steep hill. Just before a sharp bend, Richard suddenly felt anxious. The hair on his neck stood on end, and his color became white as a sheet. He stopped. "What's the matter?" asked his wife. "Why are you so frightened?"

Richard could give no answer. He just looked anxiously around, but could see nothing dangerous. They went ahead on foot. Just around the bend, the road was blocked. A lamp post had been knocked over by a car and was lying across the road. The car was also standing there, badly damaged. No warning sign had been put up. The owner of the car had gone off to find help. The couple would have ridden their tandem right into the blockage, if Richard had not been fore-warned.

What is the difference between psychic precognition and warnings from the Lord?

Psychic warnings announce an event which is inevitable. The event cannot be escaped.

God's warnings serve to preserve God's children from harm. The danger which has been announced can then be avoided. I will give another example.

Ex 276   It was in the summer of 1974. Many German vacationers were staying in Tenerife (in the Canary Islands). At the airport were one hundred eighty German vacationers, waiting for the flight to take them home. Among them was a couple from Bavaria. When the wife entered the airplane, she felt uneasy. "Come," she said to her husband, "let's get out of this plane. There are so many people here. I am afraid. Something might happen." Her husband was not very will-ing to follow his wife's wishes, but he did so nonetheless. They went back to the airport lounge, aware that they might well not be able to obtain a refund of money paid for this flight. Some hours later, news arrived that the plane had crashed. All the passengers had been killed. The man from Germany was deeply stirred. He hurried to the telephone and called his children in Bavaria. "Don't worry about us," he said. "We were not in the airplane which crashed. We have our Lord to thank, and your mother's intuition."

It is encouragement to one's faith to hear such a story in a world so full of disaster. God has not given our earth up to the demons. His hand reaches down into the chaos of this earth to help and to save. And the time is coming when God will wipe away every tear from the eyes of the children of men.

2
RESISTANCE TO THE THINGS OF GOD

One of the chief characteristics of mediumship is that mediums are immunized against the work of the Holy Spirit. A person of psychic disposition has a resistance to all that has to do with genuine Christian faith. He is insensitive to the promptings of the Holy Spirit, and he has no love for the word of God or for prayer. In cases of strong mediumship, a person will become ill to the point of vomiting when he is confronted with clear Biblical preaching.

This phenomenon of resistance to the things of God shows itself in another way also. In some cases, people suffering from occult oppression always become ill before the great festivals of the church, so that they are unable to attend the Christmas or Easter services. If an evangelistic campaign or a week of Bible teaching is planned, they always fall ill just before the week begins. It is as if the devil were continually trying to stop them from hearing Biblical preaching.

I can illustrate this best by one or two examples.

Ex 277   Some years ago a young man came to me for counseling. He had availed himself of various kinds of occult help. If he had questions he could not answer, he would go to a fortuneteller, an astrologer, or a dowser. If he was sick he would go to a notorious charmer, with the result that he would actually make a quick recovery. Since he started doing this, however, the young man suffered from fits of mania, especially before the festivals of the church or when an evangelist or missionary was due to preach in his home church. This all came out in the course of counseling, and I was able to show the young man the way to Jesus Christ.

Ex 278   The following example is of particular value because the man concerned was first examined by a Christian psychiatrist. The man in question was a preacher of the gospel who went for treatment to the famous psychiatrist Dr. Lechler, with whom I had contact for many years, and whom I highly respected. The preacher told the doctor that he had terrible struggles in performing his pastoral duties. This problem had begun as soon as he was converted. When he went to Bible school, it became worse, and he sometimes considered leaving the Bible school. He held out, however, and became a preacher; but his struggles were not over. Especially when he read the Bible, prayed, preached the word of God, and conducted the communion, he was subject to terrible attacks.

Dr. Lechler thought the preacher was overconscientious and that his anxiety not to sin had turned into an opposite reaction. Such reactions certainly do happen. I have met such things occasionally in counseling.

The treatment that the preacher was given at the Hohe Mark Clinic did not bring him relief, and so he sought my advice. I asked him to tell me his family history, not only concerning his parents but also his grandparents. It came to light that he had been charmed in early childhood. His brothers and sisters had likewise been treated by a healing practitioner who used magic charms. The result was that all of them suffered with the same symptoms.

The problem here was thus neither a psychiatric nor a psychological one, but a spiritual matter which could only be discovered by Christian counseling.

Ex 279   A certain deaconess administered a charm to another deaconess who was ill. Both sisters were one day present at a prayer meeting led by Mother Eva. During the prayer time, the sister who had been charmed began to rave. She had also found difficulty in bringing herself to attend meetings in the chapel. Mother Eva went to the heart of the matter. It turned out that the other deaconess had learned about charms from an aunt. They both confessed their sin and found deliverance through the spirit-filled ministry of Mother Eva. After the spell had been broken, however, both sisters were ill for a while. This reaction is also found sometimes; people who are freed from the ban of sorcery become ill and experience other difficulties.

Ex 280   I had a typical experience when I was lecturing in the Martin Luther Church in Curitiba, Brazil. During the service on Sunday morning there were three disturbances. A woman who was the daughter of a magic charmer and who had had all her children charmed, fell into a spiritistic trance during the sermon and heard nothing. She did not regain consciousness until I said the final "Amen." A second woman, a Salvation Army officer, ran out of the church. Later she confessed that she had been unable to bear the preaching. A voice within her had been whispering to her continually: "Cry out aloud, disturb the message!" In order not to make herself noticed, she had left the church. The third person was a girl who had likewise heard a voice saying to her during the sermon, "Curse God, blaspheme Him." She too left the church. Talking to her later, I discovered that she had been charmed against an illness as a child.

Here we have three examples of resistance to the things of God caused by sins of sorcery present in a single church service. Brazil is full of spiritism. Those who preach the gospel in Brazil come up against it nearly every day, unless they are afflicted with total blindness and avoid all problems of this sort.

Ex 281   Several times people have confessed to me in the course of counseling that although they are quite open to the gospel, they become unable to move every time they try to pick up a Bible, read, and pray. The latest example of this kind, which has not yet even been recorded in my files, is as follows. In a Catholic area in which a great deal of sorcery is practiced, a woman came for counseling. She confessed that when she wanted to read her Bible, she became stiff as a board and could neither hold nor open the Bible. The state of tonic immobility without loss of consciousness is familiar to me from the study of medicine. We find such conditions in cases of catalepsy and also in myoclonic epilepsy.

No such disorder was present in the case of this person. The disturbance only occurred when she wanted to read the Bible or to pray. I inquired about her history with regard to the occult, and was more than shocked. The whole of her family, back to her great-grandparents, had engaged in spiritism and magic of every kind. This was the origin of the frightful oppression which the woman had described to me.

The woman was willing to accept Jesus Christ as her Lord. Together we prayed a prayer of renunciation. From that time onward, she came regularly to my meetings. I am well aware that when people are as strongly affected as this, it is easy for them to fall back into being oppressed. Normally, therefore, a prayer group should be formed to intercede for a person who is under such strong psychic oppression.

It is an experience confirmed by thousands of examples that people, who are oppressed because of occult involvement, usually have peace as long as they serve the devil and avoid Christ. If on the other hand they wish to decide for Christ, dreadful struggles begin. The rule is quite straightforward: the devil leaves those who serve him in peace. Not until he is theatened with losing his victim do his attacks begin. Sadly, it is also very evident that not all those who come to Christ are at once freed of their occult oppression. If the surrender to Christ is not complete and if all the Biblical rules are not observed, the person who has decided for Christ may have weeks, months, or even years of great trouble. It is not true, as superficial and inexperienced counselors often assert, that all occult problems are over when a person is converted.

I can demonstrate this best with an example.

Ex 282 Some years ago a well-known evangelist came to me for a talk. He said that he had read my book *Christian Counselling and Occultism*. As a result his eyes had been opened. His work as an evangelist had been under a form of oppression for twenty-five years which he had never been able to account for. Now he had for the first time realized the cause. When he was a young child, his mother had had him charmed against an illness. Later he had been soundly converted to Christ, and after theological training had been serving the Lord for twenty-five years. He had always felt as if he had lead weights on his feet. I was able to show this evangelist the way of deliverance. He took my advice and said a prayer of renunciation. I declared him free in the name of the Lord, and he was delivered. Some months later he wrote me a letter in which he testified that since then his ministry had been completely changed. The lead weights had gone. This was the work of the living Lord Jesus.

3

DISTORTION OF CHARACTER

Occult oppression sometimes takes the form of extreme tendencies and traits of character. I will give a few examples.

Ex 283   In Brazil, a twenty-year-old girl came to me for counseling. She suffered from a violent temper. On one occasion she had thrown a pair of scissors at her younger sister and injured her head badly. Then she had tried to cut her own arteries, but had been stopped in time. She desired to follow Christ and was even a helper in Sunday school. But her terrible temper was a great trouble to her. In the course of counseling, it came to light that she had been charmed when ill at the age of six by a Curandeiro.

Ex 284   B., the nature healer of Appenzell, also gives treatment by telephone. The mother of a seven-year-old child telephoned him and said that the child had an inflamed appendix and would have to go to hospital for an operation. "That is not necessary," replied B. "She will be free of her appendix trouble in no time at all." The operation did prove unnecessary. The result was that the child became dreadfully depraved. At the age of ten she seduced a married man — not vice versa. At the age of twelve she had sexual relations with a man in public service, who was brought to court because of it. From the age of twenty onward she lived with a well-known public figure without being married.

Occult healing is always dearly paid for. The cost is not only the loss of salvation, but often serious disasters in a person's lifetime, or accidents, or continual illness.

Ex 285   A young boy was often caught stealing. He stole a bicycle, although he had one of his own. At school nothing was safe when he was around. He stole pens and books and rubbers, and many little things that he had already. When he was called to account, he tried to get away by lying. Finally he admitted it and said, "I don't want to steal, but I am forced to do it." In counseling it was learned that as a young boy his mother had taken him to a charmer when he was ill.

Compulsive lying, compulsive stealing (kleptomania), and compulsive arson (pyromania) are frequently the result of occult healing. In the last few years there has been much news in the papers about pyromania. A young incendiary in North Germany, for instance, set fire to a number of historic buildings and destroyed property worth millions. The boy was subjected to a psychiatric examination. But the psychiatrists never considered the possibility of connections with the sorcery practiced by a person's forebears. They will put it down to a maladjustment or faulty development.

Ex 286 A married couple were converted during an evangelistic campaign. Both husband and wife accepted Jesus as their Lord. Since their conversion, terrible attacks and troubles have come into their lives. The struggles begin usually two days before the festivals of the church or when a prayer meeting takes place in their home. Then fits of temper and quarreling break out between this Christian couple. Strangely enough, the couple's unbelieving relatives do not suffer such problems. Again, the couple are frequently ill. Their unbelieving relatives say, "That comes of your religion."

In counseling it became clear that both husband and wife come from families of sorcerers. Here we have again the oft-repeated pattern of the devil leaving in peace those who serve him. Not until they run away from his school does he begin to attack.

Ex 287 A woman from Poland came to me for counseling. She told me that as a child she had had rickets. Her mother went to a magic charmer and was given the following instructions, "Get some earth from nine different fields; tie it up together with a spell from the *Sixth and Seventh Book of Moses* in a cloth. Then pour some hot water over the earth. Then bathe the child in this water. Then take the earth back where it came from. Then the child will recover." The Polish woman obeyed the instructions. The child recovered. But the child also developed in a strange way. She was very ready to quarrel, apt to fly into a violent temper, and suffered from severe sexual perversions. She brought a great deal of disharmony and quarreling into the family.

Ex 288 A man told me, in the course of counseling, of great problems he had in his thought life. In his youth he had practiced homosexuality. He often had sexually blasphemous thoughts about Christ. This man was converted during an evangelistic campaign. He was not however freed from all these problems. I told him that I had encountered such symptoms before in connection with sins of sorcery. He admitted that this was so in his case. "When I was a soldier," he explained, "I had my palm read. Later I went also to card-layers and pendulum dowsers. My grandfather was also a man who suffered from magical oppression. On the eve of May Day, he used to stand a broom upright to ward off witches." I showed the man how he could find deliverance and prayed a prayer of renunciation with him, for he was willing to become a follower of Jesus.

Ex 289 A man of high position in the academic world came to me for pastoral advice. He told me about his mother who had practiced sorcery. His mother had once said to him in anger, "I am going to the lake of fire of my own free will. God will not have to send me there. I will not give Him the chance." The son, who was repelled by his mother's activities, sought the way to Christ in order to be free from the vicious circle. From that time on, he had terrible struggles. In fits of anger he broke the crockery in the kitchen. He beat his wife and children so badly that they ran away from him in fear. None of this had happened beforehand. This behavior only began when he surrendered to Christ.

One should not conclude from such stories that the devil is stronger than Christ. The devil is an enemy we should take seriously, and no more. The fact remains that Christ conquered him on the cross of Calvary. If we make use of all the means and possibilities of help which are shown us in the Bible, we can find complete deliverance. We shall return to this later.

4

EMOTIONAL DISORDERS

There are many things which can give rise to emotional disorders. Years ago, I was invited by Akira Hartori, the well-known radio evangelist in Tokyo, to address a meeting of ministers on the subject of depression. In my address, I described some twenty different causes of depression. Only one of the twenty is occult in character. Those who are not familiar with the medical aspect of emotional disorders are in great danger of making false diagnoses and therefore giving the wrong treatment. In this chapter I am concerned only with emotional disorders having occult causes and not with the complex subject of hereditary, reactive, or organic causes for emotional disturbance.

Ex 290 A woman in a European port told me the story of her family. As a girl, her sister had taken part in spiritistic séances. She herself had refused to do so. The medium in the séance was so strong that she only had to think about the table and not even to touch it. The table would then move and give tapping signals. The sister who took part in these séances today suffers from a compulsive neurosis. She hears voices and talks to them. The voices give her commands which she obeys. This sister under the influence of spiritism is almost driving her healthy sister out of her mind.

A psychiatrist would of course regard the voices as a symptom of schizophrenia. But there are voices which have a spiritistic background.

Ex 291 During an evangelistic campaign in Edmonton, a Christian woman came to me for help. She gave me permission to publish her story provided I mentioned no names. One morning this Christian woman woke up and said to her sister, "I saw you in a car with your friends. You had an accident. You were one of those killed." A week later the accident happened. Three girls and a young man, all of them believers, and members of Christian Endeavor, were in a car when they were hit by a truck. It was the truck driver's fault. All four of the young people died, including my informant's sister.

I told this woman that predictive dreams of this sort often originate with sorcery practiced by one's forebears or magic charms. She admitted that once she had her warts charmed. Since then she had suffered from depression, although she had been able to overcome this through faith in Christ and prayer.

Ex 292 A young man came to me for counseling, complaining of depression, suicidal thoughts, and inability to make decisions. Often he felt unable to cope with his work. He felt as if he were paralyzed. His family history presented a dismal picture. His great-aunt, who lived with the family, practiced pendulum dowsing. She used the pendulum for all the members of the family. She swung her pendulum over their daily food. She used it to solve everyday problems and to discover the future. She used it whenever decisions were to be made. The result was that the whole of their family life was disturbed. Both children and parents suffered from depression, and all sorts of other troubles afflicted them.

I have several hundred examples concerning pendulum and rod dowsers, and all are negative in character. I cannot understand those theologians and Christian workers who regard dowsing as harmless.

Ex 293 A young woman of thirty-four came to me for counseling. She told me that her great-grandmother had been a charmer and card-layer. All four generations were depressive and tended to extremes of character.

A psychiatrist would, of course, probably talk in terms of manic-depressive psychosis. This is a disorder which frequently repeats itself over four generations. Manic-depressive psychosis has different characteristics from the depressions which arise from sins of sorcery.

Ex 294 A Christian nurse came to me for a personal talk. She said she had problems. She heard voices, she suffered from depression, and her sleep was disturbed—all in spite of the fact that she read the Bible, prayed, and belonged to the Church of Christ. The history of her trouble revealed that at the age of ten she had been charmed for boils.

Ex 295 A theology student suffering from a compulsive neurosis came to me for counseling. His father and mother were believers. His grandmother was an active magic charmer. The young man had compulsive, fixed ideas, with a pronounced tendency to repetition. On one occasion he had played a practical joke on April Fools' Day. Four years later he went from house to house, asking the people to forgive him for this joke. He was well aware that some things he did were ridiculous. But this compulsion from his unconscious mind was stronger than his conscious will.

Twenty-five years ago I had an interesting experience. I pointed out to Dr. Lechler, then the head of the Hohe Mark nerve clinic, that about fifty percent of the compulsive neurotics whom I had counseled had connections with spiritism or magic in their background. Dr. Lechler was unable to comment on this, because he was not in the habit of asking patients about their occult involvement when tracing their medical history. He said, however, that he would introduce this point into his examination of patients. About fifteen years later, he wrote to tell me that he could confirm my finding. A good half of the compulsive neurotics had forebears who had come under occult influence as a result of sins of sorcery.

At this point I must again warn against ascribing all mental disorders to occult causes. Only a small percentage of emotional disorders have occult roots. Other forms of mental disorder must be treated by psychotherapists or psychiatrists. It is, however, often difficult to separate the two areas and to say whether a particular problem is spiritual or medical. We must not let these many examples make us impulsive in our judgments, or worse still, make us victims of an occult neurosis. That too is possible. I am sometimes plagued by people who want to account for anything unusual in their lives in terms of the occult. This is a form of delusion. I warn people against the occult but have no wish to make people paranoid about the occult. My opponents will want to attack me at this point. I do not mind. The problem of the occult is neglected by theologians, psychiatrists, and psychologists to such an extent that someone has to raise a warning.

5

A BREEDING GROUND FOR MENTAL ILLNESS

It must be clearly emphasized that I do not regard occult practices as the causes of mental illness, but as the breeding ground, the environment, the spiritual climate in which mental disorders can easily develop. There are, moreover, within the field of spiritism some disorders, for instance the mediumistic psychosis, which are very similar to real mental diseases. I will try to make clear what I mean by examples.

Ex 296   A missionary and his wife came to me for advice. The missionary's brother heard voices and had compulsive ideas. The doctor's diagnosis is schizophrenia. The family history revealed that both the grandfather and great-grandfather were magic charmers. Here again it must be emphasized that the practice of charming is not the cause of the mental disorder, but rather provides the conditions, the soil, in which mental disorders can easily grow.

Ex 297   A man came to me for counseling in Blumenau. He told me that he suffered from compulsive drives. He often heard voices saying, "murder your wife," or "take your own life." On being questioned, he informed me that his mother practiced spiritistic table-tapping. He also told me that all his children were abnormal. At the age of 10, 12 and 15 they still wet their beds and did other abnormal things.

Ex 298   In England, a doctor came to me for counseling. He had had a nervous breakdown and had been suspended from his profession. He had been given nine electric shock treatments at a psychiatric clinic. When I asked him to tell me the history of his illness, I discovered that his father had been a freemason and also a spiritist. His mother was a fortuneteller and spiritist healer. It is actually quite usual for such a marriage to produce children who are severely oppressed. This was the case with this doctor.

Ex 299   In England, an Anglican priest told me the story of his brother. Years before his brother had had trouble with his knee. The doctors who examined him thought that it was tuberculosis. Then a pendulum practitioner was called in. He said, "No, it is not tuberculosis." How did this man make his diagnosis? On his table he had a paper with a list of the various bacilli and bacteria. He put his left hand on this paper. To the right of the table was a transistor with an electrode and a meter connected up between. He laid his right hand on this. Then he concentrated mentally on the patient, who was also present in the room. Then he moved his left hand down the list of bacilli. The transistor gave the highest reading when he came to the right disease. As a result, the Anglican priest's brother was able to be healed. Two years later, the man who had been healed developed religious mania. Pendulum diagnosis and treatment belong within the field of occult practices.

Ex 300   A woman came to me for counseling. She complained of the disintegration of her family and her marriage. Her husband would sometimes rage and roar like a bull, and then he would become quite sensible and normal again. He had already spent some time in a mental institution. His grandfather had been an active magic charmer.

Ex 301   In Canada, a spiritist woman came to me. She told me that her grandmother had been a spiritist, and that she herself was a spiritist medium. She confessed that all four grandchildren of this spiritist grandmother were mentally abnormal. This spiritist medium came to me because she wanted to protest against my address on the subject of healing. In the address, I had declared that spiritist healings also cause oppression. She denied this and stated that she herself had been healed by a spiritist healer. She went on to say that she had the ability to make contact with good spirits. She could hear them, feel them, and sense their presence. Sometimes, it was true, bad spirits would find their way in as well, but she was able to drive these away by prayer. This confirmed my suspicions. This woman is already suffering from a mediumistic psychosis.

I fully recognize treatment given by psychiatrists in cases of genuine mental illness. There are various forms of therapy. Pharmacists have developed a number of effective medicines. In serious cases, electric shock treatment or a sleeping cure can be used. In the USA, now often used is a water cure, in which the patient is put in a bath in a fetal position. In the case of mental disorders which have developed in the context of sins of sorcery by the forebears, these forms of treatment are very often ineffective. One must simply distinguish between medical problems and Biblical, spiritual problems.

6
OPPRESSION OF DESCENDANTS

In the examples already given, it is clear in a number of cases that charmers, spiritists, and sorcerers bring oppression on their descendants to the third and fourth generations. This accords with the second of the Ten Commandments, which speaks of "visiting the iniquity of the fathers upon the children to the third and fourth generation of those who hate God." I will add a few more examples to make this clearer.

Ex 302 On a missionary journey through Thailand, I was accompanied by Mr. Pretel, a missionary who was later killed in a road accident. He told me of the following incident. In a mission church, a very-gifted, young Thai was converted. The mission raised money to send him to Bible school in the USA. He became a pastor, returned home, and was given a church to look after. Soon he went off the rails to such an extent that he had to give up his office. The background of this story is that his father had been healed by a spiritist healer.

Ex 303 While I was on a speaking tour in Brazil, a minister came to me, not for counseling, but to have a discussion with me. I had spoken against using the pendulum. This minister was in the habit of using the pendulum. He admitted that the practice could exhaust a person's nervous energy if he overdid it. He regarded it, however, as a gift of God. The minister's daughter is mentally deranged. He explained that his daughter's condition was the price he had to pay for his ability to help others with the pendulum. One must always bear some cost oneself, and in this case it was the mental illness of his daughter. A strange theology; it would be better if this minister would study the Second Commandment.

Ex 304 While I was on a speaking tour in the province of Santa Catarina, Brazil, a woman Salvation Army officer came to me for counseling. She was of psychic disposition and encountered severe attacks during the night and when praying or reading her Bible. In my addresses, I mentioned some examples similar to events in her own family, and she therefore had confidence in me. As she told the story of her life, the following facts came out. Her grandmother and her mother were active spiritists. Her mother's brother had committed suicide. Her father had been killed in an explosion. Her own husband had been killed in a road accident. Her eldest son also had a fatal accident.

This example shows us several aspects of what things are like in a spiritist's family: accidents, suicides, mental disorders, and severe attacks from the powers of darkness. If the spiritist grandmother had known what trouble she would cause with her spirits, she would perhaps have left it alone. Frequent accidents and suicides are a familiar phenomenon in the realm of the occult. This will become even clearer in the chapters which follow.

7
FREQUENT SUICIDES

Ex 305   During a series of addresses in Hamburg, a man came to me with the following story. Both his mother and sister had attempted suicide. The grandfather had been a magic charmer. He had committed suicide, as had his brother. This family's balance sheet: 2 suicides, 2 attempted suicides. Furthermore, the members of this family are well known for their hard, self-righteous, and egotistical natures. They make no contact with the world around them and of course have no links with the Word of God or with Christ.

Ex 306   When I was on a speaking tour of South Africa, a woman came to me for advice. Her mother was a card-layer. Her father had taken his own life. Her brother, likewise, had committed suicide. Her sister was a missionary but was completely emotionally unhinged. She was addicted to lesbianism, suffered from depression, and was unable to read the Bible or to pray, despite her work as a missionary.

Ex 307   Many years ago, I gave two lectures at the Geesthacht High School in Schleswig-Holstein. Dr. Rieck, who was then headmaster of the school, told me that as far as suicides were concerned, that province had the highest figures in Germany. I was not surprised, for Schleswig-Holstein, along with the Lüneburg Heath, is also known to have the largest number of magic charmers in the entire Federal Republic.

8
GHOSTS AND POLTERGEISTS RESULTING FROM
SINS OF SORCERY

Ex 308   A girl in the sixth grade at school came to faith in Christ. Her father had died as an unbeliever a year before. Several months later he reappeared in waking visions, and he spoke to his daughter. She saw him. The appearances became more and more frequent. The father's face took on increasingly sinister-looking features. Finally, he ordered his daughter to commit suicide. During these visitations, the daughter felt as if she were paralyzed. She could neither pray nor move nor even think about Jesus.

A woman minister took the girl to a critical psychiatrist, whom I know very well. Before he spoke to the girl, he said, "These are hallucinations and delusions." When he had spoken to her he said, "She has no medical disorder, she must go to a Christian counselor." To guard against any mistake, the minister took the girl to Dr. Lechler, then the most well-known psychiatrist in Germany. Dr. Lechler was a believing Christian. He, too, diagnosed no mental illness, but said that the girl was actually being plagued by spiritistic phenomena. He offered the girl some pastoral help. Dr. Lechler was not only a psychiatrist, but also a spiritual father and pastor.

Ex 309 During a speaking tour in Western Canada, a twenty-three-year-old girl came to me for counseling. She said that at night the doors in her house would open and shut without any visible cause. The radio also turned on. She heard footsteps and scratching noises, and saw glimmers of light and faces. She heard voices and bangings, although the doors were all locked securely. She was not suffering from a mental disorder. I asked her if spiritism had ever been practiced in the house or in her family. She admitted that her grandmother had been a spiritist and a magic charmer and had died in a terrible way. It is usual for spiritists' houses to be haunted by poltergeists. if spiritism has been practiced in them for years on end.

Ex 310 I received a call from a deaconesses' home, asking me for help. A young deaconess could not sleep at night. The furniture, especially the table, danced around the room. My answer was, "If it is not a case of hallucinations, then it is possibly the result of spiritism." The deaconesses confirmed that the girl's father had practiced spiritist table-tapping for many years. As a result, the daughter was psychic and was used by these dark powers as a medium. The parapsychologists would again say that this was an example of poltergeists appearing in the presence of an adolescent. As if that solved the problem! The sisters in this home did the right thing. They formed a prayer group which met and prayed in the young novice's room. Both the girl and the room were freed from the poltergeists.

9
FREQUENT DISEASES

People who come under the curse of sins of sorcery are frequently plagued with illness of every sort. Here, too, one must be on guard against over-hasty conclusions and avoid ascribing all unaccountable diseases to occult causes. It is necessary, in every case, for a qualified doctor to be asked to make his diagnosis and prescribe treatment. One must not, under any circumstances, allow himself to fall victim to an occult or hysterical *maladie imaginaire*. When the doctor's work is done, there remains a great deal of ground for the counselor to cover.

Ex 311   Brazil is the country in which I have had the greatest number of sessions with people oppressed through spiritism. This is because Brazil is one of the world's strongholds of spiritism. In the region of Ponta Grossa, a woman came to me for counseling. She had been a member of a spiritist group for eighteen years. Then she left it, because she had a complete lack of peace and wanted to find Christ. Since making this decision, she had suffered from disturbed sleep and depression, and still could find no peace. One thing she confessed was that she possessed a "letter from heaven," and that she had been charmed against an illness as a child. In addition to all her emotional disorders, she had an inexplicable skin disease, which no skin specialist had been able to cure.

It may frequently be observed that people under occult influence suffer from skin disorders. An example follows.

Ex 312   In a city in Santa Catarina, Brazil, a couple brought their son to me. He was suffering from sclerodactylia. His fingers were stiff like claws. The skin of his hand was rough and hard and was gradually peeling off. The muscles were also affected. Even the bones were atrophying. The parents had heard my addresses and thought that I might be able to give some advice. I asked about the family history and was told that both grandmothers had been charmers. Doctors who know nothing of spiritual processes will laugh at the suggestion that these facts are connected. And yet one frequently finds that incurable skin diseases appear in families whose forebears have practiced sorcery.

Ex 313   Another example shows the nature of an hysterical, or psychically caused disease. A woman came to me for an interview. She had had one disease after another. First it was a lung infection, then an inflammation around the kidneys, then a compulsive neurosis. Finally it continued so far that she practically went through the whole medical textbook, one disease following another. Her medical history was a typical pattern of hysterical illness, or of illness resulting from psychic associations. Her family history revealed that her grandmother had been a card-layer who had also had her children and grandchildren charmed. In a case of this sort, medicine can offer no deliverance. It is a spiritual problem.

Ex 314 When I was staying on the islands of Fiji, a woman came to me for counseling. She was a European settler. This woman had frequent attacks of complete motionlessness. I have already given one example of how a person can become as stiff as a board when he wants to pick up a Bible or to pray. This woman had been to a doctor for treatment. The doctor could find no reason for her condition. In his opinion, everything was in order organically. I gave the woman several examples of how in East Asia and in Africa, people sometimes experience a kind of cataleptic fit if they are under influence resulting from their forefathers' sins of sorcery. I asked the woman if her father, mother, or if she had ever practiced such things. She said they had not. On the way home, she told the woman who was my hostess that as a little girl she had taken part in table tapping. She had not regarded this as of any significance. Yet there we may see the connection.

Ex 315 A young woman suffered from remarkable fits of epilepsy. Her family doctor was unable to get to the bottom of her trouble, so he sent her to the university clinic. In this clinic it was established that the woman had a rare form of epilepsy; what is known as myoclonic epilepsy. Since this was the only case of its type in the clinic, she was used as a guinea pig. She was asked to come at certain intervals in order to try out various medicines. The treatment was free of charge. In her conversation with me, she told me that she had been charmed while she was still in her mother's womb. Her mother had tried to abort her by means of a magic charm. It had not been successful. Now she was trying to find the way to Christ, since the medical treatment she had received had not helped her.

This brings us to the end of our tour of the effects of occult oppression. I do not recommend anyone to read this book through as if it were a thriller. It is only a reference book, containing information in certain areas. People who are unstable or who are unusually sensitive and easy to influence should certainly read this book only in very small quantities. My opponents will now want to ask me, "Why do you write such books at all if you know the dangers involved?" Only those who have sufficient experience are qualified to write books on this subject. Believing Christians will perhaps understand what struggles have been involved for someone who has spent forty-five years in counseling and has heard some twenty-thousand terrible cases. Normally, no one would be able to hold out so long, even with the strongest nerves. It is a miracle of the preserving grace of God that the devil has not destroyed me long ago. At this point, I would once again ask all believing Christians to pray earnestly for my family, my work, and for me.

Let us conclude this chapter on the effects of occult involvement on a positive note.

Ex 316 Some years ago a young woman came to me for counseling. She was covered from head to foot with a dreadful skin disorder. I asked her how she ever got married in such a condition.

"This skin disease disappears now and then for a few months," she replied. "Then it comes back again." She has spent thousands of dollars going to skin specialists. None has been able to help her. I asked her if any of her forebears had practiced sorcery. She said, "Yes my grandfather produced charms for cattle and spells against disease, my father had learned these arts from the grandfather and had likewise practiced them for years." And now she had this terrible skin disease which tormented her for years, driving her to despair. I showed the young woman the way to Jesus Christ. Her dreadful plight moved me greatly. I wondered if I ought to pray with her along the lines of James 5:14. I had some reservations about this, since her disease was a result of her father's and grandfather's sins of sorcery. I asked a believing pastor, a friend of mine, what he thought about it. He was ready and willing and bold enough to lay hands on the woman and pray. He did so only as far as her disease was concerned, not in connection with the occult involvement. We both put ourselves under the protection of Christ, and then we prayed with the woman, laying our hands upon her, that she might be healed of the dangerous skin disease. I then left the area. Eighteen months later, I met the pastor again and asked him how the young woman was. He replied with a beaming smile that since our prayer for her with laying on of hands, she had been free of this terrible skin trouble. The woman had been following Jesus ever since. That is a triumph of the grace of God. Here Christ has set up a trophy of His victory. We are not simply abandoned to the power of Satan. There is a place where we can attain victory in the name of Jesus. We shall read of further examples like this in the two following chapters, on the subject of deliverance, and in the final chapter of this book.

C. DELIVERANCE

We come now to the most important point as far as Christian counseling is concerned. How can people who suffer occult oppression or are possessed by demons be delivered? If there were no way of deliverance and freedom from occult oppression, I would not have written this book. My wish now is that the Holy Spirit may give me wisdom and so inspire my writing that the reader will have the desire to seek and to find the way of deliverance.

If the examples in parts A and B of this book are compared with those in parts C and D, it will be observed that there are far more examples of occult oppression than there are of deliverance. This will be held against me by some. "Why do you not give more examples which show release and deliverance?" they will ask. I have two things to say in reply.

1. Many of the people whose oppression is mentioned in parts A and B have found deliverance.

2. The number of people who find freedom is always smaller than the number of the oppressed. Jesus says at the end of the Sermon on the Mount that there are many who go the broad way and only a few who find the narrow way. Salvation, healing, and deliverance is offered to all in Christ. But there are only a few who grasp the outstretched hand of the Lord by faith.

This is no reason for discouragement. We know of the victory. We know that God will make all the enemies of His Son a footstool for His feet. We can therefore be of good cheer, however dark and full of demons the world may seem.

On the very day I sat down to write this chapter, the Lord gave me a wonderful experience, as it were, a kind of prelude to what I am to write.

Ex 317   This morning a woman came for counseling. She comes from the East, from an area where there are no doctors, only magic charmers. She has had many kinds of oppression in her life, stemming from the time when as a little child she was taken to a charmer by her parents. She came to see me during one of my most recent missions. She confessed her sins, surrendered her life again to the Lord Jesus, and received deliverance by faith. Now, a few months later, she has come to tell me that everything in her life has changed. Here we see the power of Jesus, not the routine work of an evangelist.

In part C of this book, I want to bear witness to two things. The first is the blindness of many Christian workers. I refer the reader to what I said in my introduction and to the statement of Brother Gilgen that there is no occultism in Switzerland. I have met great numbers of Christian workers on every continent who take this view. During various evangelistic campaigns in Vancouver, Canada, brother Gebauer has told me of many instances where he has counseled people in Vancouver suffering from occult oppression. The pastor of another church said, on the other hand, that such things did not take place in Vancouver. Another incident that really shocked me was in another Canadian city. The church elders of a Lutheran church there asked me to come and speak in their church. "I cannot do so," I replied, "unless I am invited by the pastor of your church." The brethren discussed the matter with their pastor and then came back with his reply, "We do not need Dr. Koch to speak to us, for there is nothing of that sort in our church." One of the elders who brought the message remarked with bitter sarcasm, "Even though our pastor's wife practices table-tapping with the women's fellowship and the organist is involved in astrology!" Blindness upon blindness! I have experienced worse things still. It was in a city in which I also preached the gospel years ago.

Ex 318   A woman came to me for counseling and told me that as a girl she had felt an inward desire to join a certain Christian youth group. She attended several meetings of this youth group. One evening she had a nosebleed. The leader of the group gave her a prescription. She must take a piece of paper on which was written a spell from the *Sixth and Seventh Book of Moses* and put it under her tongue. The bleeding stopped at once. When she one day had a nosebleed again, she tried the spell once more. Again it worked. The woman said that since that time she had lost her inward hunger for the Word of God and for prayer. She did not join that Christian youth movement. "I had thought up until then," she said, "that people in that group would know what sorcery is. I was disappointed beyond measure."

Ex 319   The young wife of a pastor grew up in East Prussia. Her father was a member of the Christian Fellowship movement and belonged to the East Prussian prayer fellowship. It was his custom during the night before Easter Day to bring the so-called "Easter water," which is used for sorcery in many areas. The water has to be taken from a flowing stream. Nothing must be said while this is being done. Then the water is used to sprinkle the sick and to bless children. The pastor's wife also did this to her own children. Later, it became clear that all her children had developed some kind of abnormality.

This custom of bringing "Easter water" belongs to the realm of white magic, a form of sorcery. That a member of the Christian Fellowship movement should be unaware of this is another sign of terrible spiritual confusion and inadequate teaching.

Ex 320 A certain pastor is a water diviner. He uses a rod to search for water. He is still a young man but is already given to dreadful attacks of rage, at which time he beats his own wife. At the age of thirty-eight, he had two strokes. His six-year-old child is not normal. This man maintains that his gift is from God and that it is his duty to use it for the benefit of his parishioners. A counseling session revealed that his grandfather was a cattle charmer.

Ex 321 The superior of a deaconesses' house was in the habit of saying *toi-toi-toi* (a German phrase used rather like the English expression *touch wood*—translator). The new chaplain to the house was a believer and pointed out to the superior and the other sisters how superstitious this was. The word *toi* is a medieval abbreviation for *Teufel* (devil). Thereupon the superior became angry and said, "You are confusing my sisters." She did not become calm again until the chaplain had gone.

Ex 322 A woman missionary in South Africa was driving across the country with four Bantu pastors. At one point, the pastors asked her to stop. The missionary asked why. The men explained that this was the place where a chief magician was buried. "If we do not show respect to this man, we shall have an accident later today." The missionary rejected their demand but the pastors insisted. So they stopped. The missionary stayed in the car, while the four men went to the magician's grave, bowed their heads, and said a prayer. Then they drove on. An hour later they did have an accident. The Bantu pastors blamed the missionary, "It is your fault that we have had this accident, because you refused to pay the proper respect to this chief magician."

There are also people who have made a stand against this false spirit of sorcery. I would mention an old, believing pastor in the Werra valley in Germany. One day he discovered there was a man in his parish who was a magic charmer. He visited him and tried to show him the error of his ways, warning him that he might exclude him from the communion. The charmer replied, "What do you want,

Pastor? I have made charms not only over every house and family in this village, but also over all the villages in the neighborhood." The pastor reported the situation to his church council. He thought that something ought to be done against it. The elders replied that they themselves and their families had been charmed by this man. There was nothing that the pastor could do. Nevertheless he said, "When this man is buried I will make my witness at the graveside against the evil of magic charming." The charmer was at this time already in his late eighties. The pastor kept his word. When he tried to introduce a Bible study meeting in his parish, the parishioners said, "We will not go to the pastor's sect." Three men who have worked in the Werra valley as pastors and preachers have told me that the villages in that area are very ungodly; there is scarcely any spiritual life. It is no wonder, if a charmer has for decades been putting people under a spell.

Ex 323 One of my friends in South Germany, after reading my book *Christian Counselling and Occultism,* preached a series of sermons against sorcery in his church. The result was pandemonium in the village. The village had a charmer who had made charms over about seventy-five percent of all the farms and the families living there. There were many suicides and murders in this farming community. The farmers attacked the pastor so vigorously that, in the end, he had to leave this church. Those who make their witness against sins of sorcery must expect counterattacks from Satan and his helpers.

In evangelistic campaigns, one sometimes finds that no one comes forward for counseling until an address has been given attacking sins of sorcery. Wolfgang Heiner, leader of the "Frohe Botschaft" mission team, once told me, "The barriers in an evangelistic campaign are not usually broken down until one has spoken about the occult."

Ex 324 One more example, this time from an Australian evangelist, with whom I traveled for about three years. He was conducting a mission in Newcastle, England. Next to the mission tent was the annual fair with its sideshows. As the evangelist was passing a fortuneteller's tent, the fortuneteller called out to him; "I can tell you what your future holds."

"I know my future," he replied, "I do not need your help."

"You will speak to thousands of people," she cried, "and make long journeys."

"I can tell you your future, too," replied Tony, "from this Book." He held out his Bible. The fortuneteller asked,

"What is my future, then?"

"If you do not repent of your sorcery," answered the evangelist, "and receive Jesus as your Lord, you will be lost."

"What kind of book is that?" she asked.

"The Bible." She shook herself and expressed her disgust.

After this introduction, we must now go on to the question, how does one find deliverance?

I will answer this question by giving twenty suggestions. To avoid misunderstanding, I will say at once that these twenty suggestions are not a system, a method, or a template. We must simply bring together all the help which the New Testament offers us. It occasionally happens that the exalted Lord reaches down with His mighty hand into a human life and frees someone without the necessity that all twenty points be observed. I must make this clear, for many years ago a bishop said that my style of counseling was like a mold into which everyone I counseled was pressed. That is a slander even when it comes from the mouth of a bishop. Twenty-five years ago, in my first book *Christian Counselling and Occultism,* I emphasized that in the field of the occult, one cannot work according to a preconceived pattern. My opponents often raise objections against me. These objections have already been answered in my books. The pastoral suggestions I make in the following paragraphs are of great importance to me, and I have therefore numbered them and given them headings in bold type.

1. Come to Christ

If people are suffering from occult oppression, they will get no help from a psychiatrist, a psychologist, or an adherent of modern theology. Nor is help to be found in yoga, meditation, or in autogenic training. In this situation only Christ can help. This exclusive claim is made in Acts 4:12, "Neither is there salvation in any other [than Jesus Christ]: for there is none other name under Heaven given among men, whereby we must be saved." In Matthew 11:28, Jesus calls all those who are burdened to come to Him. The Greek text of this verse is a lovely invitation, *deute pros me kopiōntes kai pephortismenoi.* Freely translated it means, "Come to me all you who are wearing yourselves out and who bear heavy burdens." Not only has Jesus given us the command to come to Him, but He also gives us the promise of John 6:37, "him that cometh to me I will in no wise cast out."

He who tries to shake himself free of his burdens without Christ will be bitterly disappointed. Years ago, I held a mission in the Bergkirche in Marburg. After one of my addresses, a woman came into the vestry. "I suffer from all those things you have been talking about," she said, "please help me."

"Are you willing," I asked in reply, "to commit your life to Christ?" She flew into a rage.

"Leave me alone with your Jesus!" she cried. "I want to become well and free."

"Without Jesus, neither you nor I can do it," I replied calmly. She left the vestry quite angry.

He who would be free must be willing to commit his life completely to Christ. Otherwise there is no way of deliverance from these bonds.

2. Destroy all occult objects

Occult objects like amulets, talismans, fetishes, mascots, letters from heaven, lucky charms, threatening letters, figures of gods and cultic objects belonging to non-Christian religions are crystallization points for demonic powers. Rationalists who pour scorn on such things are doing the devil's work for him.

How often missionary wives have told me that from the moment that their husbands hung up a devil's mask in their living room, there was strife and discord in the family! It is extremely foolish and shows a great lack of experience for missionaries in their collector's zeal to bring home devil's masks and other cultic objects and to keep them in their homes.

Ex 325 A minister's wife on Prince Edward Island had collected a whole table-full of figures of gods and cultic objects from the mission field. Today she is in a mental institution.

It is remarkable how pagans who come to Christ often know, at once, that they must destroy their idols. Only Christians are without this elementary Christian knowledge. When a small revival broke out in Liberia in 1913 under Mr. Harris, the local inhabitants immediately threw away their idols. In the last five years, when revival came to the island of Rote through the ministry of Pastor Zacharias, the natives destroyed their idols and even burned the houses in which there had been idols. They said that the atmosphere of these houses had been evilly influenced by the idols.

In Africa, it sometimes happens that children are born with a kind of outer skin. This skin is known as a cowl. The native inhabitants believe that these children have special psychic powers. The cowl is usually made into an amulet by the midwife, and it is worn by the child throughout his life. Missionaries say that these amulets present a great barrier to conversion. Only those natives who destroy the cowl are able to come to Christ.

Ex 236a Following a mission in the Hamburg area, a preacher burned his copies of the books of Lorber. He said that now at last he had discovered why he experienced such strange attacks when praying or reading his Bible. The trouble ceased after the spiritualist books had been burned.

Ex 326b Another young man had exactly the opposite experience. He came to faith in Christ and burned all the things he had which were occult. But he kept his Lorber books, a leather bound edition of the *Greater Gospel of John*. This was a precious possession for the young man. He had paid several hundred marks for it. He was not at first willing to destroy these books because of their great value. He could not, however, find a real faith. He had one illness after another, and terrible struggles and temptations. The Christians who were counseling him told him, "As long as you are not willing to burn your Lorber books, we will not come to your house to pray anymore." It was several months before the young man was willing to burn them. Then at last he was freed from his occult bondage.

Ex 327 Some years ago I preached in Leith Samuel's church in Southampton, South England. Brother Leith told me how he had led a young girl to faith in Christ. But afterward she still suffered from depression and could not get free from her bondage. In the end, it came to light that she still possessed two magic books and still met with her spiritist friends. The pastor told her that she would not be free until she burned the books by Edwards and Cayce and broke contact with her spiritist friends. She did so and became free.

Ex 328 In Hawaii, a native woman came to a missionary named Birkey. The woman complained not only of depression and anxiety, but also of poltergeists during the night. Her husband had died several months previously as an unbeliever. The missionary counseled the woman and then visited her a few days later in her home. She noticed a little hut for the spirits up on the roof. The missionary asked her to take it down at once. She did so. Only then did this troubled and oppressed woman find freedom.

Ex 329 As already mentioned on page 204, a minister had to teach a class at a high school. The pupils asked him to teach them something about the occult. He ordered a copy of the *Sixth and Seventh Book of Moses* from a German publishing firm. His wife came to me for counseling and said, "Since we have had that devil's book in our house, there has been strife and discord in our family."

She had often asked her husband to get rid of the horrible book, but without success.

Those who would be free must destroy not only all occult objects but also all books written by occultists. It is, however, all right to have books written by men of God which warn against the occult.

Ex 330 It made a great impression on me when King Kusa Nope, on the island of Timor, destroyed his precious amulets. They were jewels set in gold and were of very high value. Nevertheless, he smashed them with a hammer and threw them into a rubbish pit. I heard his testimony in the church of Soe, during a great missionary conference.

I have often been asked if it is advisable to take figures carved in wood home from the mission field as souvenirs. Objects carved from new wood and those which were not consecrated to any deity are not dangerous. Unfortunately, it is the custom in some areas, like the island of Bali, to consecrate even the newly carved figures of gods to some demon. I have been to Bali five times. I have taken home no objects from this island. But one should not go to extremes of exaggerated caution.

3. Break off all mediumistic contacts and friendships

It is not enough to destroy all occult objects. We must also give up contact with people who are consciously practicing sorcery and are not willing to cease such practices. I will give some examples to illustrate this in various ways.

Ex 331 During my speaking tour of South Africa, a Baptist pastor came to me to talk things out. He had a revival in his church. Then he became ill. He went to see a healer. This man took some of his blood to use it for psychometric clairvoyance. The pastor went to this healer four times. At exactly the same time, the revival stopped abruptly. The pastor could not understand why it had stopped so suddenly. By going to this healer, he had caused a spell to be cast over the revival in his church. When he read my book *Between Christ and Satan* his eyes were opened, as he told me personally and later publicly stated at a gathering of ministers. This example shows that it is possible to come under a ban even though acting in ignorance. The excuse "I didn't know" does not protect us from the consequences.

Ex 332 When I was traveling around Peru and preaching at Pucallpa and Lima, I met Dr. Money who told me of his experiences with Christians who had done yoga exercises. His judgment was backed up by many examples. He said to me, "He who goes in for yoga loses his Christian faith." This should be said to all who think that yoga is a harmless activity which can also be practiced by Christians.

Ex 333 In Colombo, Sri Lanka, I gave several addresses in the church of the Rev. Fernando. I also met there Dr. Niles, a member of the World Council of Churches. It was Dr. Niles who told me the story which follows. A missionary in Sri Lanka was working in a village whose inhabitants were fire worshippers. The remarkable thing was that this village was often the scene of serious fires. The missionary told the villagers that these mysterious fire disasters would not stop until they stopped worshipping the fire devil. So heavy were their losses that the inhabitants were willing to stop offering sacrifices to the fire devil. Then the frequent fires in the village also ceased. A few weeks later, however, another fire occurred. The missionary called the villagers together again. It turned out that one man had again offered sacrifice to the fire devil.

Ex 334 In South Africa there are about 1.1 million Indian immigrants. These immigrants brought their Hindu gods with them. I have visited a number of communities where they live. An evangelist who works among them told me the following story. A certain Hindu family had a daughter who had been dumb for years. Since the Hindu gods were unable to help, the parents came one day to the missionary asking for his help and prayers. Brother N. visited the family and prayed with them. The first day there was no reaction to be seen in the girl. She only uttered an inarticulate cry. Brother N. went the next day, and the day after. On the third day, the girl suddenly asked a question. Everyone was filled with joy.

The events of the next days, however, showed that the girl was not completely free. One evening she started to writhe around on the ground like a snake. The father sent her to bed. The next morning he called in the missionary again. Brother N. visited the family once more and asked them to bring out all their gods. The family had some sacred Hindu nails, used to ward off the spirits. The nails were handed over. Then the missionary prayed again for the girl. She still didn't have complete deliverance. "Have you brought out everything?" the missionary asked the parents. The parents said they had. The daughter however interrupted and said: "Mother, what have you hidden in the bath?" It was a beautiful idol which the mother was very loath to part with. Nevertheless she resolved to give up this idol, too. Then the girl was freed. The child's dumbness was not organic, but the effect of a ban resulting from sorcery.

Ex 335 In Port Elizabeth, South Africa, I spoke at a ministers' meeting as well as at several meetings in the churches. A minister's wife told me of a friend of theirs who read the Bible, prayed, and was seeking Christ, but could not break through to real faith. This man is a Rosicrucian and unwilling to break with that organization.

Ex 336 In Pretoria, South Africa, a young man came to see me after I had spoken. He said that as a result of yoga exercises he had become lukewarm and slack in his Christian Life. Three of his friends had had the same experience. He added that the atmosphere of yoga was dangerous for believing Christians.

In counseling, one meets far more serious problems than these. I have often been told of situations like the following. The parents belong to a spiritist group and take their son or daughter with them to the séance. Then the son or daughter comes to faith in Christ. He must immediately stop going to the spiritist meeting. The problem then, however, is that it is very dangerous to the faith of these children who have become Christians to continue living with their parents. One often finds that these young, converted people fall away. Sometimes I advise them to find a room to rent and stop living at home with their parents. Caution must be exercised by young believers in such situations even in praying for their parents. It is best if they pray for them only when together with others. In bad cases I even advise them, "Stop praying for your parents as long as they are unwilling to give up going to the spiritist meeting." Intercession for people under occult influence who are not willing to come to Christ can be a source of continual struggle for young Christians. I pray only for people who wish to become free, and not for those who show no such willingness.

4. Recognize and confess your guilt

Ex 337 A pastor in Schleswig-Holstein told me that in his women's group, six out of eight women have been magically charmed. A neighboring pastor has three women in his group who have been charmed. Neither pastor dares to enlighten his church or women's group for fear of hurting their feelings.

How are members of a church to recognize their occult bondage and oppression for what it is, if their pastors do not point out these things to them? Here it is not only the church members who have been charmed who are guilty, but also the pastors.

Ex 338   A girl in Hamburg had her warts charmed. As a result, she was rid of these ugly growths. During a mission, she came to faith in Christ. There too she heard for the first time of the evil effects of magic charms. She confessed her guilt in the presence of a counselor and then prayed, "Lord Jesus, if it was wrong, let me have my warts return and be free of the ban." The next day her warts reappeared. The hard rule is, Better warts on earth and no warts in Heaven than no warts on earth and warts in hell.

Ex 339   An epileptic girl went regularly to a Christian youth group. Then her mother, in ignorance, allowed her daughter to be charmed. The epilepsy disappeared. But after being charmed, the girl stopped coming under the Word of God.

The pastor noticed this, visited the family concerned, and asked why she was not coming any more. The facts of the matter came out. After being told about the charming, the girl handed over an amulet, which upon examination, to her horror, contained a paper signing her to the devil. Both the mother and the daughter repented and confessed their guilt. They both started attending church. They were both able once more to read the Bible and pray. The epilepsy also reappeared.

1 John 1:9 says, "If we confess our sins, he is faithful and just to forgive us our sins, and to cleanse us from all unrighteousness." No one is delivered from occult bondage without recognizing and confessing his sin. This confession concerns not only occult sins, but everything that we recognize as sinful and which comes between ourselves and God. If the person concerned has already made such a confession, there is no need for him to repeat it. It is a basic rule that confession of sin does not need to be repeated. There are, however, some believing Christians who suffer from occult bondage because they have not recognized it. They must confess the things of which they have never repented to a counselor in the presence of God. In my many years' experience of counseling, I have never known a person who was bound as a result of occult activities, or who was demon-possessed, to be freed without first recognizing and confessing his guilt. The apostle James wrote, "Confess your sins one to another, and pray one for another" (James 5:16).

5. Renounce and declare yourself free from Satan and the sins of sorcery of your forebears

Sins of sorcery represent an unconscious pact with Satan. Satan believes that one's practice of sorcery gives him a right to control that person. This relationship exists also where a person's parents or grandparents have been involved with occult things. It is one of the mysteries of God's government of the world that children are affected and oppressed through the sins of their forebears. This is in accord with the second commandment. And it is confirmed a thousand times over in counseling.

Therefore a person who is under occult bondage or oppression must pray once, or possibly several times, a prayer of renunciation. This can take some such form as this, "In the name of the Lord Jesus Christ I renounce the devil and all of his works, I renounce the sins of sorcery of my ancestors and in my own life, and I subscribe myself to Jesus my Lord for time and for eternity, in the name of the Father and of the Son and of the Holy Spirit. Amen." This prayer must not be regarded or used as a magical formula. That would be "white magic." The prayer can also be phrased in one's own words.

Ex 340 A pastor in Brazil was charmed as a child against epilepsy. Before one of his epileptic fits, his mother had taken some froth from the child's mouth, spread it on some bread and given it, together with a spell from the *Sixth and Seventh Book of Moses,* to a cat to eat. The cat died. The boy never had any more fits. Later, when he was already a pastor, he came to me for counseling. The conversation revealed that he suffered greatly from the effects of this charm. In my presence he declared himself free in the name of Jesus and was delivered from the effects of sorcery. At the same time, the pastor came to see clearly that magical healing has nothing to do with divine healing. Originally, he had regarded his healing from epilepsy as the work of God.

Ex 341 In England, a woman with one leg shorter than the other went to a spiritist healer. The leg stretched itself back to the normal length, not suddenly, but in the course of several weeks. During this remarkable healing, the woman lost her peace and the assurance of salvation. This made her aware that there must be something wrong about the healing. She repented, renounced this strange healing and recovered her peace. The leg which had been healed grew shorter as it was before.

Of course I am aware that doctors do not accept such stories.

Yet they do happen, especially in areas where strong spiritism reigns, like in Haiti, Brazil, and some East Asian countries.

Ex 342 The director of a missionary society, whom I know very well, told me of the following incident. One day a sorcerer came to him who had such strong psychic powers that he was able to kill animals at a distance. The missionary was alarmed at this and called in a believing pastor to assist in counseling.

The sorcerer confessed that he had sold himself to the devil with his own blood. In return for his powers he had to perform two services for Satan every week. If he cursed a chicken house, the chickens would lay no more eggs. If he cursed a cowshed, the cows would produce no more proper milk, but a brown liquid. If the cows were taken away to another village, however, they produced normal milk again.

The sorcerer wanted at all costs to become free, for he knew that he was gripped in the power of Satan. He came for several counseling sessions. One day he got one of the pastors to give him a candle, some matches, a needle, some paper, and a penholder. He made the needle red-hot in the flame, pricked his finger, and wrote a message in his own blood declaring himself free from the devil. From that time onward he received no more orders from Satan and he no longer saw the devilish figure that had plagued him previously.

This was not therefore a case of mental illness resulting in hallucinations, but the result of a blood pact.

I must here repeat what I have said earlier in this book. I never advise people to declare themselves free from the devil by writing a statement in their own blood. I know that there are some counselors who do give such advice. If, however, people who are suffering from oppression or who have signed a blood pact with the devil believe that that is what they ought to do, I do not hinder them.

We know too that certain men of God in the past have sometimes done something similar. I think of Tersteegen, who signed himself over to the Lord Jesus in his own blood. Anyway in this particular instance the magic charmer evidently knew more about what he was doing than did his counselors.

Ex 343 On a speaking tour in Argentina I was accompanied by Pastor Albert Renschler, who introduced me to various Protestant churches. Our tour through Entre Rios was very interesting. After one of my talks, a pastor from this region told me that he had been healed by a magic charmer. He had also received an amulet from this man. We asked him to open the amulet. He did so and was horrified to find, inside the amulet, a piece of paper containing a pact with the devil. He burned the paper and the amulet and declared himself free of the devil in the name of Jesus. His illness thereupon reappeared.

It is a good sign when illnesses reappear after the spell of a magic charm has been broken. For it means that the spell can no longer bind that person. This example also demonstrates that even pastors can enter into this kind of pact through ignorance.

Ex 344   I was invited by Pastor Seifert to conduct a mission in Lüneburg. When it was over, a young man who had been charmed for a disease in childhood, came to me. He confessed his guilt and surrendered his life to Jesus. He was freed from this occult ban. A few days later he came back again and said that his illness had returned. Then his mother also came and complained to brother Seifert that it was wrong to so confuse the boy that he had become ill once more. "Do you want your son, then," brother Seifert asked her, "to remain under the curse of sorcery and go to hell?" The woman was surprised. Brother Seifert continued, "Jesus can do as much as the devil and more, yes, a thousand times more!" He prayed, and the boy was made well.

It is a common experience to find that people are healed by Jesus when the spell of sorcery has been broken and the old illness has returned.

Ex 345   While touring Australia and New Zealand, I met Peter Jamieson several times. He is chief of the Wongai tribe in West Australia. As chief of the tribe, he accepted the Lord Jesus in faith and felt called to preach the Gospel to the aboriginal tribes. He told me that all the aborigines who were converted had fallen away. The reason is that they did not renounce their former sorcery. Missionaries are generally unaware that this is necessary.

Ex 346   During my speaking tour in England and Scotland, a student at Bible school, in Glasgow, came to me for counseling. This young man was constantly troubled with suicidal thoughts and tried several times to take his life. He did not know the background of this desire to commit suicide. In the end, his ninety-year-old grandmother admitted that, for several generations, sorcery, and in particular spiritism, had been practiced in the family. The young man confessed his sins and declared himself free from the sorcery of his forebears. I noticed how sincere and earnest he was in doing this. I felt free to declare him free in the name of Jesus Christ. This act of declaring someone free is based on Matthew 18:18. The young man had come to the end of his own strength. Now he was able to begin again with Jesus, as a disciple who had been freed from his bondage.

Ex 347 Unfortunately, it is also possible to come under a ban as a result of mediumship with a religious covering. While I was in England, an Irish believer came to me for counseling. He had already been a disciple of Jesus for several years. His friends had invited him to a conference of the Pentecostal movement. He joined them in prayer and received the gift of speaking in tongues. At the same time, he lost his peace and the assurance that he was forgiven. As a result, his eyes were opened. He said to himself, that if the gift of tongues resulted in the loss of assurance, forgiveness, and peace, something was not in order. He repented, confessed the whole incident, and declared himself free of the spirit of tongues. He was freed from speaking in tongues and found his peace once more. I have many such examples.

6. Accept forgiveness by faith

In pastoral work with the victims of occult oppression, faith plays a decisive part. Paul wrote, "That if thou shalt confess with thy mouth the Lord Jesus, and shalt believe in thine heart that God hath raised him from the dead, thou shalt be saved" (Romans 10:9). "But without faith it is impossible to please him; for he that cometh to God must believe that he is, and that he is a rewarder of them that diligently seek him" (Hebrews 11:6). Without faith we cannot appropriate the good things God offers us in salvation. But it is a fact of experience that people under occult oppression find it particularly difficult to come to faith. For this reason we must avail ourselves of all the aids which the New Testament offers us in order to overcome the dead, inward area of unbelief.

7. Don't get stuck halfway

Both in history and in the present we have examples of people who have been converted but who have not become free at once of all their occult oppression. I will begin with an example from Chicago.

Ex 348 Dwight L. Moody, the great American evangelist, used to be accompanied on his tours by the singer, Henry Drummond. Originally Drummond was able to influence and hypnotize people at a distance of fifty miles. After his conversion, he had difficulty in overcoming these occult powers. While ministering at Moody's meetings, he occasionally noticed that the audience was being influenced by his psychic powers. He was very troubled about this and asked the Lord to free him from these occult powers. The Lord answered his prayer.

Ex 349 In Kotzebue, Alaska, an Eskimo woman came to me for counseling. She was able mentally to see people coming to her house before they were there. Before her conversion, she was aware that this was a psychic power. After she was converted, she thought her occult powers would end. She was mistaken—her occult powers remained. So she came to me for counseling, she confessed her sins, and declared herself free from these powers.

Naive counselors on both sides of the ocean often maintain that with conversion all a person's problems are solved once and for all. This is not so. We often have to suffer the effects of earlier occult activity. This may be shown by an illustration from another field. If a young man has, as a result of a life of debauchery, contracted syphilis, and then comes to faith in Christ, his sins are forgiven but the disease is still there.

It is hard to say how many people become free and how many continue to drag their occult oppression around with them. It could be as many as half of those who have experienced conversion. If they discover psychic powers after they have begun to follow Jesus, they must ask Christ to free them and give them an even fuller measure of the Holy Spirit.

There are, then, some believers who are still under occult influence in spite of their conversion. This becomes still clearer in the examples which follow.

Ex 350 A young man of twenty-one, who comes from an ungodly family, was converted. He became a local youth leader. He is gifted, and everyone is attracted by his personal charm. He is always the center of attention, and others are impressed by him. He conducts Christian houseparties, gives talks on prayer, counseling, and confession, yet he refuses to join his wife in prayer. He also refuses to accept any pastoral help. If his wife goes to a pastor or counselor for help with a problem, he becomes furious with the pastor and with his wife.

His wife came to me, and I sent him a message saying I should like to speak to him, too. He flew into a rage and said to his wife, "You can bring ten men like him to me, but you won't get me to go. And if you go on like this, you can pack your bags." His parents are ungodly people. If they come to visit the home, an oppressive atmosphere comes over the family. There is a ban upon this believing man, who behaves differently in the world outside from the way he behaves at home. Many Christian tyrants have some kind of occult influence in their background, which was not cleared away at their conversion.

Ex 351 A Jamaican Christian came to me for counseling. He told me that at night he had to struggle against evil spirits. Not until he looked to Jesus in faith and called to Jesus for help would these dark powers go away. I asked him whether he had been charmed as a child by an Obeah. Obeahs are the magicians of the Carribean islands. He replied that he had been ill as a boy. No doctor had been able to help him. His parents had taken him to a "godly man" who had healed him with the Word of God in three days. That was white magic. White magic has the same effects as black magic. We can see the result. This Christian was still troubled by dark powers even after his conversion, because at his conversion, he had no counselor to give him the right advice.

Ex 352 A young woman came to see me in Brisbane. She had gone to a fortuneteller in 1960. The occult woman had said to her, "I can only tell your future as far as 1965. In 1965 something will happen in your life which will change it. Beyond that I can see nothing." In 1965 the girl came to faith in Christ. She found forgiveness, but not real peace. She was pursued by thoughts which she could not overcome. This is another example of a conversion where the occult oppression did not totally disappear.

Ex 353 In Los Angeles, I gave some addresses at the Church of the Open Door. While I was there, a Christian woman came to me for help. She had suffered with eczema since childhood. Treatment by dermatologists had been without effect. The woman told me that her mother was an atheist. My suspicion that this eczema had occult roots proved to be right. Our conversation revealed that her mother had been engaged in occult activity for years. The believing woman had prayed for her mother for years. This was why this believing daughter often suffered great trials. In spite of her conversion, the eczema with its occult background did not disappear. In such cases, I prefer to advise a daughter not to pray for her mother, because the mother is not willing to give up her sorcery. A believer only comes under more oppression by praying for such a person. Moreover, this woman did not have the support of a prayer group. It is extremely difficult in Los Angeles to find prayer groups which have spiritual power and authority. All these examples show that conversion does not always mean at the same time the end of occult oppression. Many Christians get stuck half-way.

8. Seek out a counselor who has spiritual authority before whom to declare yourself free

Renunciation, or declaring oneself free, is an act of faith on the part of an oppressed person who wishes to become free. Declaring a person free is an act of faith on the part of the counselor, who has the authority in the name of Jesus to loose a person who is bound. This declaration is based on Matthew 18:18, "Whatsoever ye shall bind on earth shall be bound in heaven: and whatsoever ye shall loose on earth shall be loosed in heaven."

As a young pastor, I was sometimes too hasty in declaring people free who were suffering from occult oppression. The result was that I myself was severely attacked from the realm of darkness. I have become, therefore, more cautious. In every single case I ask the Lord Jesus whether or not it is right for me, acting on His authority, to declare a person free. I have often refused to do so, but in some cases I have felt free to do so.

Ex 354   A forty-two-year-old woman came and confessed that in her youth she had her warts charmed in the following fashion. Her mother put salt on the warts, pronounced a spell from the *Sixth* and *Seventh Book of Moses,* and said the names of the Holy Trinity. Then the salt was thrown into the fire. The warts disappeared. Ever since that time, however, she had gone astray sexually and had also become a compulsive liar and thief. When she wanted to accept Christ, she found that she could not.

In my presence, she confessed all the sins of her life, and in the name of Jesus declared herself free of her mother's sorcery. I then claimed the authority of Matthew 18:18 and, in the name of Jesus, commanded the powers to depart from this woman and declared her free from her bondage. This woman was helped through the aid of God.

The counselor never has any authority in himself. He is only a representative, speaking on the authority of the exalted Lord.

Ex 355   In Paris, a young man, who had become involved in sorcery in both an active and a passive capacity, came to me for counseling. He made a general confession and was willing to give his whole life to Christ. I prayed with him a prayer of renunciation and then declared him free in the name of Jesus. I was a young pastor at this time. Many years later I met this man again. He was completely free and happy and an active worker in a Baptist church.

Ex 356 Many years ago I was invited by Pastor Fritz Taddei to take a mission in Verden. He told me the following story. A young Christian couple had been to him for counseling. At two o'clock each morning, they saw a dark man. Taddei said, "Then either you or the people who lived in the house before you must have been practicing sorcery." The couple made the following confession. They had often been ill and had found that the doctor could not help them. So they had sought out a charmer, who was able to help them each time. One day the charmer told them, "I am getting old and infirm. Soon I shall not be able to come any more. You can learn how to do it for yourselves." He wrote the formula for them. After this, the husband tried the formula and found that it worked. In the end, people started calling him in as a charmer. Then came the time when both husband and wife decided for Christ. This was also the time when they began to see the dark man at night. They were troubled with this problem for a long while, until they finally asked Taddei to help them. They confessed their sins and renounced the sorcery. Taddei declared them free in the name of Jesus.

When the dark figure appeared again at night, the husband and wife said, "We are not following you any more. Jesus has made us free. We renounce you." Since then they have enjoyed peace. Here again we see the fact that believing people can be affected by occult powers even after their conversion, until they declare themselves free and are declared free by a counselor.

9. Join a prayer group

The counseling of those who suffer from occult oppression is team work. Often a single counselor is unable to break through on his own; he needs the backing of a prayer group. Sadly there are few active prayer groups among Christians.

Ex 357 A missionary who had worked for many years in China came home. He was no longer able to read the Bible or pray. He seemed up against a spiritual brick-wall. This drove his own children to repentance. First, his daughter rededicated her life to the Lord Jesus; then her brother did the same. They formed a prayer group to pray for their father. After a long while of faithful prayer, God granted their request and their father was again able to pray.

Ex 358 During a speaking tour in Argentina, I met Professor Winter. He had the following experience in Cordoba, Argentina. He came into contact with a woman who had been practicing spiritism and magic for years. Professor Winter spoke to this woman about the influence of evil spirits on our life and about psychic gifts. She listened attentively and observed that Professor Winter knew something of what he was talking about. On his second visit, the woman accepted Christ. From that moment on the spirits began to seek their revenge. She saw frogs jumping out of her mouth, and her bed was rocked. She was afflicted with convulsions. Several Christians joined to form a prayer group and met together over a period of several months. Finally she was delivered. Her deliverance was very evident. She placed herself completely at the disposal of the Lord Jesus and His work.

Ex 359 Some years ago I was invited to speak by Dr. Martyn Lloyd-Jones. He had gathered twenty-two doctors and psychiatrists together for a conference. The subject assigned me was demon possession. Two psychiatrists attacked me. Two others defended me. Now I want to record the experience of one of these psychiatrists, who is a believing Christian. He lives near the New Forest, where much magic is practiced. One day a young man came to him who had originally been involved in one of these magic groups. He wanted to be free, for this magic group always ended up in sexual orgies. They used to meet regularly in a thicket of the Forest. The psychiatrist brought together a group of people to pray near that meeting place. The magicians and spiritists began their rituals, but such a storm blew up in the forest that they had to stop. The doctor stayed there, praying with his group of Christians, until the magicians lost interest in starting their meeting again.

Ex 360 A man came to see me in Port Elizabeth, South Africa. He is now a member of the Salvation Army. His uncle was a magic charmer. In 1947 he decided to follow Christ. At the same time, psychic abilities began to manifest themselves in him. He was able to stick nails through his tongue, cheeks, and hand, without feeling any pain. He could also swallow fire.

A prayer group began to pray for him and continued to do so for a long time. Through the faithful ministry of these people of the Salvation Army he became free again. To this day, however, he cannot feel fire. He can burn his fingers or touch hot objects without noticing it. This shows that a residue of his psychic powers has remained. In other words, the work of the prayer group should go on praying until the man has been freed of the last remnant of his occult powers.

It is a great problem all over the world, that there are many Christians, but few prayer groups ready to go into action and to be faithful and authoritative in the ministry of intercession.

Our authority for prayer groups is found in the promise of Matthew 18:19, "If two of you shall agree on earth as touching anything that they shall ask, it shall be done for them by my Father which is in heaven." If necessary then, two people suffice to form a prayer group if no more can be found.

A Biblical example of two people joining together to pray is found in Acts 16:25, where we read: "About midnight Paul and Silas were praying and singing hymns to God." Also in Acts we are told of a very large prayer group which met in the house of Mary. In Acts 12:12 we read, "He [Peter] came to the house of Mary . . . where many were gathered together praying." Such prayer cells are the places where the Lord Jesus reveals His glory.

10. Practice praying and fasting

We find authority for prayer and fasting in Matthew 17:21, "This kind goeth not out but by prayer and fasting."

Prayer and fasting has almost become forgotten. The Catholic Church has turned fasting into a work through which one may obtain merit. But that is not the purpose of fasting. Fasting only means intensive prayer. One must also use common sense with regard to fasting.

Ex 361 A woman missionary went to Israel and resolved to spend forty days in prayer and fasting. She had nothing to drink. After twelve days she collapsed. She was taken to a hospital, but her life could not be saved. Those who fast must at least take the necessary amount of drink each day. In my book *Jesus auf allen Kontinenten* and in my English book *The Wine of God* I tell the story of Father Daniel of Madras, who used to take the month of June each year as a month of prayer with fasting. Father Daniel was a man of a rare spiritual authority. He was able to bring the help of God's grace to many people who suffered under severe oppression.

Ex 362 On one of my tours of East Asia, I met Dr. Eitel, who for many years was head of the Changsa hospital. He told me the following story. A city in Kweichow had been surrounded by a

powerful band of robbers. Within the city walls were the magis-
trate's soldiers, but they were inferior in numbers. For ten days,
the soldiers held off the robbers. Then they ran out of ammunition.

Although she knew nothing of these events, Eva von Thiele-
Winckler, in far away Germany, felt an inner urge to fast and pray
for China for ten days.

At the end of ten days, the robbers strangely went off. At the
same hour, Eva von Thiele-Winckler rose and began to eat again.
She knew that the danger was over, although she knew nothing
of the details.

Ex 363   About twenty years ago I gave some addresses in
Coburg. There a believing pastor told me this story. A woman in
his church had been undergoing treatment from a psychiatrist for
years. She had been diagnosed as schizophrenic. The woman saw
devil faces at her window, was melancholy, and had thoughts of
suicide. The pastor then formed a prayer group, which began to
intercede for the woman, with fasting. The woman changed visibly
under the spiritual influence. She was evidently suffering not from
schizophrenia but from occult oppression as a result of the sorcery
of her forebears.

Ex 364   Now for a dramatic case which I experienced some
years ago in company with my friend and counselor Gottlieb Weiland. It is a long story. I will try to recount it briefly. It was Easter
Monday, 1962. The gospel singer Franz Knies brought in a young
man for counseling whom he had been unable to help. There were
three of us: Franz Knies, Gottlieb Weiland, and myself. Franz
Knies asked the young man, "Horst, what is the matter with you?"

"I am not Horst," came the reply, "I have Horst."

Then Franz Knies commanded the spirit in the name of Jesus.
The voice began to wail, "Don't drive me out. I will not go out.
Where else shall I go? I have nowhere to live."

Gottlieb Weiland then took the young man into another room
and talked with him. The boy made a general confession and said
that he wanted definitely to follow Jesus. Then Gottlieb Weiland
called us into the room. At the same moment Horst's face changed.
He put on a mocking grin. Weiland said, "Let us get on our knees
and pray."

"But not I," said Horst. As we prayed, Horst interrupted us.

"Stop praying," he cried, "and leave me in peace." We continued
to pray. Horst jumped up and began to attack us physically. He
stood in front of me and put his hands round my neck as if he

were going to choke me. I put myself under the protection of Jesus. The possessed man was unable to touch me.

"Between you and me," I said, "stands Jesus." Horst let himself drop on the floor. We continued in prayer. Once more the voice came from the possessed young man, "I will not go out, for else I must wander around. I need a person to live in." In the name of Jesus we commanded these powers to go out of him.

Suddenly the possessed man said, "If I must go out, then let me go into a drunk who is sitting this afternoon in the ale house down the road."

We replied: "In the name of Jesus, go to the place where Jesus sends you."

Then we brought reinforcements. In the house were two deaconesses whom we called to come and pray with us. The possessed young man was still lying unconscious on the floor. Various voices spoke from him, talking about Horst in the third person. We went into another room for further prayer. Weiland said, "This must be one of those people to whom the words of Jesus apply when he said, 'This sort will not go out except by prayer and fasting.'"

11. Place yourself under the protection of Jesus' blood

Some years ago I visited a number of mission stations on the Ivory Coast. Among other things, I had a conference with the missionaries working in Man, whom the missionary Walter Hadorn had called together. At this conference I heard the following story. The local pagans had tried to poison the president of all the Protestant churches in the area of Man, a man who was a faithful evangelist. They had used the gall of a crocodile and of a leopard. The evangelist should have died within ten minutes. But all he had was a mild stomach ache. A year later, the man who had tried to murder him admitted, "I would have poisoned you. But your God is stronger than my god."

The missionaries who work in these dangerous parts place themselves daily under the protection of Jesus' blood, that the enemy may have no power over them. They also know of particular Bible promises which they may claim in faith. These include Zechariah 2:5, "For I, saith the LORD, will be unto her a wall of fire about, and will be the glory in the midst of her." Also in Luke 10:19, "Behold, I give unto you power to tread serpents and scorpions, and over all the power of the enemy: and nothing shall by any means hurt you."

Ex 365 Dr. Eitel told me of a friend of his who was a pastor in Switzerland. In this village a great deal of sorcery is practiced. The pastor and his wife often prayed against this sorcery. Then the pastor's wife became possessed and was never free again for the rest of her life. The pastor said, "We did not often enough place ourselves under the protection of Jesus' blood."

In such cases my advice is different. I do not recommend believers to pray generally about the sorcery of a whole village, but rather for those people who have become victims of the sorcery, especially for those who are willing to break with their practices. I have heard of a number of examples from the mission field of missionaries who regarded it as their duty to pray against the priests of a Buddhist or Hindu temple, and who in doing so, have lost their reason.

Counselors who help and minister to those who suffer from occult oppression must place themselves daily under the protection of Jesus Christ. Similarly those who have been delivered from occult oppression need to place themselves daily under the protection of Jesus Christ, especially at night when they go to bed.

The blood of Jesus Christ is our banner. (See Hebrews 9:14, 10:22; Ephesians 1:7.)

12. Command the enemy in the name of the Lord

The way this commanding is to be carried out was spoken of by the apostle Paul in Acts 16:16-18. Faced with the spirit of divination in this fortuneteller of Philippi, the apostle Paul commanded it in the name of Jesus Christ, and the woman was set free. It is not only when we are counseling others that we may use this authority to command; we may also command in the name of Jesus when the enemy attacks us personally. Commanding in the name of Jesus is a stronger form of prayer and believing. Every Christian ought to practice it in order to win in the struggle with the powers of darkness. Hell trembles before the name of the Lord. In Revelation 14:1, we are told that the elect have the name of the Lamb of God and the name of the Father written on their foreheads. We have His name, and therefore we are on the side of the conqueror.

Ex 366 In 1964, I traveled among a number of Indian tribes in the upper Amazon area. I also visited the Bible school near Pucallpa. One night I was called out to see a young Indian woman. I found that she had gone to sorcerers five times, and that she drank Ayahuasca, a magic potion. She would fall into a trance just like the sorcerer himself, and then begin to sing in a very high-pitched voice. As far as the Christian faith was concerned, she was totally closed to it. And now I had been called out to help her at half past one in the morning. She had been singing her magic songs for the past hour. I prayed with her, placing myself under the protection of Jesus' blood. Then in the name of Jesus Christ, I commanded the powers to go out from her, and also commanded her to cease at once from her magic song. She stopped at once and sang no more.

Ex 367 During a mission in the neighborhood of Zofingen, Switzerland, a believing brother came to me for counseling. His sister lived in a haunted house. Her husband was not a Christian. When he went to bed, the bed would rise in the air and swing to and fro. This phenomenon of swinging, and also of gliding, is found particularly in the houses of spiritists. The man's Christian wife told him that he ought to call on the name of Christ when such things began to happen. Another time he had already gone to sleep. He was awakened by invisible powers and felt someone pressing down on both his shoulders. He grabbed at the one who was doing it and found he was holding an animal's paws. Following his wife's advice, he called on the Lord Jesus, and the paws disappeared.

On other occasions there would be a loud bang in the room, or he would hear hundreds of pigeons flying out of the room, although all the windows and doors were shut. These were not the hallucinations of someone who was mentally ill. The four other families who rented apartments in the same house also experienced these and even worse things. They wanted to move out, but none had succeeded in finding suitable accommodation.

Here we have an unbelieving man calling on the name of the Lord Jesus, and the Lord actually answering. This is a fulfilment of the promise, "Whosoever shall call upon the name of the Lord shall be saved" (Acts 2:21). The name of Jesus, however, must never be used as a magic formula, or it will bring even more trouble and oppression on the person who uses it. Bible texts and the name of Jesus are not magic formulae. We may also learn that unbelievers who use the name of Jesus in a moment of anxiety will receive help for a time. But the attacks always continue to come until the person concerned *commits himself totally* to Christ.

Ex 368 At a ministers' meeting which I had been asked to

address in San Francisco, one of the ministers told of the following experience. A young woman in his church had been converted and had also begun to attend the prayer meeting. During the prayers, she always lost consciousness and went around the room in a trance, crying, "watch and pray!" The pastor saw this happen three times. His church members thought it was a wonderful thing, but the pastor took a different view. In the name of Jesus, he commanded the woman to cease. The woman was delivered, and she rejoiced at her deliverance. It turned out that earlier this woman had gone to spiritist gatherings. It was there that she had acquired the ability to go into a trance. In spite of her conversion, she was still under occult oppression until the pastor commanded the spirits in the name of Jesus Christ.

Here we see again that, at the time of a person's conversion, all the occult bondage does not immediately disappear. If this does happen, it is a mighty act of God. But sometimes such people need specialized counseling.

The question of commanding in the name of Jesus also leads us to ask what we ought to think about exorcism. Just a few brief notes on this question. In Mark 1:27 we read it said of Jesus, "With authority commandeth he even the unclean spirits, and they do obey him." Disciples of the Lord have been given the same authority by their Master. In Matthew 10:1 we are told, "He [Jesus] gave them [His disciples] power against unclean spirits, to cast them out." These texts give us evidence that both Jesus and His disciples practiced exorcism.

Some supporters of dispensational theology say that this authority came to an end at the close of the first century. Since we have had the canon of Scripture, all or most of the gifts of the Spirit have disappeared. This theology is only partially true. There are some gifts—for instance, in my opinion prophecy about the last days—which ceased with the closing of the canon of Scripture. There are other powers and gifts which are part of the permanent armor of the Christian, and one of these is the authority to command and drive out evil spirits in the name of Jesus. Nearly all the great men of the Church in the nineteen hundred years of her history have practiced it. I therefore find it impossible to understand why men of the twentieth century who are otherwise of good repute declare in their magazines that this gift belongs to the past. I can only counter this statement by saying that these men have absolutely no experience in dealing with the possessed. If they had, they would not adopt this unscriptural view.

Neither can one dismiss exorcism by pointing out that pagan sorcerers and followers of non-Christian religions like Muslims, Hindus, and Buddhists also have forms of exorcism. The only genuine exorcism is that which is done in the name of the Lord Jesus Christ.

In the Middle Ages, the Roman Catholic Church often made exorcism into a spectacular religious show. This has brought real exorcism into disrepute. Nevertheless, one must give credit where it is due and say that the Catholic Church has discussed the questions of possession and exorcism more thoroughly than the Protestants. I say this as a Protestant and not as a Catholic, and this gives what I say especial weight. A very recent example:

Ex 369 This is from a report in a South German daily newspaper on December 15, 1975. Writing in the weekly paper of the Vatican, the Observatore Romano, Monsignor Balducci says "There are people who are possessed." Balducci freely admits that in the old days many cases which were thought to be cases of possession really belonged to the realm of psychiatry. Nevertheless there are, he says, definite criteria for believing that a demon can gain possession of a man. The symptoms of possession are different from the natural symptoms to be observed in psychiatry and parapsychology.

The question of demon possession is terribly confused by the pronouncements of fanatics who often regard easily diagnosed disorders as possession. Further confusion is caused by sensational films like *The Exorcist,* which distort the problem of possession in a satanic fashion. Even if out of every hundred cases of exorcism ninety-nine are unscriptural, there still remains a few genuine cases of possession which also require a genuine exorcism. I am quite familiar with authentic cases of this sort. Together with my circle of friends, I have witnessed people who were possessed, and who displayed unquestionable symptoms of possession, being delivered through the name of Jesus Christ. Thanks be to God, that even in the twentieth century we may still know and experience something of the victory of Jesus Christ.

13. Make diligent use of the means of grace

In Acts 2:42, the means of grace are listed, "They continued steadfastly in the apostles' doctrine and fellowship, and in breaking of bread, and in prayers." Here the four elements which form the spiritual bricks for building up the Christian life are named: the

Word of God, the fellowship of believers, the Holy Communion, and private and corporate prayer. Many people suffering from occult oppression allow themselves to be brought to the point of saying a prayer of renunciation. Some think then, "Now we have arrived, now we are free from this oppression once and for all." Sometimes, however, it happens that, in spite of having renounced these things, the oppression continues. This is because the person who has been delivered is not faithful in making use of the means of grace. He who does not feed his spiritual life by these means of grace will not remain free but will be a continual target for Satan's attacks. It is an important point in our life of faith and in following Jesus, that we make faithful and diligent use of the means of grace.

Ex 370 A woman traveled from a large city in Bavaria to see me. She was in great spiritual trouble. Her mother and her grandmother had practiced spiritist table tapping. She herself had read my books and had come to see that her troubles were the effect of the spiritism of her forebears. She went to see a believing pastor in her city, and he, in his ignorance and lack of experience, told her that her telepathy and second sight were a gift of God. She rightly saw that it was a form of oppression, and that is what prompted her to come and ask my advice. She made a confession of all her sins and rededicated her life to Christ. I prayed with her a prayer of renunciation. In spite of this, she still felt as if there were a wall between herself and God, as she told me later. I replied that she ought to look around the city where she lived and see if there were not some Christians who would join her to form a prayer group. At the same time I urged her to be faithful in using the means of grace which are mentioned in Acts 2:42.

Ex 371 During a mission in Switzerland, a man of about forty years came to me for counseling. He had suffered from headaches for ten years. He had been to see two well-known healers in Appenzell and also a woman charmer. All three had told him, "We cannot get through. Someone is disturbing us, there are counterforces." The man's wife is a faithful woman of prayer, who makes use of all the aids and promises given in the Bible.

He who does not feed his spiritual life diligently and faithfully each day will not be freed from his occult past and is always an easy prey for Satan's attacks.

14. Put on the spiritual armor

In Ephesians 6:10-18, Paul devotes a whole section of his letter to the spiritual armor that God provides. He speaks of the whole armor of God; the breastplate of righteousness, the shield of faith, the helmet of salvation, and the sword of the Spirit.

These words are all taken from the language of war. Paul uses these military terms to show us that, in our struggle with Satan and his demons, we are on a battlefield where live ammunition is used.

The enemy does not always fight with his visor open. Many of his attacks have a religious camouflage. This is why Paul speaks in Ephesians 6:11 of the wiles of the devil. When I was in Toronto, Mary Klee, a sister from the Marburg mission, told me, "With the cults of Satan, one knows immediately where one is. With the so-called charismatic movements and the various branches of the Pentecostal church it is often impossible to see clearly. It all sounds so spiritual. The distinctions are blurred." This sister was saying the same thing as was Paul when he spoke of the wiles of the devil.

We may see from the story of Christ's temptation in Matthew 4 that the devil uses the Bible in making his attacks. The devil knows the Bible. Jesus, however, knows it even better, and is able to counter the pious-sounding attacks of Satan with other Bible texts.

The Bible should be read with a pencil in one's hand. We should underline all the things we want to note and which we can use in the battle against Satan's attacks. At the time of Satan's worst attacks on me, I have only been able to save myself by the use of Bible texts, which have carried me through all my struggles. When spiritual-sounding demons try to confuse us, we must say as Jesus did, "Again it is written." Against the misuse or distortion of words from the Bible, we must answer with a proper use of the Bible.

Ex 372 During one of my speaking tours in Canada, Pastor C. told me that a woman in his church maintained that God had given her an ability to tell the future. The pastor tried to enlighten her, but she did not accept his advice. When he prayed with her at the end of the interview, an uncanny power came out of her eyes in his direction. It was like a dark cloud trying to overshadow him. He could only flee to Jesus for protection and ask for the armor of God: the shield of faith, and the helmet of salvation. Let us think carefully about these pieces of military equipment. The armor, the breastplate, the shield, and the helmet are defensive armor to help us ward off the attacks of the evil one. The sword is an aggressive weapon. In the Ephesians passage four kinds of defensive armor are mentioned and one offensive weapon. This shows what dangers surround us.

15. Realize the victory of Jesus over the powers of darkness

Ex 373 I had the following experience in Liberia. I was visiting a farm which employed a hundred men. The manager of the farm had originally belonged to a secret society. When he came to Christ, he left the secret society, and as a result, had made some deadly enemies. He gathered some believing Christians in his house and read the Bible and prayed with them. One day his ten-year-old son came home in agonizing pain. An hour and a half later, he was dead. It turned out that he had been poisoned by members of the secret society. Six months later, another boy came home, complaining of terrible pains. This time, however, the father and his believing friends were prepared. They prayed and proclaimed over the boy the victory of Jesus. For a while the boy was totally blind. But he recovered when they had prayed with him and laid hands on him. He regained his sight and health. At the first attack, these Christians had been surprised by the powers of darkness. On the second occasion, they were warned and able to claim the victory of Christ.

Ex 374 A believing woman was spending the night in Würzburg. Before she went to sleep, she had a waking vision of a woman who had come into the room, although the doors and windows were closed. The woman cried out something about cutting her throat. The believing woman became paralyzed. She was unable to pray. Finally she succeeded in calling out, "Jesus, Jesus, Jesus." As she cried out, the paralysis left and the apparition disappeared.

Ex 375 At Manila in the Philippines, I gave an address in the Union Church. Suddenly the electric light went out. Someone brought out two candles and put them before me. The flame grew smaller and smaller. Then a missionary held his hand cupped around the light. Although there was no wind in the church and the flame was protected by the missionary's hand, the light looked as if it were going to go out. At this moment, I became aware that this was an attack by the powers of darkness, and in my heart I said, "In the name of Jesus, I command you powers of darkness to depart." The flame became normal again. "That," I said to the missionary who was with me, "was the devil." Later it turned out that there was a Hilot (sorcerer) in the church. He came out of the meeting dripping with perspiration. I spoke to him, because he was standing quite near me. He readily admitted that he had extinguished the electric light by magical power, and he said he would also have extinguished the candles if a stronger power had not prevented him. This Hilot also claimed to be able to kill people at a distance by magic power.

I know from conversations I have had with missionaries that this is possible. The Hilots in the Philippines, the Karunas in Hawaii, and the Saugumma in New Guinea have the power to perform "death magic."

Ex 376 During a mission in Southern Württemberg, two men came to me to talk. They belonged to a family of four, two brothers and two sisters, who owned a mill. Another miller came to work at the mill. He had soon set his eyes upon the younger sister. He was a spiritist. He practiced table tapping, used the *Sixth and Seventh Book of Moses,* and practiced mental suggestion. At night he would call to the girl he had chosen, "Come!" She would then go like a sleepwalker to the miller's room. They were married. When the young wife had to go to the hospital, the older sister heard the same call about ten times during the night, saying "Come!" But she called on the name of Jesus and withstood the call of the miller.

The two brothers who came to me were being terribly troubled by this spiritist. They heard poltergeists, noises and bangings, and saw black creatures coming toward them. But if they called on the name of Jesus and prayed, these poltergeists disappeared.

The miller has said that he will not leave them in peace until he has put all three of them under six feet of earth. He wants the mill and the inheritance of the three for himself. Up until now he has not succeeded, for the two brothers, the sister, and also his young wife are all believing Christians. The only mistake was that the younger sister agreed to marry this dreadful man.

Ex 377 Now an example from Switzerland. This is something which happened to one of my friends. The evangelist O.H. was holding a mission in the Swiss Jura. The valley in which he was working is renowned for its sorcery. During the night following the first meeting, he suddenly saw a dark figure in his room, although the door was shut. The dark figure said, "I am the lord of this valley. Go away, or I will kill you."

The next morning, the evangelist phoned a number of friends and asked them to pray for him, telling them what had happened during the night. He did not leave the valley. Following the second meeting, he again saw the apparition. "I give you twenty-four hours," said the figure, "and if you have not disappeared by then, you will be a dead man." The evangelist felt as if he were paralyzed. He could not even move his lips to pray. He could only call out in his heart again and again, "Jesus, Jesus, Jesus."

The next morning, he called yet more people to pray for him.

After the third meeting, the dark figure appeared no more. Everything was quiet. The mission was richly blessed. A large number of people came to faith in Christ, and many of them were freed from occult bondage. We see here a fulfilment of the promise in 1 John 4:4, "He who is in you is greater than he who is in the world."

I must, however, plead that people should not take this word and use it irresponsibly in situations for which it is not appropriate. I have come across many irresponsible Christians who justify their actions by such words as these and then in their superficiality are shot down by Satan. He who knows the power of Satan will not underestimate him—but he also knows still more of the wonderful, victorious power of Jesus, which he may claim in faith.

I will close this section with an illustration from the Old Testament. The people of Israel were standing before the Red Sea. Pursuing them were the Egyptians. The position of Israel was hopeless. They cried to Moses, "Why have you led us out of Egypt? Now save us from the hands of the Egyptians." Moses cried to God. The Lord answered him, "Why is this people complaining and moaning and crying? Tell the people of Israel to move forward." God made it clear to Moses that the victory was already determined. "The victory is there: claim it." Then Moses lifted up his rod over the sea, the waters parted, and the people of Israel went through the sea on dry ground and so gained the victory which God had prepared for them.

So too on the cross of Calvary God has prepared for us the victory, and in our struggles He calls to us, "Why are you crying to me? The victory is there: claim it." As the refrain of one American hymn puts it, "Realize the victory!" That is a command.

16. Guard against the return of the demons

In Luke 11:24 we are warned that demons which have been cast out are eager to return. They find the house swept and in order, enter in, and the last state of the man is worse than the first.

Anyone who has had anything to do with counseling the possessed is familiar with the problem of spirits which have been cast out returning and making matters worse. I have experienced this several times in my own counseling.

It also happens sometimes that demons will go out of one person and then enter another member of the family or a friend. One or two examples follow.

Ex 378 During a speaking tour in Paris, Vaux and Nogent, I counseled several different people. The housekeeper of a Bible school told me of one girl student who had earlier taken part in spiritist séances. Following this, the girl was still wetting her bed at twenty years of age. Previously she had not done so. The housekeeper prayed intensively for the girl. The result was that the girl stopped wetting her bed, but the housekeeper started to do so. She therefore sought out some believing brethren, who came and laid hands on her and prayed. Then the housekeeper stopped wetting her bed but the girl started again. These events demonstrate that the counseling received by the housekeeper and the girl was not adequate. There are some believers who are not thoroughly familiar with the counseling of those suffering from occult oppression.

Ex 379   While I was on a speaking tour in Australia, I spoke among other places at Riverwood. After one of my talks, a young man came to me for counseling. He confessed his sins, surrendered his life to Christ, and, because he previously had had dealings with spiritism, he said a prayer of renunciation. A week later he came back saying that, since he had become a Christian, he had been subject to attacks from the unseen world. In other words, he was either not yet completely free of the effects of spiritism, or he was not sufficiently well armed to ward off these unseen powers. In one counseling session, one cannot tell a person everything about deliverance and about remaining free. Normally I give such people a copy of my book *Heilung und Befreiung* (if they are German), or *Occult Bondage and Deliverance* (in the English-speaking world), or in France *Esclavage occulte et délivrance*.

Ex 380   During one of my missions in Switzerland, a woman came to faith in Christ. From that moment on, she became raving mad, for she suffered severe occult oppression. One of her friends was a Christian woman, and she took care of the woman who had gone mad. During one of the attacks, the woman died. After the death of the woman, her Christian friend, who had been praying for her, became melancholy. Since then she has had no time for the things of God. What we have here is the process of evil spirits leaving one person and entering another. Demons will not remain in a corpse: When a person dies, they leave that person and look for another suitable place to live. Sometimes they enter another member of the family or a friend. This example shows that one must not simply pray for an oppressed or possessed person without further thought. One must put oneself under the protection of the blood of Christ, and if need be—in cases of severe oppression—pray for the person only within the fellowship of a prayer group. There are many inexperienced, and therefore unprotected, Christians.

17. Be willing to dedicate yourself fully to Jesus

Those who are only half-hearted, as far as Jesus is concerned, will not be able to overcome and to withstand the attacks of Satan.

Ex 381   A young man came to me for counseling in Zurich. He told me that he had belonged to the "spiritual lodge" for five years. He left the lodge and gave his life to Christ. It then became evident that he was under a very strong ban and terrible oppression. He was unable to believe or pray properly. There was a real blockage, and he could not find assurance of salvation. Perhaps it was because he was unwilling to burn the literature of the spiritual lodge or to break with his former friends. Those who are not whole-hearted in following Jesus Christ do not gain the victory.

Ex 382   I think too of the worst case of possession I have encountered, which was in the Philippines.[53] I was lecturing in a theological seminary near Manila, and a young man came to me for counseling. As I prayed with him, he fell into a trance, and other voices spoke from him. Some of the voices spoke in languages which the young man had never learned. He only spoke his own Filipino dialect and English. The demons which spoke through him spoke in fluent Russian and other languages. It was the longest counseling session of my life. It lasted nineteen and one-half hours, during which time I was supported by the believing lecturers of the seminary. We asked the voices: "Why are you in this young man?" They answered in English, "We possess him because he did not make a full surrender." Every incomplete surrender of a life to Jesus leaves the door open for the fresh entry of demonic forces. After this long counseling session, the young man confessed various things which he had not mentioned at his conversion and in the course of his first confession. The testimony of the demons was true.

Half-heartedness is a dangerous thing in the kingdom of God. My friend, the evangelist Gottlieb Weiland, has sometimes asked his hearers, "How many wholes do one-thousand halves make?" Some of the class will then answer: "Five hundred." "No," he replies, "a thousand half-Christians do not make one, single, whole Christian." We understand the meaning of this illustration. Jakob Vetter, the founder of the German tent mission, sometimes declared to his hearers: "Halbheit taugt in keinem Stück, sie tritt noch hinters

Nichts zurück." (Incompleteness is no use in anything, it is even less than nothing.)

18. Understand clearly that deliverance is possible only through Christ

Various aspects of the truth in this exhortation need to be considered carefully.

a.   Every person who is under occult oppression must be urgently advised to go to an experienced counselor. The occult labyrinth is so dangerous that it is almost impossible for the person who has become caught in it to find his own way out. But one needs to see a counselor or one or two brethren who are familiar with this field. I have found on a number of occasions that theologians, pastors, and ministers have regarded occult abilities as gifts of God or of the Holy Spirit.

b.   What is an oppressed person to do if there is no counselor to be found in the area where he lives? God is certainly more merciful than we men. He does not need our help. He can make paths in the trackless wilderness. For example, one day I received a letter from France. A woman wrote to tell me that she had read my books about the occult and had taken the advice I gave. By the goodness of God, she had found deliverance.

Ex 383   I heard a similar story in New Zealand. I was preaching in a Baptist church in Otorohanga. After the service, a woman came to see me in the vestry. She said that she was the Sunday School superintendent. Earlier, she said, she had practiced sorcery. A friend had given her a copy of my book *Between Christ and Satan*. Her eyes were opened. She asked the Lord Jesus Christ to make her free and was delivered without the help of a counselor. She had not been able to find one in the area where she lived.

Ex 384   I had an experience of a similar sort in Australia. At the airport I was met by a woman, who told me her story. Her husband and only son had previously practiced black and white magic. She herself was a believer. Then one day she saw in a shop window my book *Between Christ and Satan*. She bought it. The book brought about a revolution in their family. Her son Allan stopped practicing magic and repented. He accepted the Lord Jesus. When I next go to Australia, he wants to accompany me on my tours as a musician.

c.   These are all exceptional cases. They are not the rule. Let us note the words of John 8:36, "If the Son therefore shall make you free, ye shall be free indeed."

The Lord Jesus is able to make men free with or without the

aid of a counselor. "Except the Lord build the house, they labor in vain that build it." We can apply this by saying, unless the Lord does the counseling, those who counsel, counsel in vain. To finish this section, another case is offered.

Ex 385 A woman told me her life story. At the age of twelve she had been charmed for warts. Later she practiced fortunetelling, both actively and passively. Then followed yoga and meditation, just to fill up the measure of her bondage.

At the age of thirty-four she found Christ during a mission, after being counseled by the evangelist. Following her conversion, disorders began to appear. If a believing Christian prayed with her with authority, she found her mind wandering and she felt as if she would burst. The worst thing was that she developed an absolute scotoma. A scotoma is a partial or total blindness in the retina of the eye. She was scarcely able to see. The troubled women sought out several brethren, who prayed for her and laid on hands, according to James 5:14. The prayer was answered, and the Lord honored the request of these brethren.

If men trained in counseling are working with an oppressed person, they must never come between Jesus and the person seeking help. The way must be left open for the person to see Jesus.

19. Obey the Lord in all things
The story is told that Field Marshall Moltke was one day visiting a deaconesses' home, and there delivered an address to the sisters. It was the shortest address of all time. He said, "Sisters, be obedient!" An address only three words long.

In the Indonesian revival on the island of Timor, one word played a very important part. It was the word *taat,* obedience.

Even for believing Christians it is very hard to obey the Lord in all things. We are very reluctant to give up the reins to another. We make our own plans, act and decide for ourselves, and do not like being told what to do.

Those who, after conversion, are not obedient to the Lord will experience many setbacks and defeats.

Obedience in the things of every day, both large and small, brings with it great blessing. Disobedience paralyzes our spiritual power.

It is said of Jesus in Philippians 2:8, "He became obedient unto death."

It was part of Paul's commission to bring about the obedience of faith (Romans 1.5).

Peter speaks of obedience to the truth (1 Peter 1:22).

Ex 386   Many years ago an elderly brother who worked within the Fellowship movement poured out his heart to me. When he came home at the end of World War I, he prayed that God would give him a life partner. He was already a believer. One day he met a pretty girl who attracted him at once. Unfortunately, she was not a believer. He was so much in love that he thought he could bring her to Jesus by his love. In a corner at the back of his mind he heard a warning voice: "Be ye not unequally yoked together with unbelievers" (2 Corinthians 6:14). He ignored the warning and married this unbelieving girl. Even in the first year of their marriage, problems began to appear. "I will go to church," she said, "but with ten horses you will not get me to your Fellowship." This caused a disharmony between them, and he had to admit that he had not been obedient to the warning voice of his conscience. As far as this brother was concerned, marriage became a martyrdom. His wife was domineering and made the decisions. He became more and more quiet for the sake of peace. He reaped the fruit of his disobedience for the rest of his life. His wife was not converted. She did not even go to the church services as she had promised at first. One day, however, she met her match. Her daughter was as pretty as she had been and just as unbelieving. When she got married, the mother thought she would be able to dominate the young marriage just as she had dominated her own. She had not reckoned with her resolute son-in-law. On several occasions he told her to stop "ordering him about." When she took no notice of this, he gave her such a box on the ears that she lost her desire to dominate. Where did things start to go wrong? When the Fellowship member was disobedient in the matter of marriage and married an unbelieving girl. He had to bear the consequences of this wrong decision to his dying day.

20. Be filled with the Spirit!

In these days, there is much talk about the Holy Spirit. More of it is unscriptural than is Scriptural.

Ex 387   I visited a ministers' meeting in South Germany. The chief speaker was Erich Schnepel. Bender, then the provincial bishop, was also there. The subject under discussion was the Holy Spirit. A young woman theologian stood up and said, "We receive the Holy Spirit when we are baptized as babies." My hair stood on end at this, for no one rose to disagree. In Germany, ninety percent of the population have been baptized as babies. Accordingly, we are to suppose that ninety percent of Germans—the bank robbers, the murderers who kill for the sake of gain; the sex murderers; and also the self-righteous, self-satisfied, well-to-do citizens—have the Holy Spirit. The idea is ludicrous. Yet this was said in the presence of 140 ministers of the national church. In the break which followed, I went to the chief speaker and asked him to declare his disagreement with this unscriptural statement. I was still a young minister at the time, and Bishop Bender had already more than once "hauled me over the coals" for my protests.

My request of the chief speaker was not granted. Schnepel was always an over-cautious brother, who did not want to hurt anyone.

The other extreme is the over-heated atmosphere of some fanatical groups who place more value on speaking in tongues than on genuine, Scriptural life in the power of the Holy Spirit. The following is an example of this from Soe in Indonesia.

Ex 388   After revival had broken out in Soe, several American Pentecostal pastors came over to observe the revival. Before they arrived, the leading brethren in Soe were warned by the Lord, "Men are coming who have a false teaching about the Holy Spirit. They must not be allowed to speak here, or they will confuse the church." The Americans came and soon made themselves popular among the people by giving away a lot of money. At the great conference in the church, they took their place on the platform as visitors. The meeting went on for hour after hour. Many speakers gave their testimonies. The Americans were not allowed to speak. Finally they became impatient and asked, "May we give our testimonies?" "No," replied Pastor Daniel, who was acting as chairman, "The Lord has warned us that you have a false doctrine of the Holy Spirit." That was rather a cold shower for men who had traveled 6,000 miles!

Between the cold lifeless "churchianity" of the official church and the over-emotional atmosphere of the extremists, lies the truth.

The truth is revealed to us quite clearly in the Scriptures.

We receive the Holy Spirit when we are born again. No one can call Jesus Lord without the Holy Spirit (I Corinthians 12:3). Infant baptism is not the same as rebirth.

We have no need of a second great experience in addition to the second birth, whether in the form of a "second blessing" or an additional "baptism in the Spirit." I would not follow a Lord who had only two blessings to give. Every day that we live with Him is a blessing.

All the passages in the Bible which speak of the Holy Spirit are of great importance to me. But we do not have the right to take these passages and build them into a false doctrine. I refer the reader at this point to my book *Charismatic Gifts.*

To summarize the teaching of the Bible briefly we must say:

a. We receive the Holy Spirit when we are born again. At our second birth, we are filled and sealed with the Holy Spirit.

b. We must not stand still at this starting point. Paul, who had experienced the filling with the Holy Spirit of the believers at Ephesus (Acts 19:6), writes to the same people in Ephesians 5:18, "Be filled with the Spirit." This means that we do not need a baptism of the Spirit as a second experience of full salvation. We need a continual filling with the Holy Spirit after we have become members of the Church of Christ through the second birth. There are of course many questions left unanswered here. They are dealt with in the book already mentioned, *Charismatic Gifts.*

The person who has been delivered from the sphere of occult power and influence must stand firmly in the sphere of the Holy Spirit's power and follow Jesus. The *civitas diaboli,* the realm of Satan, is left behind, and the believer becomes a member of the *civitas Dei,* God's kingdom.

If I have still not made it clear to anyone that these twenty points are not a blueprint, I hope it will not be taken amiss if I repeat that point. We do not need a blueprint, nor a routine, nor a method, nor a system, but Jesus Christ Himself. He is the only one who is able to rescue us from the power of Satan.

But it has been essential to show those who are oppressed what possibilities the Holy Scriptures contain for finding freedom.

D. IN THE CONQUEROR'S TRAIN

In history it has often been the custom for victorious generals to take along the leaders of their conquered enemies in their triumphal processions.

We find an example in 1 Samuel 15. King Saul had conquered the Amalekites and then led along Agag, their king, as a prisoner in his train.

The same custom was observed in ancient Rome. Homecoming conquerors would be allowed a triumphal procession, and among those who followed them would be their vanquished foes.

Isaiah 53:12 speaks of the mightiest conqueror of all time in these terms, "I will divide him a portion with the great, and he shall divide the spoil with the strong." (German version reads: "he will have the mighty as his spoil").

Who is this mightiest of conquerors? Who has the mighty as his spoil? The following chapters will give the answer.

1
FROM THE SATANISTS TO CHRIST

In 1975, the Lord allowed me to meet a former satanist. He gave me permission to publish his life story and asked at the same time for the prayers of those who receive my news sheet. Several months after our meeting, David Hansen—that is this brother's name—sent me a short autobiography. It is too long to be printed here in full, so, let's use only the introduction to the letter, in order to give background to the following story.

Dear Dr. Koch,

Thank you for the time I was able to spend with you after the service at Trinity Baptist Church in Santa Barbara, California, on March 19th. That was a very crucial meeting for me, one of encouragement and blessing.

I praise God for your committed life to Christ and the work our Lord has brought you into. As I read your book, *Wine of God* (Kregel, Grand Rapids, Mich.) I was again blessed, encouraged, and challenged. The Lord has used your life of commitment to Him to encourage and strengthen me every time I delve into one of your books. I uphold you in prayer daily now.

And now for the story of this man, who is a high school teacher. The Christianity he heard about at home and at church left him unsatisfied. He saw with open eyes the great gulf existing between Christian teaching and practical living. He was also honest enough to acknowledge the discrepancy between willing and doing in his own life. He therefore sought for a solid foundation for his life. He strove to find a power which would make it possible to live the kind of life he wanted to live.

One evening he heard a Satanist talking on television. The Satanist was extolling the power of Satan. This child of darkness said, among other things, "If you want power, we will give you it. If you are looking for fulfilment in life, we can offer you that. Christianity has long since gone out of business. In any case, it has never offered its followers anything. It has just fed them with empty promises."

That evening, this physical education teacher who was searching for something to live for made his decision. He asked for the address and meeting place of the nearest cult of Satan. It was at Skeleton Canyon, near Thousand Oaks, a place between Santa Barbara and Los Angeles.

For two years, the teacher was a member of this group. Normally they met on a Saturday, from 4 P.M. until midnight, or even later, in Skeleton Canyon, celebrating the black mass and holding orgies. David had surrendered everything to Satan: his life, his soul, his home, his income, his car, and his family. This total surrender, however, did not bring him peace. The power of darkness reached out after his soul, and suicidal thoughts plagued him.

One day he found himself praying once more to Satan, his lord. He cursed God, one of the requirements for genuine prayer to Satan. Then there came into his mind the words of the Bible in 1 John 4:4b, "He who is in you is greater than he who is in the world." Despite these words from the Bible, he continued to curse God with all the hate he could muster. Then he felt a great peace spreading through his heart and throughout the room. The atmosphere overpowered him. It was sent by God. Suddenly David sat up in bed and asked God for help. God heard his prayer and his cry.

From that moment on, David's life was set on a new course. He took the Bible out and daily he studied the Scriptures eagerly. His peace became deeper still.

Then came Saturday. His former friends would be gathering in Skeleton Canyon. David prayed for guidance as to what he should do. He decided that he would once more attend the meeting, to tell them that he was leaving and to bear witness to Jesus Christ among his friends.

This is something nobody ought to imitate. As a counselor, I would never advise a person to visit the scene of a devilish meeting like that. In this case, however, not only did David feel an inward freedom to go, but he was also given the necessary strength and authority.

He went to Skeleton Canyon. When all the members had gathered, he explained that he was leaving and testified that Jesus Christ was his Deliverer and Redeemer. His friends were astonished, but strangely enough they did not contradict him. They only said, "Why are you doing this? What are you getting for it?" David was ready to give an answer.

"I am making this step because life in our fellowship has brought me nothing but lack of peace, despair, and thoughts of suicide. What I have already gained with Christ is an inner peace which passes all understanding."

His witness for Christ and the discussion which followed went on for nine hours, until midnight. The result was that a number of his friends said, "We will join you. Your problem is our problem, too. We are also seeking this peace which you say Christ can give."

The result of this meeting shows that David had a commission from the Lord to go to the sect meeting.

Those who would escape from Satan's clutches must be prepared for Satan's counterattacks. During the night following this mighty victory of Jesus Christ at the cult's meeting place, David experienced the personal intervention of Satan. "You belong to me," said the evil one. "If you try to escape from me I will kill your child and make you a poor man." But David was resolved that, come what may and whatever the Lord allowed, he would remain true to Jesus.

The next morning his child was severely ill and had to go to a hospital. The hospital treatment lasted three weeks. Then the child died. The bill amounted to about $3,000.

Satan had carried out his threat. The child was dead and the family faced financial ruin.

At this point, I must interrupt the story. I have already given a short account of David's experiences in a news-letter. As a result,

I received a number of letters asking me to omit this side of the story. Some Christians are offended because they believe that when a person is converted everything is forgiven and all his problems are solved. This view is to be found particularly in American and Canadian churches.

One thing is true: when a person is converted all his sins are forgiven. But not all the consequences are wiped out—not by a long way. The Bible does not provide us with a superficial unthinking theology.

An illustration which I have often used may help us to see this more clearly. Let us say that a playboy, as a result of his life of debauchery, has contracted syphilis. Then he finds Christ, and so too forgiveness for his dissolute life. This does not mean that his disease is cured. It will probably require a lengthy period of medical treatment.

There are some Bible passages which make any superficial theology look absurd. Think of Isaiah 45:7, "I make peace, and create evil." God creates evil? Think of Amos 3:6, "Shall there be evil in the city, and the Lord hath not done it?" God brings evil?

Unthinking, superficial Christians forget the holiness and righteousness of God and underestimate the power of Satan.

David had signed himself over to the devil and had often cursed God. It is God's business if He allowed the death of the child and David's financial ruin. Moreover, David told me that the child had been consecrated to Satan while it was still in its mother's womb.

Despite these terrible setbacks, David did not let anything stop him from following Jesus. After this, he took to placing himself and his family daily under the protection of Jesus. The advice given in my book *Occult Bondage and Deliverance*[54] became a blessing to him.

As an additional help, he tried to find some believers to support him in prayer. He was greatly disappointed. The Christians were afraid of him and avoided him. It is a tragedy that Christians in the Western world have so little interest in prayer cells, which can come to the aid of troubled and threatened Christians.

Since then David has been a blessing in many churches. Wherever he is invited, he gives his testimony as to how Christ freed him from the bonds of Satan. God has equipped this brother to counsel those who suffer from occult oppression. Many churches have opened their doors to him.

Such a ministry requires the prayer support of understanding

Christians. I take this opportunity of asking all those who pray for me to engage in such prayer for him and to continue faithfully in it.

This experience from 1975 is a first answer to the question, "Who is the man who has the mighty as his spoil?" We know Him.

2

ASTROLOGY AND CHRISTIANITY?

In 1972 I gave a talk in a French church in Quebec on the subject of fortunetelling. After the talk there was a discussion. A long-haired young fellow got up and said, "I am both an astrologer and a Christian." Then he began to contradict some of the things I had said. I replied, "Either you are an astrologer or you are a Christian. You cannot be both at once."

"Why not?" asked the long-haired lad.

"Go home and read Isaiah 47:12-14." I then quoted the three verses. That was the end of the discussion with this young man.

About six months later I received through the mail a twenty-three-page booklet. On the front were two photos. The top one was of a long-haired fellow, the one underneath was a young man with hair cut short. There was no visible similarity between the two. The top one had a beard, "Absalom's locks" and a dark look; the one below no beard, a happy face and military-style haircut. Between the two pictures was the title: *Pourquoi j'ai quitté l' Astrologie, Why I Left Astrology.*

This booklet contained the testimony of Ives Petelle. Let us read his story in brief.

Petelle came from a Catholic family who lived in Montreal. His father worked in a factory belonging to a Canadian.

As he grew up, Ives took an interest in art and the theater. He wanted to study at the Conservatory of Dramatic Art. He went in for the entrance examination. The head of the Conservatory turned him down for the following reason: no lack of talent, but insufficient discipline and adaptability. Anyone who knew Petelle's wild life before his conversion will understand this comment.

After several more unsuccessful attempts to become a student of fine arts, he lost interest. The succession of disappointments drove him to drugs. He wanted to forget the unpleasant experiences of his life, to shake off the past.

Drugs did not bring him the sense of meaning and fulfilment he hoped for, so he took up astrology.

For three years he studied astrology, making it his speciality. He cast horoscopes in order to give medical diagnoses. With the aid of a sky chart, he tried to predict future events. He also practiced character analysis and attempted psychotherapy. This was how he earned his living.

How did the great turning point of his life come about? The disappointments regarding his professional training and his addiction to drugs had probably left a certain vacuum which Petelle unconsciously wanted to fill.

He received encouragement to find a new direction for his life when a friend of his was converted, at the end of 1971. Petelle noticed the great change in character of his friend after he had decided for Christ. This spurred Petelle on to read the Bible. He began to read parts of it at random.

The next step towards a reorientation of his life was my sermon in a French church in Quebec, which was mentioned earlier.

Petelle struggled through to the recognition that there was no more supernatural power and wisdom in the constellations of the sky than in a crystal ball or a pendulum. These supernatural abilities do not lie in the person who practices fortunetelling by such means: this supernatural power comes from Satan alone. Many Bible passages like Isaiah 47, Deuteronomy 18:9-12, had led him to realize this.

Although he knew these things, it did not lead at once to a practical change in his life. He needed to have one more thing pointed out to him. This happened a short while after my seventeenth lecture tour in Canada.

A series of lectures on the occult was advertised at the salon of international occult sciences in Montreal. Petelle, who was still unsure of where he stood with regard to astrology,—particularly since it was his means of earning his living—went to these meetings. The total revulsion, which he felt while he was there helped him to come to the point of breaking completely with occult practices.

At this occult festival in Montreal, Petelle talked with a Catholic priest. The latter advised him to use a crystal ball to clarify his unsolved problems. In other words, the priest told Petelle to seek help through soothsaying.

The young man was now upset and could find no rest. He realized that astrology and all the arts of divination were inconsistent with the Christian faith. On May 28, 1972 he made his decision for Christ. This was the beginning of a completely new life for Petelle.

The effects of his radical conversion soon became evident. Petelle opened a small pizza restaurant in the city of Quebec. The first people whom he led to Christ were his assistants. It was a remarkable experience for me to see his assistants during my eighteenth tour of Canada. They went into the restaurants with Bibles under their arms and began the day with Bible reading and corporate prayer.

Eighteen months after his conversion, Petelle had already led twenty-three young people to Christ. When I gave an address at the Bethel Bible School, one student who spoke to me had been led to Christ by Petelle. Petelle is not ashamed to speak to customers about spiritual things and to pray with them.

Anyone who is so active in serving the Lord must expect the counterattacks of Satan. They came with great force. Petelle was due to be shot down like many others in the kingdom of God. For this reason I have twice in my news-letters asked people to pray for him. At this point, I call on all my prayer partners to engage in earnest intercession for him. The church of Christ has often failed those who are fighting in the front line. Petelle is a witness who is involved in hand-to-hand fighting with the enemy, for he sometimes travels around giving talks and warning people against the occult and astrology, which he himself once practiced.

3
THE MAGICIAN

On the mission fields I have often encountered men like Elymas in Acts 13 who practice their dark arts and keep people from coming to Christ. I have written enough already about sorcery in this book. What interests us in this chapter is only the question of how magicians have become free through Christ.

I remember Gandi in New Guinea. I was visiting the stations of the Australian South Sea Mission. Sister Lisbeth Schrader introduced me to a former magician who had become a Christian. His story has already been related in my book *Unter der Führung Jesu.*

Among all peoples there are magicians who practice their dark arts and, by acting as the devil's henchmen, bring about much suffering.

For instance, years ago a magician in Holstein, Germany, told me he had killed three people through the power of Satan. Today he is a disciple of Jesus.

One experience has left a deep impression on my memory. It

was the conversion of a sorcerer whom I was able to point to Christ.

After I spoke in a Lutheran church, a man came rushing into the vestry where I was. Before I could stop him, he was on his knees weeping and confessing his sins. He was so deeply moved that he could no longer control himself. It takes a powerful blow to make a man weep.

He had heard my talk attacking magic and charming, and his conscience had been pricked. He made a clean break from it before God. It was easy to lead him to Christ. The Holy Spirit was obviously at work. I prayed a prayer of renunciation with him and declared him free in the name of the Lord (Matthew 18:18).

The next day I had to travel elsewhere, and I lost touch with the man. About two years later I visited a place not far from that town. The former magician was unable to come himself, but he sent a friend with the message, "Tell Dr. Koch that I became free that day, and since then I have been following Jesus." That was an encouraging message amid all the difficulties of my ministry.

Then for years I heard no more of him. Eight years later, I was speaking at a missionary conference two-hundred-seventy miles from where he lived. Among the people present at the conference who came to talk to me was a man who said, "Do you still know me?" I said I did not. "I am the former magic charmer whom you led to Christ. And I am still following Him." My joy was great.

I have not finished the story yet. The brother said, "You don't know everything yet. When I came to you then, I had a lung disease. I had never told you that when I was converted, my tuberculosis came to a halt. I wanted to wait until I was quite sure. Now it is almost ten years since. The Lord has done a threefold miracle for me: He forgave all my sins, He freed me from the bondage of Satan, and He healed me from tuberculosis."

Here then is an illustration of Jesus' original commission to His disciples when He sent them out. In Luke 9:1-2 we read, "He gave them power and authority over all devils, and to cure diseases. And he sent them to preach the kingdom of God and to heal." Preaching—healing—casting out demons, these are the three notes of Jesus' commission. There are many Christian workers who believe these verses apply only to the apostolic age. The age of the apostles, of course, was different in character from what developed in the later church. But many servants of Jesus make a cushion for themselves out of this reference to the apostolic age. As long as it says in my Bible "Jesus Christ the same yesterday, today and forever" (Hebrews 13:8), I will not spend my time investigating what does not belong to us, but rather I shall ask for what does belong to us. And that is more than short-sighted people would have us believe.

4
CONQUEST OF THE MIGHTY

Some of the strongest forms of spiritism and magic are found among the Macumba groups in South America, voodoo in Haiti, the Zombis in Africa and Asia, and the Shamans of Siberia and Alaska. I have visited these areas, but have not heard of many examples of deliverance there. The few experiences of victory, however, are tokens of the triumph of Jesus in the dark regions and areas of the world. Let us notice them.

a.   *From Macumba to Christ*

The story of Otilia Pontes is a beacon light, showing that Jesus really can rescue people from the deepest hell of sorcery and make them into His instruments. For a complete account of Otilia, see my book *Jesus auf allen Kontinenten,* pp.544ff. Here I will erect just a small victory memorial.

Otilia Pontes was a textile worker in a factory in Rio de Janeiro. There she fell into the hands of her manageress, who caused her, by means of psychic powers, to join the Macumba. Otilia was introduced to the cultic ceremonies in the Brazilian jungle. Because of her strong, hereditary, psychic powers, she quickly progressed through all the stages and passed all the tests.

One of the tests was to take some burning wool out of boiling oil with her bare hands without burning her fingers. Out of fifty candidates, only Otilia and one other novice were able to do this.

The most difficult test was the command to offer up her own son as a cultic sacrifice. At midnight, the boy was brought to the festal gathering. At the same time, a he-goat was bound and placed next to the boy. The demon had to decide whether he would rather have the life of the child or that of the goat. Child sacrifice is practiced by the Macumba to this day. The state has strictly forbidden it. But the meeting places of the cult are so hidden in the jungle that the police would never find them.

At midnight, the demon Joao Caveira entered the cult mother and announced that he would accept a substitute. Thereupon the goat was killed and sacrificed. The boy would undoubtedly have been sacrificed if the demon had so demanded.

Let it be said at this point that this boy is now a servant of Jesus.

After the final test, Otilia became Baba de vovo Rosario, or cult mother of the rose vow. She developed extraordinary mediumistic powers. She was able to heal and cause illness, to cast spells and to loose them. When she was in a trance, she could receive a message and transmit it to others. What Otilia found surprising was that her power proved ineffective where true Christians were involved. She came to know that there was something even stronger than Satan and the demons.

Otilia held a leading position among the Macumba for twenty-three years. Then she heard the call of Christ. First of all, her child became so ill that his recovery seemed almost out of the question. A servant of Christ who visited her said, "Christ can heal your child. Please come next Sunday to the service."

A cult mother go to a Christian service? An impossible notion! But she loved her child. And so for a whole week she struggled with the question of whether she ought to go. All kinds of difficulties came in the way. Moreover, her predecessor, the old cult mother, tried to prevent her. Otilia put a spell on her in her house. The old Baba had to stand motionless until Otilia returned. That was the strength of the young Baba's powers.

She did not content herself with going to the church service just once. Amid fearful struggles, Otilia found the way to Christ and renounced the Macumba cult. A cult mother who leaves the Macumba would normally forfeit her life. Otilia was aware of this. But she accepted the risk. She knew that she was now under the protection of a mightier One. Her child recovered completely. Otilia herself became an evangelist, and has since gone around Brazil speaking to large meetings of women. When I met her in Rio and heard her testimony from her own lips, she had already spoken in one-hundred-thirty churches. She needs our prayers, because Satan pursues any person who has once served him and then escaped from his clutches.

b. *From Voodoo to Christ*

This story can be told quickly, but there is much between the lines. I learned about voodoo in Haiti. I have many reports from missionaries, but also some observations of my own from my counseling experiences.

It was early in the fifties. A young negro came to me for counseling. He had been healed in childhood by a voodooist in Port au Prince, Haiti. His parents always went to the voodooist whenever they needed help.

The effects were obvious. He had undergone a change of character; there was a blockage in his spiritual life; there was bondage of many sorts. The young man told me his whole life story. I prayed with him a prayer of renunciation. In the presence of two believing brethren I then declared him free of voodoo in the name of the Lord. I must confess that I felt afraid of doing this. I know the counterattacks of the powers of darkness, which are much more terrible than superficial and inexperienced Christians like to think.

After this I lost touch with the young man. Then in 1966, at the World Conference on Evangelism, he suddenly came up to me and said, "Do you remember me? About ten or twelve years ago, I came to you for counseling." The whole scene came back to me. How glad I was to hear that this brother is now preaching the Gospel in his home country and is one of the leaders of the Christian church. The Lord sometimes puts to shame the smallness of our faith.

c. *From Yoga to Christ*

Years ago I gave some addresses in San Diego, California. After one of the meetings a young woman came to me and said that she had been involved in yoga for many years. After much practice, she had mastered the second grade. She could control her visceral nervous system by mental concentration. She could accelerate or slow down her circulation. Her unconscious bodily functions were controlled by concentration and meditation.

In her exercises she had chosen Jesus as her guru. Note well: Jesus was only an example, only the great man of wisdom, not her Redeemer and Savior. The young woman thought she had a balanced philosophy of life. Then her security was shattered.

Living near her were some Christian believers who prayed for her. They used to invite her to services and gave her Christian literature to read. They also argued that it was not enough to give Jesus a title of honor and to choose Him as one's guru. No, Jesus wants to be Lord of all our life.

With this, one stone was knocked out of the system of teaching which she had constructed. Others followed. It was a painful process, but at last she surrendered her life to Christ.

She had the account of her conversion to Christ printed. It is a little booklet of thirty-two pages. She gave me a copy while I was in San Diego. The booklet is entitled *From Yoga to Christ.*

d. *The Country Devil Becomes a Christian*

It was in Liberia. I was visiting Kingsville where the missionary Graham Davies was working. Brother Davies was a fine Christian. He has since died.

After I had spoken, a seventy-year-old man came to me for counseling. The missionary warned me that this old man was a much-feared sorcerer, who was nicknamed the Country Devil. He was the president of the sorcerers in Liberia.

I felt uncomfortable about having such a man with me for counseling. But I was in for a surprise.

The sorcerer said forthrightly, "I want to confess my sins and become a Christian." Then he began to reveal all the things he had done during his life. He had no difficulty in accepting forgiveness and deliverance through faith in Christ. This interview also enabled me to see what goes on behind the scenes in Liberian magic. A lot of this magic depends on suggestion, but there is also much satanic sorcery involved.

It was obvious to me that as far as this man was concerned, I was only the last link in a long chain. The missionaries had prepared the ground excellently. Without the ministry of these faithful witnesses of Jesus on the mission field, the sudden conversion of the old sorcerer, who was so clear about what he was doing, would not have been possible.

I was also enabled to see clearly how great is the power of Jesus Christ, when a chief sorcerer can surrender to the Son of God.

e. *A Muslim Sorcerer Becomes a Christian*

In South East Asia I have three times met Brother N.N. It is better if I do not give his name, as he might otherwise be open to attacks.

His parents lived in Sumatra, in a district controlled by the Muslims. Their son was gifted and went not only to high school but also to the university. The parents' plan and hope was that their son would become a Muslim priest. During the vacations, the young priesthood candidate would go to an old priest and learn all the things one cannot learn at university. The old disciple of Mohammed introduced his eager pupil to the art of magic. Evidently the boy had a strongly psychic disposition, and he gained a great mastery of the art. By magical power, he could open closed doors and windows, put out a burning flame, or light one. During all these experiments, his teacher made it clear that every fully qualified

Muslim priest must also learn and master the art of magic.

To round out his studies, the young man had to go abroad and attend a leading Koran university. Here for the first time he met genuine, convinced Christians. For no reason he began to hate them. No wonder, for through his magical practices he was caught in the hands of Satan.

In order to translate his hatred into action he formed an anti-Christian action group among the students. The object of this group was to fight any open activity by the Christians. Wherever Christian services were being held, this group broke the windows and made such a row around the church that the services were disturbed. The Christians did not receive help from the police, for the police were Muslims and felt similar hatred against Christians. The Christians did not think of asking the police for protection. They knew there was no point. Instead they prayed, among other things in the words of Psalm 124:8, "Our help is in the name of the Lord."

In the church, surrounded by the uproar outside, the Christians got on their knees and prayed for those who were making the disturbance. At another service one Sunday evening, the leader and preacher of the Christian church got the idea of inviting the group of Muslims to a discussion in the church. While the leader went outside, the others in the church prayed for the Lord's protection for him. It was an answer to prayer when the ringleader of the Muslims said he was willing to join in a discussion. Students all over the world are, of course, always ready for a discussion.

A little uneasily, other Muslims, with defiant and aggressive looks on their faces, entered the Christians' meeting room. Supported by the prayers of all the Christians who were present, the leader quietly explained to the young hotheads what they as Christians wanted to do. The discussion was much quieter than one might have expected.

That evening, the two groups parted without any further disturbance.

The one who thought most about what the Christians had said was the student who was preparing for the priesthood. He lost his desire to instigate any further disturbances. His friends continued the campaign, but not at the "discussion church."

The young priesthood candidate even went a step further. One evening he slipped into the Christian service and sat down in the back row. The message which he heard touched a chord in his heart. God's Spirit had begun to work in his heart.

Storms and struggles followed, but the young man nevertheless firmly resolved to have a personal talk with the leader of the church. This pastor then took the student to an evangelistic meeting which a missionary, a man of spiritual authority, was conducting in the city. This was the final impulse—the disciple of the Koran, the candidate for the Muslim priesthood, became a disciple of Jesus. Just as radical as had been his opposition to the Christians was his decision to be a witness for Jesus Christ.

He signed up to go to Bible school, in order to study the New Testament thoroughly. Then he went back to his old homeland to work as a missionary.

I have not lost touch with this brother, who was to have been a Muslim priest and instead became a Christian missionary. Other missionaries have kept me informed of his much-blessed ministry.

Let me tell just one more experience, which for me was an example of the Lord's guidance. For years my Bible and Literature Mission has supported a number of missionaries on every continent. It is not always easy to send money to other continents. Once I sent a large sum of money through the State Bank of Madras in South India. The State Bank held up the money for six months before they paid it to the recipient. And then they claimed twenty percent in foreign exchange duty. According to Western standards that would be a swindle. First they use the Western money for six months without paying interest, and then they take a large proportion for themselves.

Now for the little incident with Brother N.N. One day I felt moved to send him a check. The letter had to be sent to him through a middle man. This time it went through extraordinarily quickly. After only three weeks I received confirmation that he had received it. "A year ago," he wrote, "I got married. Now we are expecting our first child. We were completely out of money when you wrote. My wife could not buy anything for the baby. There was not even enough for diapers and baby food. We prayed earnestly to the Lord to help us. Then as God's answer, an answer to our prayers, your check came. Thanks be to God!"

This time it did not take months because the Lord knew that it was urgently needed. I had no idea of the situation at all. I did not even know that Brother N.N. was married.

The Lord knows how to strengthen our faith through both great and small experiences.

The great experience in this story is the fact that a candidate for the priesthood, who had been trained in all the arts of sorcery, escaped from the service of Satan, became a Christian, and is today working on the mission field as a messenger for the Lord!

    f. *It's Your Fault!*

I was giving a series of addresses in the Aubette (Festival Hall) in Strasbourg when two young men confronted me in this way:

"What have I done wrong, for you to accuse me?"

"A year ago you spoke here in this same hall against fortunetelling. Our mother heard you, and afterward came home and told us children, 'That is the end of that. I am not going to carry on with my work any longer.' "

"What work was your mother doing?"

"Well, that's obvious, isn't it? She used to help people who sought her advice, with cards, crystal ball, and pendulum. She made a lot of money out of it. The whole family was very comfortable. Now that is over. We all have to go out to work because our mother is so obstinate and will not use her gifts any more."

"Do you not understand that fortunetelling is the devil's work, and that it causes some people to forfeit a chance for salvation?"

"But our mother did a lot of good with it. She didn't ask for any money, either. Her clients gave it to her of their own free will. Some of those who came for advice were important people in high positions. They would not have come if our mother had been doing something that was not right."

I was unable to convince these young people. They were angry because they now had to earn their own living instead of drawing on their mother's ever-ready supply.

I was glad to hear of it. I saw some fruit of my talks in the previous year. In Isaiah 55:11 the Lord says, "So shall my word be that goeth forth out of my mouth: it shall not return unto me void." In Strasbourg, God's Word stopped a fortuneteller's money supply. But it did more than that. Someone whom Satan had bound was delivered and "blessed with the riches of the house of God."

    g. *Blood Pacts*

In the last twenty years, tens of thousands of young people have signed their souls to the devil in their own blood. What is the background of these dreadful blood pacts?

Some young people, like fourteen-year-old Heidi in Switzerland, try it out of curiosity, to see if a blood pact has any effect.

Other young people are put off by the rigidity and lifelessness of the church, or feel revolted by the comfortable, self-righteous Pharisaism of people who call themselves Christians.

For others the blood pact is only one further step in their pursuit of enjoyment or of finding a purpose for an empty life. They progress through the whole catalog of what the devil has to offer: sex, alcohol, drugs, demonic music, religious fanaticism, and finally, total surrender to Satan.

In counseling I fear blood pacts more than any other form of possession. I have recorded about one-hundred such cases. I know of only four young people who have been delivered.

The most wonderful experience I have had in this connection was in Zurich. A young man confessed to me while I counseled him that he had signed his soul to the devil in his own blood. My heart sank.

Nevertheless I listened patiently to what the young man had to tell me. He confessed his sins and announced his resolve to surrender his life to Jesus. I prayed with him a prayer of renunciation. I dared not declare him free, for I had not the faith to feel free to do so. I simply gave him a copy of my book, *Heilung und Befreiung,* in which I have given instructions about counseling those involved in the occult. I was not even faithful in praying for him, because bad experiences in similar cases have made me cautious.

All the greater, therefore, was my joy some eight months later, when I heard that the young man had been delivered and was preaching the Gospel.

Here the Lord Jesus has set up a trophy of His triumph, an encouraging sign which shows that no bondage or oppression is too hard for Him to overcome. To Him is given all authority in Heaven and on earth.

> Jesus! the name high over all,
> In hell or earth or sky;
> Angels and men before it fall,
> And devils fear and fly.
> Jesus the prisoner's fetters breaks,
> And bruises Satan's head;
> Power into strengthless souls He speaks,
> And life into the dead.

To those who have signed themselves over to the devil in their blood, the New Testament gives a threefold guarantee:

Purified by the blood of Christ from dead works, Hebrews 9:14
Redeemed through His blood, Ephesians 1:7
Ransomed for God by Jesus' blood, Revelation 5:9

The blood of Jesus Christ, the Son of God, is the banner of victory for all those who have come under Satan's spell and who wish to be freed or have already found deliverance.

72

UFO

I have never seen a UFO, nor do I particularly wish to see one. My knowledge of unidentified foreign objects comes from friends, from reading, and above all from pastoral counseling sessions.

Here are some examples.

I traveled in South American countries nine times and listened to UFO stories there. One of my friends was at the beach one hot day. Thousands were there looking for relief from the heat. At three in the afternoon, the bathers were craning their necks watching a group of nine flying objects in the sky moving in an arrow formation. There was no sound. These objects did not correspond in shape to ordinary aircraft. About a thousand witnesses can testify to what happened there. The incident was reported in the newspaper.

On another occasion a believer friend in France witnessed a similar phenomenon. A brother in Christ was driving his car up a road in the Vosges Mountains. A saucer-shaped aircraft approached his car. It was noiseless. The motor of the car stalled at once. The starter would not work. When the flying object disappeared on the horizon, there was no difficulty starting the motor.

One can number such experiences by the tens of thousands. When I gave lectures in Colorado I learned that a Professor Saunders had more than 50,000 such cases in his records.

A second source of my information is in material published by a believing Christian. I mention as worthy of commendation the writings of Weldon Levitt: *Encounters with UFO's and Close Encounters — A Better Explanation*. The conclusions reached in these books correspond largely to my own views.

The most important data to shape my judgment and give it some clarity came to me in my work as counselor. As an example, I cite an experience from South Africa.

A white woman was visiting the mission station Kwa Sizabantu. The proclamation by Erlo and the other brethren touched her conscience. She decided to go to confession. Without mentioning names, in her confession she reported that her parents were spiritualists and that she had attended spiritualist seances in her youth. In 1972 many

UFO's had been sighted in South Africa and in Southwest Africa (now called Namibia). At such a place, where there had been numerous appearances of UFO's, the woman reported this exciting experience.

It had been her wish for years to be able to communicate with UFO pilots. This wish was to be fulfilled in an unexpected way. During the night she noticed a whirlwind, as if a helicopter were hovering overhead.

She was taken out of her house. She didn't know how this was happening. It was a riddle to her. She wondered if perchance her mind was going off on a mental excursion. She was not merely familiar with such spiritualistic tricks — indeed she had formerly practiced them herself.

Inside the UFO she saw robot-like figures. They examined her body with many instruments. The whole procedure was not without pain. One robot said, "You people are not yet fully developed, since you still have pain; we have developed further than you."

It was a telepathic conversation. The woman's language was not used. Before she was brought back to her house the robots declared, "You may make a wish for yourself, if you want. Ask whatever you would like. We want to give it to you. God is not going to answer your prayer anyway. But we can fulfill your wish." The woman answered, "I should like very much to get married." The UFO crew responded, "What a trifle! Don't you want something greater? You could have demanded more."

After the instruments were removed from her, a robot took her back to her house. She was still not free from pain. A short time later the robot came again and said, "We forgot an instrument." He disconnected it and disappeared. Since her pain didn't go away, the woman tried to find out why her leg hurt so much. Here she discovered a big, blue spot where the instrument had been attached. The area remained blue for days.

The UFO crew kept its word. The woman had an opportunity to marry. The marriage, however, didn't turn out happy.

The nature of this experience is clearly recognizable:

1. This UFO crew represented a denial of God whom she wished to downgrade.

2. Before this UFO encounter the woman was able to pray and read the Bible. After this encounter her life was devoid of these.

3. The connection between Spiritualism and the UFO encounter is of negative value.

4. The fulfillment of her wish to marry did not bring happiness.

The main point would be lost if the outcome of this counseling were not reported. The woman confessed everything that had been exposed to her as sin. She also vowed to have no more to do with Spiritualism or with UFO's and to surrender her life to Jesus Christ.

There are essentially three theories for the explanation of UFO's: the humbug theory, the assumption of the existence of extra-terrestial persons, and the demon theory.

Those who theorize along the humbug line explain all UFO phenomena as a deception of the senses. They maintain that what is reported are really cloud formations or atmospheric apparitions similar to the *fata morgana* — external projections of the human fantasy. These rationalistic denials are simply unsatisfactory in view of the tens of thousands of reliable sightings. One should strongly advise these humbug theorists to start doubting the capability of their own reasoning powers.

The extra-territorialists assume that UFO's are inter-planetary flying cbjects manned by extra-terrestrial beings. In part, they base their view on the passage in Genesis 6:4 where presumably extra-terrestrials have married earthly women. In the Hebrew of this passage the designation "B'ne Elohim" is used. The context shows that fallen angels, (demons) had dealings with the daughters of earth. Generations of giants have resulted from this. If indeed we were considering beings from other worlds, then certainly Christ would have had to die for the inhabitants of each and every populated heavenly body in order to bring them salvation. To be sure, the UFO crews are not sinless. This is abundantly clear from their crimes: murder, assault, robbery, and rape. The continuous repetition of the sacrificial act of Jesus is reflected clearly and unambiguously in Hebrews 9:25. More arguments could be adduced to show that we are not dealing here with extra-terrestrials — but we must be brief.

The explanation that these UFO beings are to be thought of as materialized demons has the most justification. The mass of evidence for this is truly overwhelming. I should have to write a whole book about it, as John Weldon has done. But in Germany and in Switzerland we have not often, indeed very rarely, seen and considered UFO's. UFO's appear most frequently in countries where the cult of Satan flourishes. This provides us with our chief arguments. UFO's and occult practices run parallel. It is clear they have the same origin.

Regarding the parallelism with Satan cults, the following should be pointed out. Brazil has 50 million spiritualists and innumerable Satan cults. The USA has its Satan-Pope in San Francisco — Anton Szandon la Vey, who boasts a Satan church of 200,000 members. Outside San Francisco, however, there are countless Satan cults, in Los Angeles and indeed in all of California. In the murder of 30,000 Christian Huguenots in 1572, France rooted out the spiritual and intellectual mainstay of the country and later confirmed it in the godless Revolution of 1789. South Africa and Southwest Namibia according to the report of a one-time high priest of the Satanists, has 40,000 Satanists, — Brazil, Haiti, USA, France are likewise all countries in which many UFO's are sighted.

Placing Satanism and UFO on the same level is only one indication that both movements have the same origin. There are many more such indications.

The whole manner of communication between UFO's and contact persons proceeds in thousands of cases, according to occult rules. Frequently telepathy is the means of transferring messages. The UFO people also communicate by automatic writing, by use of the ouija board while in trance. All the spiritualistic rules of the game are practiced; levitation, teletransport, apports, telekinesis, psychokinesis, materializations, astral traveling and many more. UFO manifestations all arise from the same demonic morass.

Likewise, the religion and philosophy of the UFO people shed light on their anti-biblical position and activities. They tell their contact persons that the Bible is full of errors. Christ is not the Son of God but rather a Venusian. Three contemporary Venusians are the real saviors of mankind. Mediums like Uri Geller are allies of these Venusians. The same can be said for other mediums like Adamski or Puharich, who are said to have the assignment on earth to give reality to the ideas of the UFO beings. The obvious purpose of these beings is to destroy faith in Christ and the Bible and to replace it with a fuzzy web of whimsies.

Everything that is said here is just a tiny sample from the witches' cauldron of the UFO people. To evaluate all of this we go to the Scriptures.

The testimony of the apostle Paul in Ephesians 6:12 takes on enormous actuality today: "For we wrestle not against flesh and blood, but against principalities, against powers, against the rulers of the darkness of this world, against spiritual wickedness in high places." Because these evil spirits know that they have but little time, they often step out of their invisibility by means of materializations to create the greatest possible confusion.

UFO's are also the heralds of the coming Antichrist. In 1956 "The Aetherius Society" was founded in California. This cult has put down roots in USA, Australia, and in Europe. In its documents, based on information from UFO sources, we are told that Globe Master, a ruler of the world, is to come — a stranger who will be more powerful than all the armies on earth. He will remove all those from the earth who do not respect his word. We already have such a reference in the Bible. The UFO people come pretty late with their announcement of the Antichrist. The great seer, the apostle John, said in his Book of Revelation (13:15 ff): "And he had power to give life unto the image of the beast, that the image of the beast should both speak, and cause that as many as would not worship the image of the beast should be killed . . . and that no man might buy or sell except that he had the mark of the beast . . . . "

Without a doubt the UFO's are phenomena of the end-time even though already in previous centuries a few UFO's were observed. Today they turn up in ever greater concentrations, as we approach the time of the return of Jesus. Lucifer sends his elite troops ahead. He is arming for the final battle. We Christians, equipped with the Bible, are in a position to understand and interpret all these power struggles. The last world ruler will not be the Antichrist. The Antichrist is only the next to the last. The ultimate ruler will be Jesus Christ, to whom all power in Heaven and on earth has been ceded by the Father in Heaven. The final victory belongs to Him.

FOOTNOTES

[1] Mark Duke, *Acupuncture* (Palm Springs, CA: Pyramid, 1972), p. 162.

[2] "Mit fünf Nadeln im Ohr zum Nichtraucher," Illutrierte Bunte (Jan. 23, 1975).

[3] *Religion in Geschichte und Gegenwart* (n.p., n.d.), vol. 1.

[4] *Rhein-Neckar-Zeitung*, (n.p., Jan. 22, 1975).

[5] Carl Gustav Jung, *Über die Psychologie des UnbewuBten* (n.p., n.d.), p. 120.

[6] Carl Gustav Jung, *Symbolik des Geistes* (n.p., n.d.), p. 394.

[7] Immanuel Kant, *Religion Within the Limits of Reason* (New York: Harper, n.d.).

[8] Kevin Ranaghan and Dorothy Ranaghan, *Catholic Pentecostals* (Paramus, N.J.: Paulist-Newman, 1969).

[9] Vim Malgo, *Mitternachtsruf* (n.p., 1974-75).

[10] Cardinal Suenens, "The Holy Spirit: My Hope," in *New Covenant* (n.p., May 1975), p. 43.

[11] Archbishop George Pierce, *New Covenant* (n.p., Feb. 1975).

[12] H. A. Baker, *Visions Beyond the Veil* (Monroeville, Pa: Banner, 1973), p. 18.

[13] Mary Baker Eddy, *Miscellaneous Writings* (Denver: First Church, 1883-1896), p. 29.

[14] Ibid., p. 34.

[15] Ibid., p. 42.

[16] Ibid., p. 89.

[17] Agnes Sanford, *Healing Light* (n.p., n.d.).

[18] Kurt Koch, *Uns, Herr, Wirst Du Frieden Schaffen* (n.p., n.d.), p. 329.

[19] Adolf Rodewyk, *Dämonische Bessessenheit* (n.p., n.d.), p. 46.

[20] Professor Bettex, *Bibel und Gemeinde* (n.p., n.d.), 69/1, p. 56ff.

[21] E. W. Bullinger, *The Foundations of Dispensational Truth* (n.p., n.d.), p. 249.

[22] W. G. Broadbent, *Hente Noch in Zugen Reden? The Doctrine of Tongues* (Germany: Liebenzeel Mission, n.d.), p. 171.

[23] Fritz Hubmer, *Zungenreden, Weissagung* (n.p., n.d.), p. 162.

[24] F. C. Endres, *Das Geheimnis des Freimaurers* (n.p., n.d.), p. 19.

[25] Esperanto is an artificial language, based on the most common words in the major languages, invented in 1887 by a Russian philologist and intended for international use.

[26] Professor Jaensch, *Iris diagnostik* (n.p., n.d.), p. 30.

[27] Ibid., p. 28.

[28] Rutherford, *The Truth Will Make You Free* (n.p., n.d.), p. 296.

[29] Malgo, op. cit.,[9] p. 10.

[30] Christliche Gemeinschaft innerhalb der Laudeskirche is a widespread body of evangelicals who belong to the national church but who hold their own meetings also.

31 Hans Bender, *Essays on Parapsychology* (n.p., n.d.), p. 10.

32 Ibid., p. 29.

33 See Kurt Koch, *Name über alle Namen Jesus* (n.p., n.d.), p. 60ff.

34 Kurt Koch, *World Without Chance* (Grand Rapids, MI: Kregel, 1974), p. 56.

35 Kurt Koch, *Jesus auf allen Kontinenten* (n.p., n.d.), p. 465.

36 Ibid., p. 544ff.

37 Doreen Irvine, *From Witchcraft to Christ* (Concordia Press: London, n.d.).

38 Ibid., chap. 12.

39 Ibid.

40 Ibid.

41 Ibid., p. 95.

42 Ibid.

43 Ibid.

44 *Religion in Geschichte und Gegenwart* (n.p., n.d.), vol. IV, p. 2108.

45 Albert Magnus in "Meisterung des Leben" (n.p., n.d.), p. 19.

46 Ibid., p. 15.

47 Kurt Koch, *The Strife of Tongues* (Grand Rapids: Kregel, 1966) and Kurt Koch, *Charismatic Gifts* (Grand Rapids: Association for Christian Evangelism, 1976). See also George E. Gardiner, *Corinthian Catastrophe* (Grand Rapids: Kregel, 1975).

48 Hubmer, op. cit.[23], p. 41.

49 Carlson and Lindsey, *Satan kämpft um diese Welt* (n.p., n.d.), p. 34.

50 Rammurti S. Mishra, *The Textbook of Yoga Psychology* (New York: Julian, 1963).

51 Maurice Ray, *Joga, ja oder Nein?* (Germany: Bibellesebund, n.d.), p. 68.

52 Carlson and Lindsey, op. cit.[49], p. 33.

53 See Kurt Koch, *Unter den Führung Jesu* (n.p., n.d.), pp. 254ff.

54 Kurt Koch, *Occult Bondage and Deliverance* (Grand Rapids, Mi: Kregel, 1970).

55 Frederick A. Tatford, *Satan, The Prince of Darkness* (Grand Rapids, Mi: Kregel, 1974).